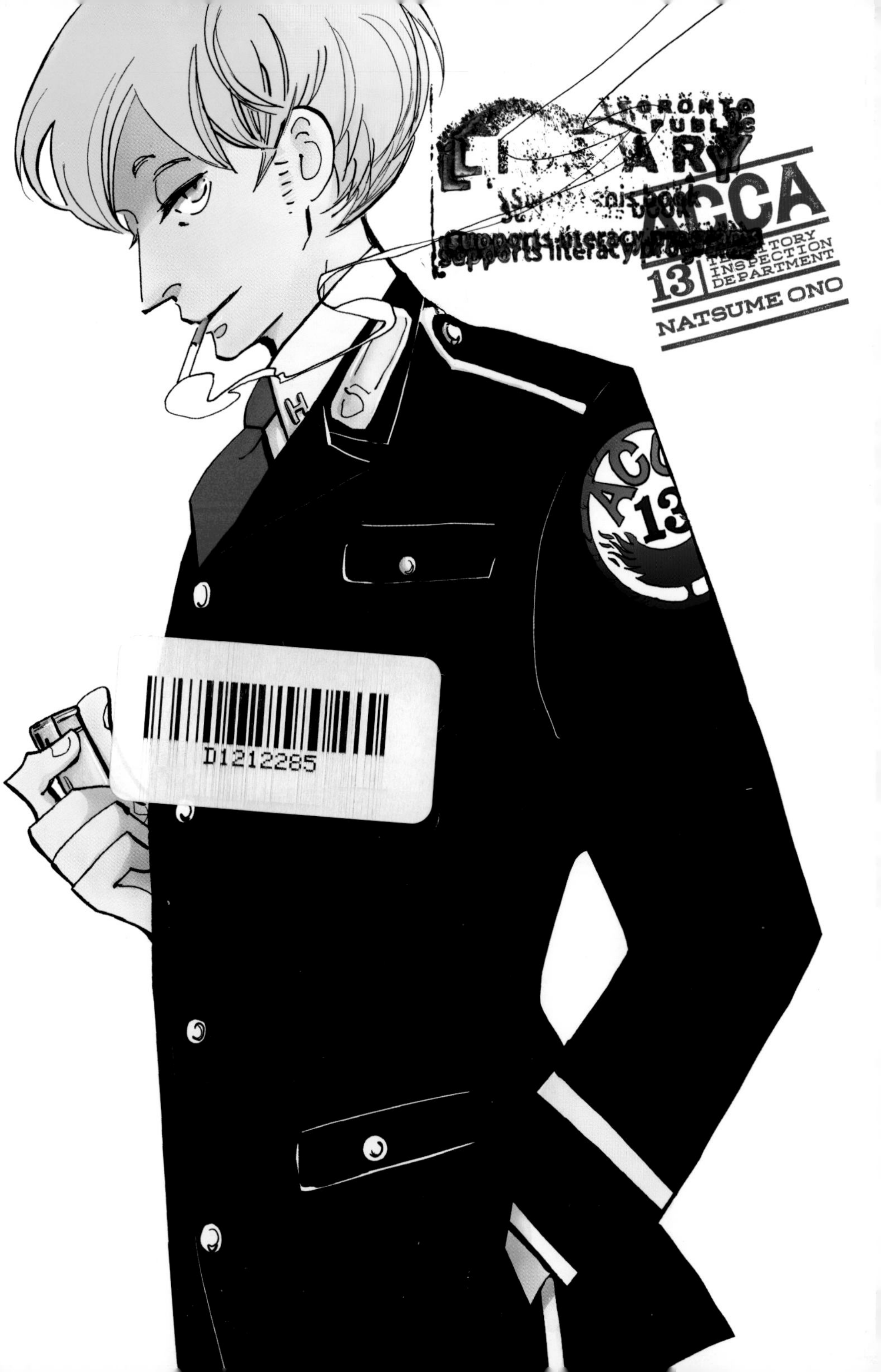
ACCA
13-TERRITORY INSPECTION DEPARTMENT
NATSUME ONO
ACCA
13

ACCA 1

13 TERRITORY INSPECTION DEPARTMENT

CONTENTS

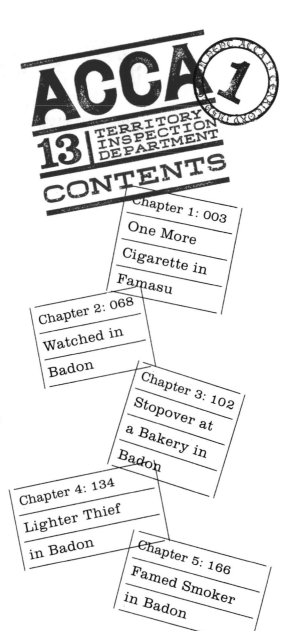

A C C
13 Terr Insp Dep
Natsume Ono

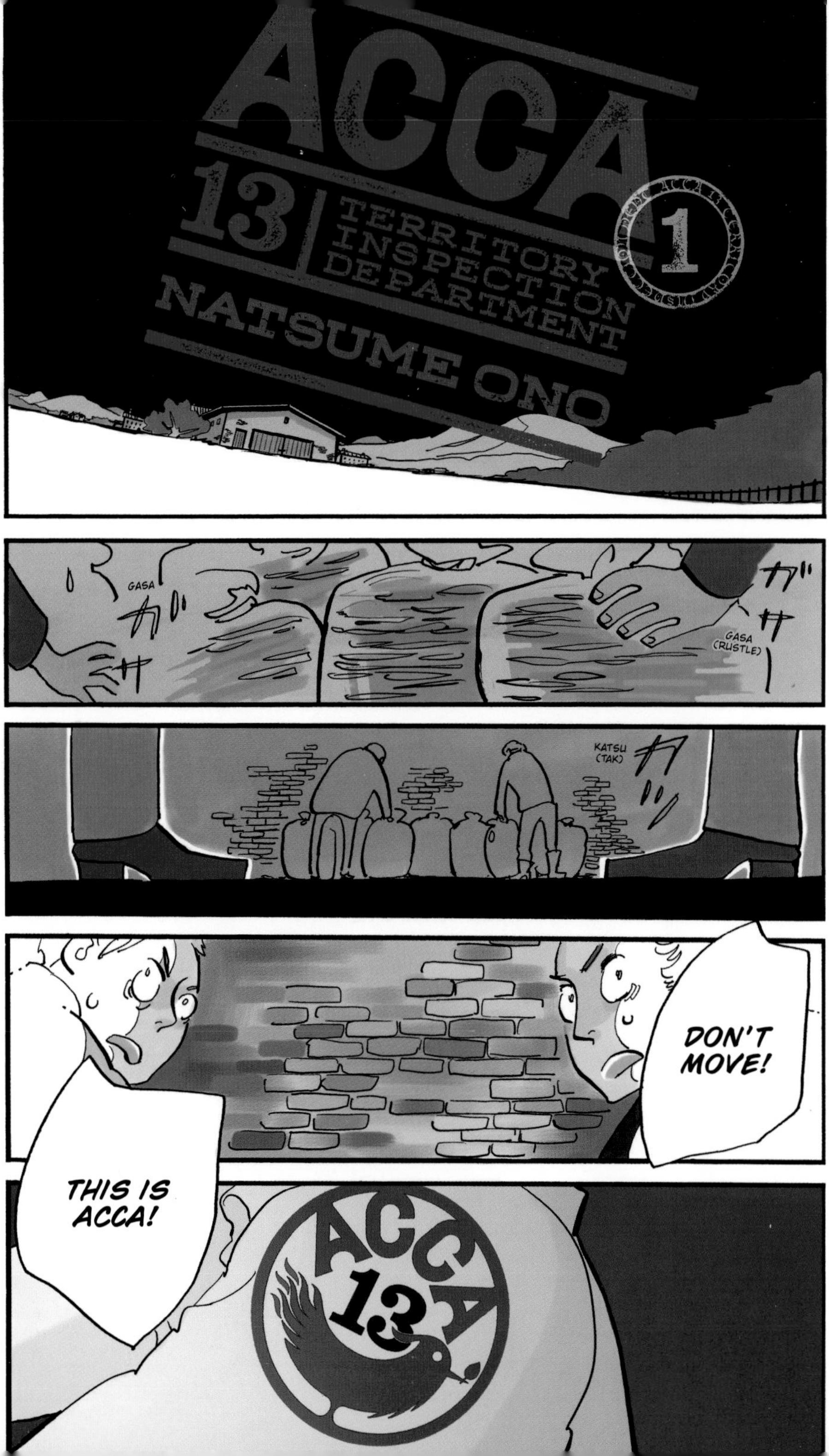
ACCA
13
TERRITORY INSPECTION DEPARTMENT
1
NATSUME ONO
ガサ
GASA (RUSTLE)
ガサ
GASA
カツ
KATSU (TAK)
DON'T MOVE!
THIS IS ACCA!
ACCA 13

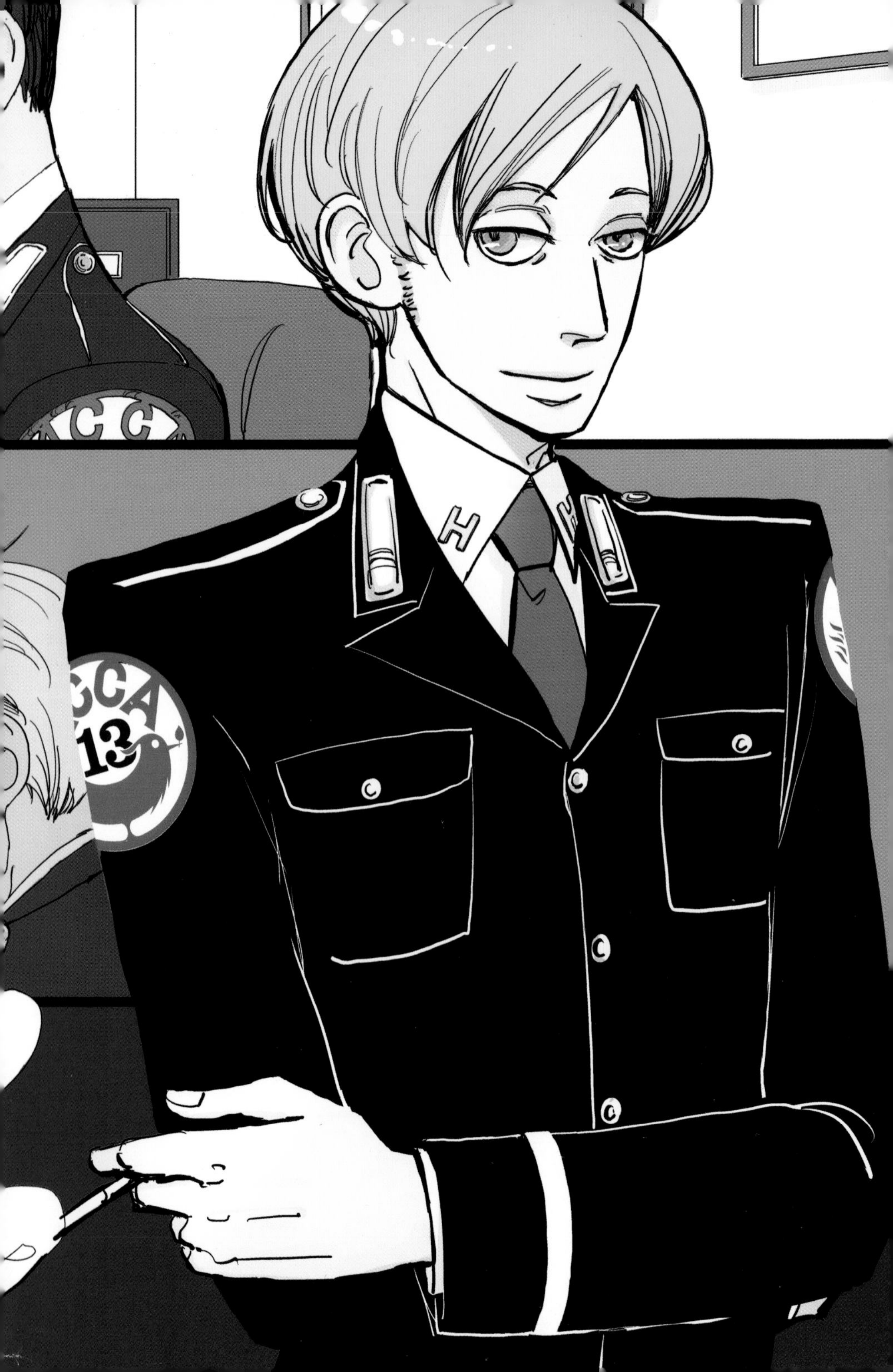

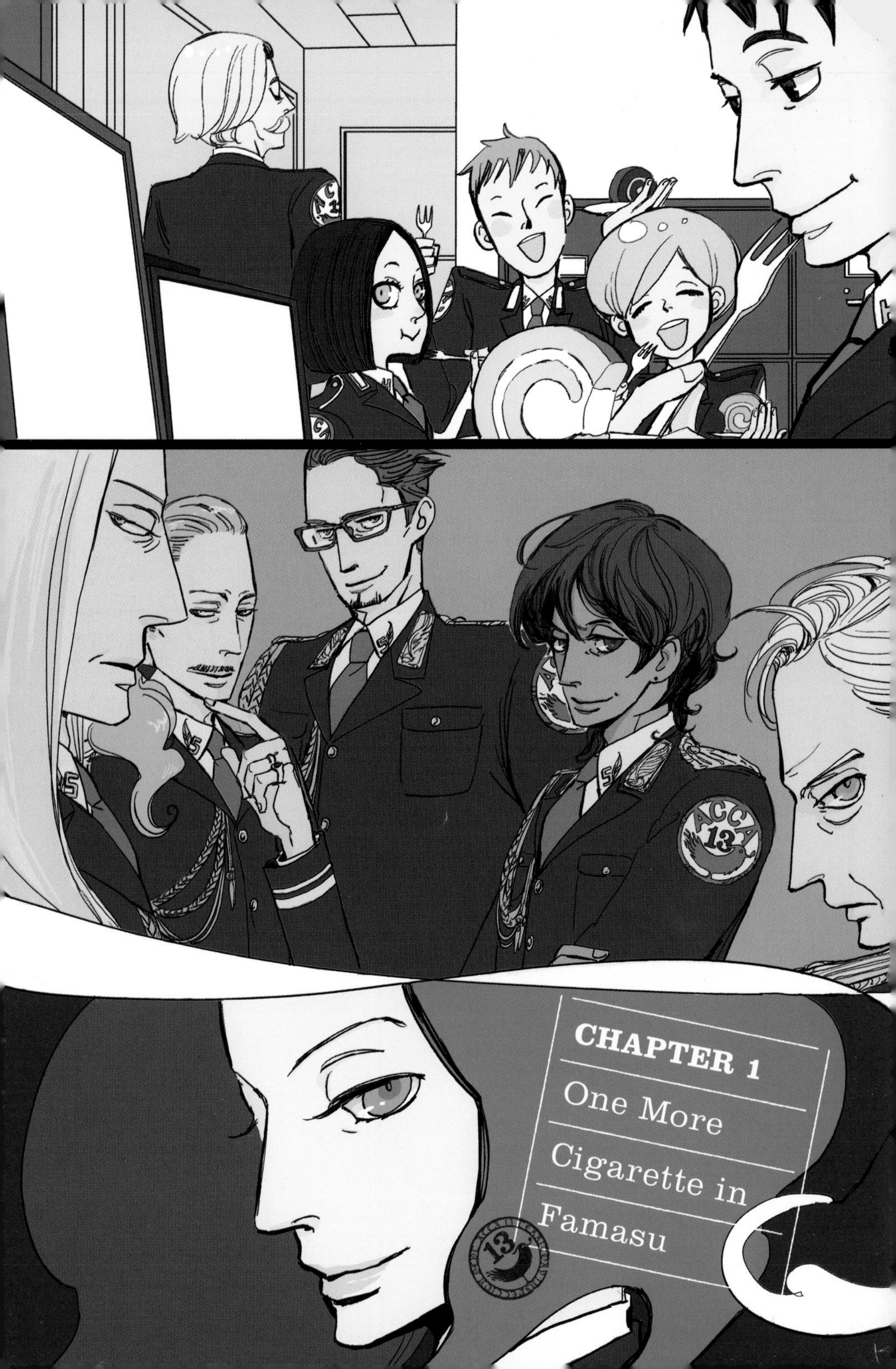
CHAPTER 1
One More Cigarette in Famasu

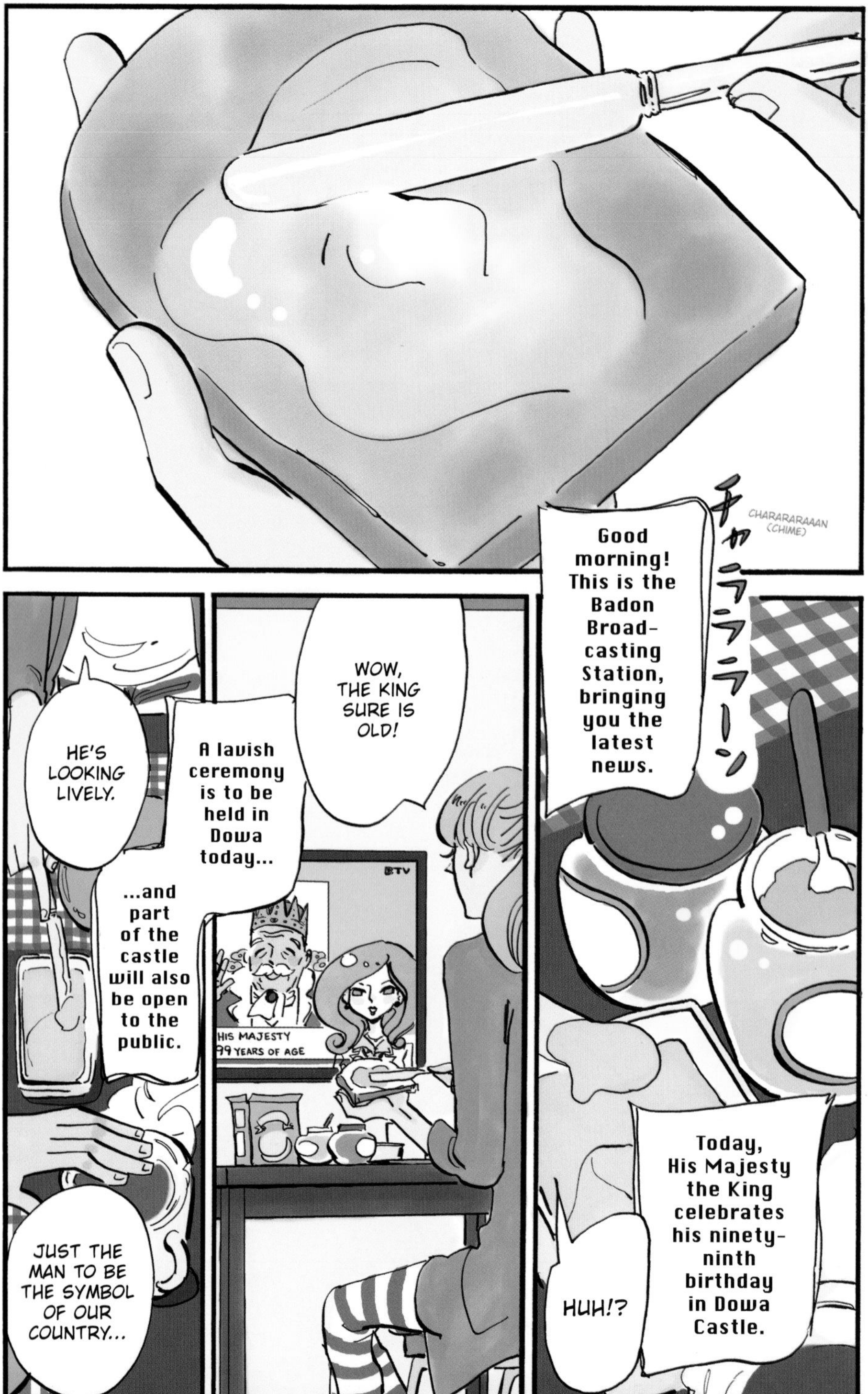
チャラララーン
CHARARARAAAN (CHIME)
Good morning! This is the Badon Broadcasting Station, bringing you the latest news.
Today, His Majesty the King celebrates his ninety-ninth birthday in Dowa Castle.
HUH!?
WOW, THE KING SURE IS OLD!
A lavish ceremony is to be held in Dowa today...
...and part of the castle will also be open to the public.
BTV
HIS MAJESTY 99 YEARS OF AGE
HE'S LOOKING LIVELY.
JUST THE MAN TO BE THE SYMBOL OF OUR COUNTRY...

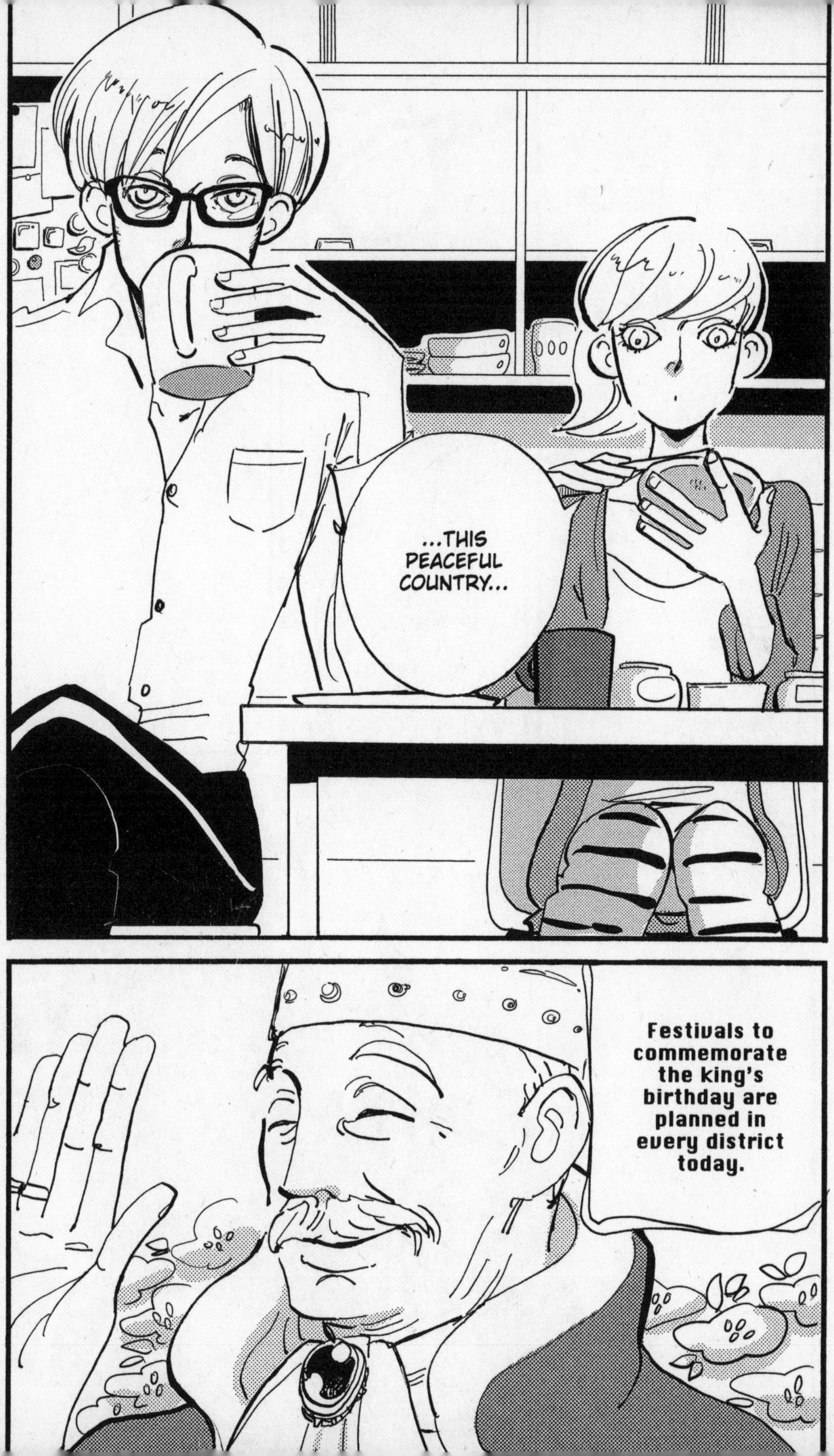
...THIS PEACEFUL COUNTRY...
Festivals to commemorate the king's birthday are planned in every district today.

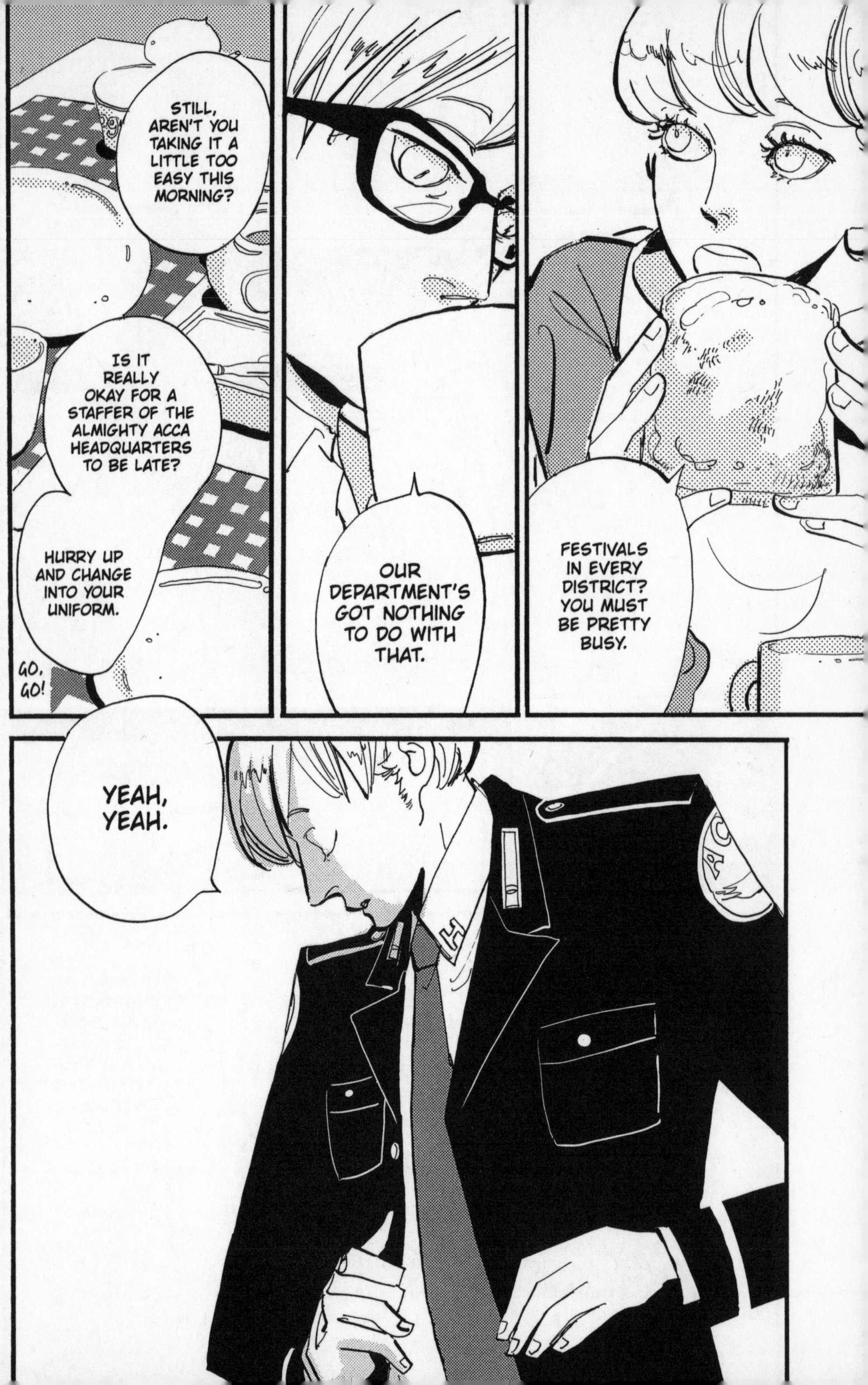
FESTIVALS IN EVERY DISTRICT? YOU MUST BE PRETTY BUSY.
OUR DEPARTMENT'S GOT NOTHING TO DO WITH THAT.
STILL, AREN'T YOU TAKING IT A LITTLE TOO EASY THIS MORNING?
IS IT REALLY OKAY FOR A STAFFER OF THE ALMIGHTY ACCA HEADQUARTERS TO BE LATE?
HURRY UP AND CHANGE INTO YOUR UNIFORM.
GO, GO!
YEAH, YEAH.

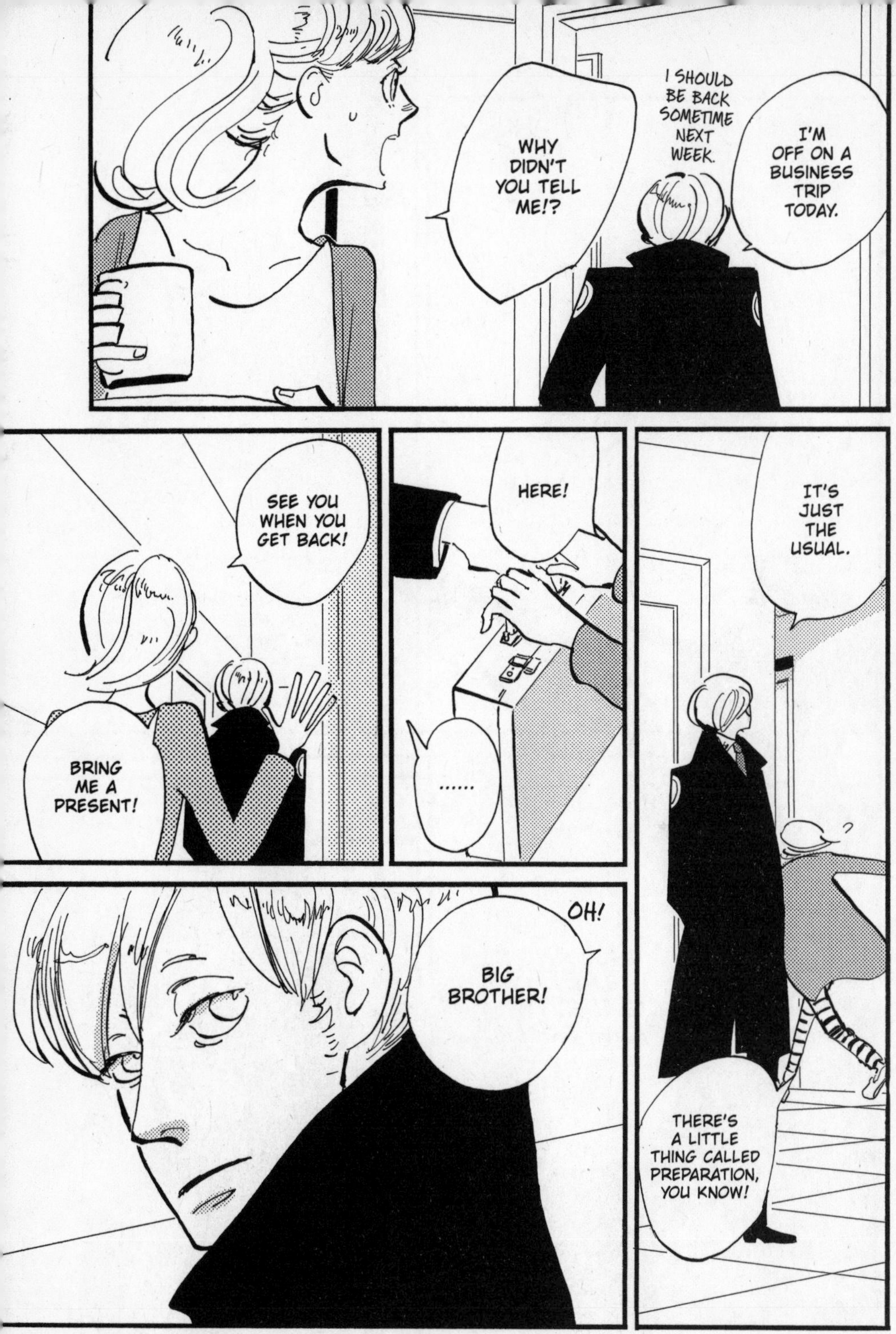
I'M OFF ON A BUSINESS TRIP TODAY.
I SHOULD BE BACK SOMETIME NEXT WEEK.
WHY DIDN'T YOU TELL ME!?
IT'S JUST THE USUAL.
THERE'S A LITTLE THING CALLED PREPARATION, YOU KNOW!
HERE!
......
SEE YOU WHEN YOU GET BACK!
BRING ME A PRESENT!
OH!
BIG BROTHER!

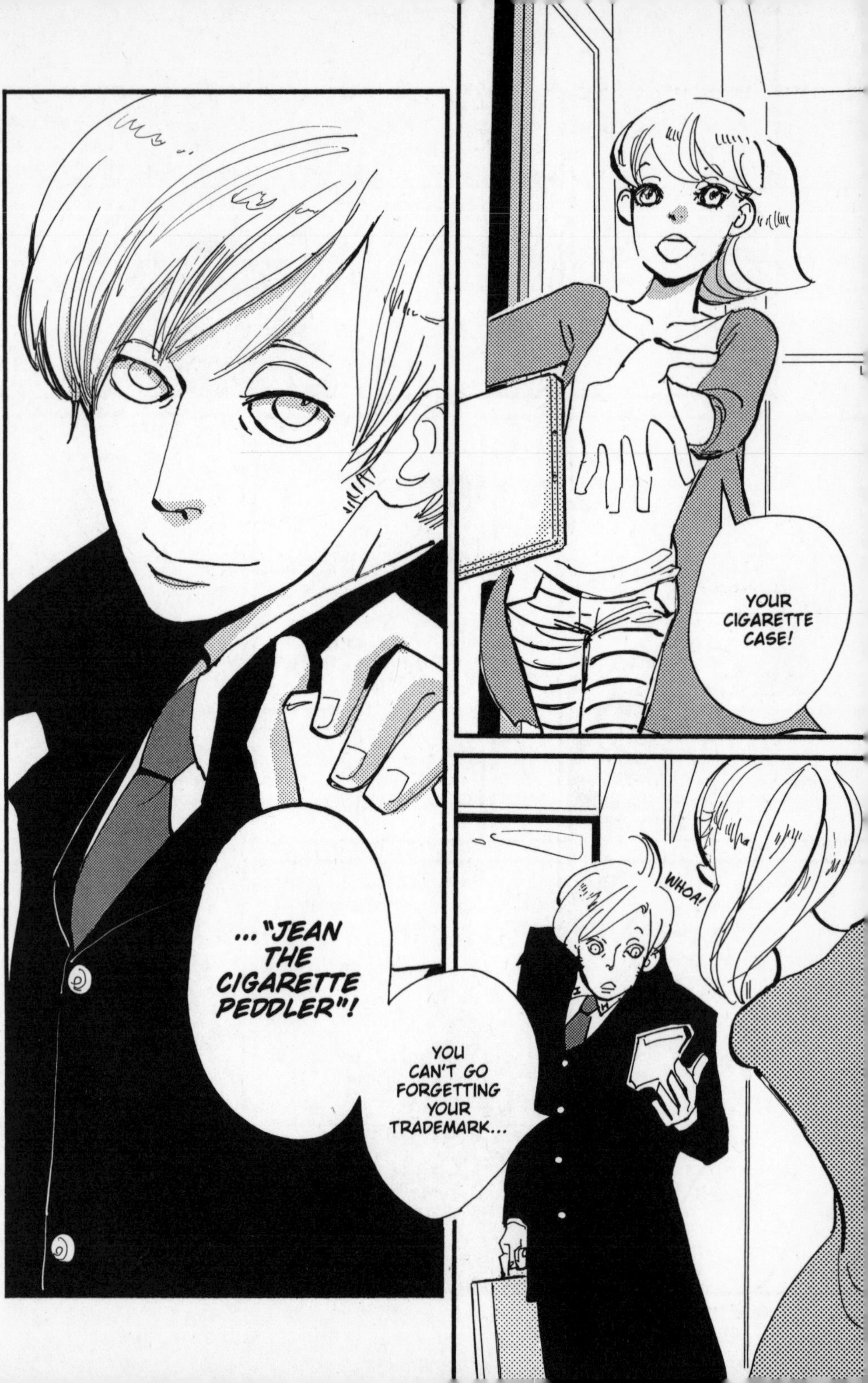
YOUR CIGARETTE CASE!
WHOA!
YOU CAN'T GO FORGETTING YOUR TRADEMARK...
..."JEAN THE CIGARETTE PEDDLER"!

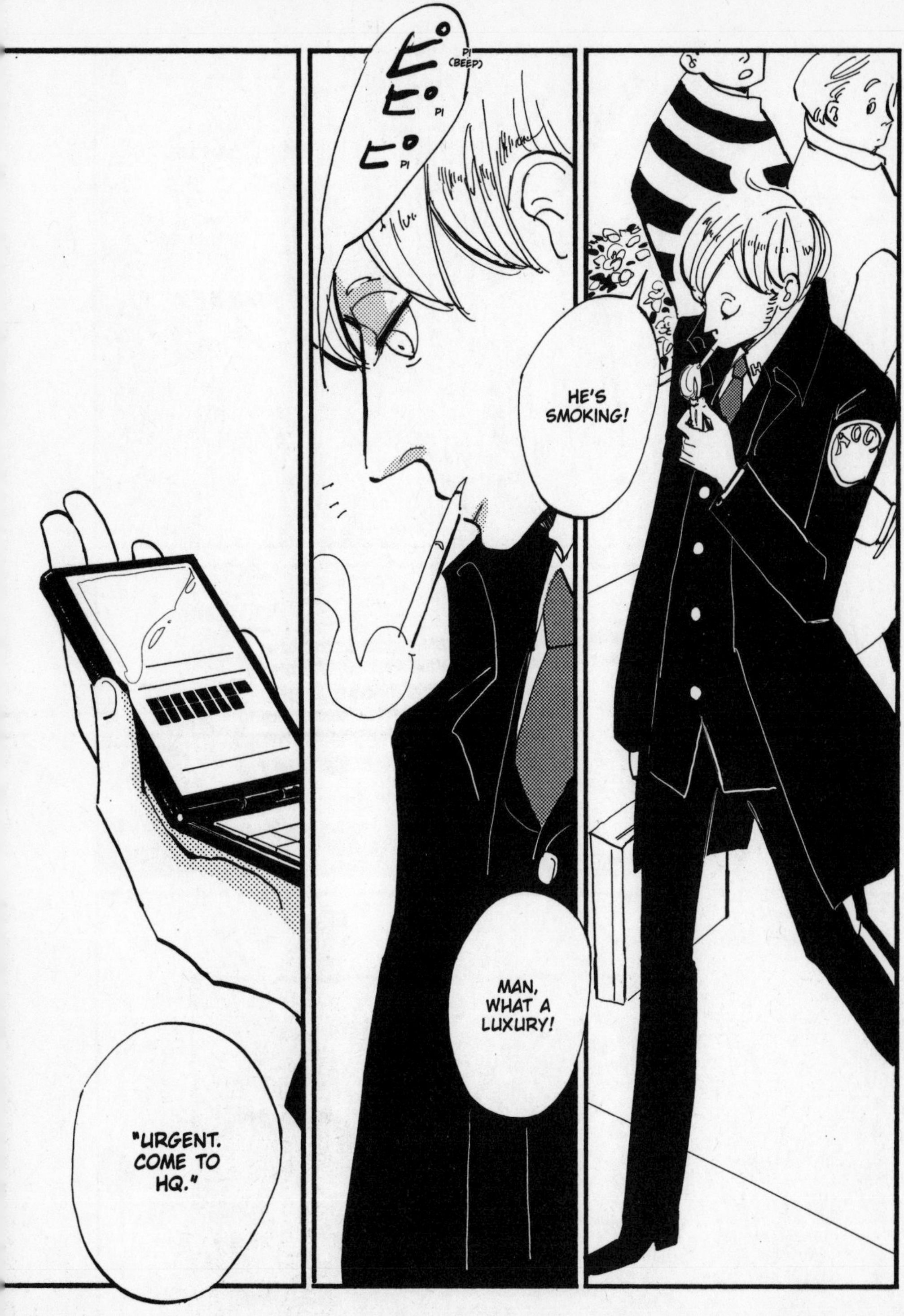
HE'S SMOKING!
ピ PI (BEEP)
ピ PI
ピ PI
MAN, WHAT A LUXURY!
"URGENT. COME TO HQ."

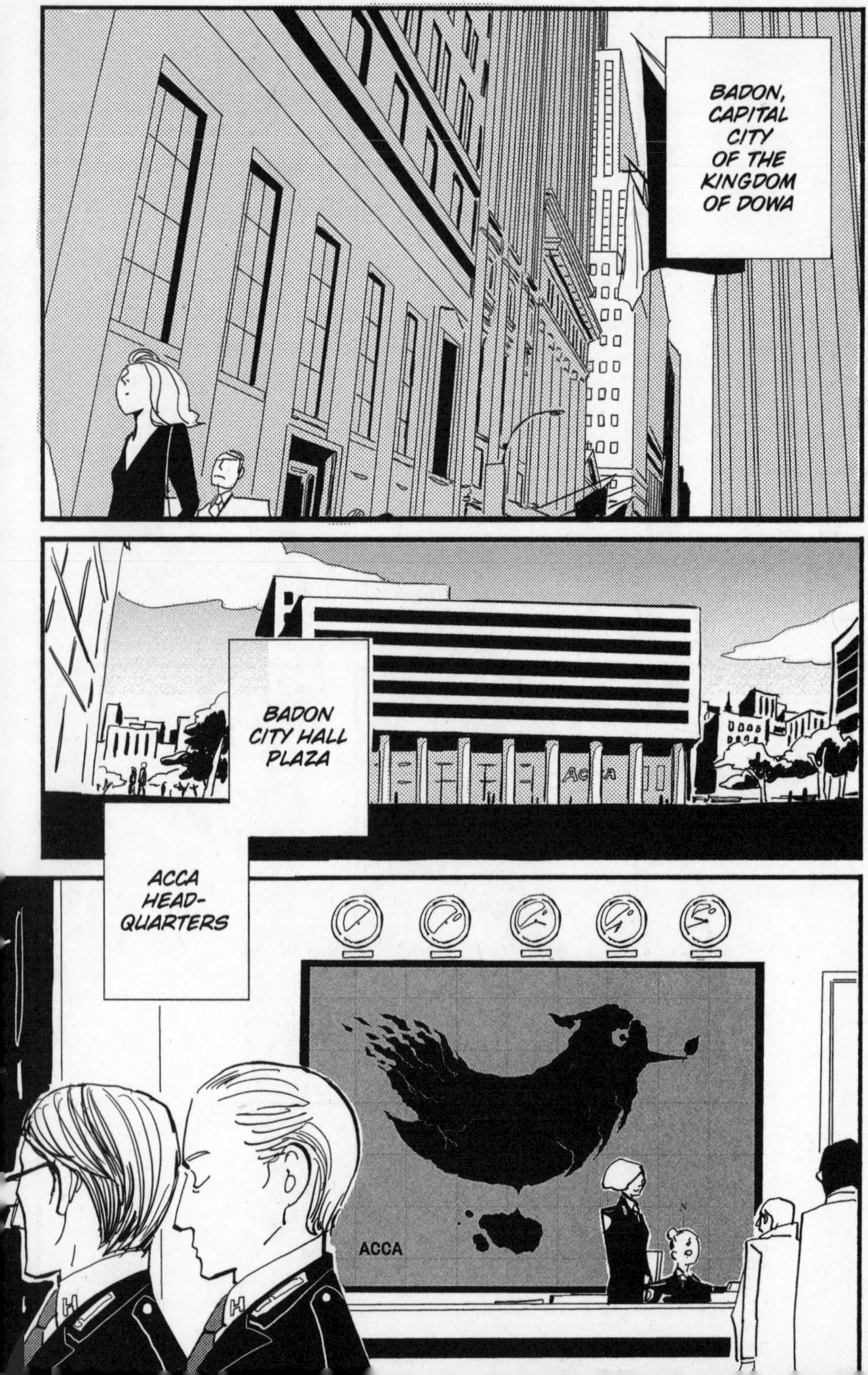
BADON, CAPITAL CITY OF THE KINGDOM OF DOWA
BADON CITY HALL PLAZA
ACCA HEAD-QUARTERS
ACCA

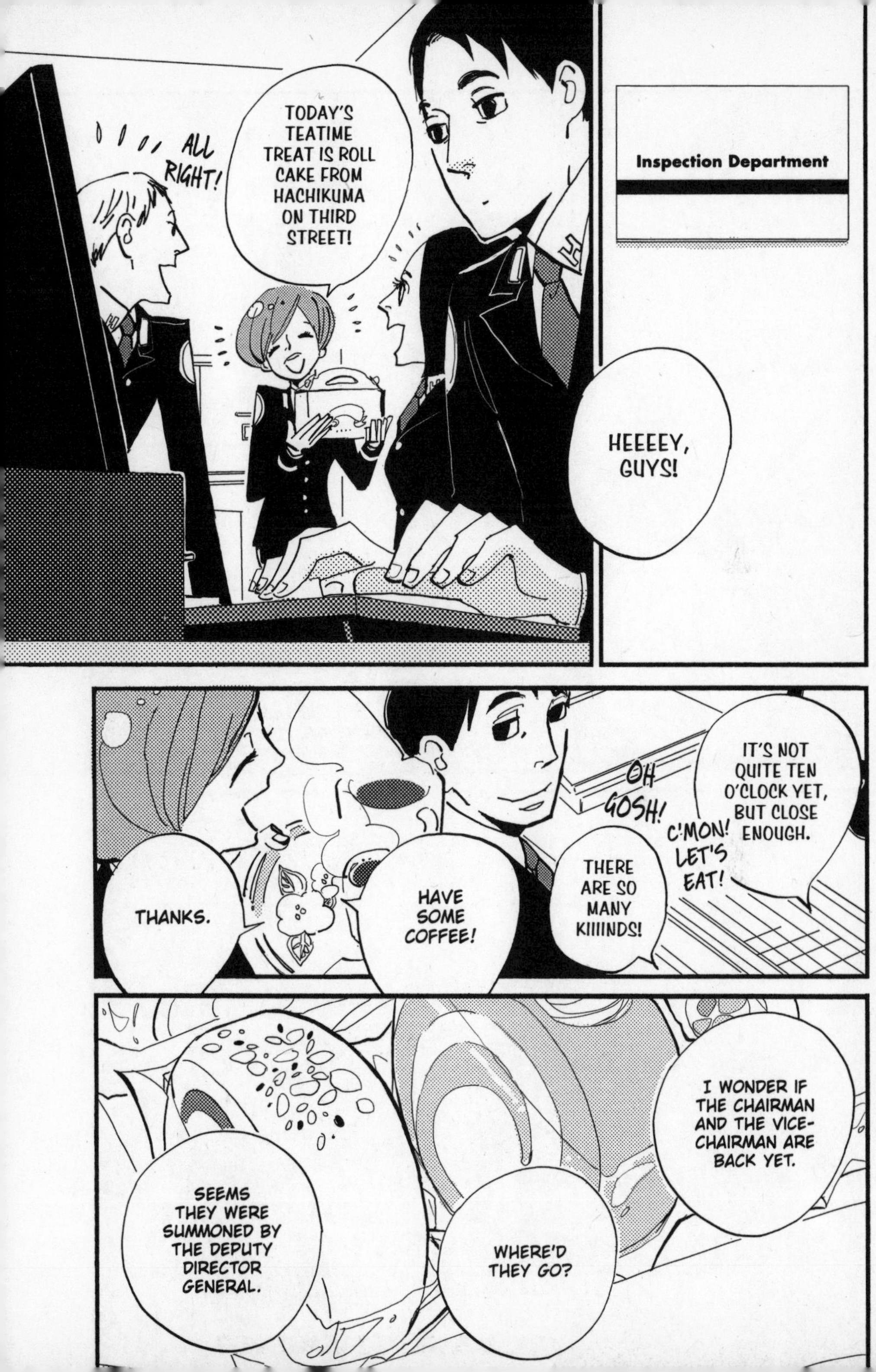
Inspection Department
HEEEEY, GUYS!
TODAY'S TEATIME TREAT IS ROLL CAKE FROM HACHIKUMA ON THIRD STREET!
ALL RIGHT!
IT'S NOT QUITE TEN O'CLOCK YET, BUT CLOSE ENOUGH.
C'MON! LET'S EAT!
OH GOSH!
THERE ARE SO MANY KIIIINDS!
HAVE SOME COFFEE!
THANKS.
I WONDER IF THE CHAIRMAN AND THE VICE-CHAIRMAN ARE BACK YET.
WHERE'D THEY GO?
SEEMS THEY WERE SUMMONED BY THE DEPUTY DIRECTOR GENERAL.

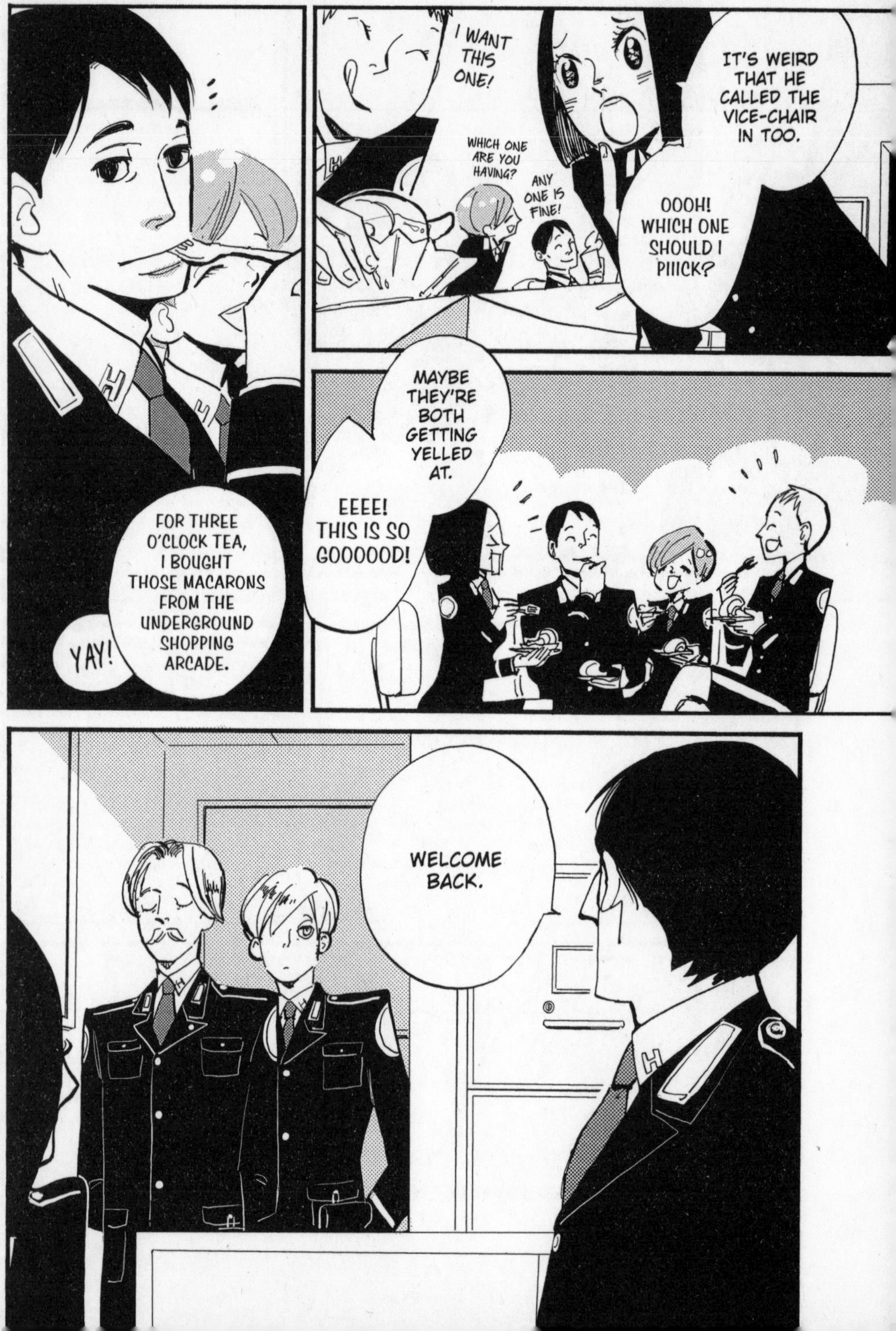
IT'S WEIRD THAT HE CALLED THE VICE-CHAIR IN TOO.
OOOH! WHICH ONE SHOULD I PIIICK?
I WANT THIS ONE!
WHICH ONE ARE YOU HAVING?
ANY ONE IS FINE!
MAYBE THEY'RE BOTH GETTING YELLED AT.
EEEE! THIS IS SO GOOOOOD!
FOR THREE O'CLOCK TEA, I BOUGHT THOSE MACARONS FROM THE UNDERGROUND SHOPPING ARCADE.
YAY!
WELCOME BACK.

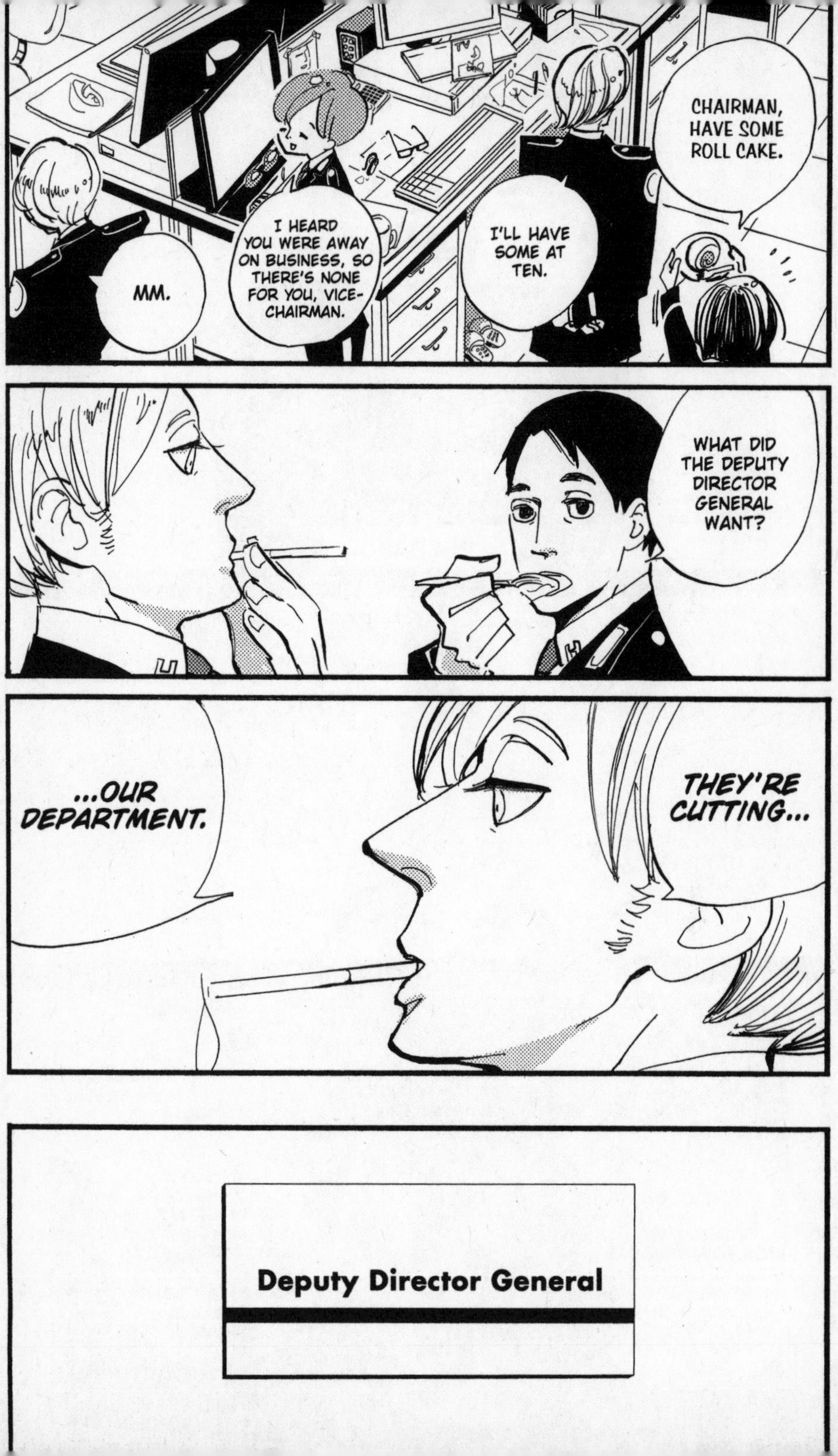
CHAIRMAN, HAVE SOME ROLL CAKE.
I'LL HAVE SOME AT TEN.
I HEARD YOU WERE AWAY ON BUSINESS, SO THERE'S NONE FOR YOU, VICE-CHAIRMAN.
MM.
WHAT DID THE DEPUTY DIRECTOR GENERAL WANT?
THEY'RE CUTTING...
...OUR DEPARTMENT.
Deputy Director General

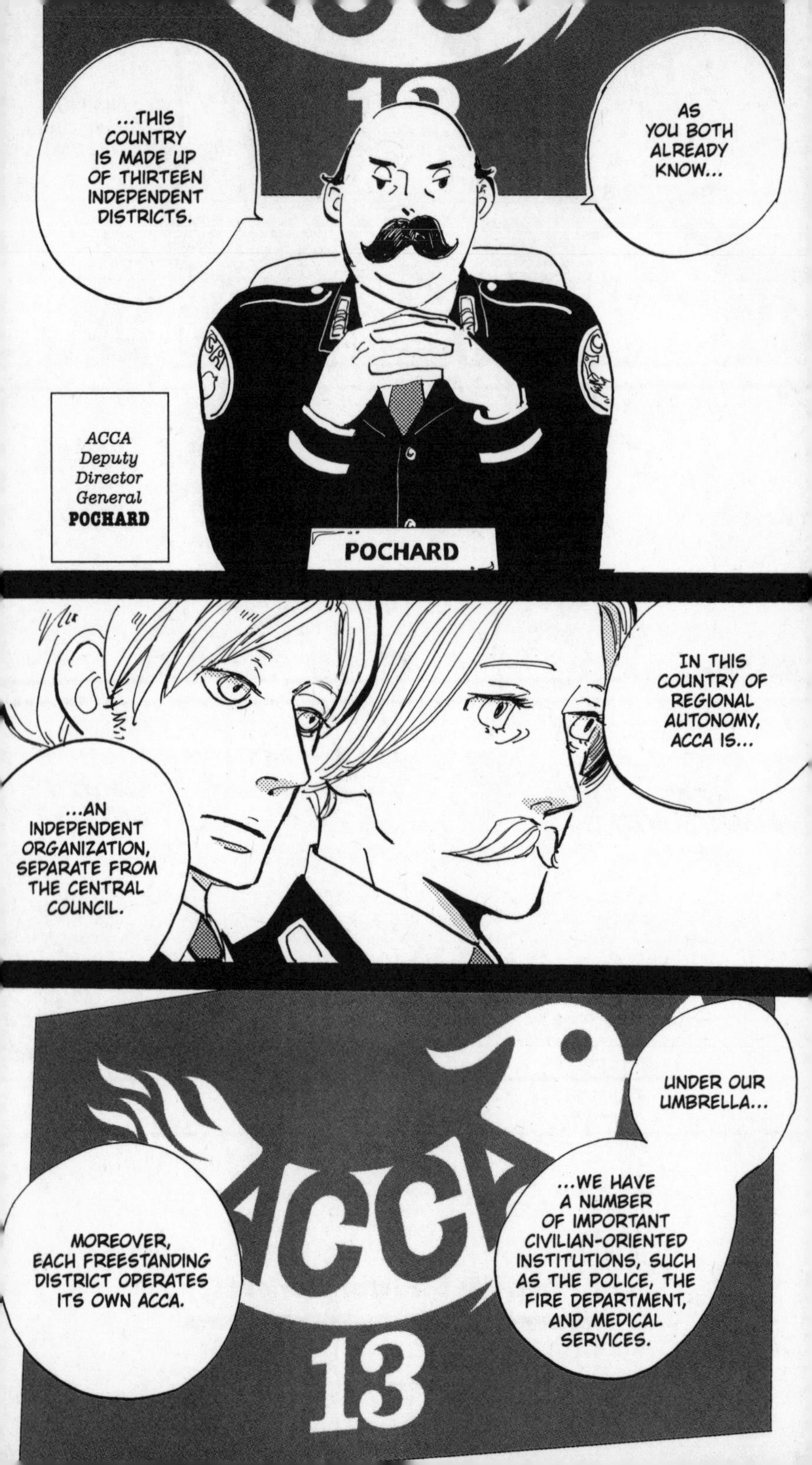
AS YOU BOTH ALREADY KNOW...
...THIS COUNTRY IS MADE UP OF THIRTEEN INDEPENDENT DISTRICTS.
ACCA Deputy Director General POCHARD
POCHARD
IN THIS COUNTRY OF REGIONAL AUTONOMY, ACCA IS...
...AN INDEPENDENT ORGANIZATION, SEPARATE FROM THE CENTRAL COUNCIL.
UNDER OUR UMBRELLA...
...WE HAVE A NUMBER OF IMPORTANT CIVILIAN-ORIENTED INSTITUTIONS, SUCH AS THE POLICE, THE FIRE DEPARTMENT, AND MEDICAL SERVICES.
MOREOVER, EACH FREESTANDING DISTRICT OPERATES ITS OWN ACCA.
13

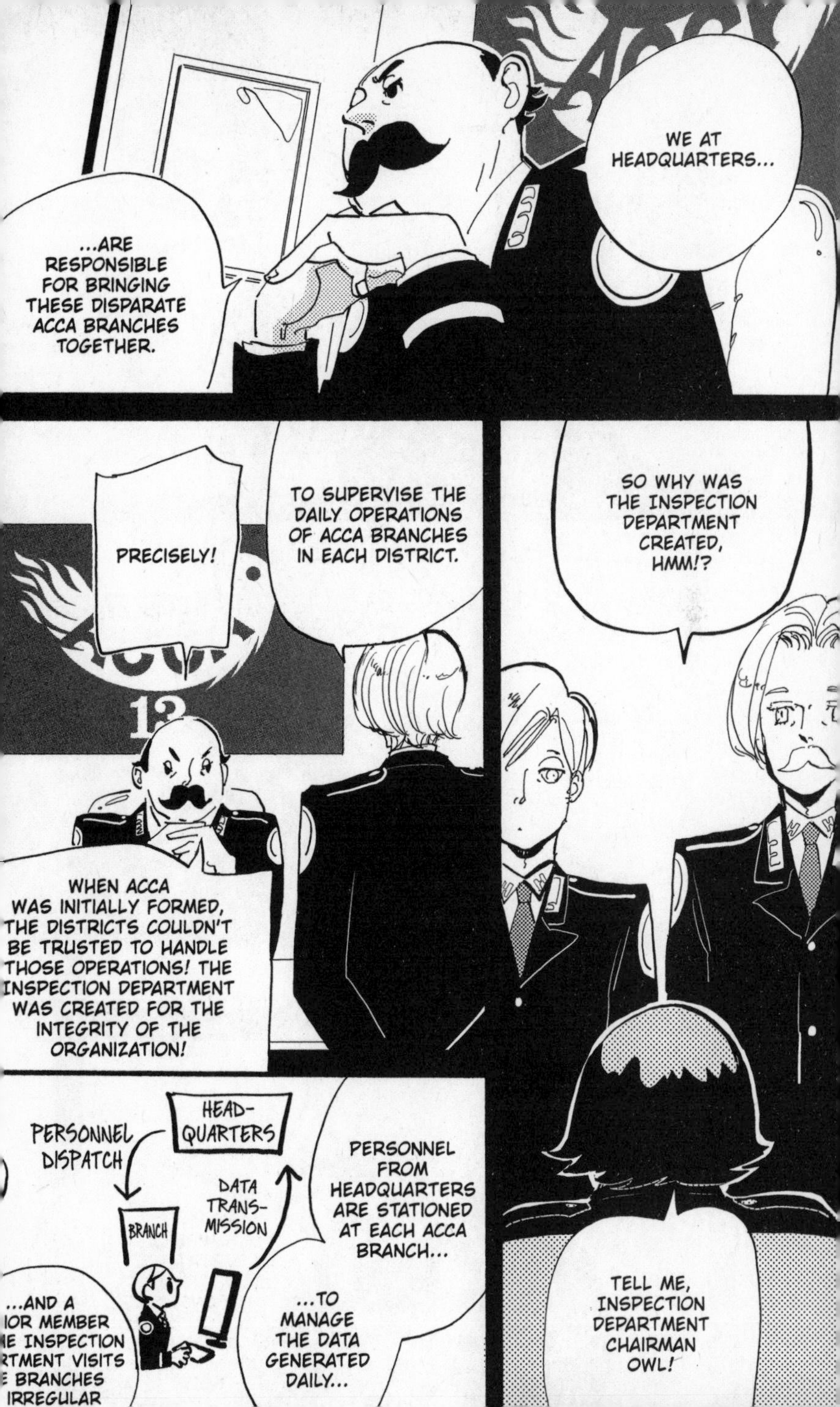
WE AT HEADQUARTERS...
...ARE RESPONSIBLE FOR BRINGING THESE DISPARATE ACCA BRANCHES TOGETHER.
SO WHY WAS THE INSPECTION DEPARTMENT CREATED, HMM!?
TO SUPERVISE THE DAILY OPERATIONS OF ACCA BRANCHES IN EACH DISTRICT.
PRECISELY!
13
WHEN ACCA WAS INITIALLY FORMED, THE DISTRICTS COULDN'T BE TRUSTED TO HANDLE THOSE OPERATIONS! THE INSPECTION DEPARTMENT WAS CREATED FOR THE INTEGRITY OF THE ORGANIZATION!
TELL ME, INSPECTION DEPARTMENT CHAIRMAN OWL!
PERSONNEL FROM HEADQUARTERS ARE STATIONED AT EACH ACCA BRANCH...
HEAD-QUARTERS
PERSONNEL DISPATCH
DATA TRANS-MISSION
BRANCH
...TO MANAGE THE DATA GENERATED DAILY...
...AND A
IOR MEMBER
IE INSPECTION
RTMENT VISITS
E BRANCHES
IRREGULAR

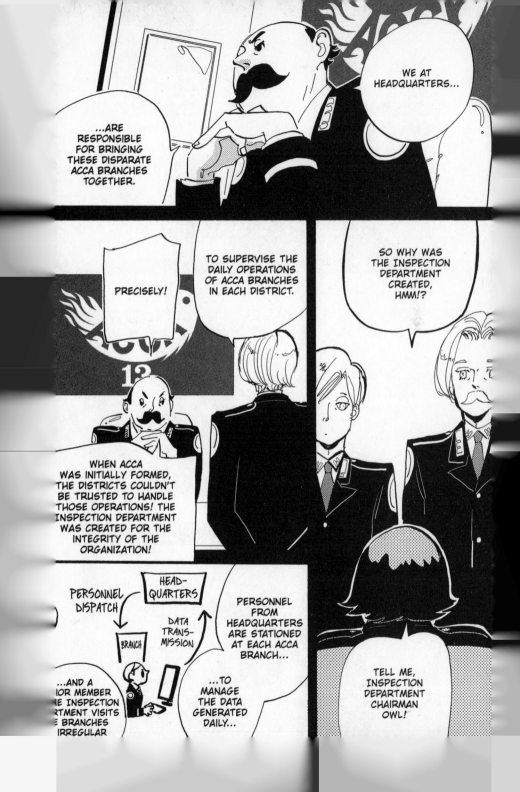

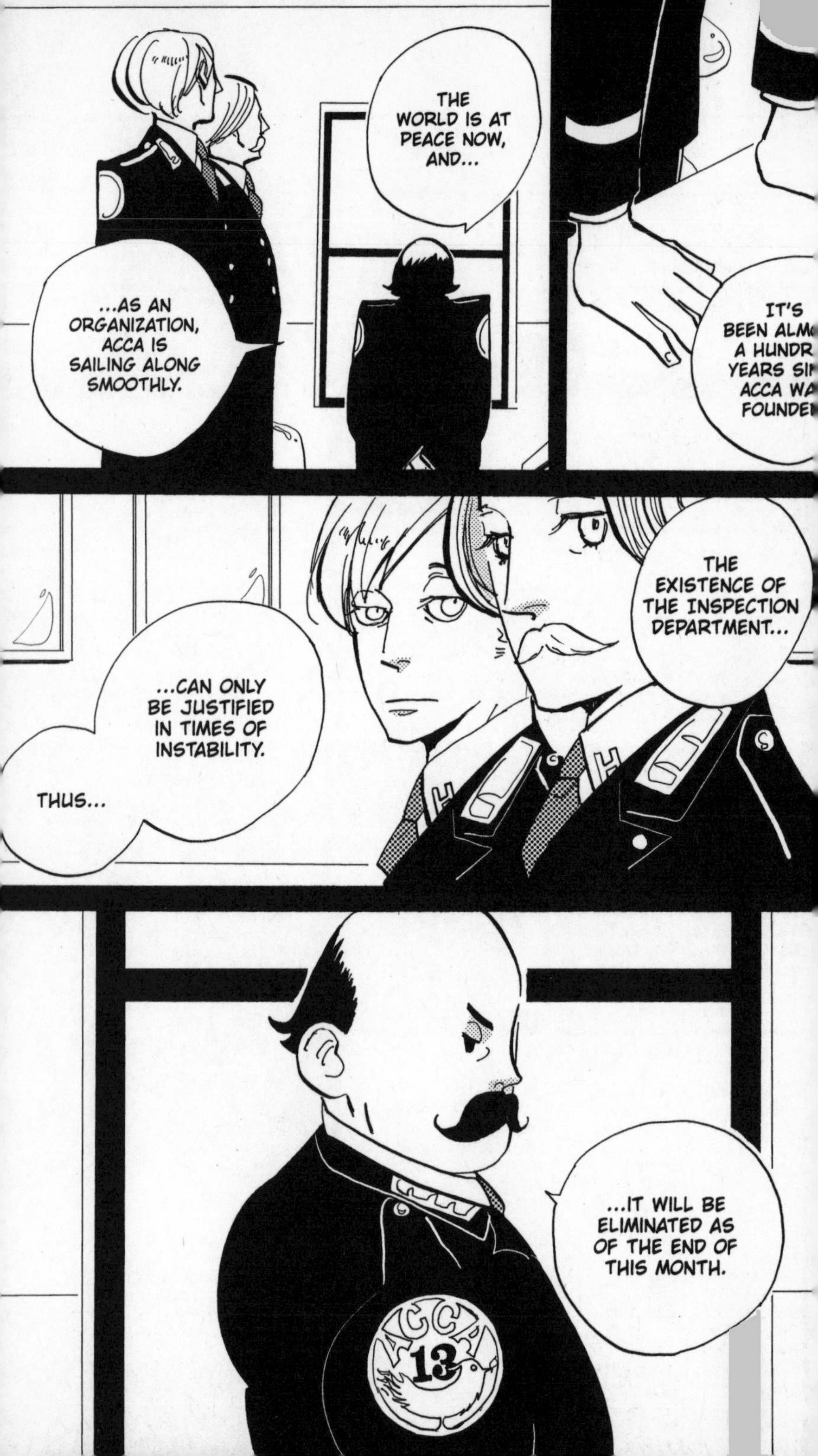
IT'S BEEN ALM A HUNDR YEARS SI ACCA WA FOUNDE
THE WORLD IS AT PEACE NOW, AND...
...AS AN ORGANIZATION, ACCA IS SAILING ALONG SMOOTHLY.
THE EXISTENCE OF THE INSPECTION DEPARTMENT...
...CAN ONLY BE JUSTIFIED IN TIMES OF INSTABILITY.
THUS...
...IT WILL BE ELIMINATED AS OF THE END OF THIS MONTH.
ACCA
13

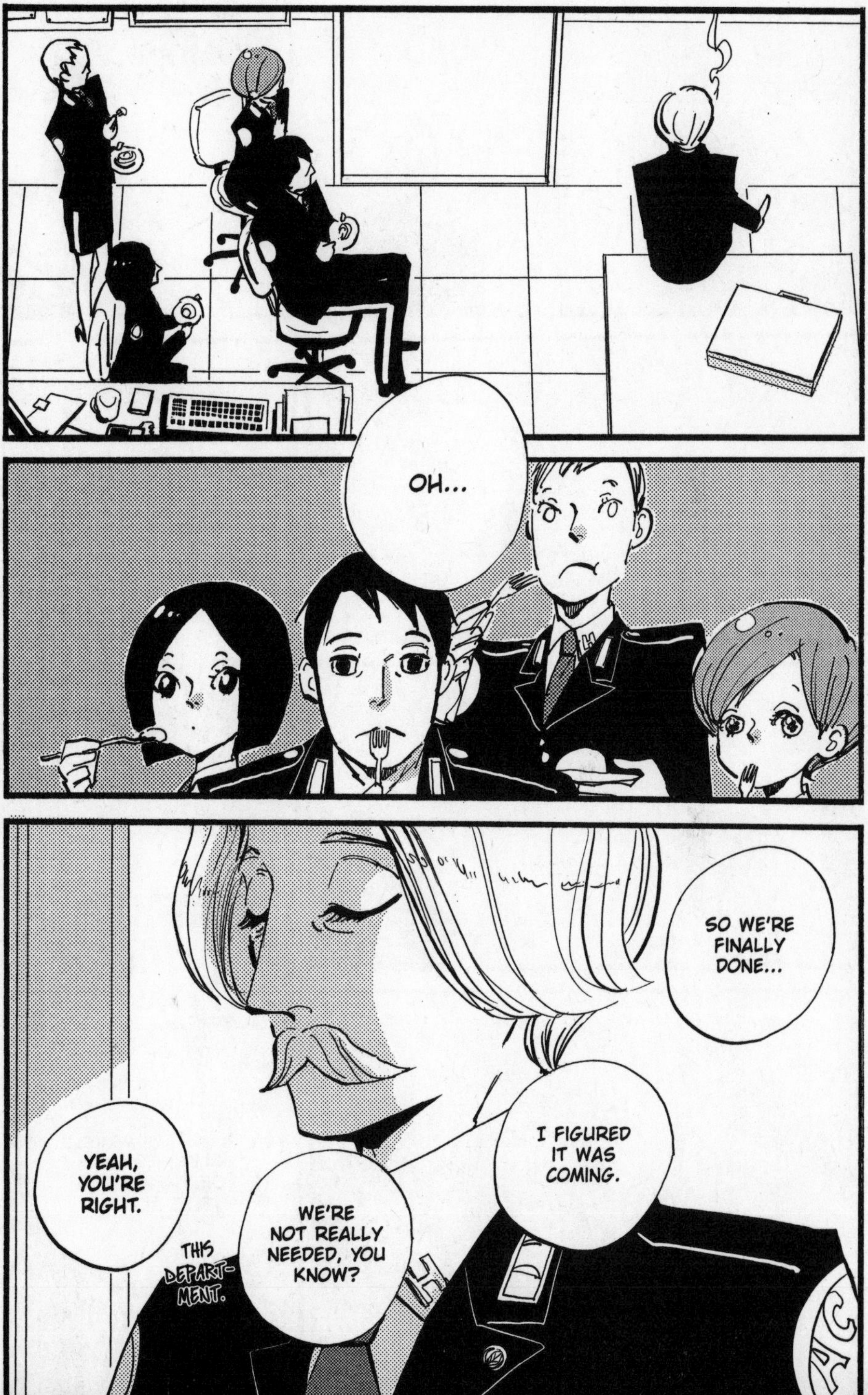

OH...
SO WE'RE FINALLY DONE...
I FIGURED IT WAS COMING.
WE'RE NOT REALLY NEEDED, YOU KNOW?
THIS DEPART-MENT.
YEAH, YOU'RE RIGHT.

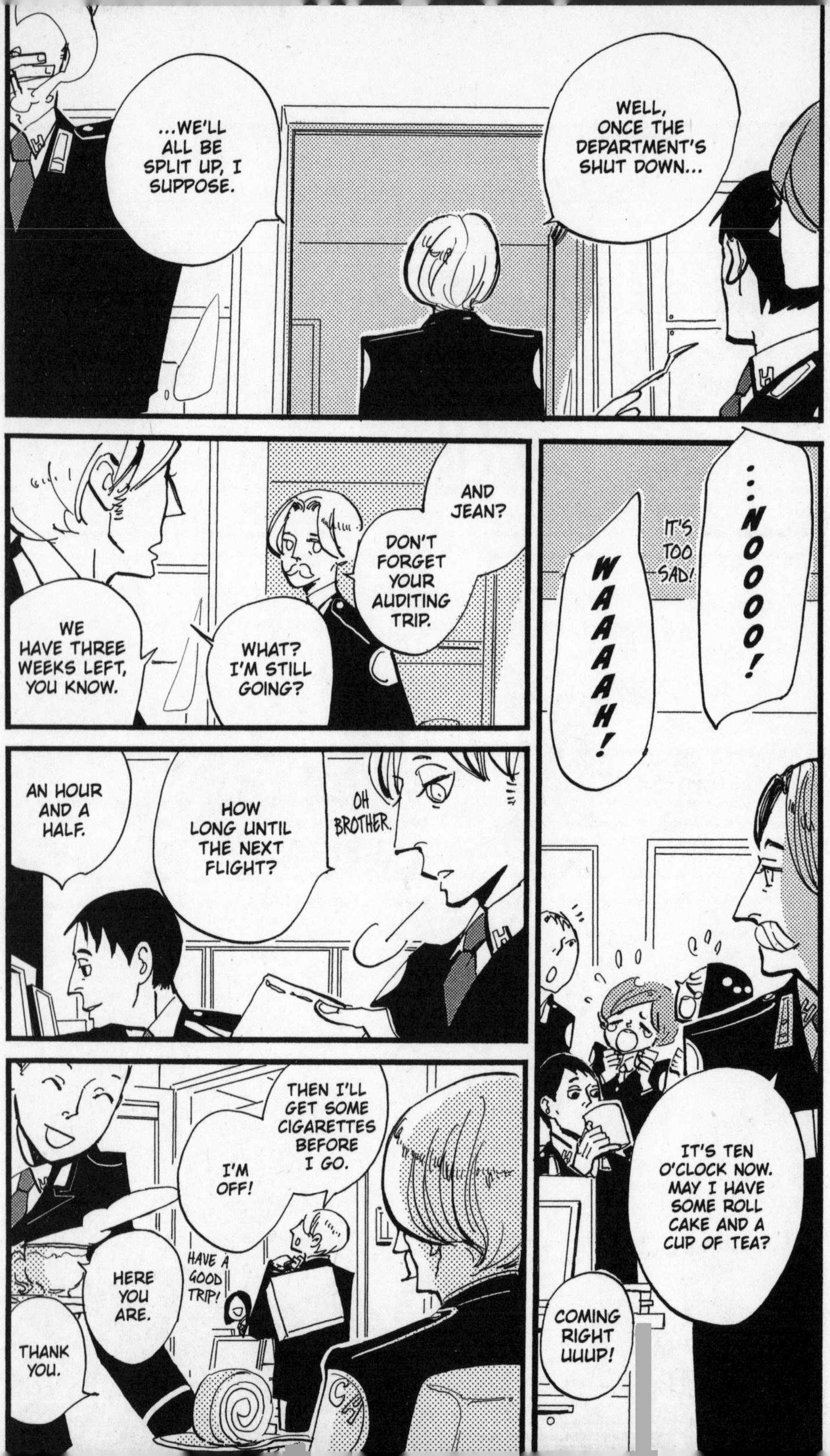
WELL, ONCE THE DEPARTMENT'S SHUT DOWN...
...WE'LL ALL BE SPLIT UP, I SUPPOSE.
...NOOOOO!
IT'S TOO SAD!
WAAAAAH!
AND JEAN?
DON'T FORGET YOUR AUDITING TRIP.
WHAT? I'M STILL GOING?
WE HAVE THREE WEEKS LEFT, YOU KNOW.
OH BROTHER.
HOW LONG UNTIL THE NEXT FLIGHT?
AN HOUR AND A HALF.
THEN I'LL GET SOME CIGARETTES BEFORE I GO.
I'M OFF!
HAVE A GOOD TRIP!
IT'S TEN O'CLOCK NOW. MAY I HAVE SOME ROLL CAKE AND A CUP OF TEA?
COMING RIGHT UUUP!
HERE YOU ARE.
THANK YOU.

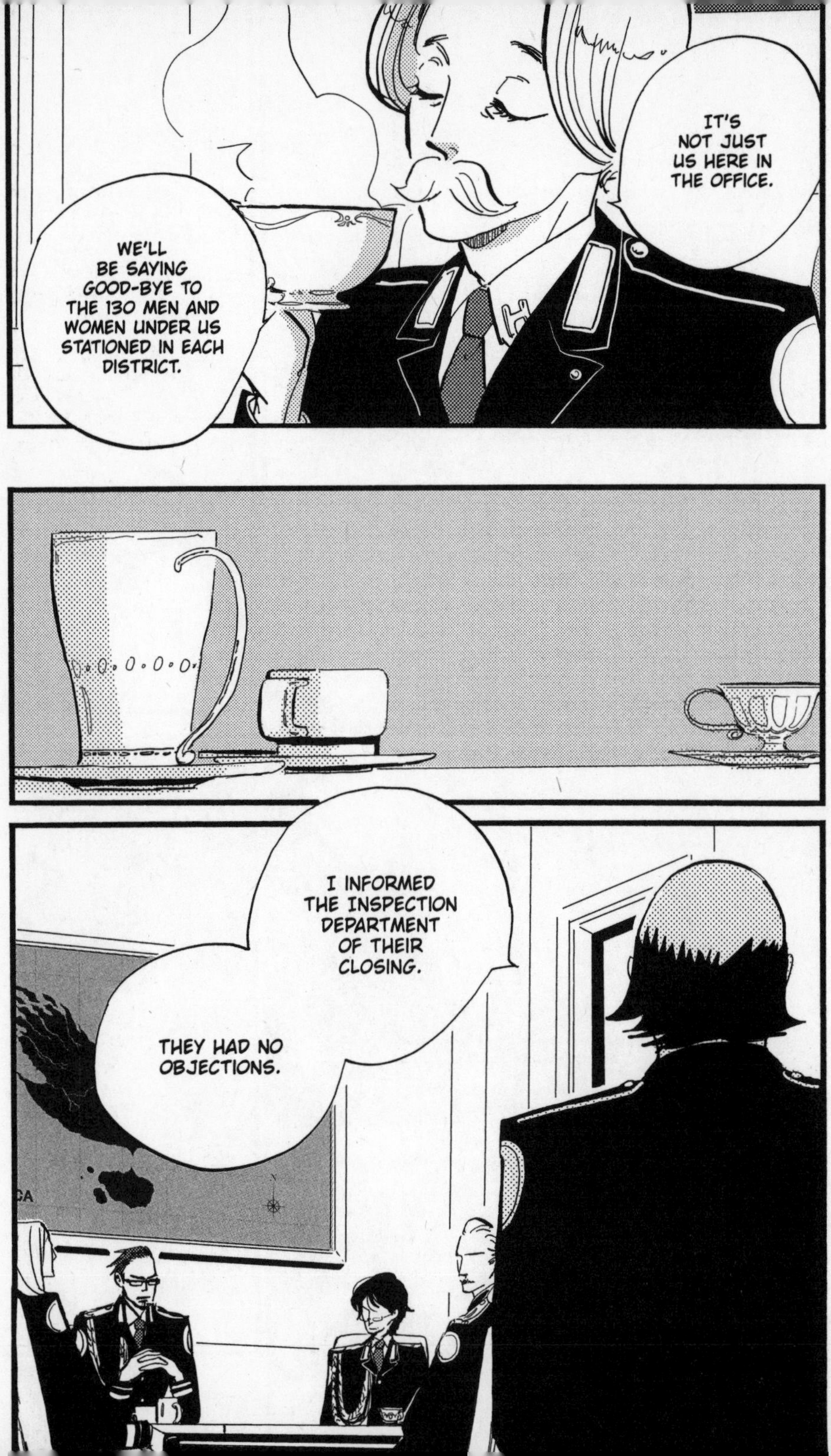
IT'S NOT JUST US HERE IN THE OFFICE.
WE'LL BE SAYING GOOD-BYE TO THE 130 MEN AND WOMEN UNDER US STATIONED IN EACH DISTRICT.
I INFORMED THE INSPECTION DEPARTMENT OF THEIR CLOSING.
THEY HAD NO OBJECTIONS.

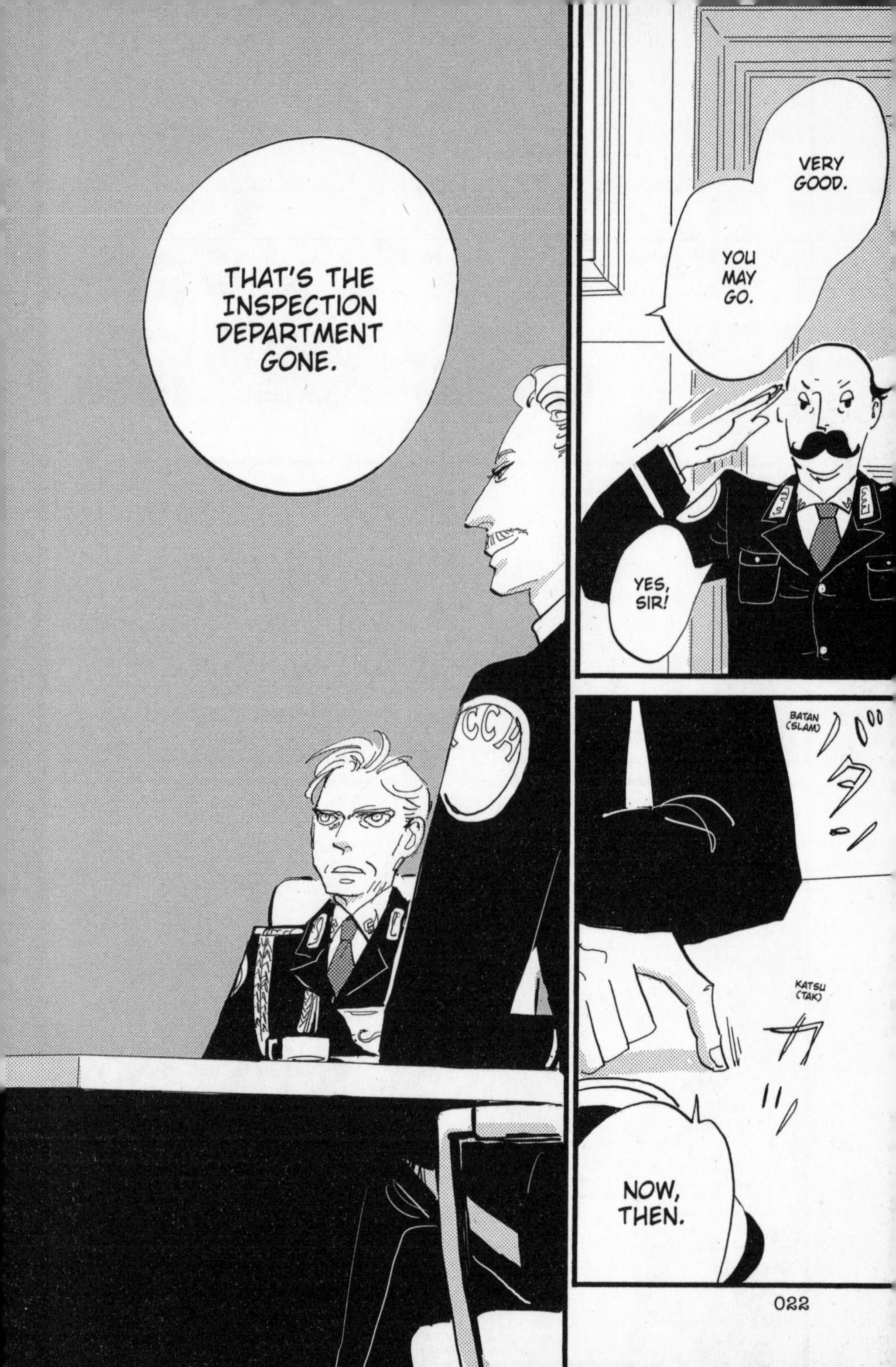
VERY GOOD.
YOU MAY GO.
YES, SIR!
THAT'S THE INSPECTION DEPARTMENT GONE.
BATAN (SLAM)
KATSU (TAK)
NOW, THEN.

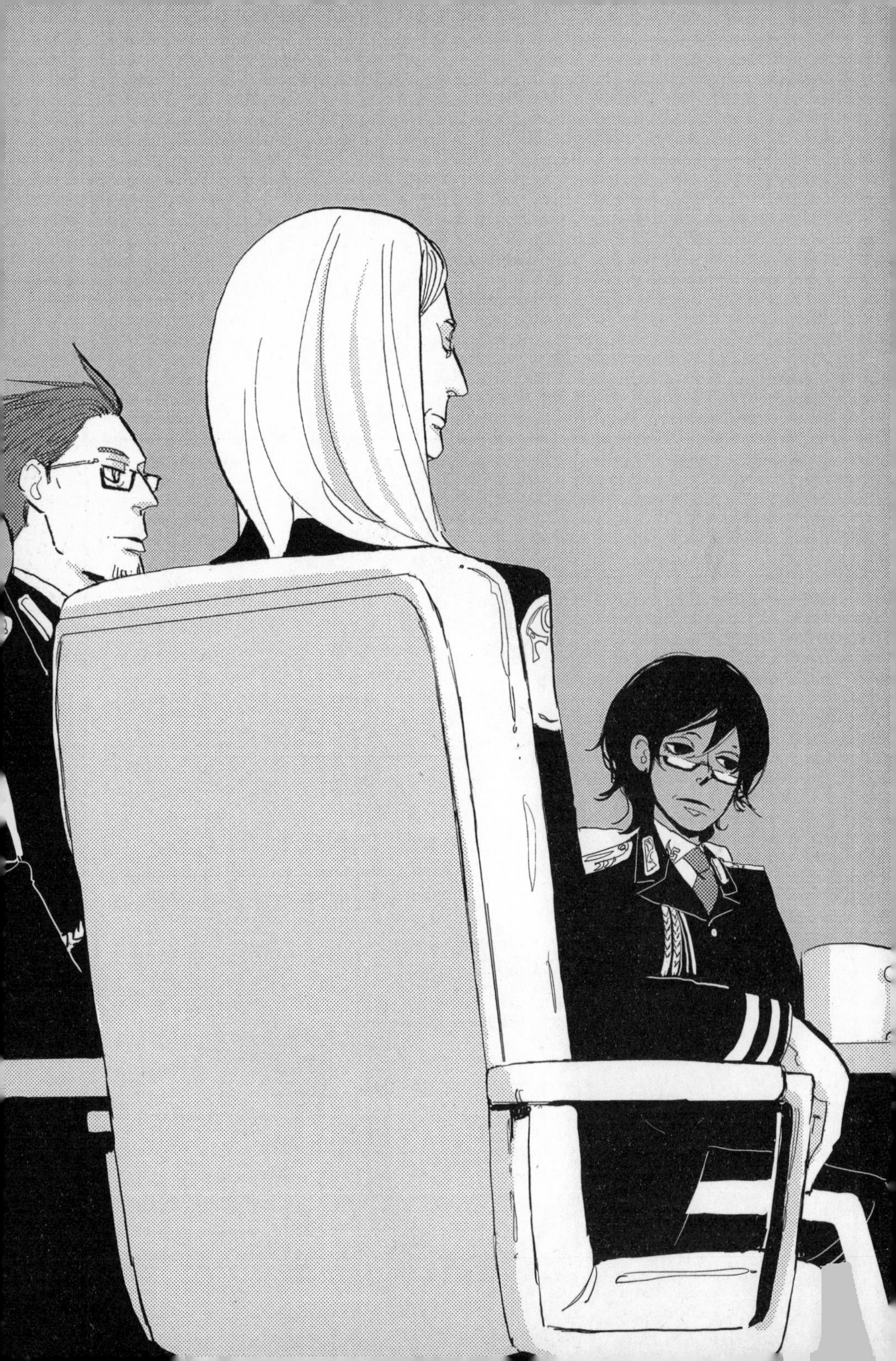

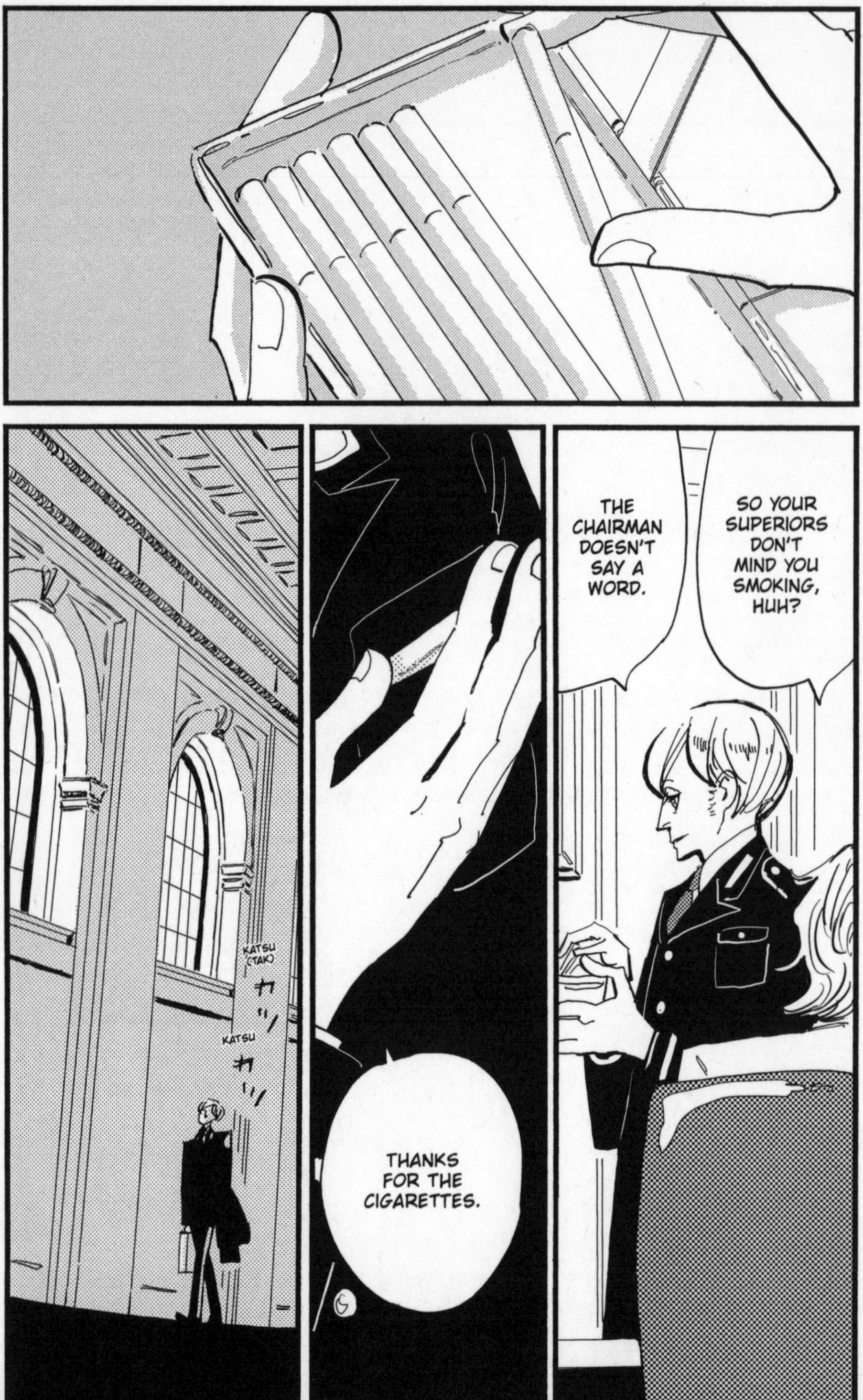
SO YOUR SUPERIORS DON'T MIND YOU SMOKING, HUH?
THE CHAIRMAN DOESN'T SAY A WORD.
THANKS FOR THE CIGARETTES.
KATSU (TAK)
カッ
KATSU
カッ

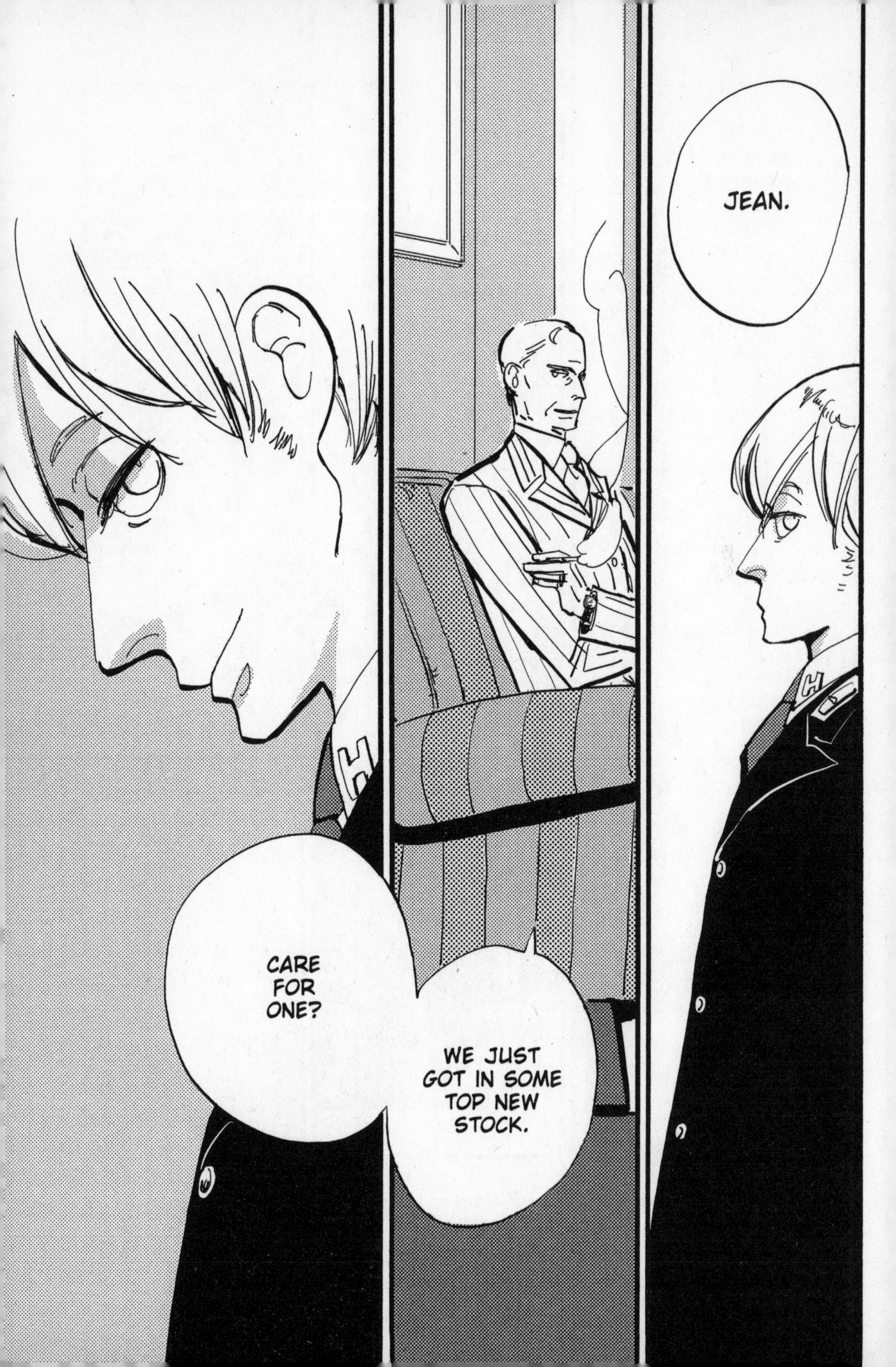
JEAN.
WE JUST GOT IN SOME TOP NEW STOCK.
CARE FOR ONE?

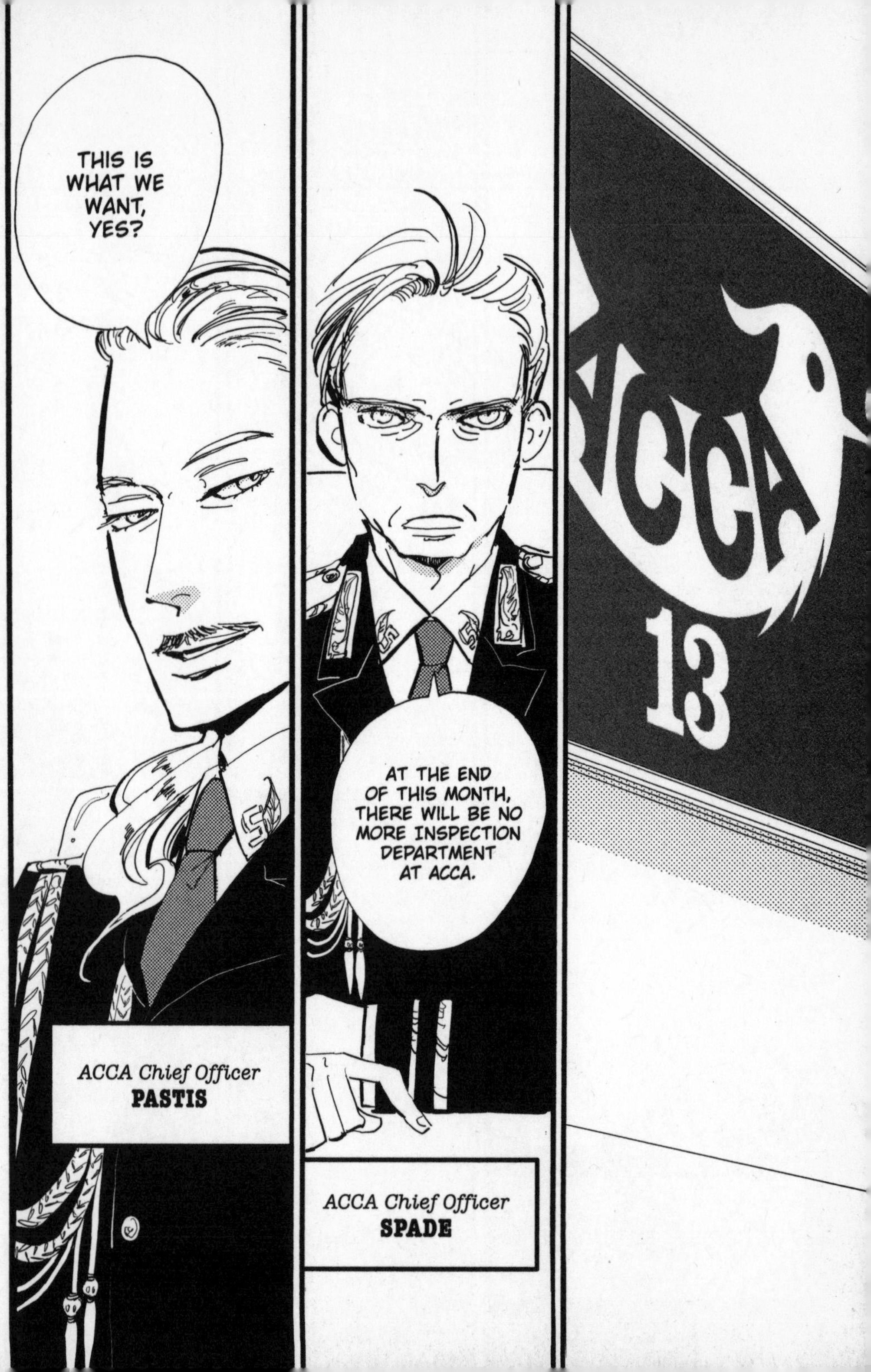
13
AT THE END OF THIS MONTH, THERE WILL BE NO MORE INSPECTION DEPARTMENT AT ACCA.
ACCA Chief Officer
SPADE
THIS IS WHAT WE WANT, YES?
ACCA Chief Officer
PASTIS

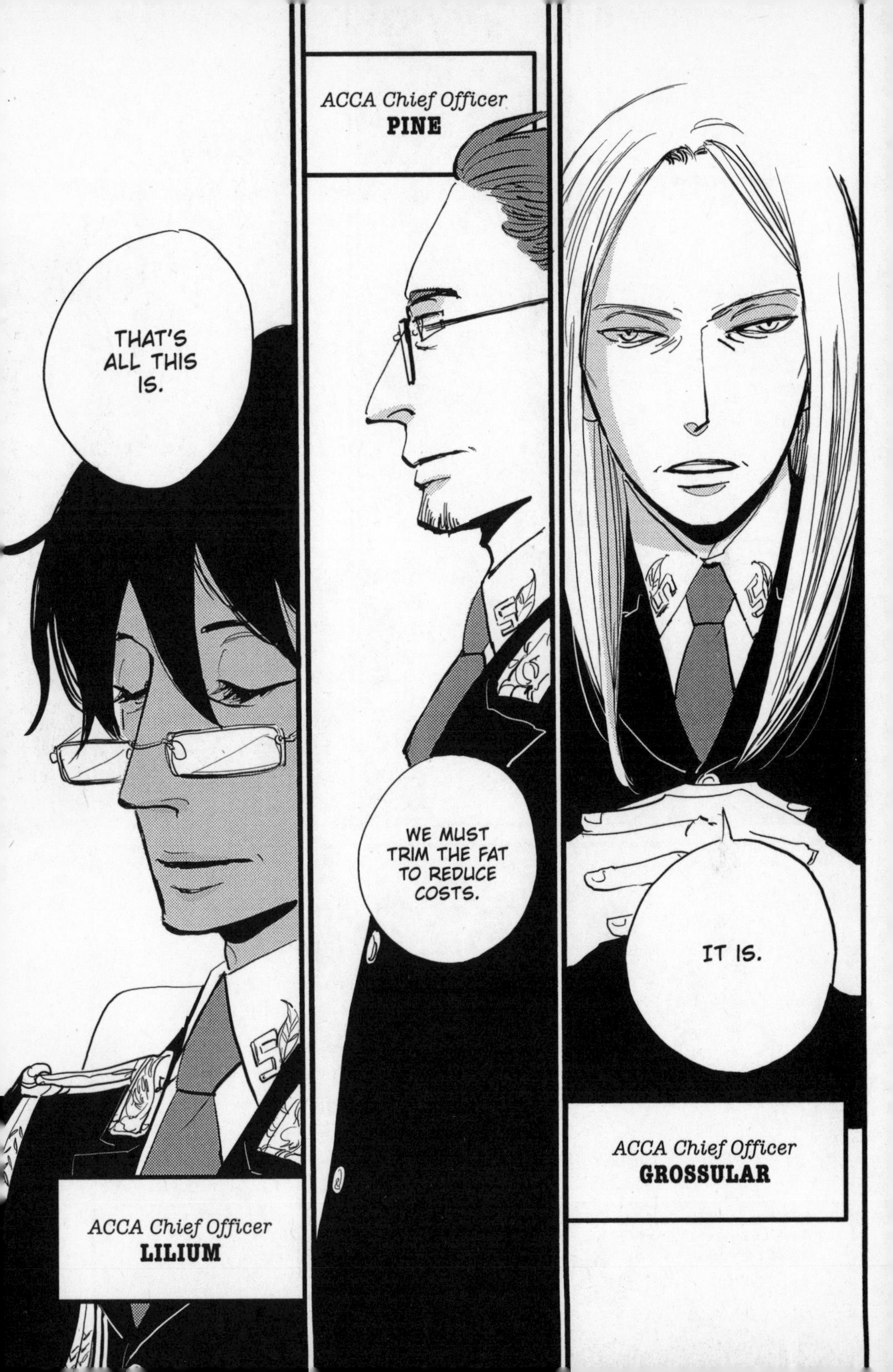
ACCA Chief Officer
PINE
THAT'S ALL THIS IS.
WE MUST TRIM THE FAT TO REDUCE COSTS.
IT IS.
ACCA Chief Officer
GROSSULAR
ACCA Chief Officer
LILIUM

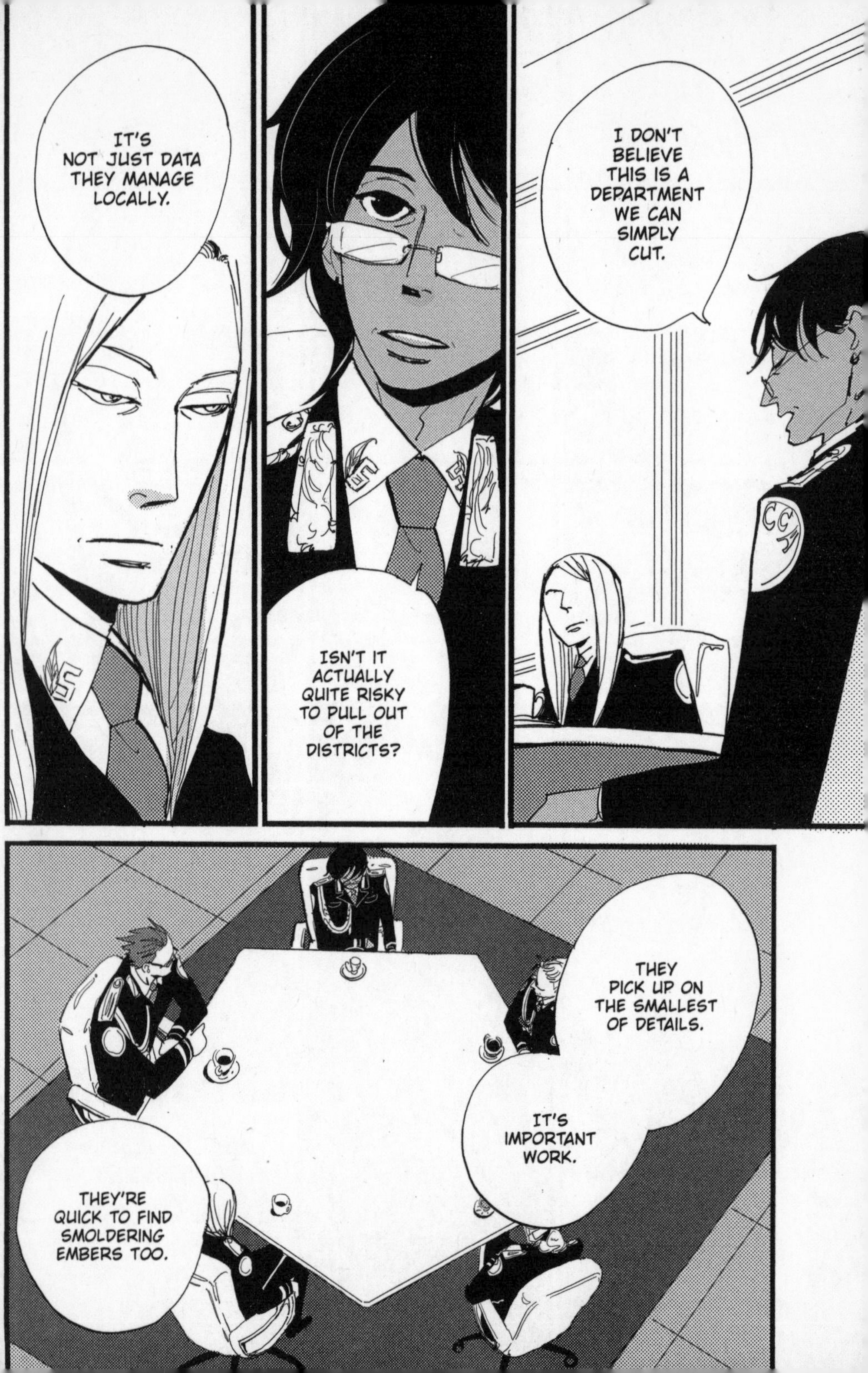
I DON'T BELIEVE THIS IS A DEPARTMENT WE CAN SIMPLY CUT.
ISN'T IT ACTUALLY QUITE RISKY TO PULL OUT OF THE DISTRICTS?
IT'S NOT JUST DATA THEY MANAGE LOCALLY.
THEY PICK UP ON THE SMALLEST OF DETAILS.
IT'S IMPORTANT WORK.
THEY'RE QUICK TO FIND SMOLDERING EMBERS TOO.

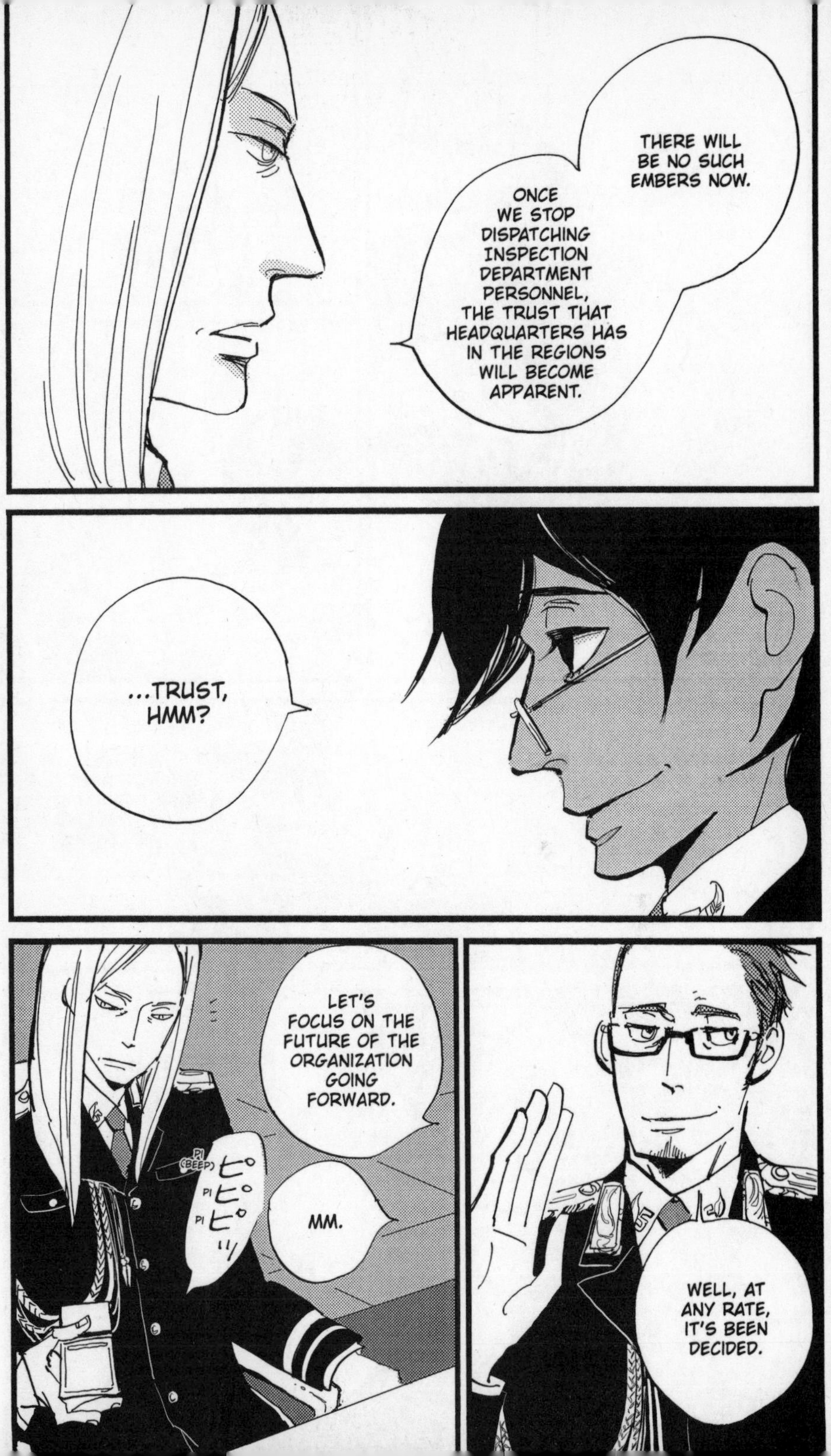
THERE WILL BE NO SUCH EMBERS NOW.
ONCE WE STOP DISPATCHING INSPECTION DEPARTMENT PERSONNEL, THE TRUST THAT HEADQUARTERS HAS IN THE REGIONS WILL BECOME APPARENT.
...TRUST, HMM?
WELL, AT ANY RATE, IT'S BEEN DECIDED.
LET'S FOCUS ON THE FUTURE OF THE ORGANIZATION GOING FORWARD.
MM.
PI (BEEP) PI PI
ピピピッ

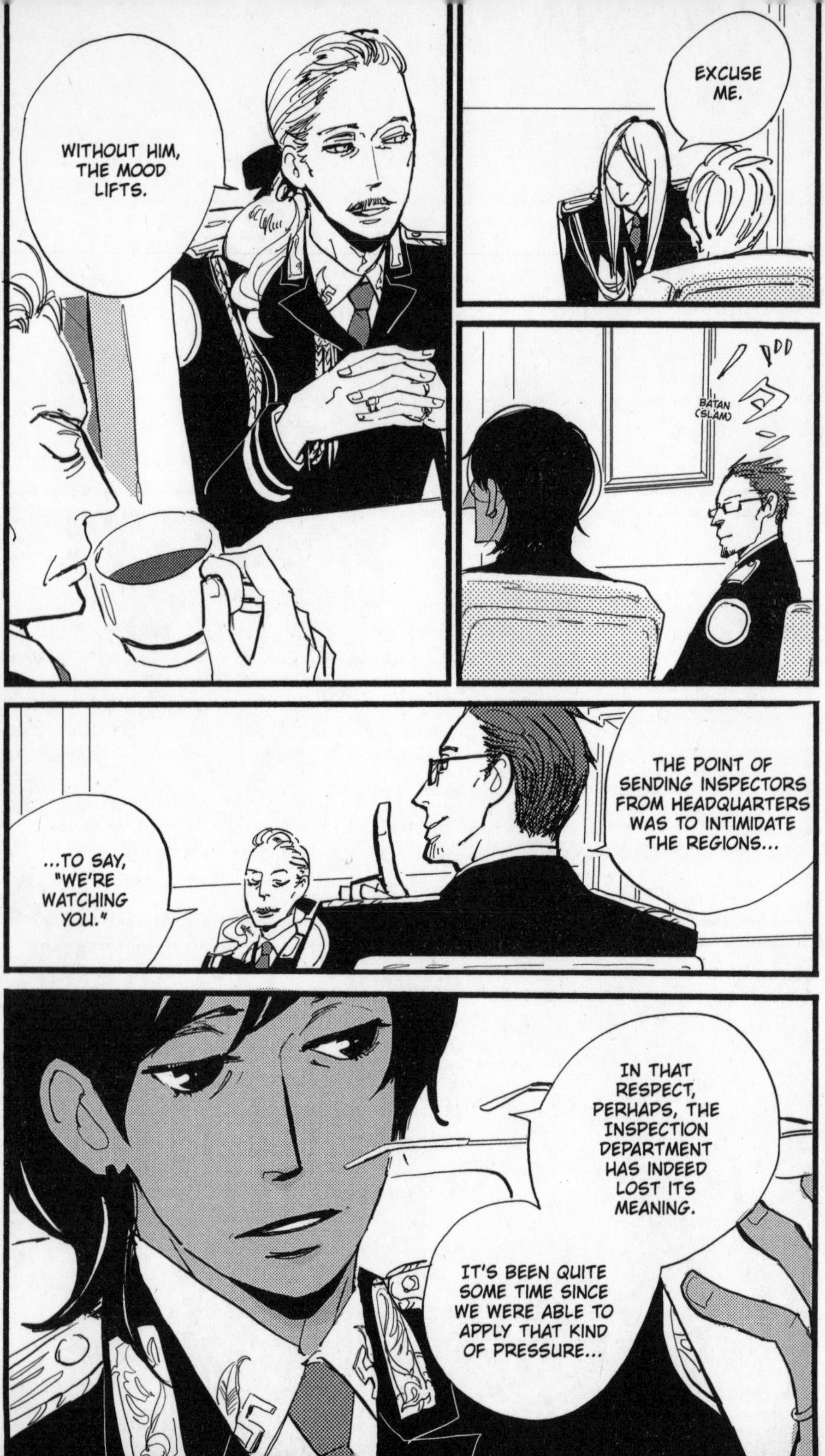
WITHOUT HIM, THE MOOD LIFTS.
EXCUSE ME.
BATAN (SLAM)
...TO SAY, "WE'RE WATCHING YOU."
THE POINT OF SENDING INSPECTORS FROM HEADQUARTERS WAS TO INTIMIDATE THE REGIONS...
IN THAT RESPECT, PERHAPS, THE INSPECTION DEPARTMENT HAS INDEED LOST ITS MEANING.
IT'S BEEN QUITE SOME TIME SINCE WE WERE ABLE TO APPLY THAT KIND OF PRESSURE...

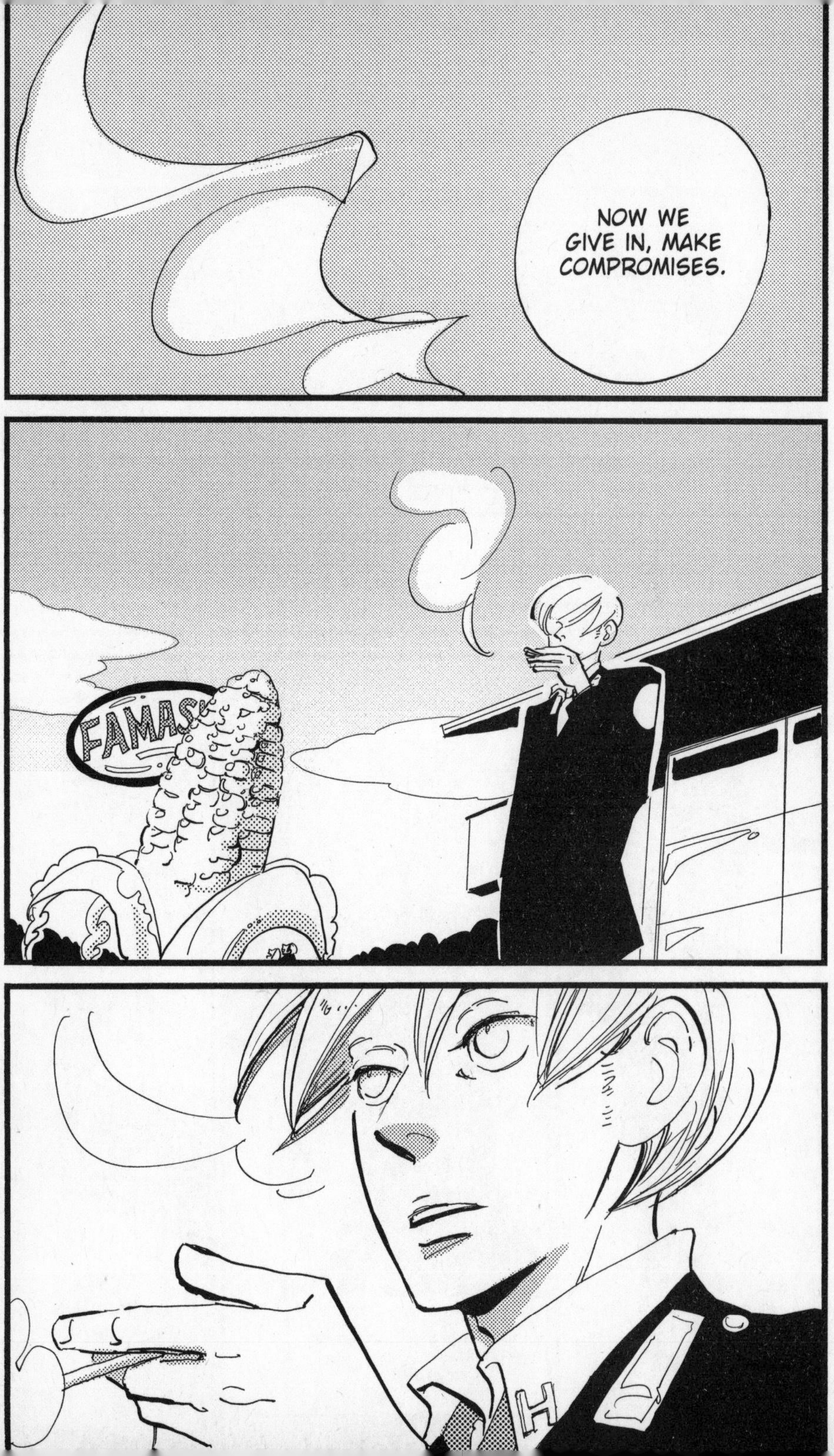
NOW WE GIVE IN, MAKE COMPROMISES.
FAMAS

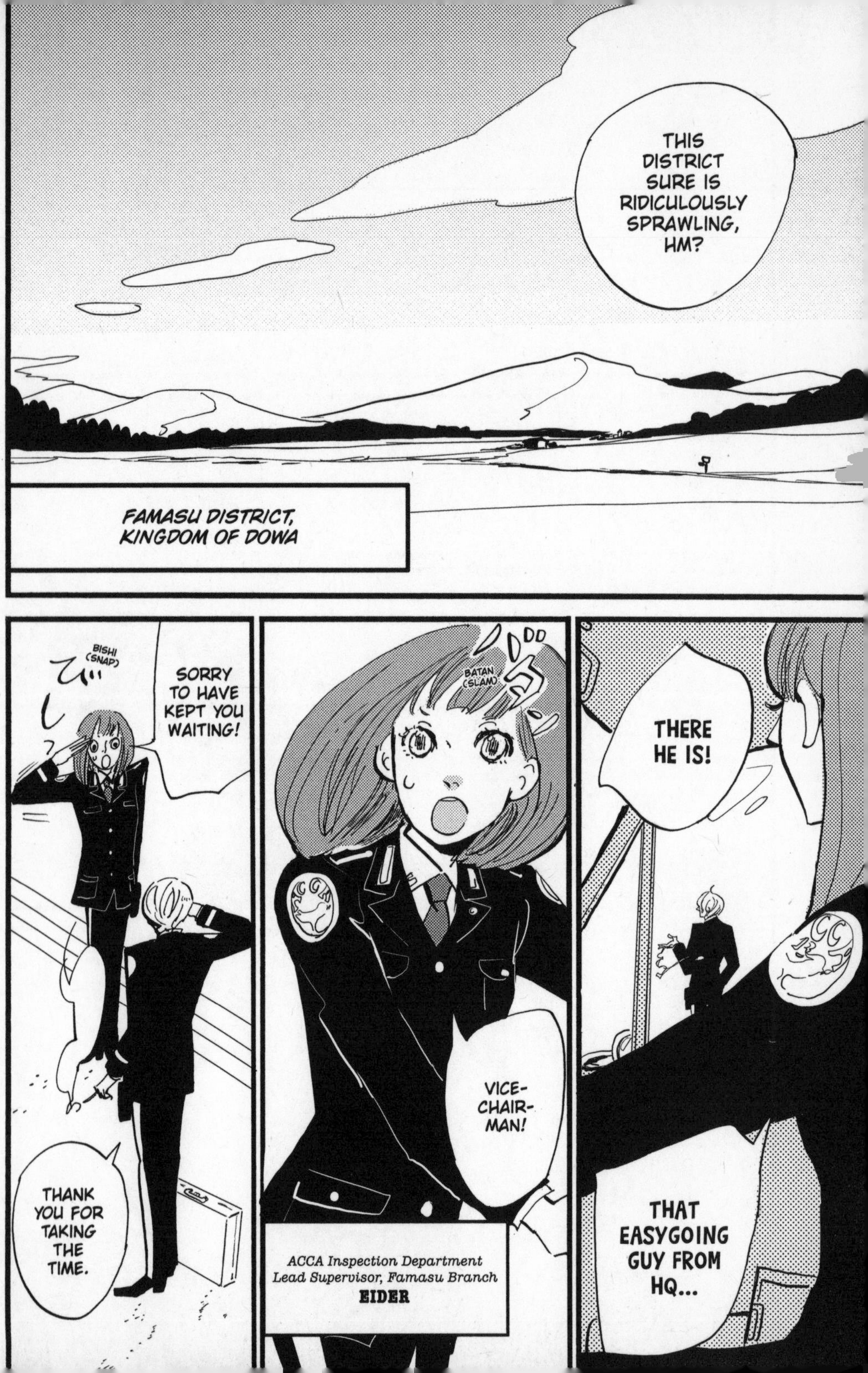
THIS DISTRICT SURE IS RIDICULOUSLY SPRAWLING, HM?
FAMASU DISTRICT, KINGDOM OF DOWA
BISHI (SNAP)
SORRY TO HAVE KEPT YOU WAITING!
THANK YOU FOR TAKING THE TIME.
BATAN (SLAM)
VICE-CHAIRMAN!
ACCA Inspection Department
Lead Supervisor, Famasu Branch
EIDER
THERE HE IS!
THAT EASYGOING GUY FROM HQ...

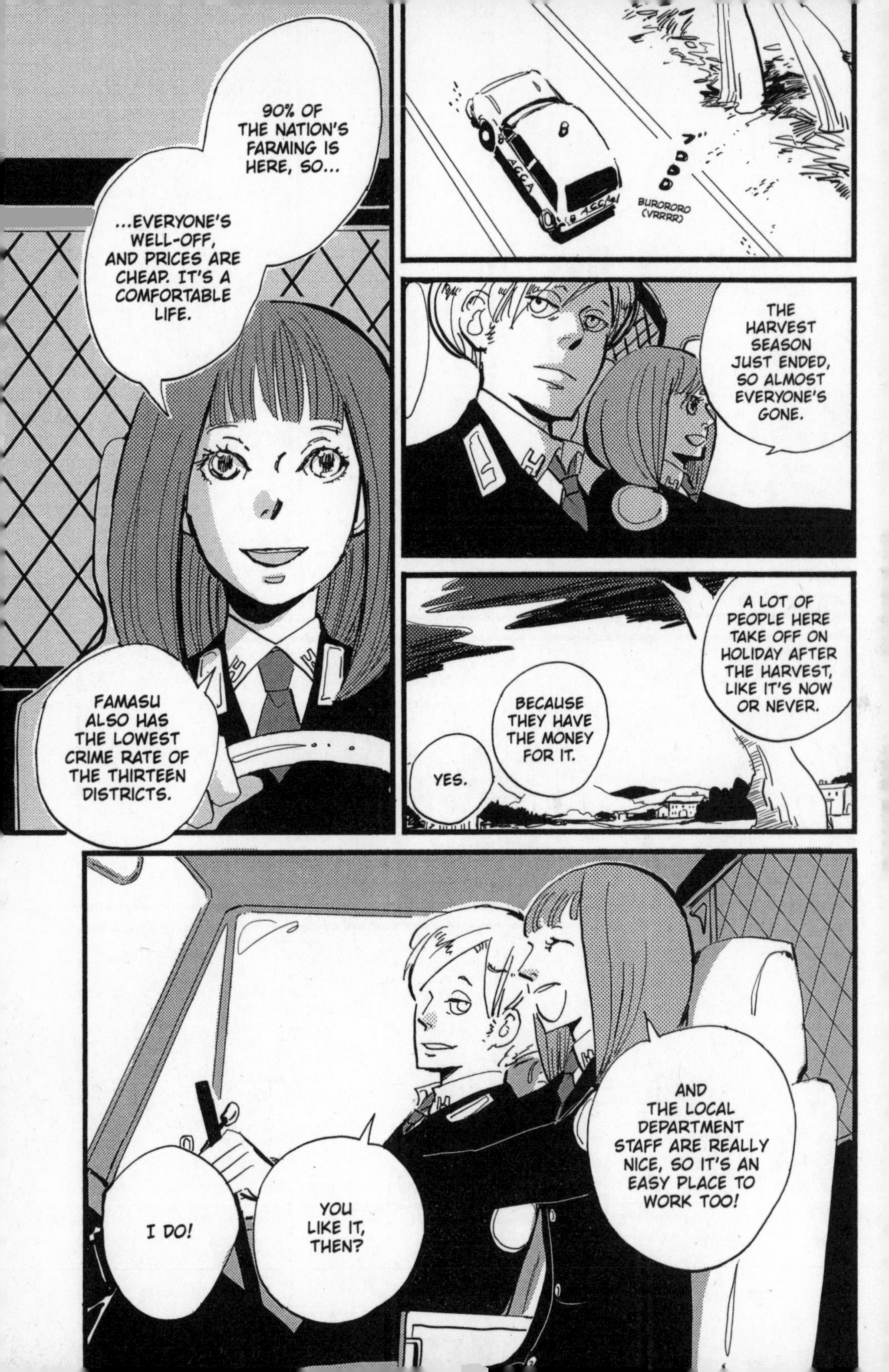
BURORORO (VRRRR)
90% OF THE NATION'S FARMING IS HERE, SO...
...EVERYONE'S WELL-OFF, AND PRICES ARE CHEAP. IT'S A COMFORTABLE LIFE.
FAMASU ALSO HAS THE LOWEST CRIME RATE OF THE THIRTEEN DISTRICTS.
THE HARVEST SEASON JUST ENDED, SO ALMOST EVERYONE'S GONE.
A LOT OF PEOPLE HERE TAKE OFF ON HOLIDAY AFTER THE HARVEST, LIKE IT'S NOW OR NEVER.
BECAUSE THEY HAVE THE MONEY FOR IT.
YES.
AND THE LOCAL DEPARTMENT STAFF ARE REALLY NICE, SO IT'S AN EASY PLACE TO WORK TOO!
YOU LIKE IT, THEN?
I DO!

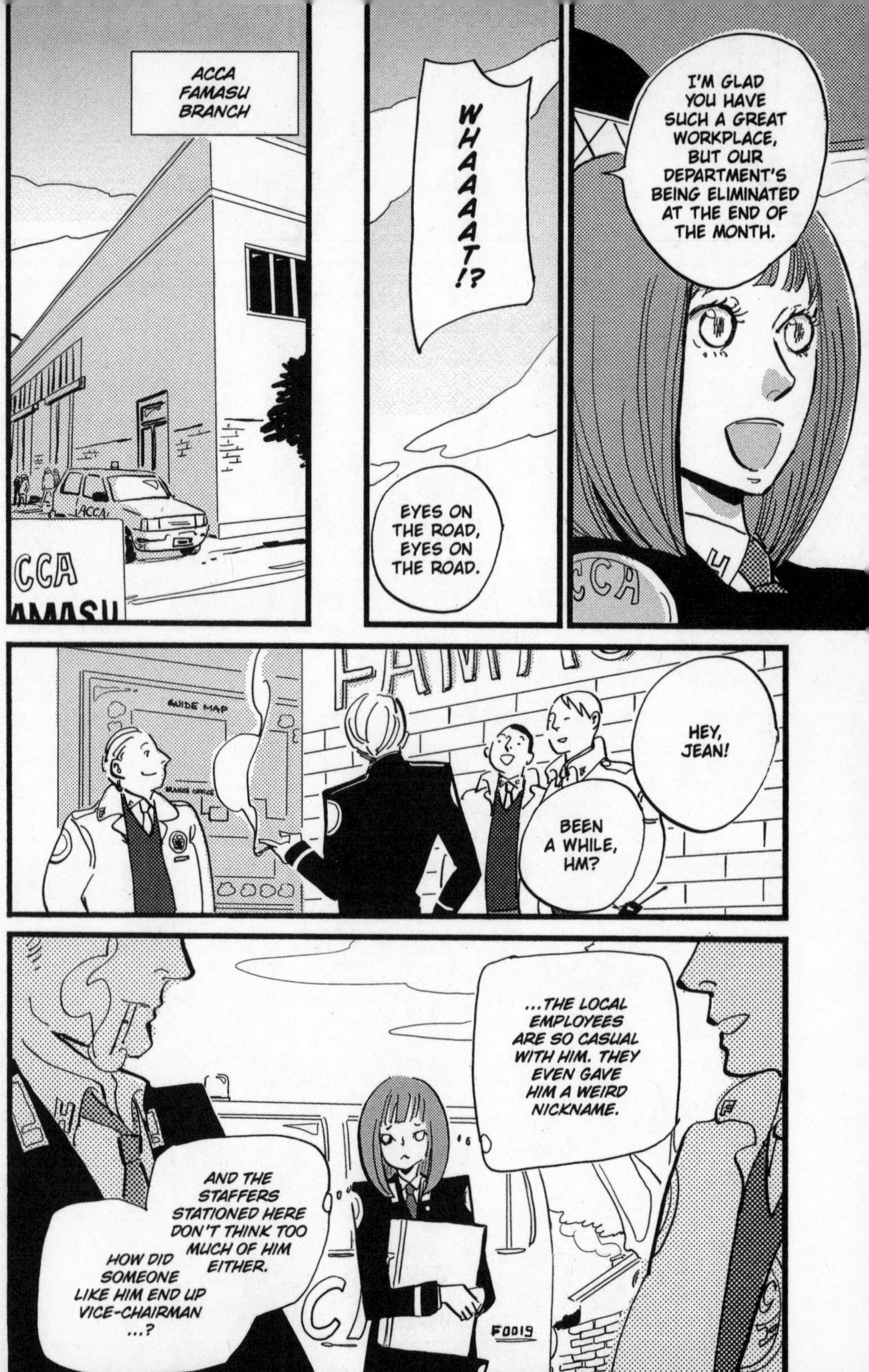
ACCA FAMASU BRANCH
CCA AMASU
ACCA
WHAAAAAT!?
EYES ON THE ROAD, EYES ON THE ROAD.
I'M GLAD YOU HAVE SUCH A GREAT WORKPLACE, BUT OUR DEPARTMENT'S BEING ELIMINATED AT THE END OF THE MONTH.
CCA
GUIDE MAP
HEY, JEAN!
BEEN A WHILE, HM?
...THE LOCAL EMPLOYEES ARE SO CASUAL WITH HIM. THEY EVEN GAVE HIM A WEIRD NICKNAME.
AND THE STAFFERS STATIONED HERE DON'T THINK TOO MUCH OF HIM EITHER.
HOW DID SOMEONE LIKE HIM END UP VICE-CHAIRMAN ...?
F0019

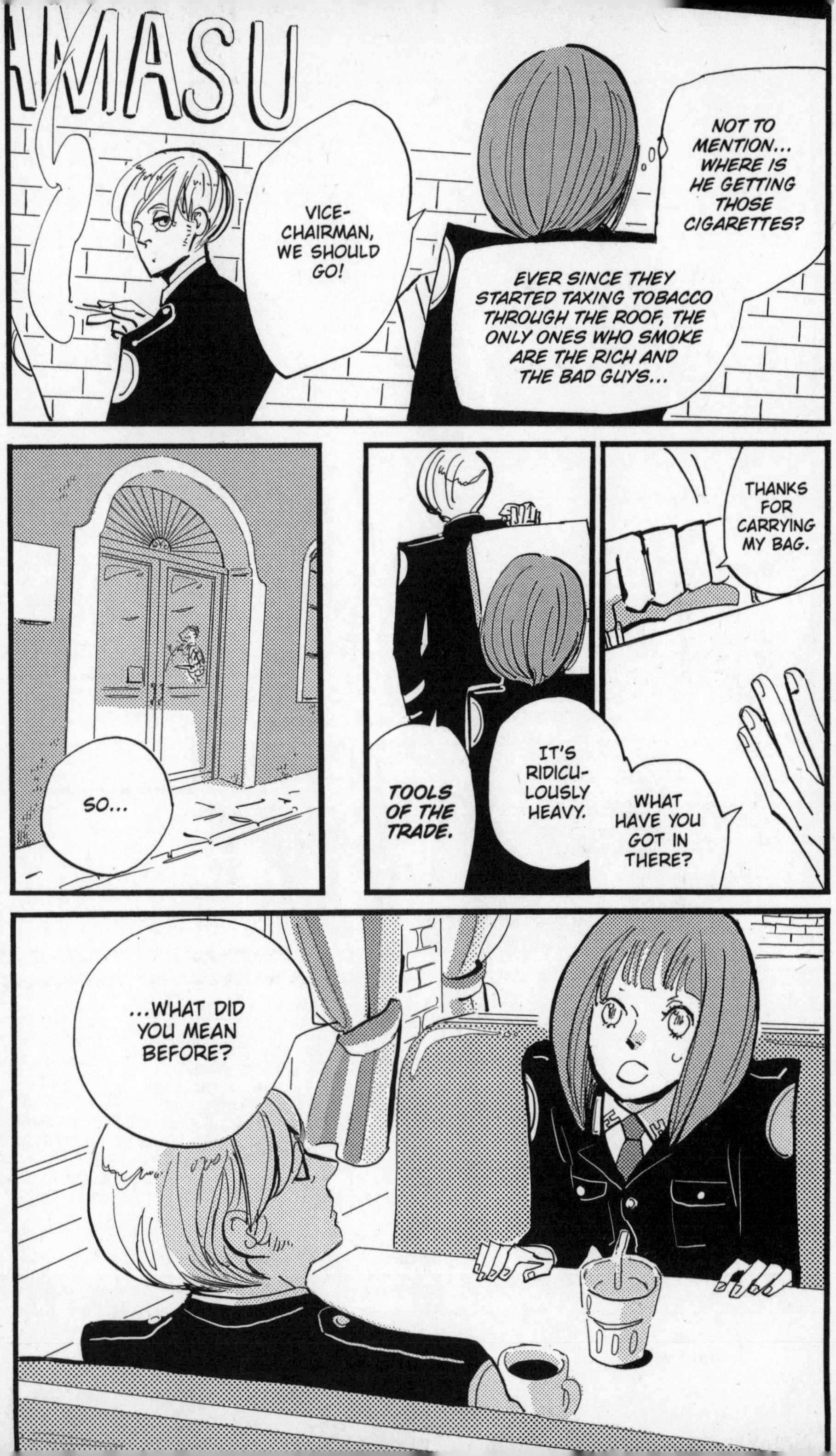
AMASU
NOT TO MENTION... WHERE IS HE GETTING THOSE CIGARETTES?
EVER SINCE THEY STARTED TAXING TOBACCO THROUGH THE ROOF, THE ONLY ONES WHO SMOKE ARE THE RICH AND THE BAD GUYS...
VICE-CHAIRMAN, WE SHOULD GO!
THANKS FOR CARRYING MY BAG.
WHAT HAVE YOU GOT IN THERE?
IT'S RIDICU-LOUSLY HEAVY.
TOOLS OF THE TRADE.
SO...
...WHAT DID YOU MEAN BEFORE?

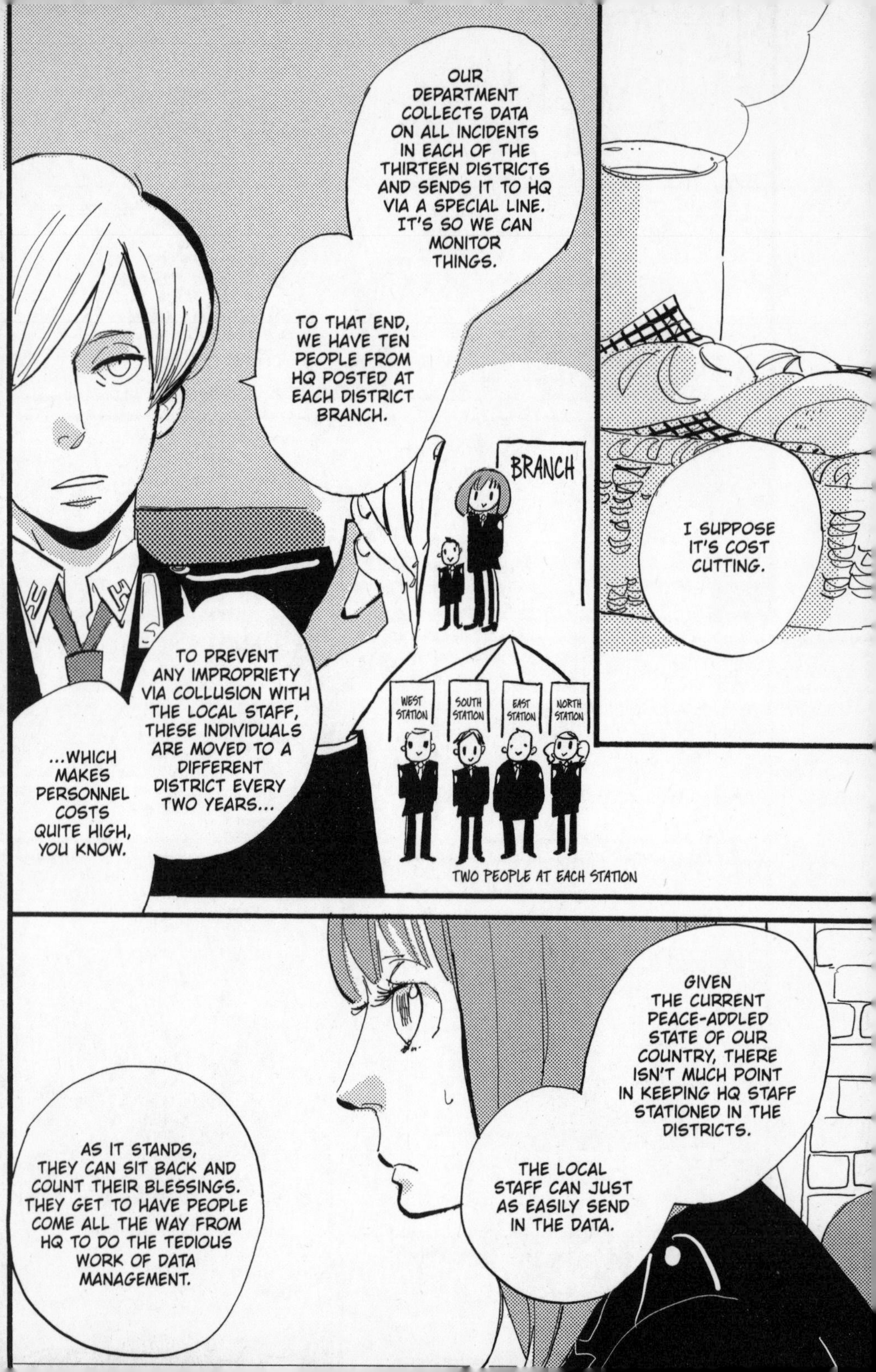
OUR DEPARTMENT COLLECTS DATA ON ALL INCIDENTS IN EACH OF THE THIRTEEN DISTRICTS AND SENDS IT TO HQ VIA A SPECIAL LINE. IT'S SO WE CAN MONITOR THINGS.
TO THAT END, WE HAVE TEN PEOPLE FROM HQ POSTED AT EACH DISTRICT BRANCH.
BRANCH
WEST STATION
SOUTH STATION
EAST STATION
NORTH STATION
TWO PEOPLE AT EACH STATION
TO PREVENT ANY IMPROPRIETY VIA COLLUSION WITH THE LOCAL STAFF, THESE INDIVIDUALS ARE MOVED TO A DIFFERENT DISTRICT EVERY TWO YEARS...
...WHICH MAKES PERSONNEL COSTS QUITE HIGH, YOU KNOW.
I SUPPOSE IT'S COST CUTTING.
GIVEN THE CURRENT PEACE-ADDLED STATE OF OUR COUNTRY, THERE ISN'T MUCH POINT IN KEEPING HQ STAFF STATIONED IN THE DISTRICTS.
THE LOCAL STAFF CAN JUST AS EASILY SEND IN THE DATA.
AS IT STANDS, THEY CAN SIT BACK AND COUNT THEIR BLESSINGS. THEY GET TO HAVE PEOPLE COME ALL THE WAY FROM HQ TO DO THE TEDIOUS WORK OF DATA MANAGEMENT.

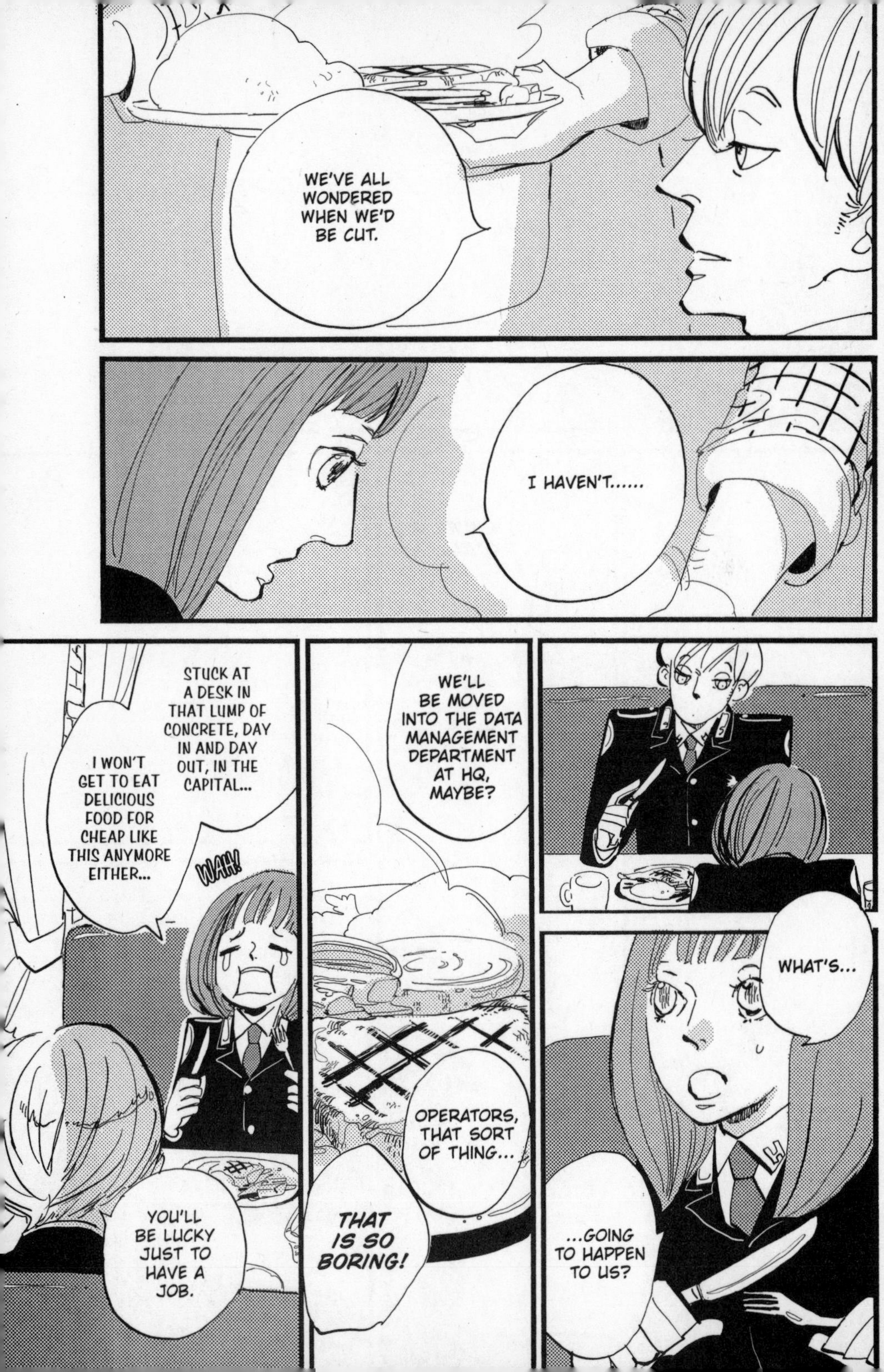
WE'VE ALL WONDERED WHEN WE'D BE CUT.
I HAVEN'T......
WHAT'S...
...GOING TO HAPPEN TO US?
WE'LL BE MOVED INTO THE DATA MANAGEMENT DEPARTMENT AT HQ, MAYBE?
OPERATORS, THAT SORT OF THING...
THAT IS SO BORING!
STUCK AT A DESK IN THAT LUMP OF CONCRETE, DAY IN AND DAY OUT, IN THE CAPITAL...
I WON'T GET TO EAT DELICIOUS FOOD FOR CHEAP LIKE THIS ANYMORE EITHER...
WAH!
YOU'LL BE LUCKY JUST TO HAVE A JOB.

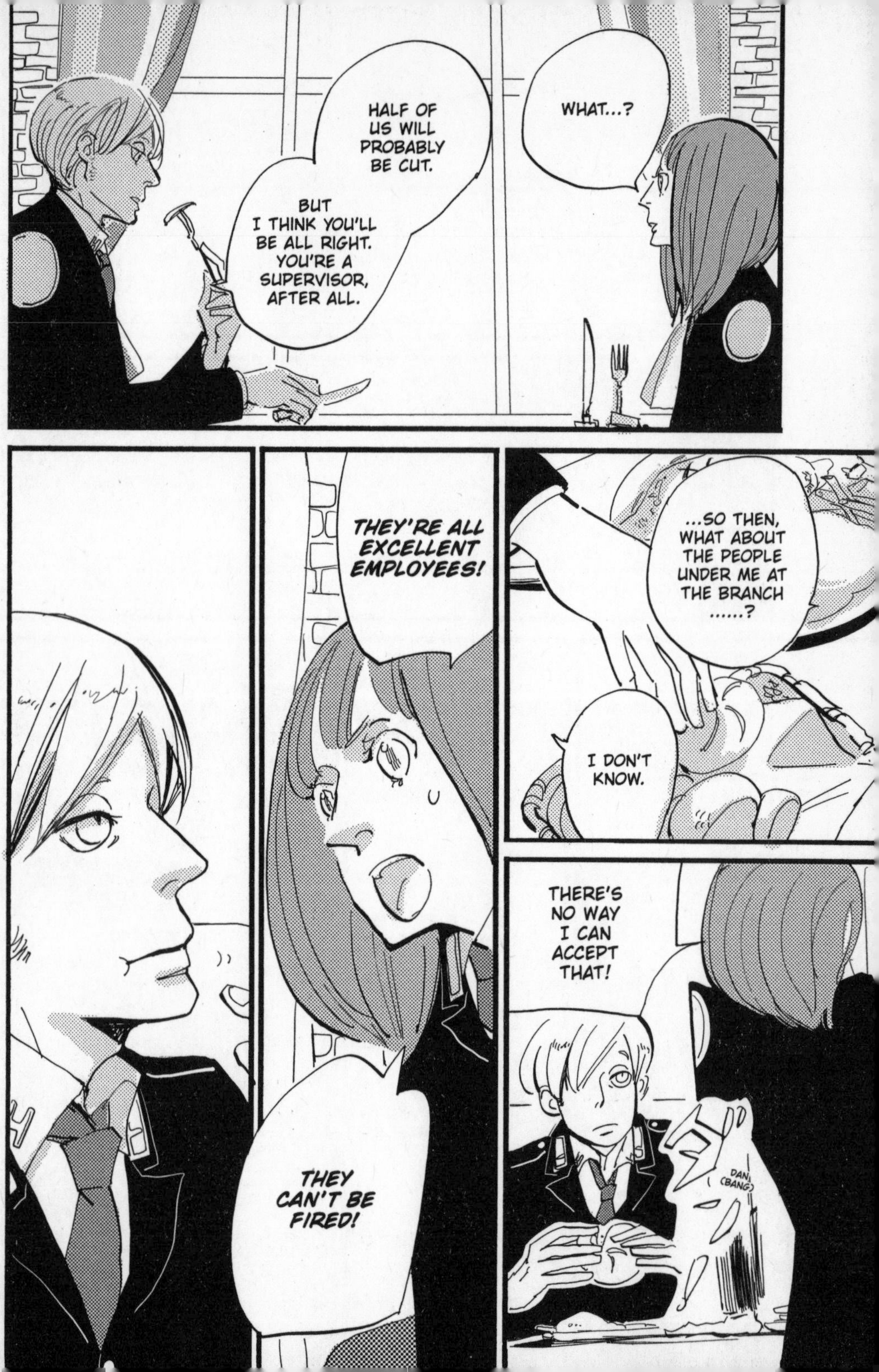
WHAT...?
HALF OF US WILL PROBABLY BE CUT.
BUT I THINK YOU'LL BE ALL RIGHT. YOU'RE A SUPERVISOR, AFTER ALL.
...SO THEN, WHAT ABOUT THE PEOPLE UNDER ME AT THE BRANCH ......?
I DON'T KNOW.
THERE'S NO WAY I CAN ACCEPT THAT!
DAN (BANG)
THEY'RE ALL EXCELLENT EMPLOYEES!
THEY CAN'T BE FIRED!

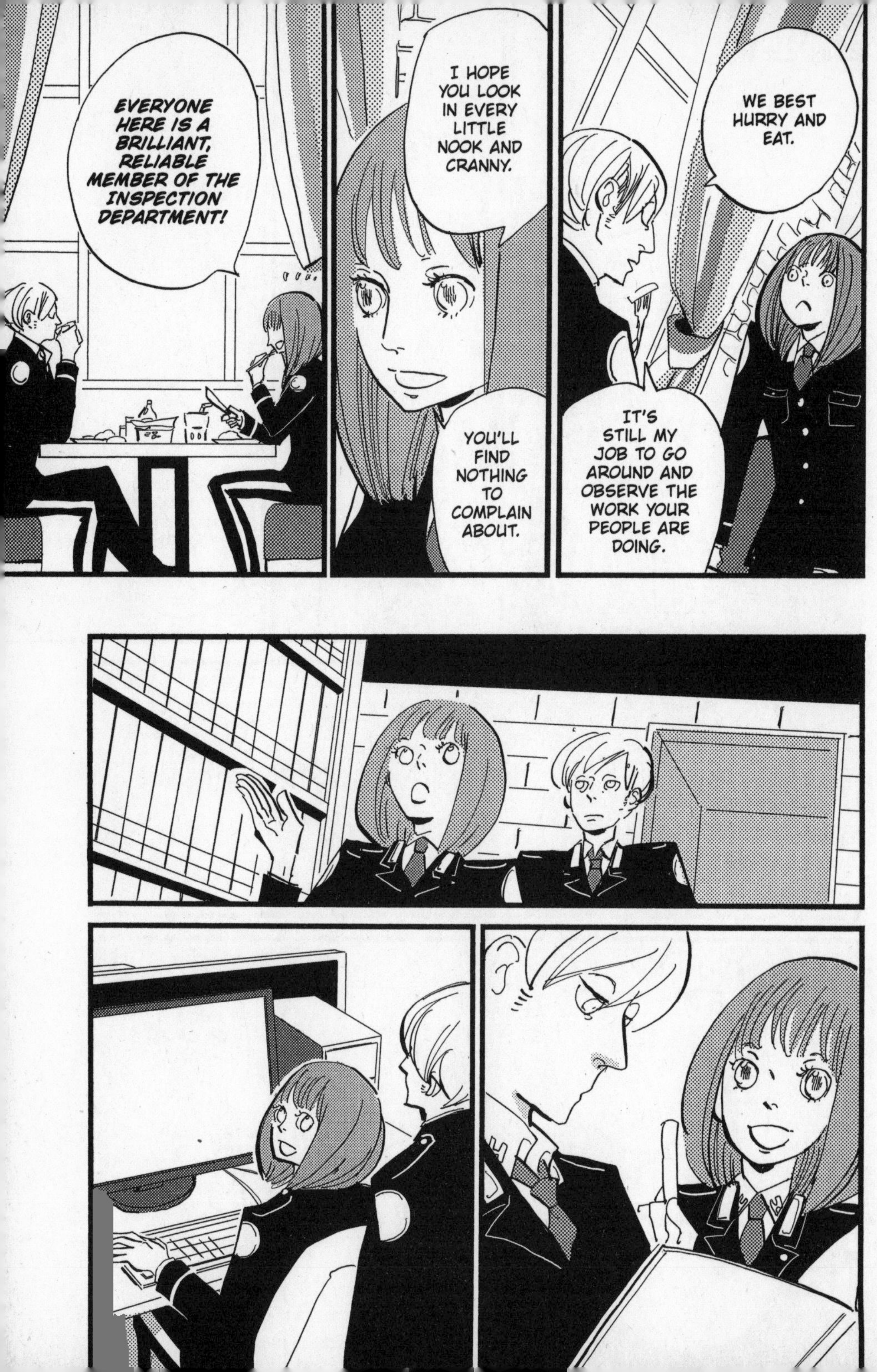
WE BEST HURRY AND EAT.
IT'S STILL MY JOB TO GO AROUND AND OBSERVE THE WORK YOUR PEOPLE ARE DOING.
I HOPE YOU LOOK IN EVERY LITTLE NOOK AND CRANNY.
YOU'LL FIND NOTHING TO COMPLAIN ABOUT.
EVERYONE HERE IS A BRILLIANT, RELIABLE MEMBER OF THE INSPECTION DEPARTMENT!

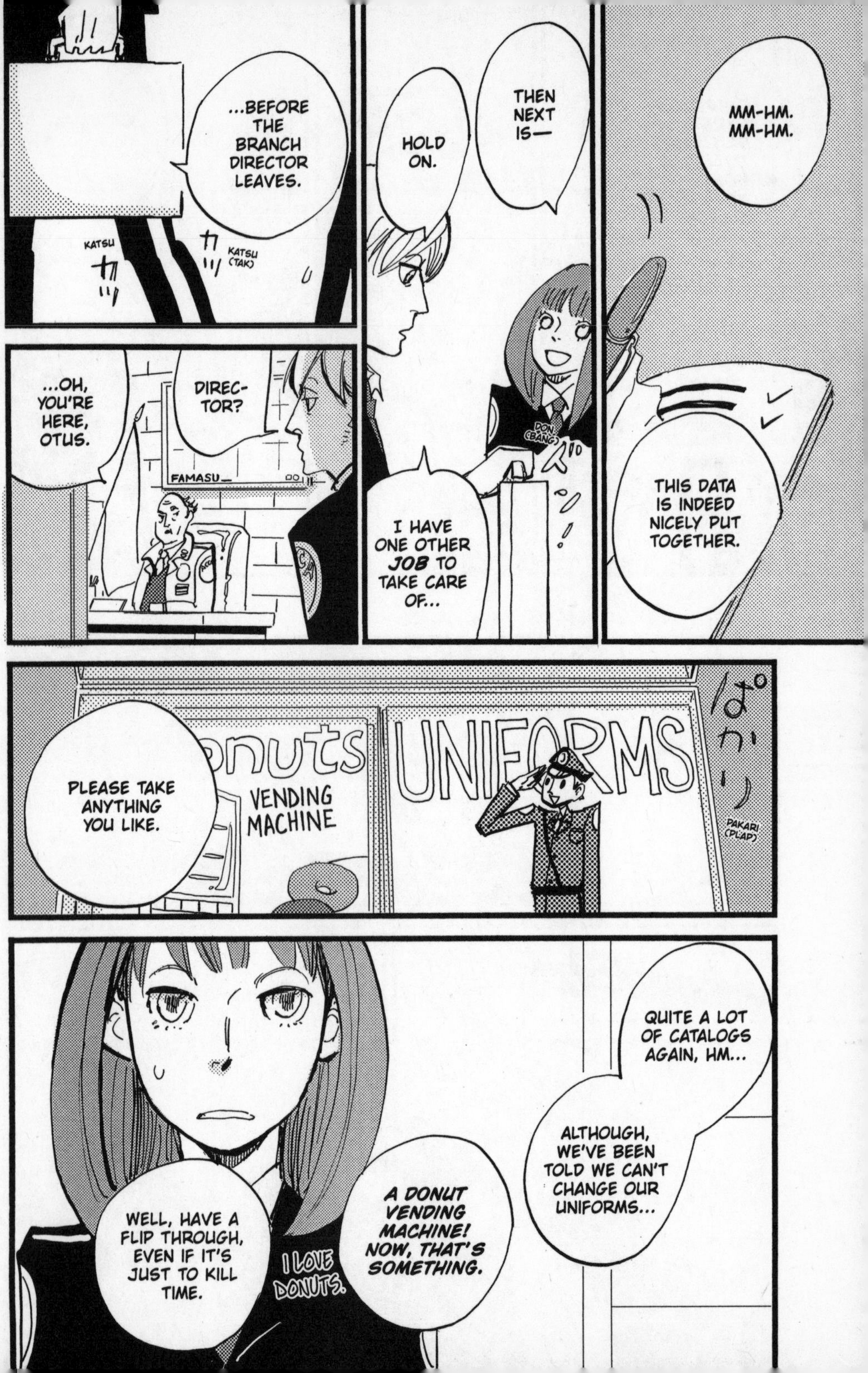
MM-HM. MM-HM.
THIS DATA IS INDEED NICELY PUT TOGETHER.
THEN NEXT IS—
HOLD ON.
DON (BANG)
I HAVE ONE OTHER JOB TO TAKE CARE OF...
...BEFORE THE BRANCH DIRECTOR LEAVES.
KATSU (TAK)
KATSU
DIRECTOR?
...OH, YOU'RE HERE, OTUS.
FAMASU
PAKARI (PLAP)
UNIFORMS
VENDING MACHINE
PLEASE TAKE ANYTHING YOU LIKE.
QUITE A LOT OF CATALOGS AGAIN, HM...
ALTHOUGH, WE'VE BEEN TOLD WE CAN'T CHANGE OUR UNIFORMS...
A DONUT VENDING MACHINE! NOW, THAT'S SOMETHING.
I LOVE DONUTS.
WELL, HAVE A FLIP THROUGH, EVEN IF IT'S JUST TO KILL TIME.

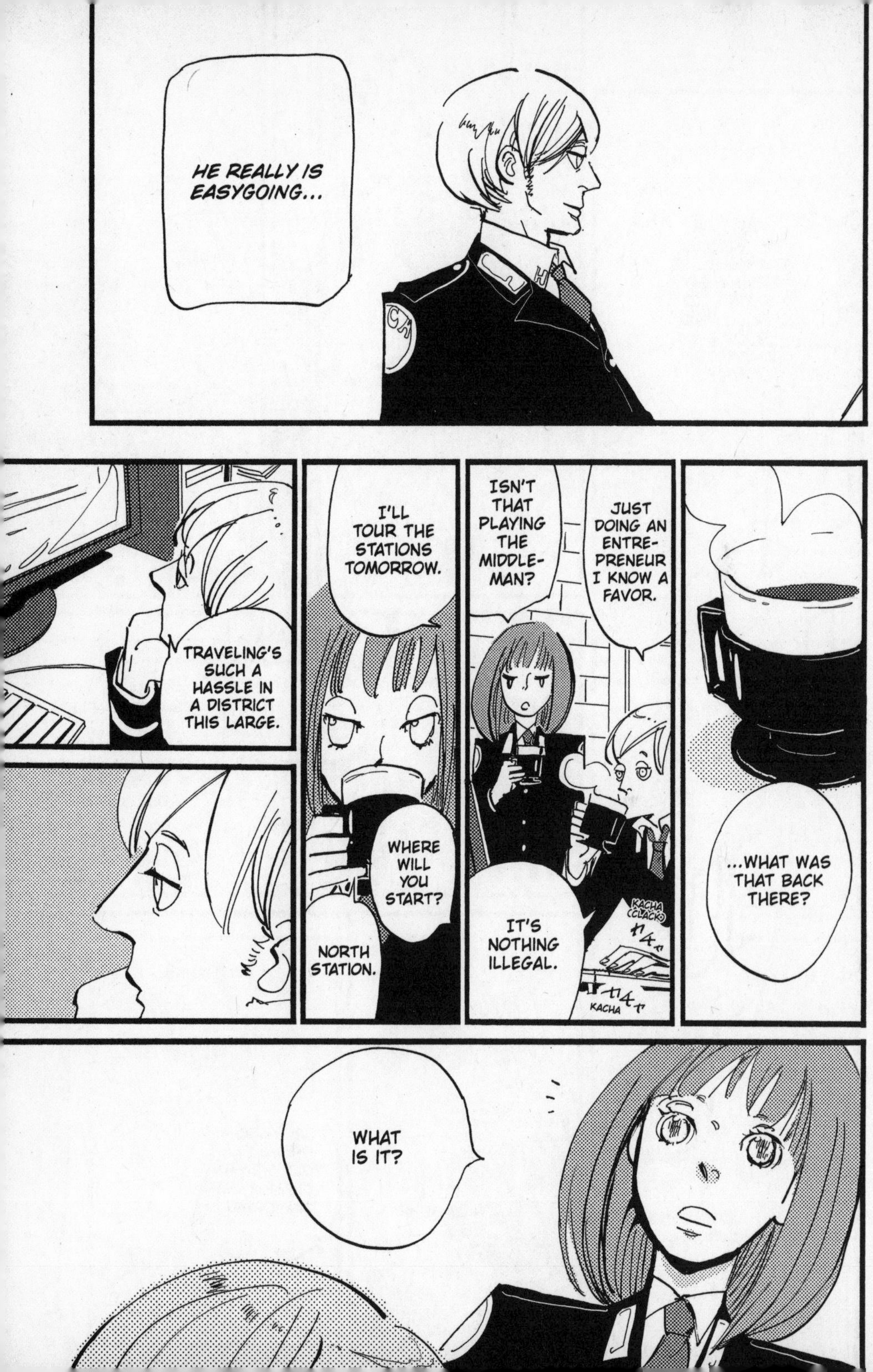
HE REALLY IS EASYGOING...
...WHAT WAS THAT BACK THERE?
JUST DOING AN ENTREPRENEUR I KNOW A FAVOR.
ISN'T THAT PLAYING THE MIDDLE-MAN?
IT'S NOTHING ILLEGAL.
KACHA (CLACK)
KACHA
I'LL TOUR THE STATIONS TOMORROW.
TRAVELING'S SUCH A HASSLE IN A DISTRICT THIS LARGE.
WHERE WILL YOU START?
NORTH STATION.
WHAT IS IT?

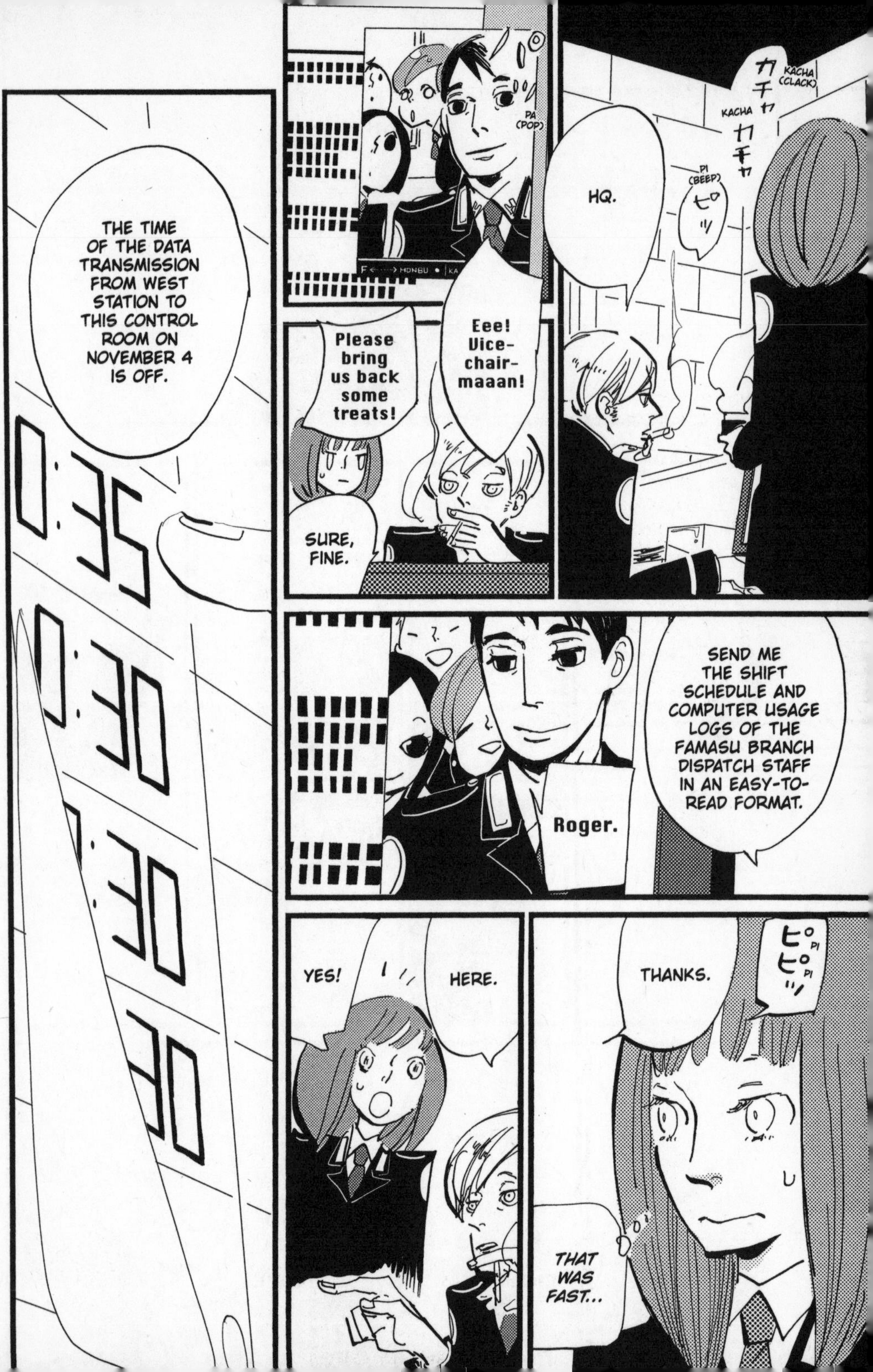

KACHA (CLACK)
KACHA
HQ.
PI (BEEP)
PA (POP)
Eee! Vice-chairmaaan!
Please bring us back some treats!
SURE, FINE.
SEND ME THE SHIFT SCHEDULE AND COMPUTER USAGE LOGS OF THE FAMASU BRANCH DISPATCH STAFF IN AN EASY-TO-READ FORMAT.
Roger.
PI PI
THANKS.
HERE.
YES!
THAT WAS FAST...
THE TIME OF THE DATA TRANSMISSION FROM WEST STATION TO THIS CONTROL ROOM ON NOVEMBER 4 IS OFF.
0:35
0:30

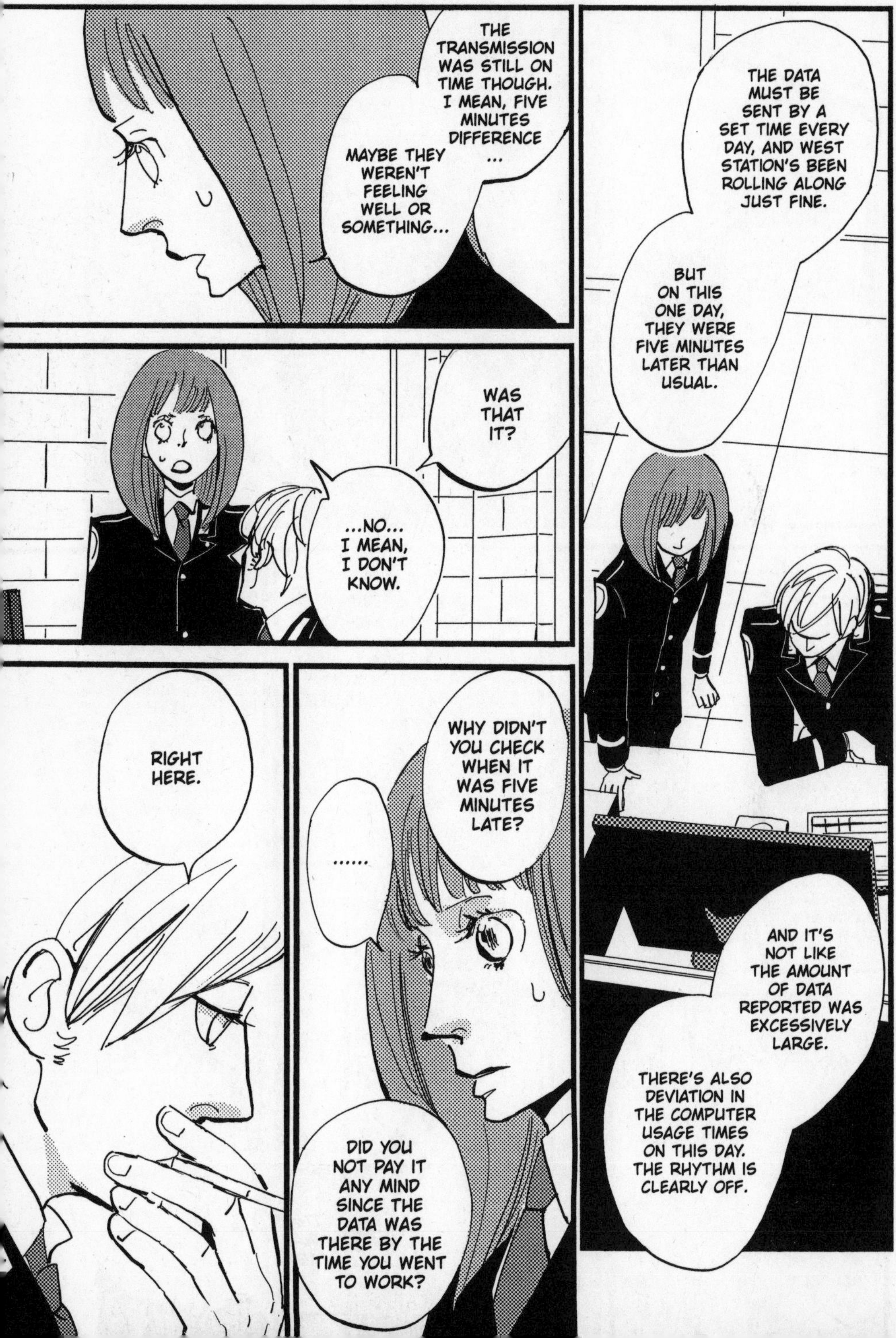
THE DATA MUST BE SENT BY A SET TIME EVERY DAY, AND WEST STATION'S BEEN ROLLING ALONG JUST FINE.
BUT ON THIS ONE DAY, THEY WERE FIVE MINUTES LATER THAN USUAL.
THE TRANSMISSION WAS STILL ON TIME THOUGH. I MEAN, FIVE MINUTES DIFFERENCE ...
MAYBE THEY WEREN'T FEELING WELL OR SOMETHING...
WAS THAT IT?
...NO... I MEAN, I DON'T KNOW.
AND IT'S NOT LIKE THE AMOUNT OF DATA REPORTED WAS EXCESSIVELY LARGE.
THERE'S ALSO DEVIATION IN THE COMPUTER USAGE TIMES ON THIS DAY. THE RHYTHM IS CLEARLY OFF.
WHY DIDN'T YOU CHECK WHEN IT WAS FIVE MINUTES LATE?
......
DID YOU NOT PAY IT ANY MIND SINCE THE DATA WAS THERE BY THE TIME YOU WENT TO WORK?
RIGHT HERE.

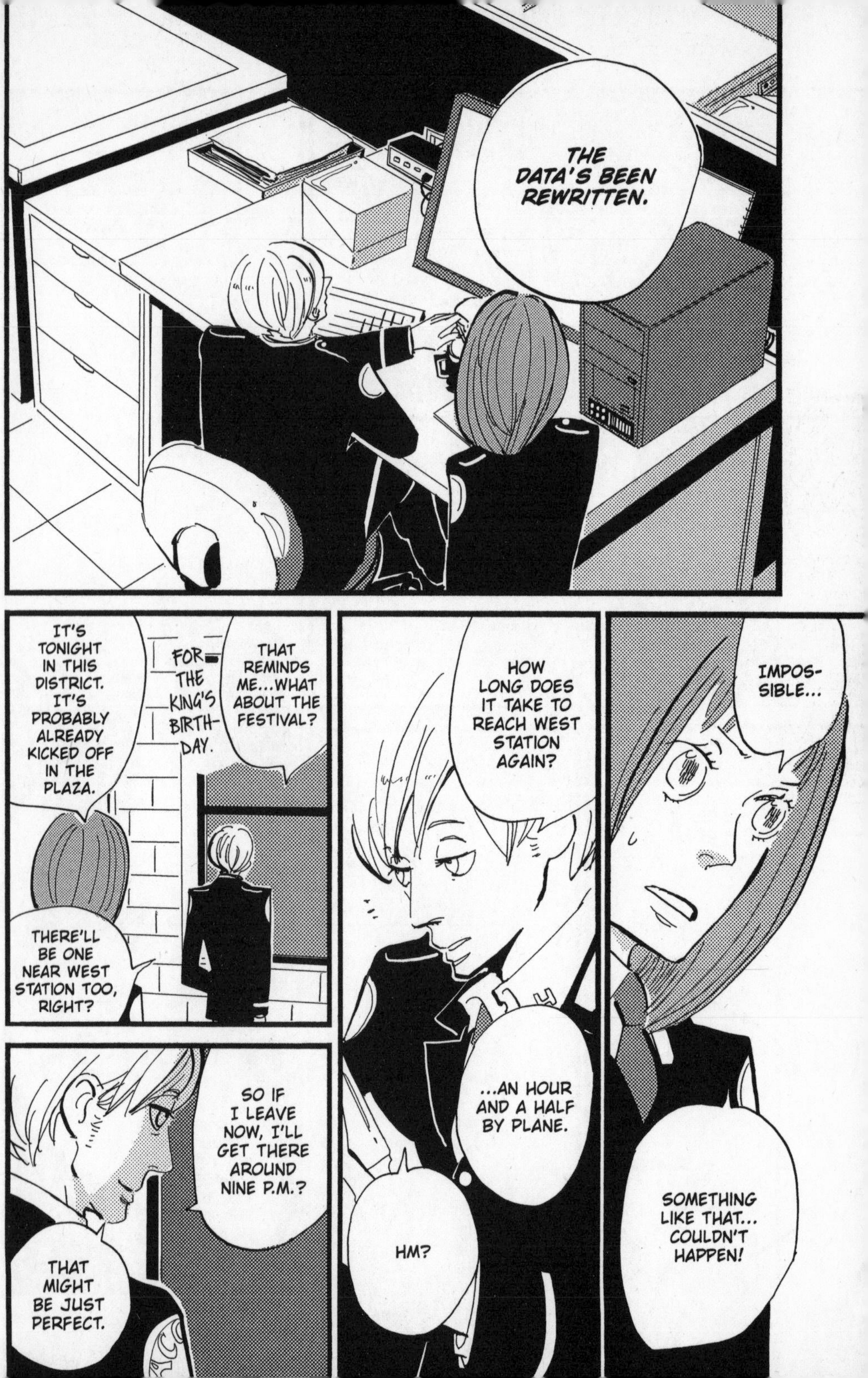
THE DATA'S BEEN REWRITTEN.
IMPOSSIBLE...
SOMETHING LIKE THAT... COULDN'T HAPPEN!
HOW LONG DOES IT TAKE TO REACH WEST STATION AGAIN?
...AN HOUR AND A HALF BY PLANE.
HM?
THAT REMINDS ME...WHAT ABOUT THE FESTIVAL?
FOR THE KING'S BIRTHDAY.
IT'S TONIGHT IN THIS DISTRICT. IT'S PROBABLY ALREADY KICKED OFF IN THE PLAZA.
THERE'LL BE ONE NEAR WEST STATION TOO, RIGHT?
SO IF I LEAVE NOW, I'LL GET THERE AROUND NINE P.M.?
THAT MIGHT BE JUST PERFECT.

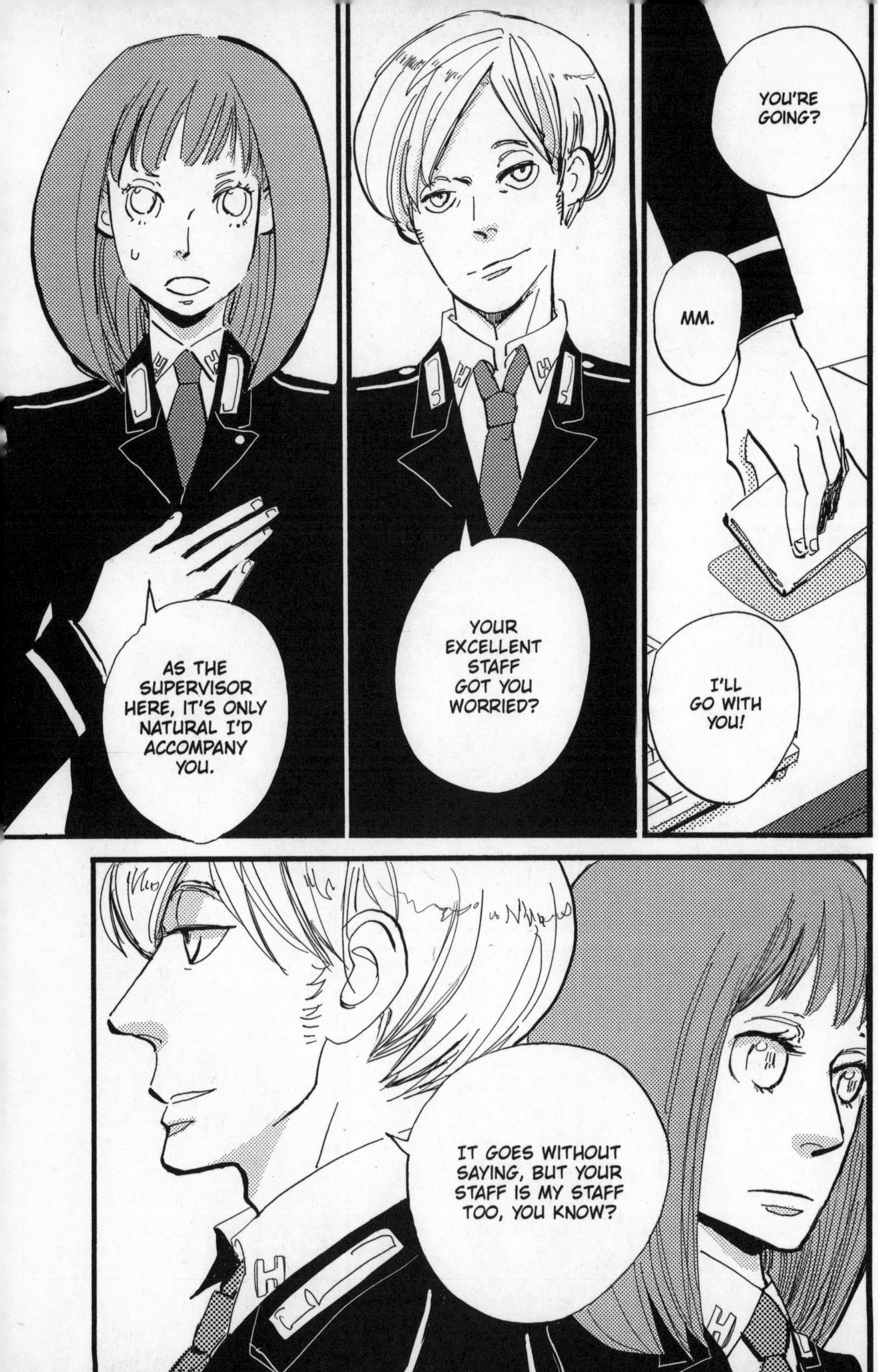
YOU'RE GOING?
MM.
I'LL GO WITH YOU!
YOUR EXCELLENT STAFF GOT YOU WORRIED?
AS THE SUPERVISOR HERE, IT'S ONLY NATURAL I'D ACCOMPANY YOU.
IT GOES WITHOUT SAYING, BUT YOUR STAFF IS MY STAFF TOO, YOU KNOW?

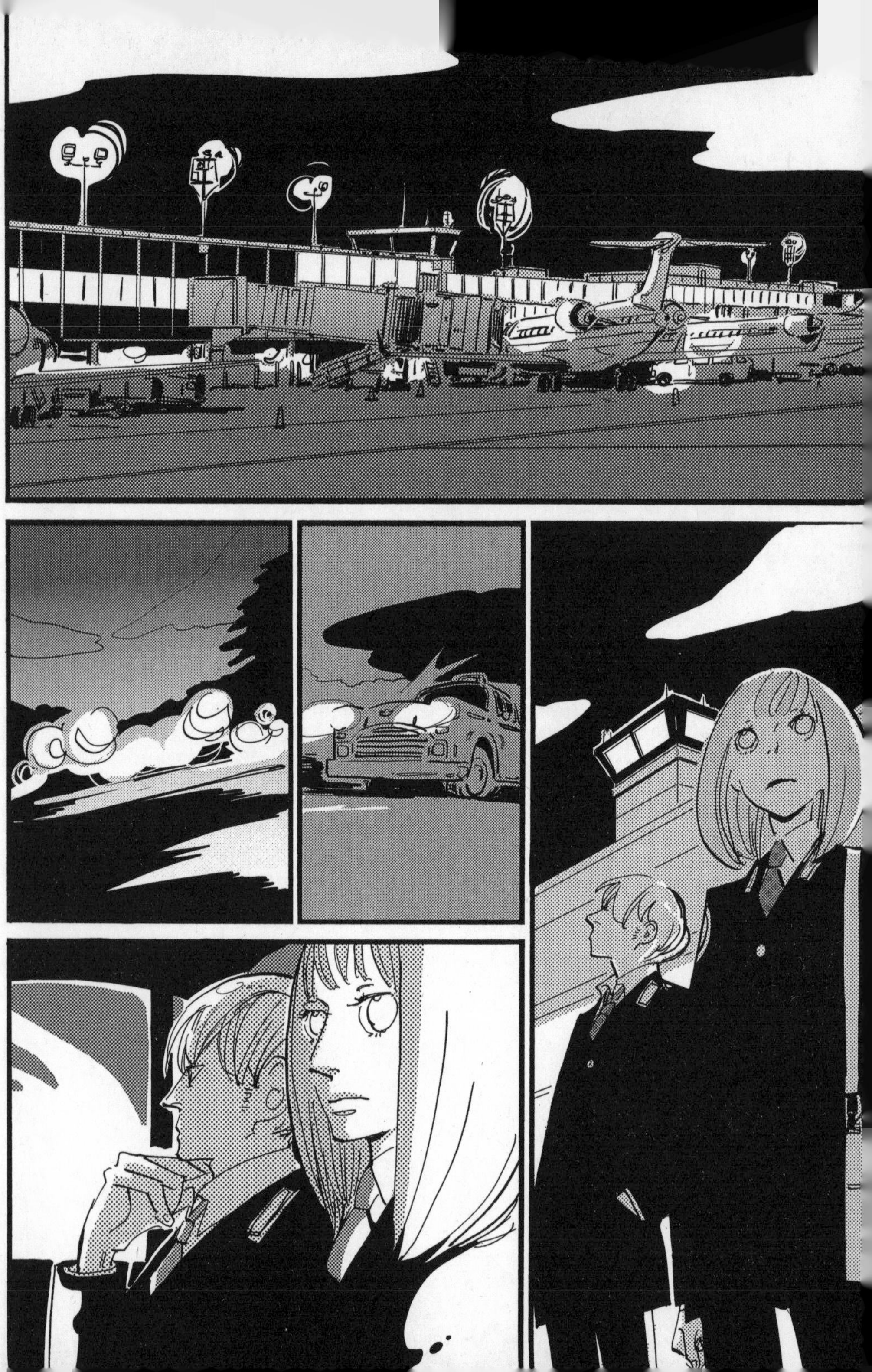

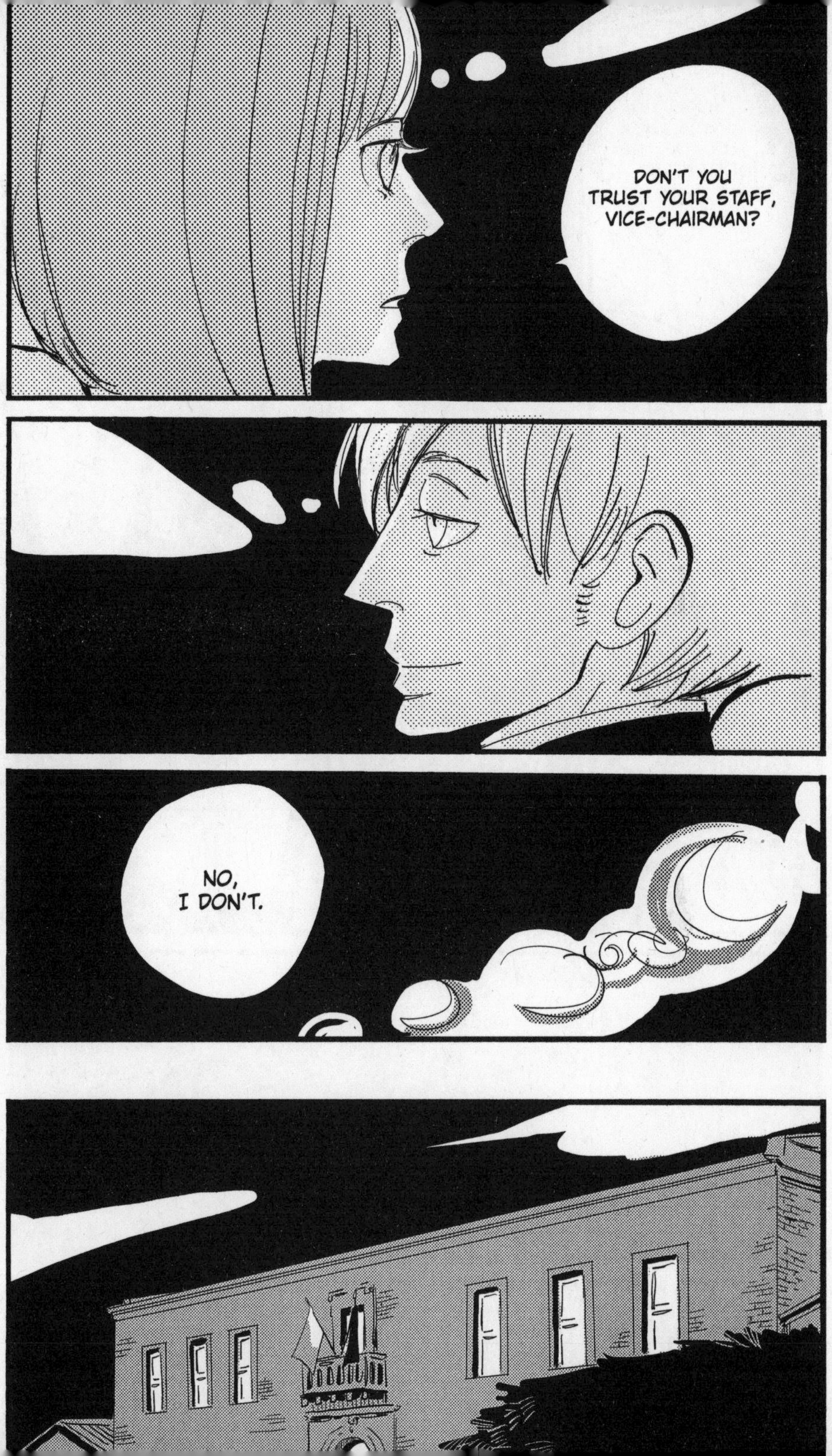
DON'T YOU TRUST YOUR STAFF, VICE-CHAIRMAN?
NO, I DON'T.

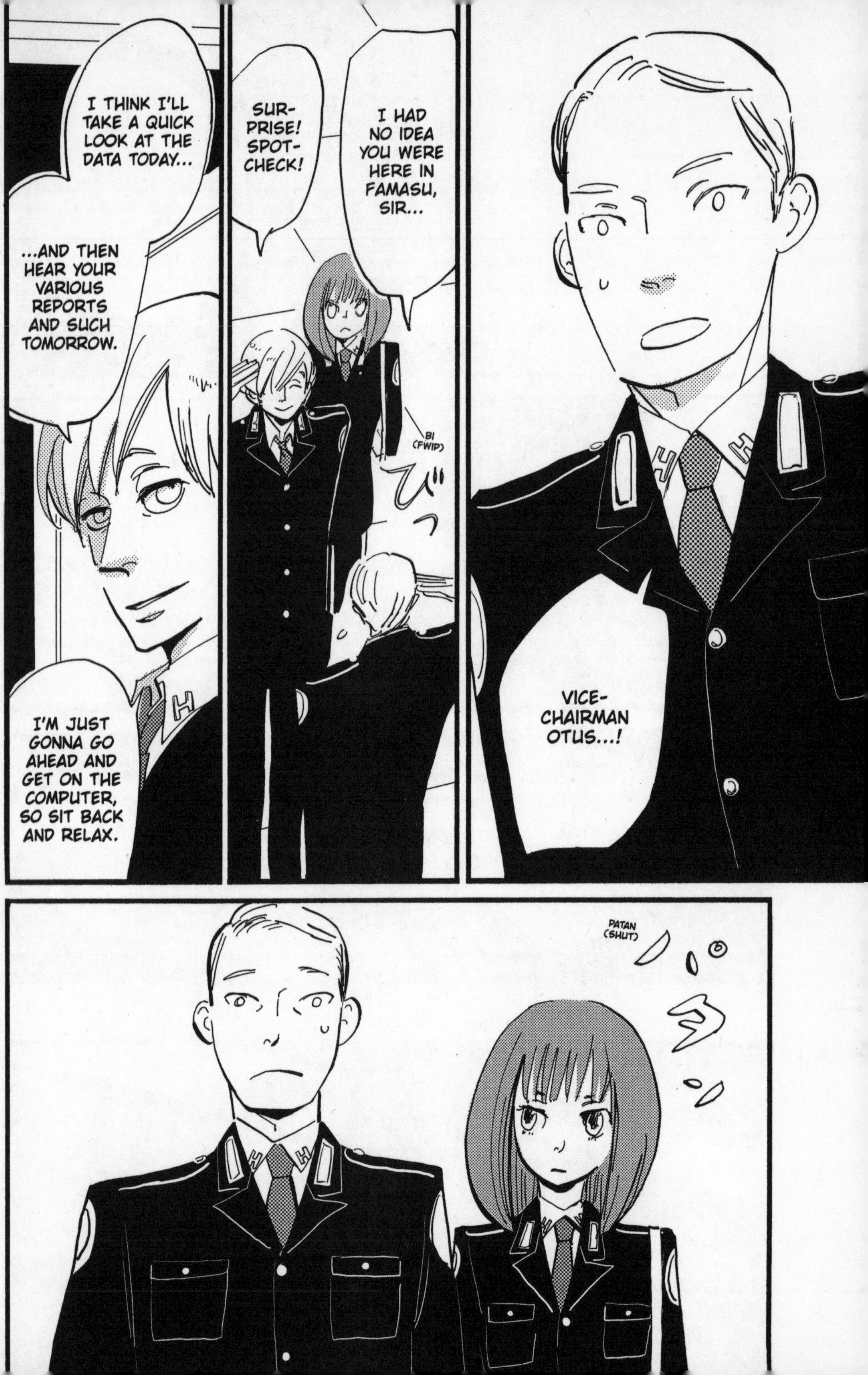
VICE-CHAIRMAN OTUS...!
I HAD NO IDEA YOU WERE HERE IN FAMASU, SIR...
SUR-PRISE! SPOT-CHECK!
BI (FWIP)
I THINK I'LL TAKE A QUICK LOOK AT THE DATA TODAY...
...AND THEN HEAR YOUR VARIOUS REPORTS AND SUCH TOMORROW.
I'M JUST GONNA GO AHEAD AND GET ON THE COMPUTER, SO SIT BACK AND RELAX.
PATAN (SHUT)

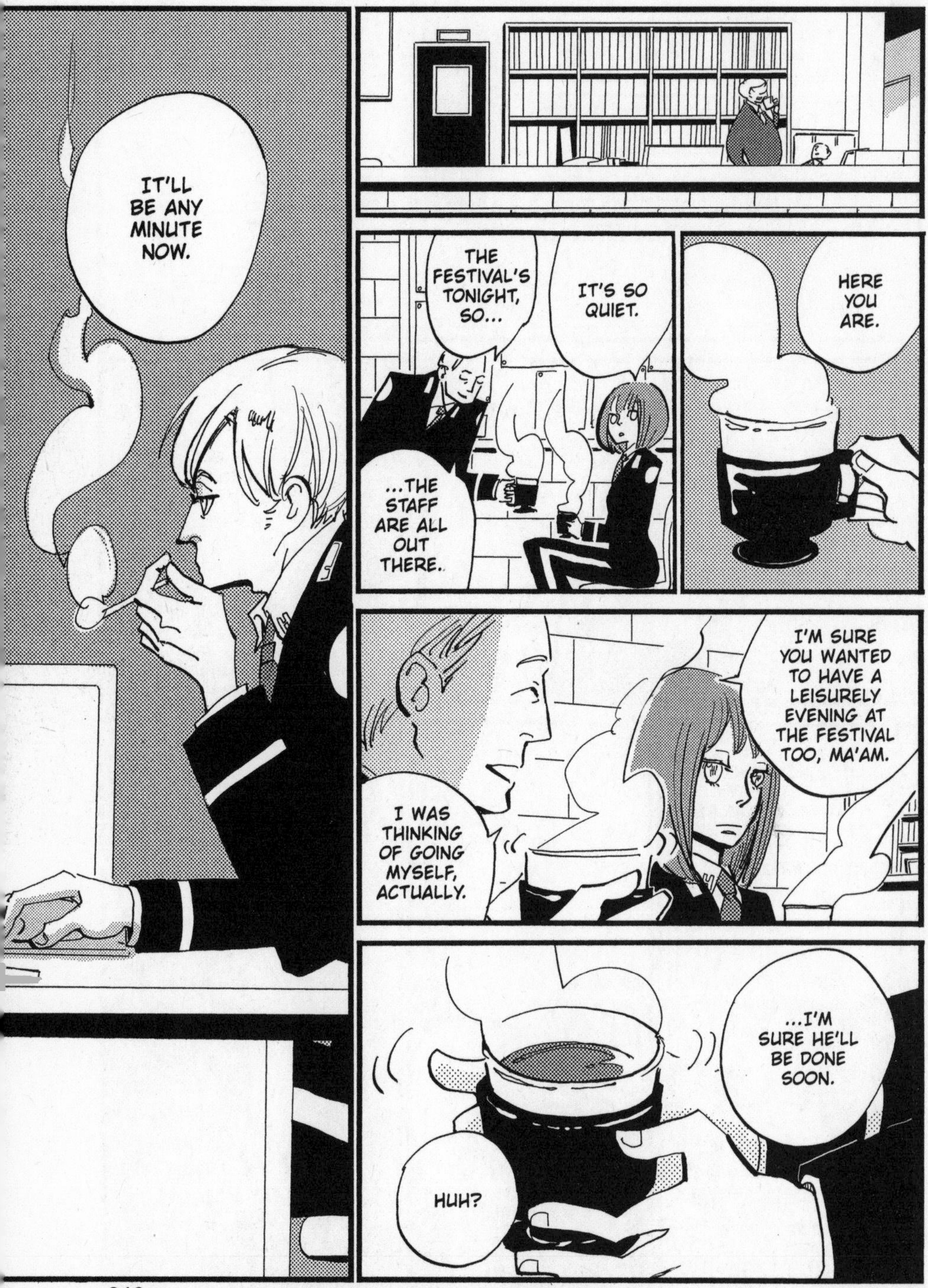
IT'LL BE ANY MINUTE NOW.
THE FESTIVAL'S TONIGHT, SO...
IT'S SO QUIET.
...THE STAFF ARE ALL OUT THERE..
HERE YOU ARE.
I'M SURE YOU WANTED TO HAVE A LEISURELY EVENING AT THE FESTIVAL TOO, MA'AM.
I WAS THINKING OF GOING MYSELF, ACTUALLY.
...I'M SURE HE'LL BE DONE SOON.
HUH?

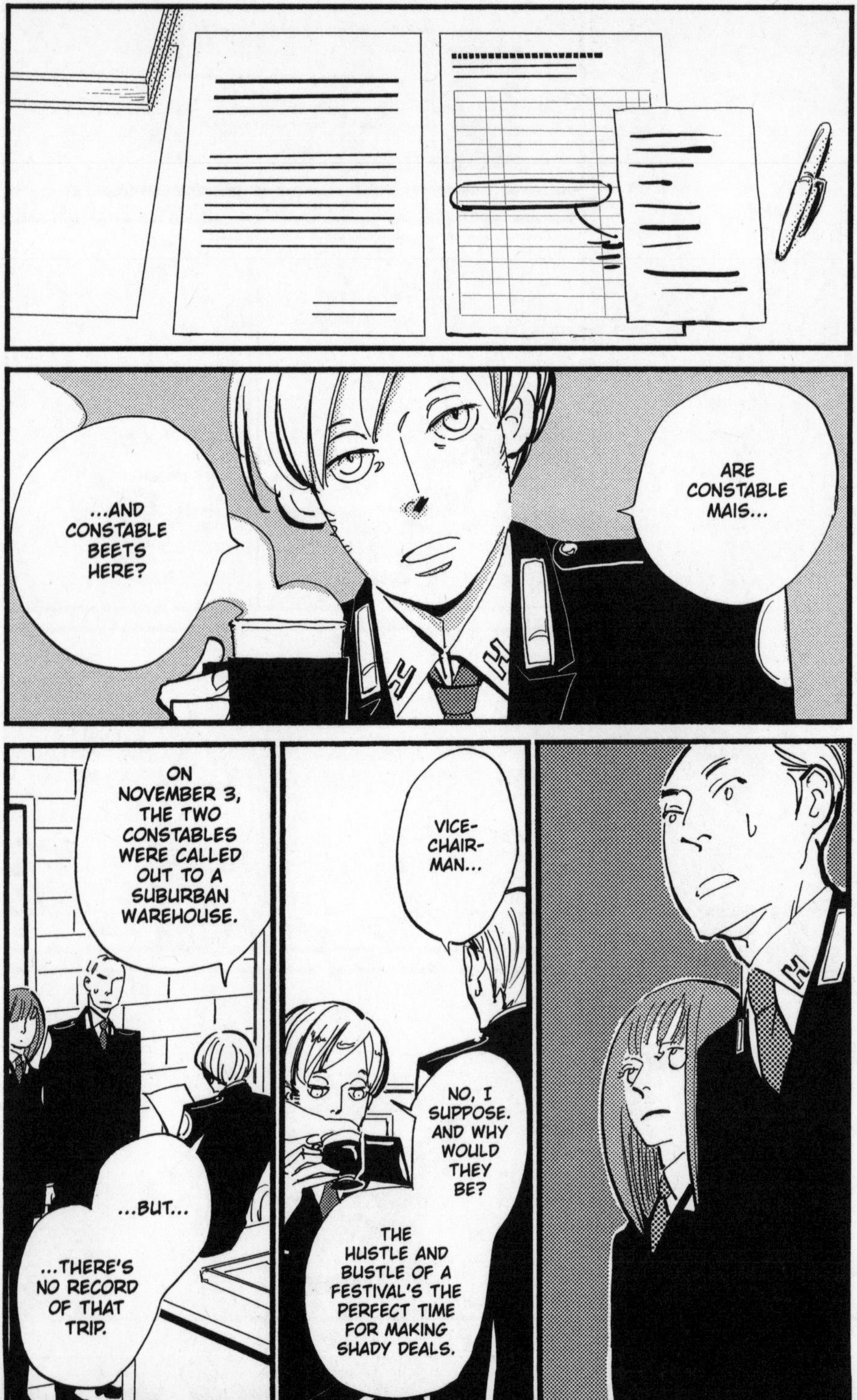
ARE CONSTABLE MAIS...
...AND CONSTABLE BEETS HERE?
VICE-CHAIRMAN...
NO, I SUPPOSE. AND WHY WOULD THEY BE?
THE HUSTLE AND BUSTLE OF A FESTIVAL'S THE PERFECT TIME FOR MAKING SHADY DEALS.
ON NOVEMBER 3, THE TWO CONSTABLES WERE CALLED OUT TO A SUBURBAN WAREHOUSE.
...BUT...
...THERE'S NO RECORD OF THAT TRIP.

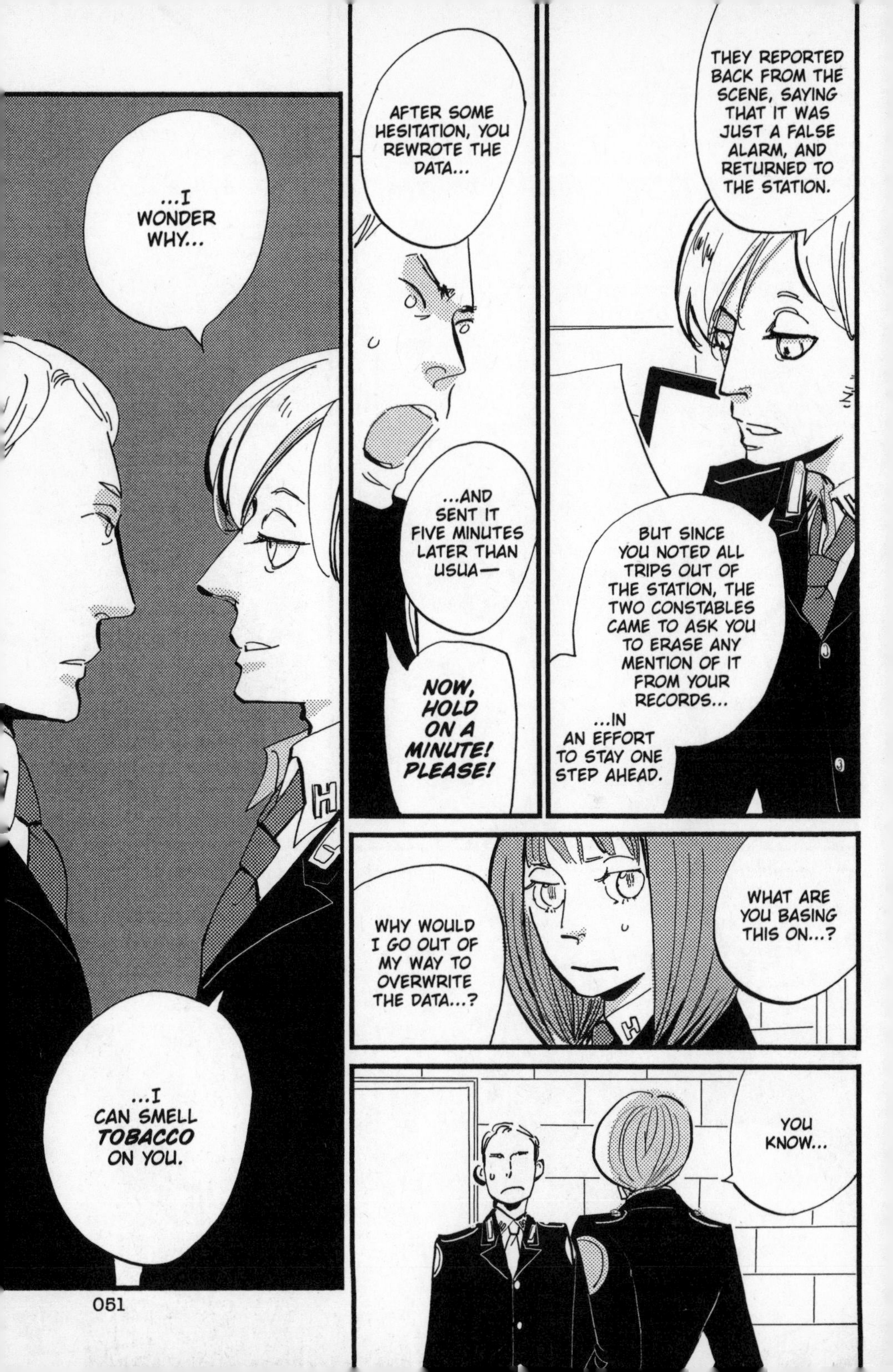
THEY REPORTED BACK FROM THE SCENE, SAYING THAT IT WAS JUST A FALSE ALARM, AND RETURNED TO THE STATION.
BUT SINCE YOU NOTED ALL TRIPS OUT OF THE STATION, THE TWO CONSTABLES CAME TO ASK YOU TO ERASE ANY MENTION OF IT FROM YOUR RECORDS...
...IN AN EFFORT TO STAY ONE STEP AHEAD.
AFTER SOME HESITATION, YOU REWROTE THE DATA...
...AND SENT IT FIVE MINUTES LATER THAN USUA—
NOW, HOLD ON A MINUTE! PLEASE!
WHAT ARE YOU BASING THIS ON...?
WHY WOULD I GO OUT OF MY WAY TO OVERWRITE THE DATA...?
YOU KNOW...
...I WONDER WHY...
...I CAN SMELL TOBACCO ON YOU.

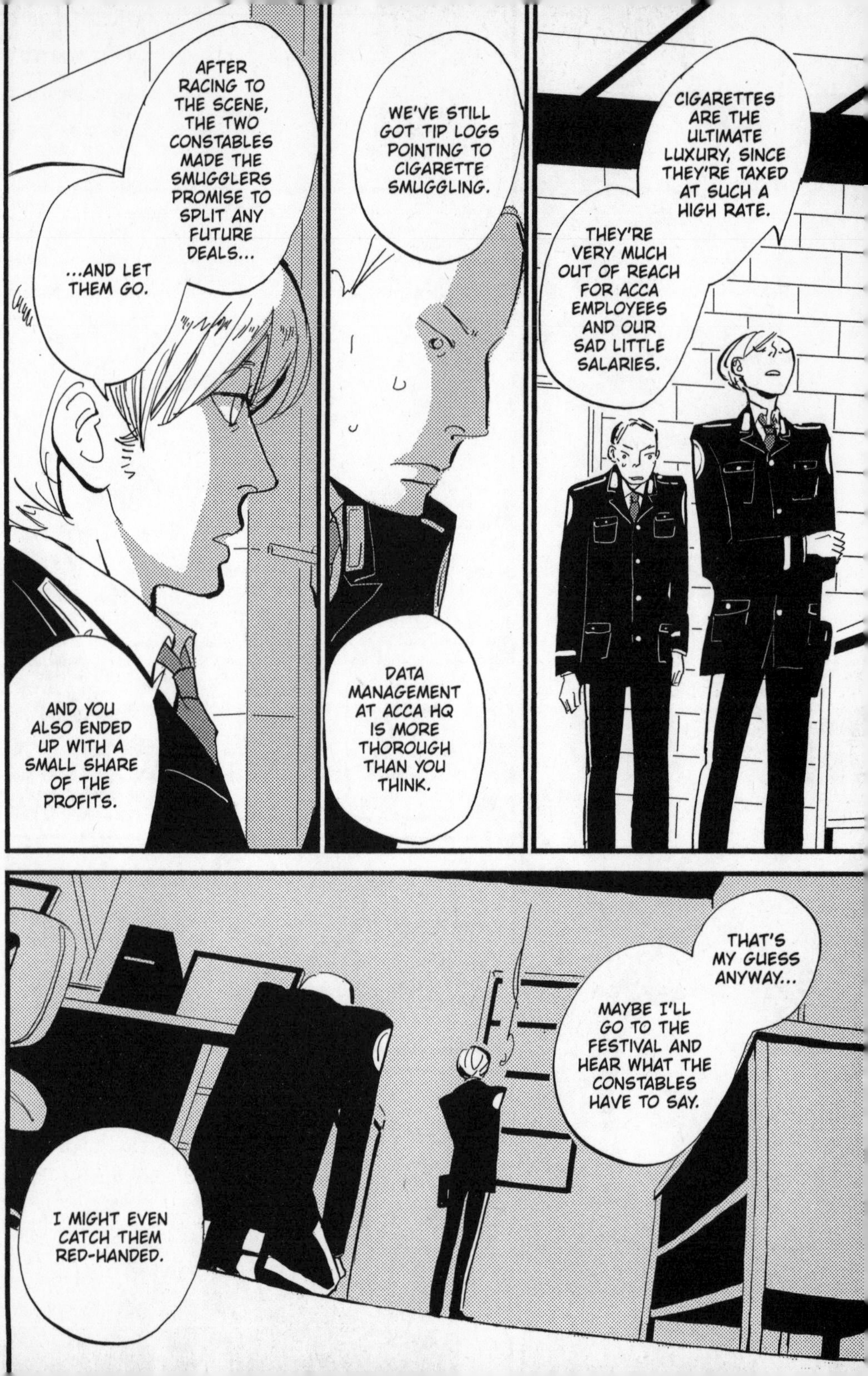
AFTER RACING TO THE SCENE, THE TWO CONSTABLES MADE THE SMUGGLERS PROMISE TO SPLIT ANY FUTURE DEALS...
...AND LET THEM GO.
AND YOU ALSO ENDED UP WITH A SMALL SHARE OF THE PROFITS.
WE'VE STILL GOT TIP LOGS POINTING TO CIGARETTE SMUGGLING.
DATA MANAGEMENT AT ACCA HQ IS MORE THOROUGH THAN YOU THINK.
CIGARETTES ARE THE ULTIMATE LUXURY, SINCE THEY'RE TAXED AT SUCH A HIGH RATE.
THEY'RE VERY MUCH OUT OF REACH FOR ACCA EMPLOYEES AND OUR SAD LITTLE SALARIES.
THAT'S MY GUESS ANYWAY...
MAYBE I'LL GO TO THE FESTIVAL AND HEAR WHAT THE CONSTABLES HAVE TO SAY.
I MIGHT EVEN CATCH THEM RED-HANDED.

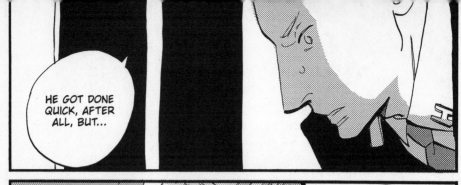

HE GOT DONE QUICK, AFTER ALL, BUT...

...YOU WON'T BE GOING TO THE FESTIVAL.

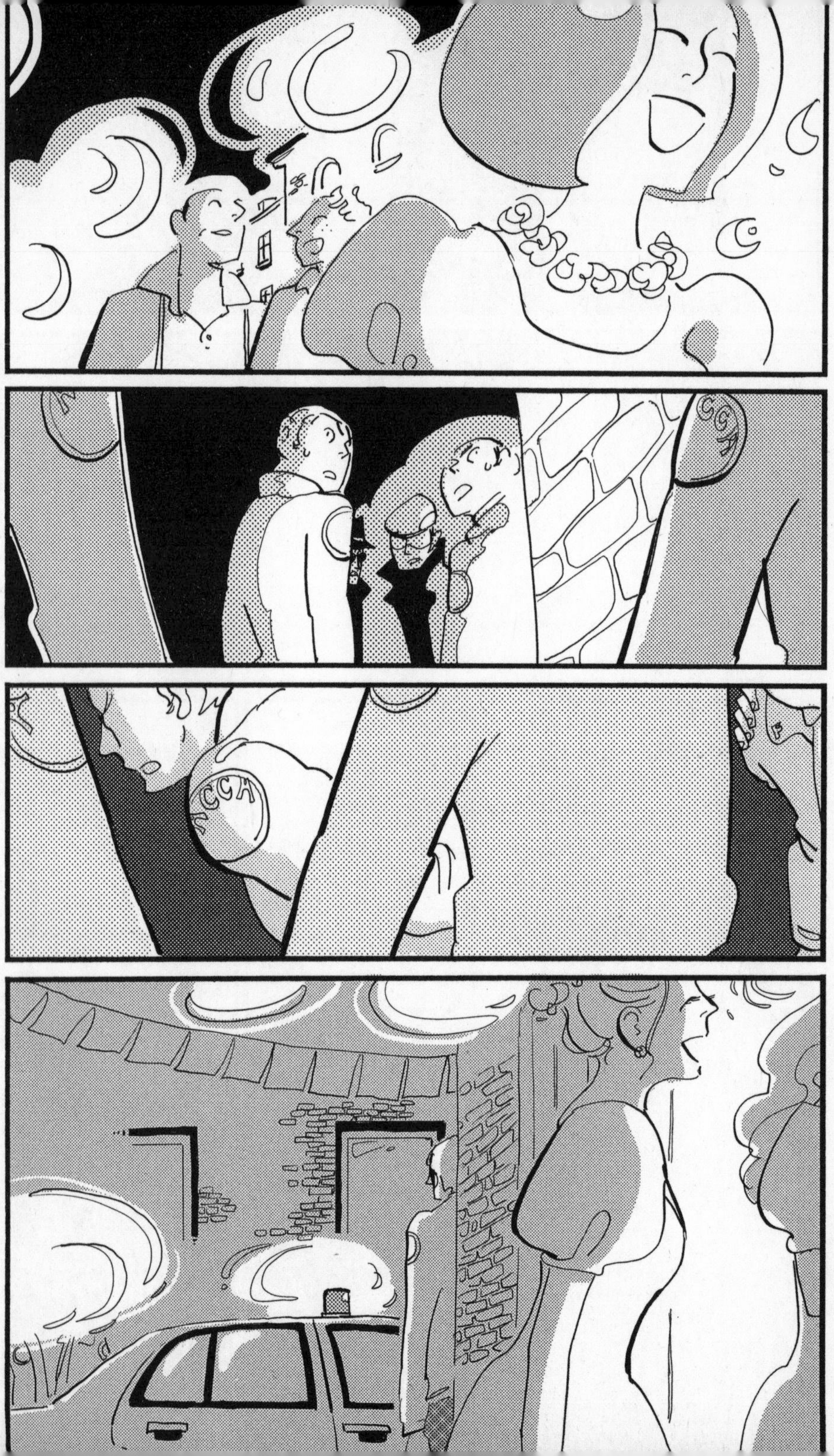
CCA

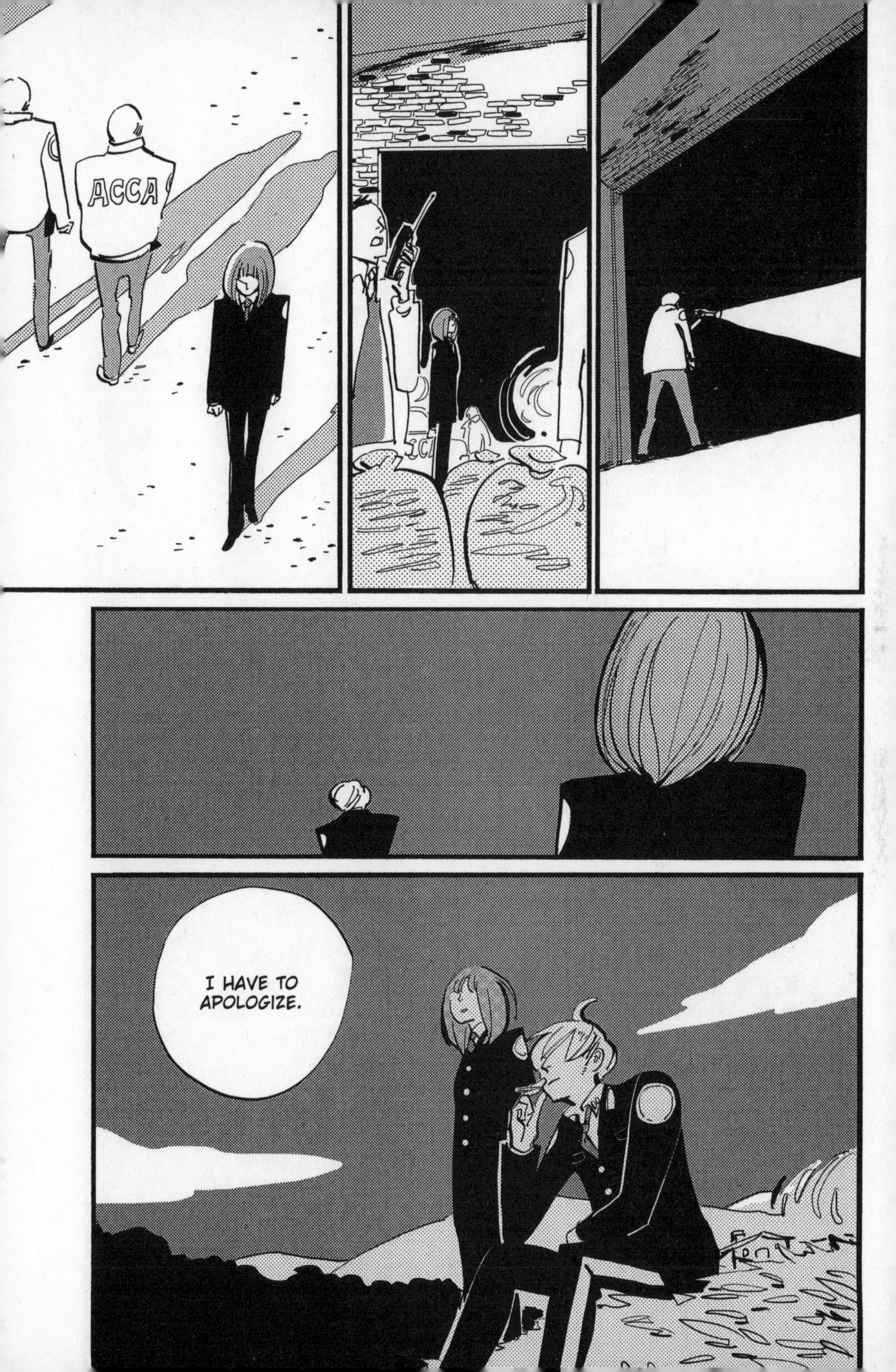
ACCA
I HAVE TO APOLOGIZE.

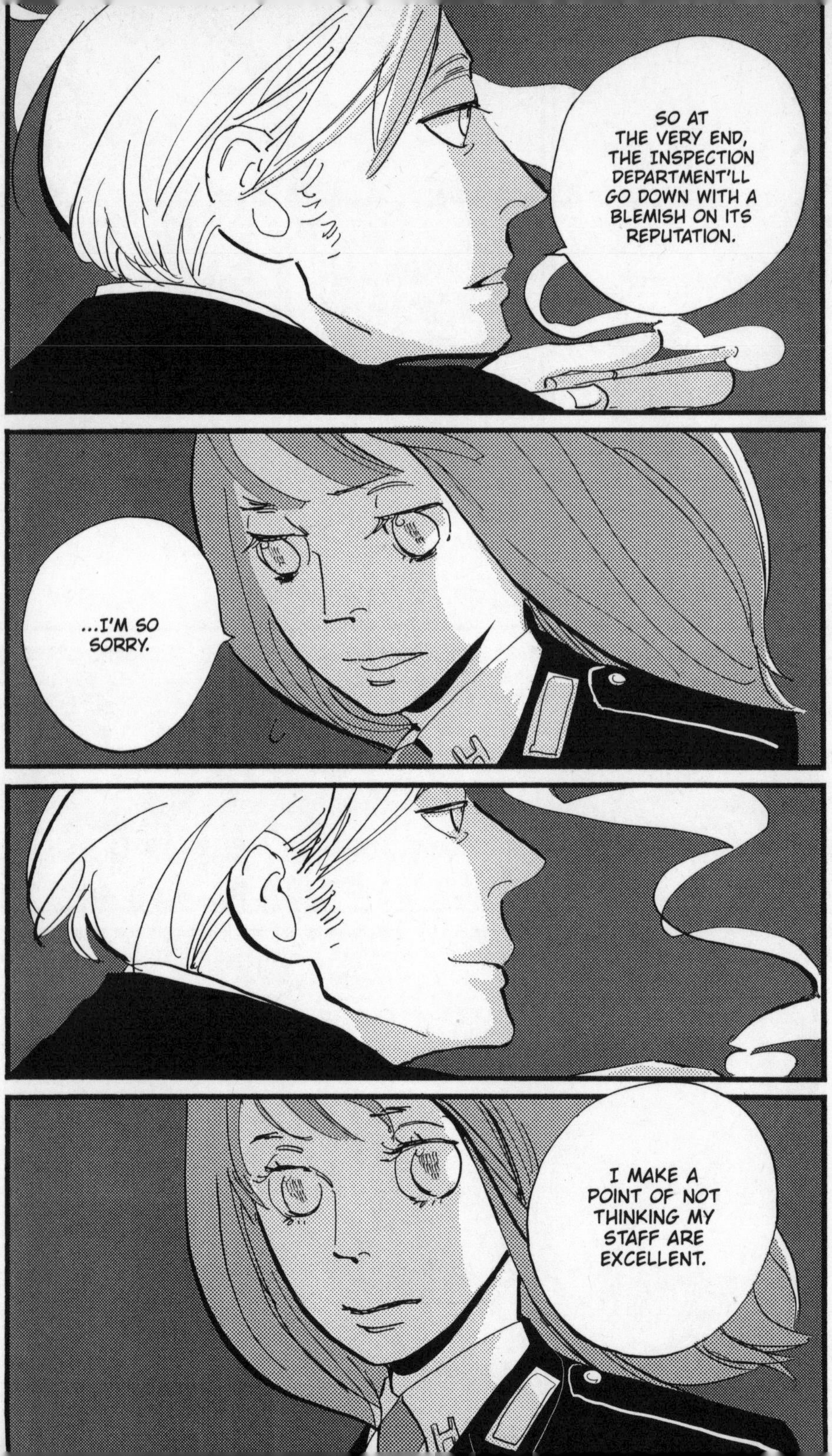
SO AT THE VERY END, THE INSPECTION DEPARTMENT'LL GO DOWN WITH A BLEMISH ON ITS REPUTATION.
...I'M SO SORRY.
I MAKE A POINT OF NOT THINKING MY STAFF ARE EXCELLENT.

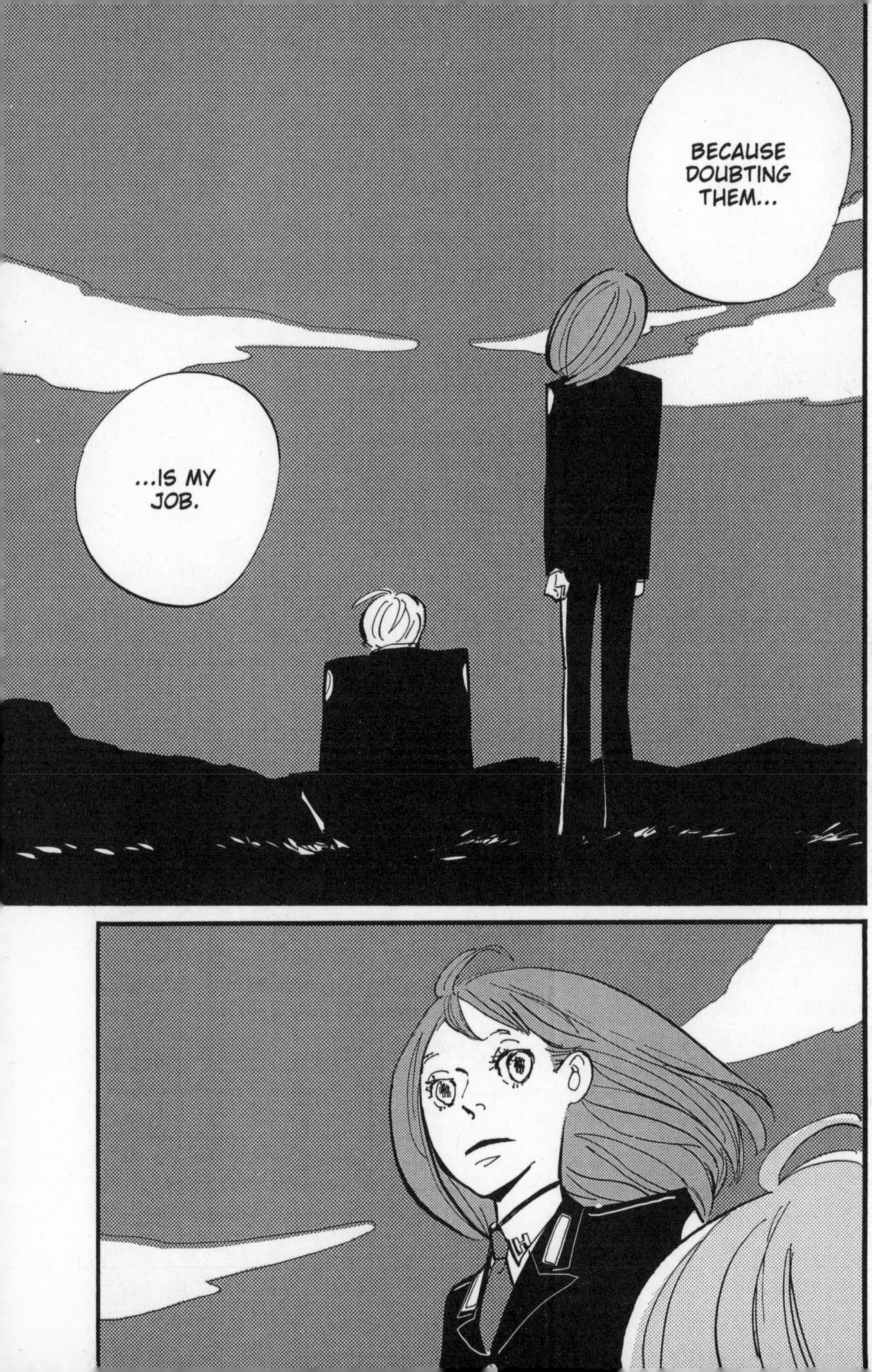
BECAUSE DOUBTING THEM...
...IS MY JOB.

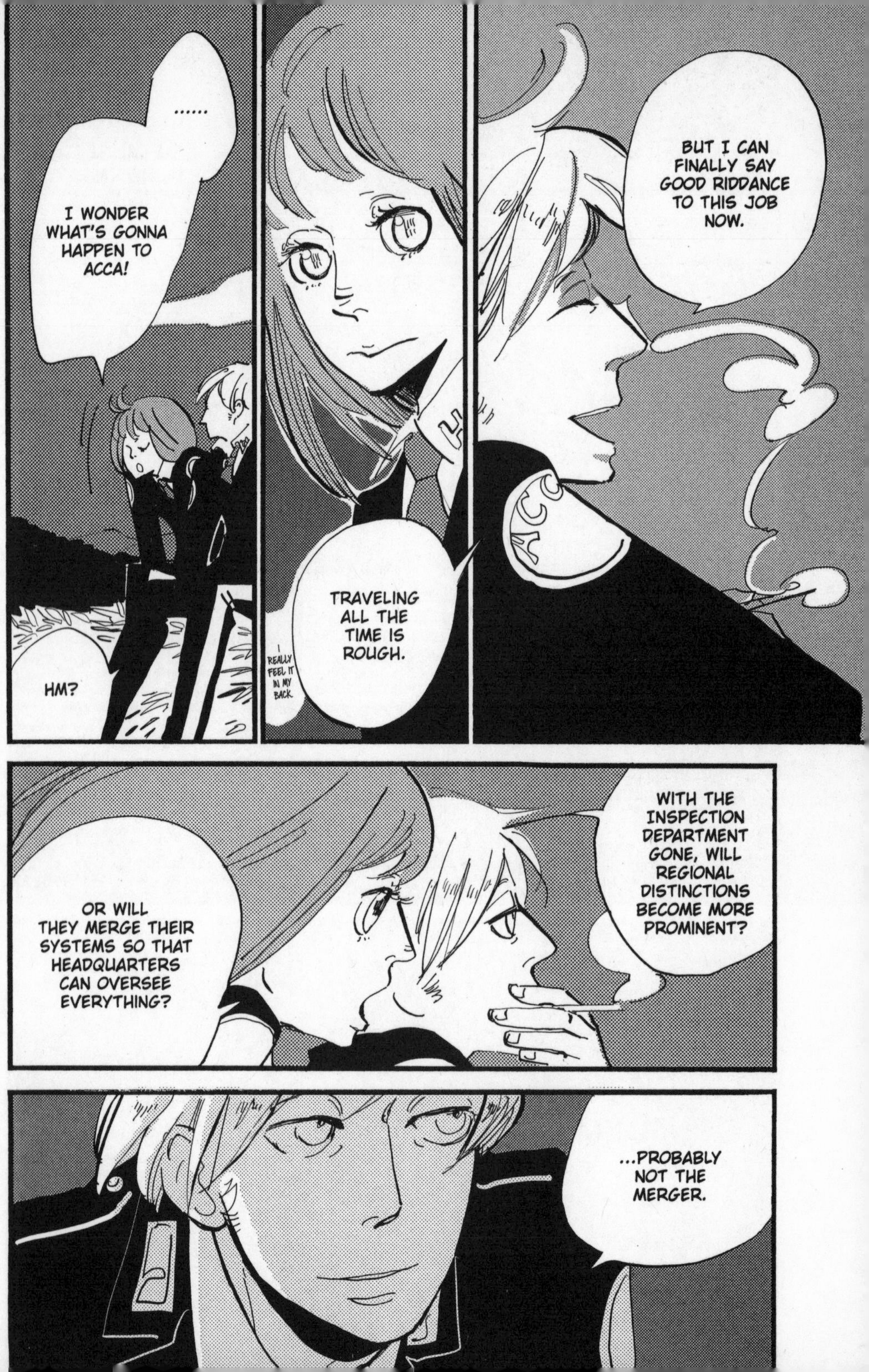
......
I WONDER WHAT'S GONNA HAPPEN TO ACCA!
HM?
TRAVELING ALL THE TIME IS ROUGH.
I REALLY FEEL IT IN MY BACK.
BUT I CAN FINALLY SAY GOOD RIDDANCE TO THIS JOB NOW.
WITH THE INSPECTION DEPARTMENT GONE, WILL REGIONAL DISTINCTIONS BECOME MORE PROMINENT?
OR WILL THEY MERGE THEIR SYSTEMS SO THAT HEADQUARTERS CAN OVERSEE EVERYTHING?
...PROBABLY NOT THE MERGER.

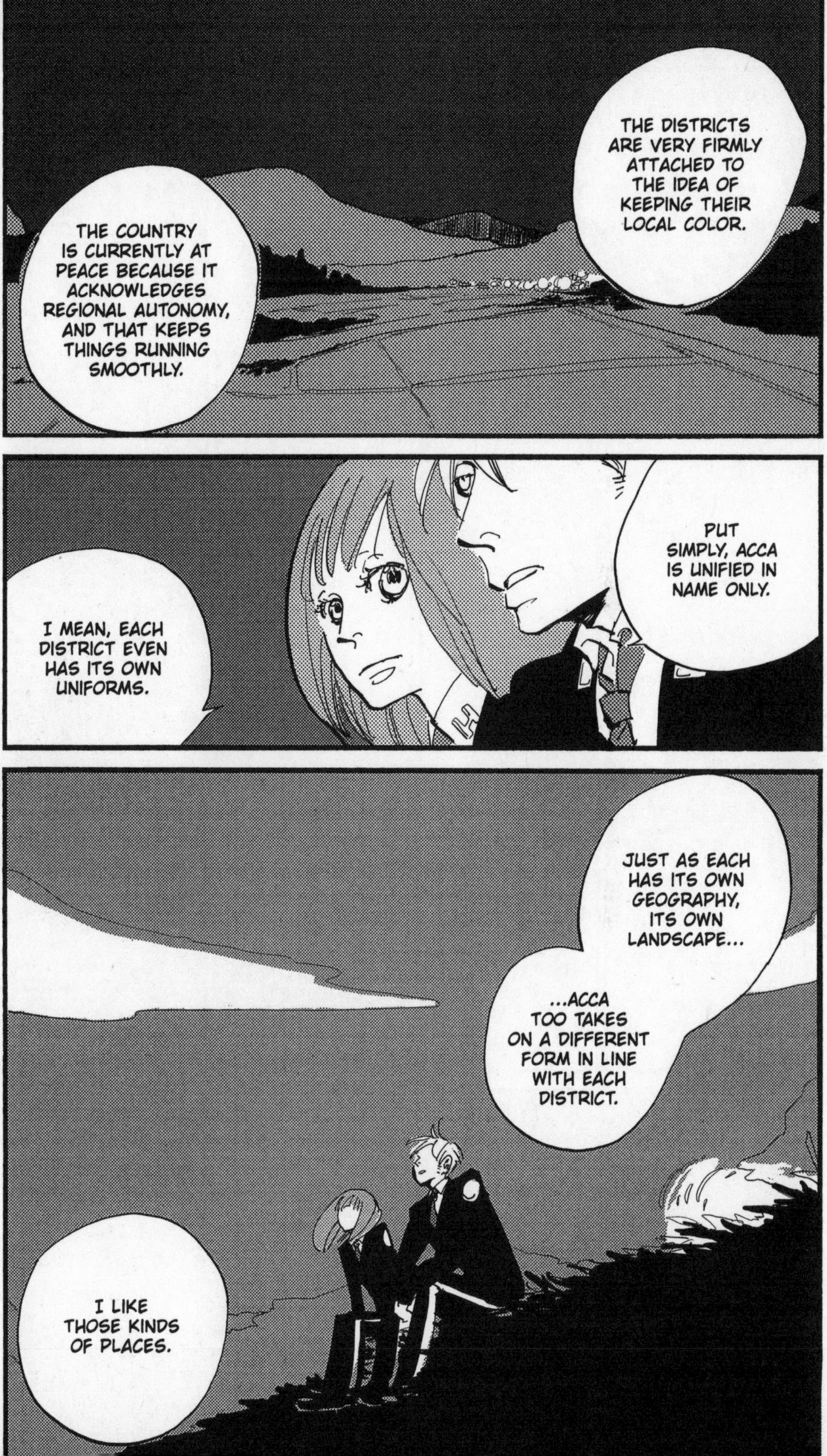
THE DISTRICTS ARE VERY FIRMLY ATTACHED TO THE IDEA OF KEEPING THEIR LOCAL COLOR.
THE COUNTRY IS CURRENTLY AT PEACE BECAUSE IT ACKNOWLEDGES REGIONAL AUTONOMY, AND THAT KEEPS THINGS RUNNING SMOOTHLY.
PUT SIMPLY, ACCA IS UNIFIED IN NAME ONLY.
I MEAN, EACH DISTRICT EVEN HAS ITS OWN UNIFORMS.
JUST AS EACH HAS ITS OWN GEOGRAPHY, ITS OWN LANDSCAPE...
...ACCA TOO TAKES ON A DIFFERENT FORM IN LINE WITH EACH DISTRICT.
I LIKE THOSE KINDS OF PLACES.

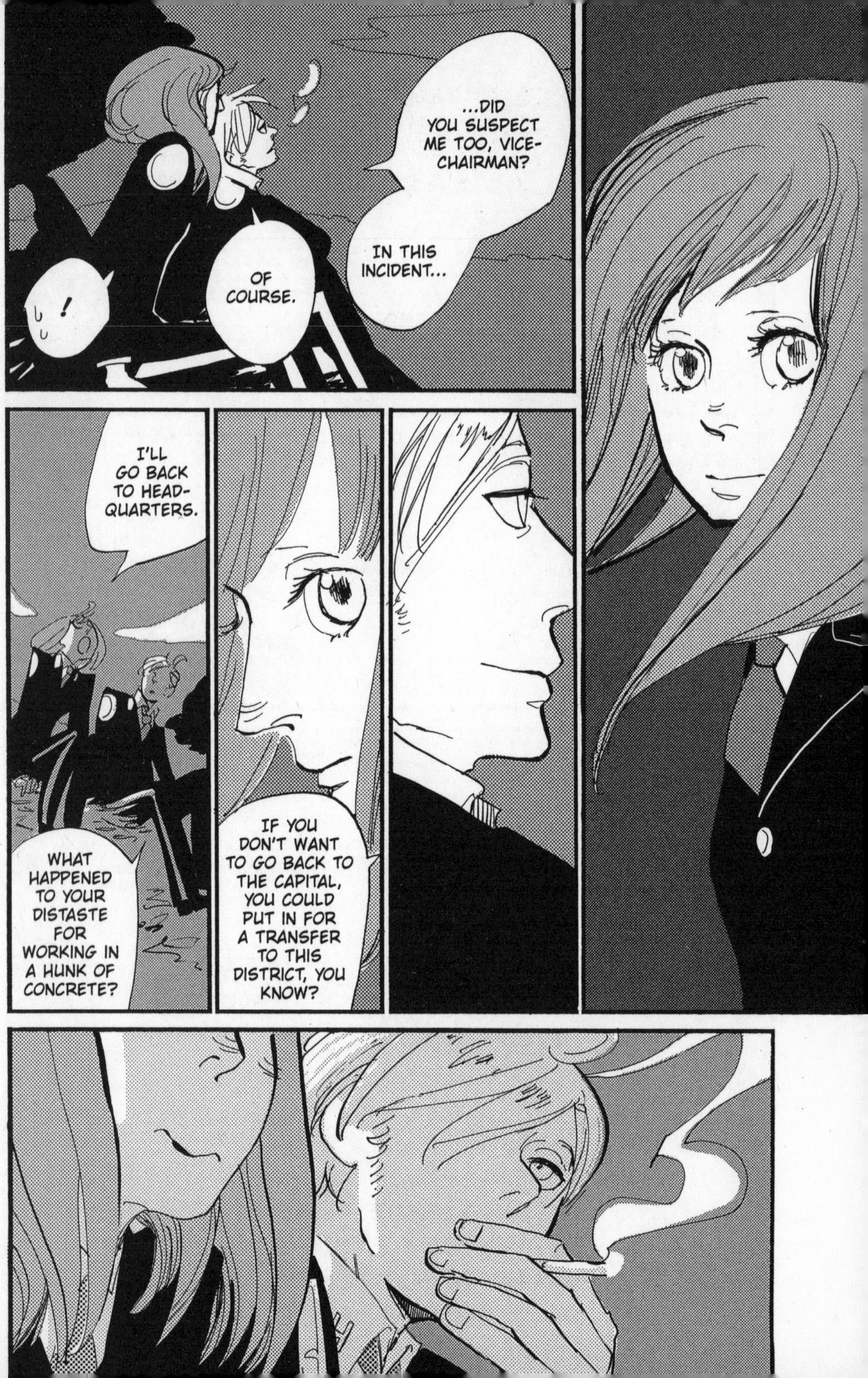
...DID YOU SUSPECT ME TOO, VICE-CHAIRMAN?
IN THIS INCIDENT...
OF COURSE.
!
IF YOU DON'T WANT TO GO BACK TO THE CAPITAL, YOU COULD PUT IN FOR A TRANSFER TO THIS DISTRICT, YOU KNOW?
I'LL GO BACK TO HEAD-QUARTERS.
WHAT HAPPENED TO YOUR DISTASTE FOR WORKING IN A HUNK OF CONCRETE?

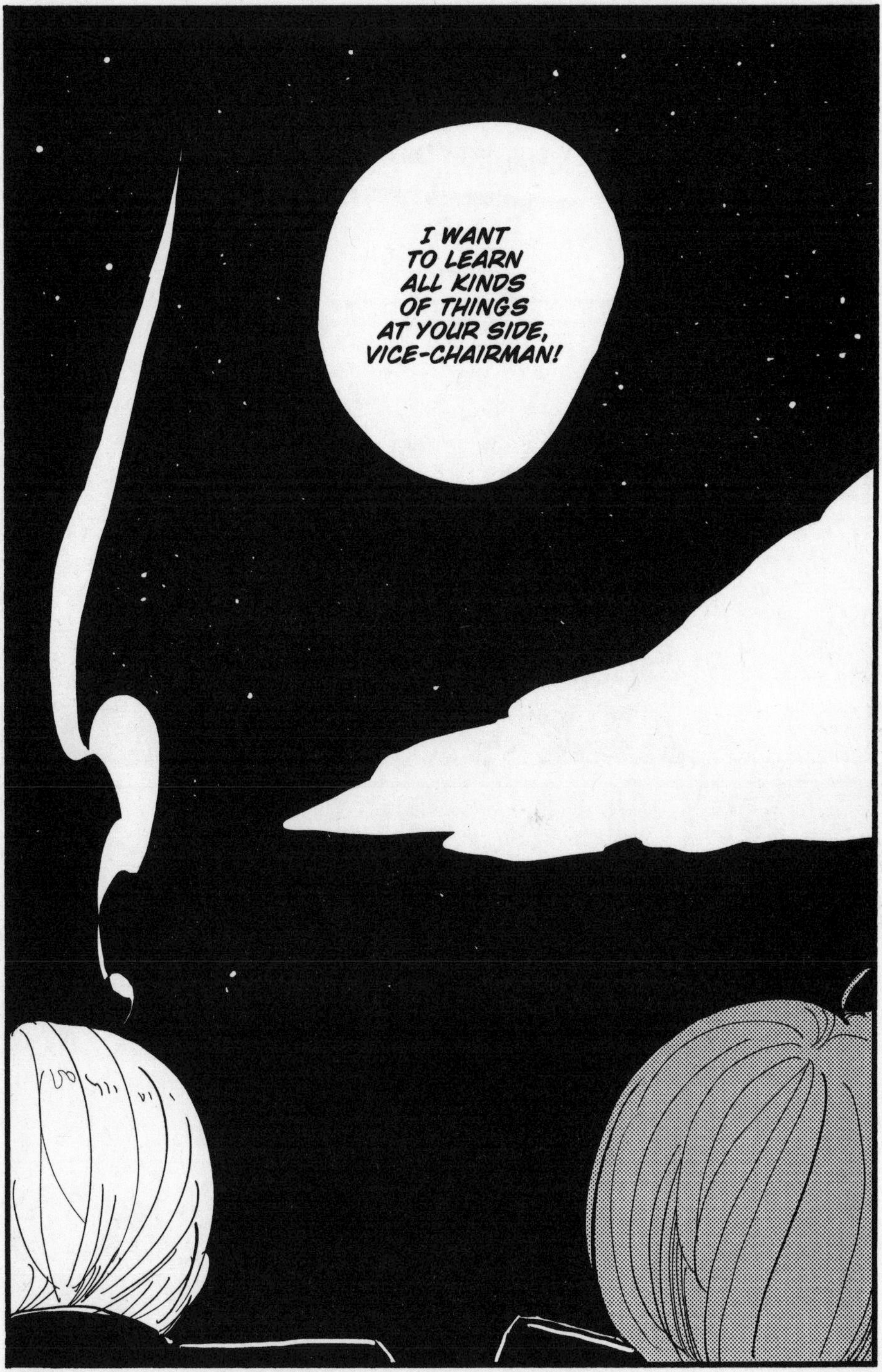
I WANT TO LEARN ALL KINDS OF THINGS AT YOUR SIDE, VICE-CHAIRMAN!

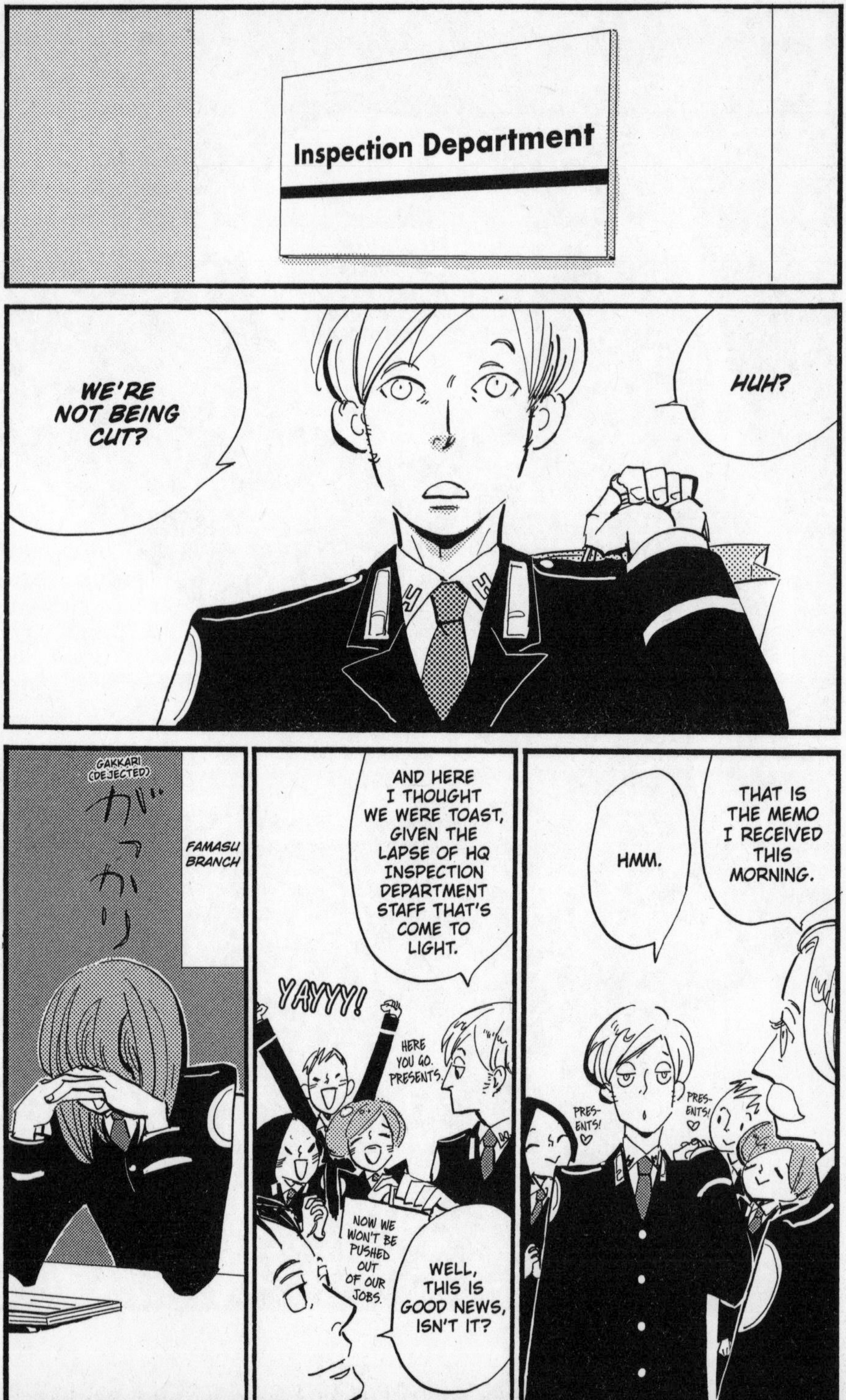
Inspection Department
HUH?
WE'RE NOT BEING CUT?
THAT IS THE MEMO I RECEIVED THIS MORNING.
HMM.
PRES-ENTS!
PRES-ENTS!
AND HERE I THOUGHT WE WERE TOAST, GIVEN THE LAPSE OF HQ INSPECTION DEPARTMENT STAFF THAT'S COME TO LIGHT.
YAYYY!
HERE YOU GO. PRESENTS.
WELL, THIS IS GOOD NEWS, ISN'T IT?
NOW WE WON'T BE PUSHED OUT OF OUR JOBS.
FAMASU BRANCH
がっかり
GAKKARI (DEJECTED)

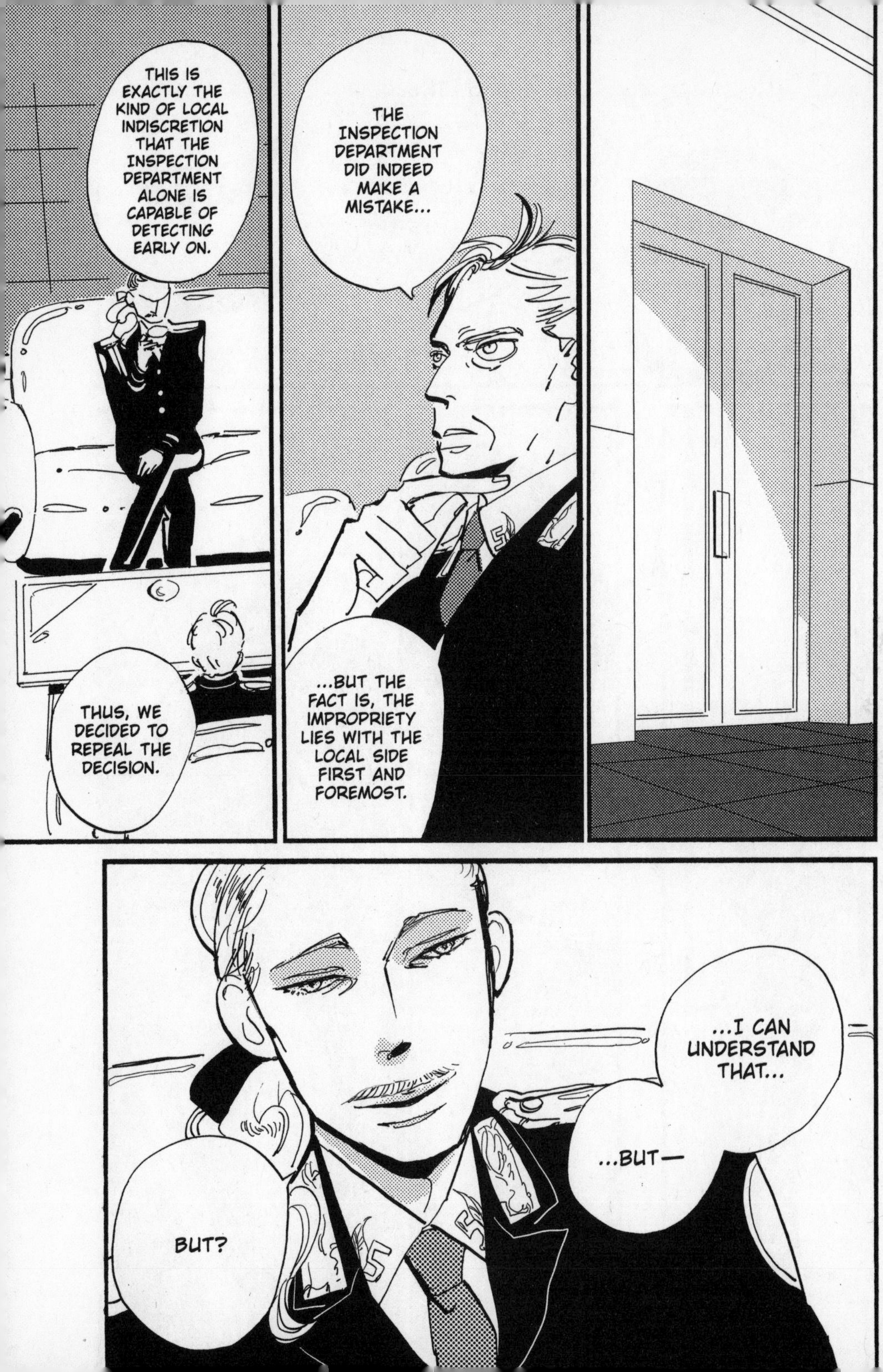
THE INSPECTION DEPARTMENT DID INDEED MAKE A MISTAKE...
...BUT THE FACT IS, THE IMPROPRIETY LIES WITH THE LOCAL SIDE FIRST AND FOREMOST.
THIS IS EXACTLY THE KIND OF LOCAL INDISCRETION THAT THE INSPECTION DEPARTMENT ALONE IS CAPABLE OF DETECTING EARLY ON.
THUS, WE DECIDED TO REPEAL THE DECISION.
...I CAN UNDERSTAND THAT...
...BUT—
BUT?

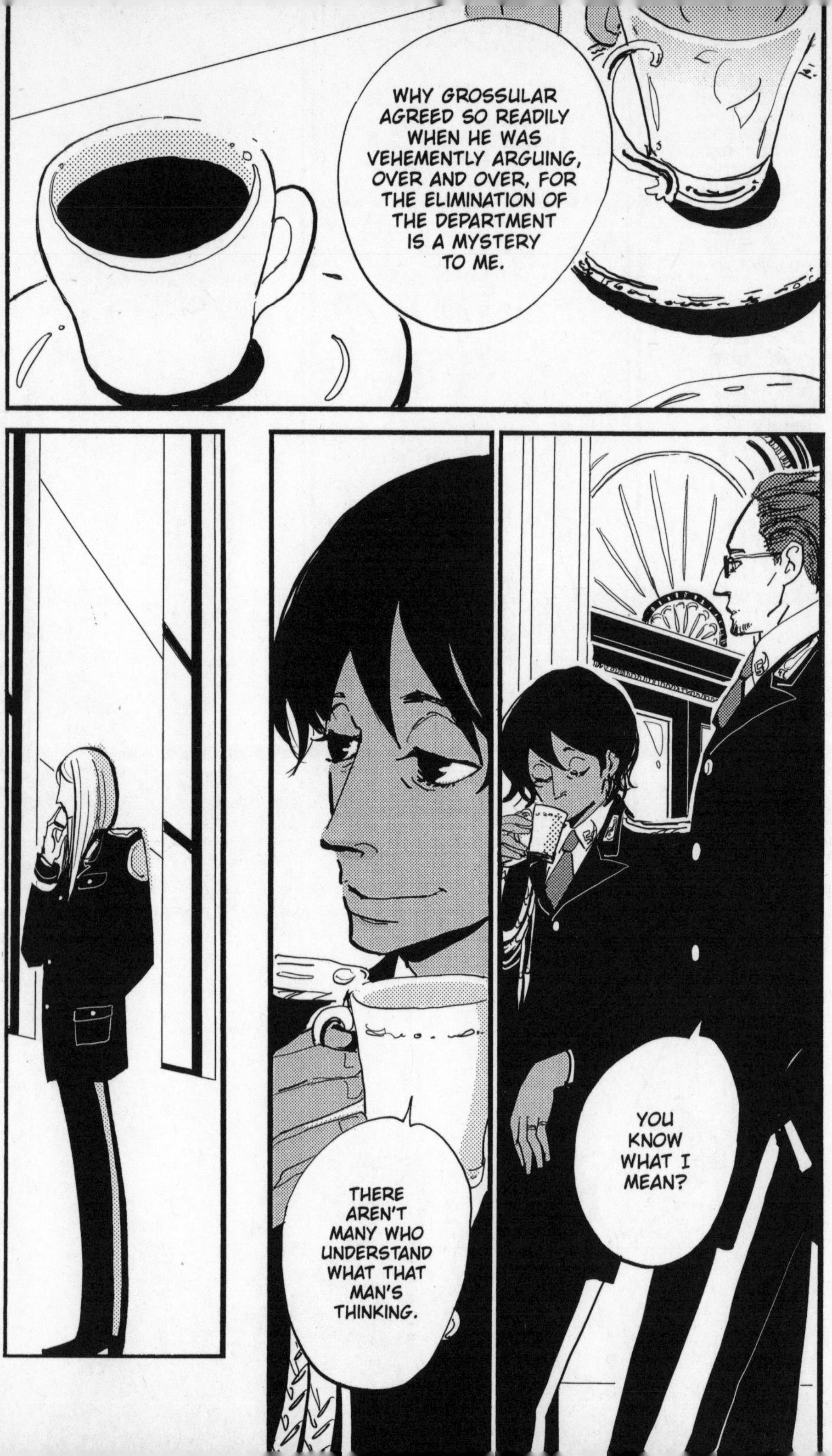
WHY GROSSULAR AGREED SO READILY WHEN HE WAS VEHEMENTLY ARGUING, OVER AND OVER, FOR THE ELIMINATION OF THE DEPARTMENT IS A MYSTERY TO ME.
YOU KNOW WHAT I MEAN?
THERE AREN'T MANY WHO UNDERSTAND WHAT THAT MAN'S THINKING.

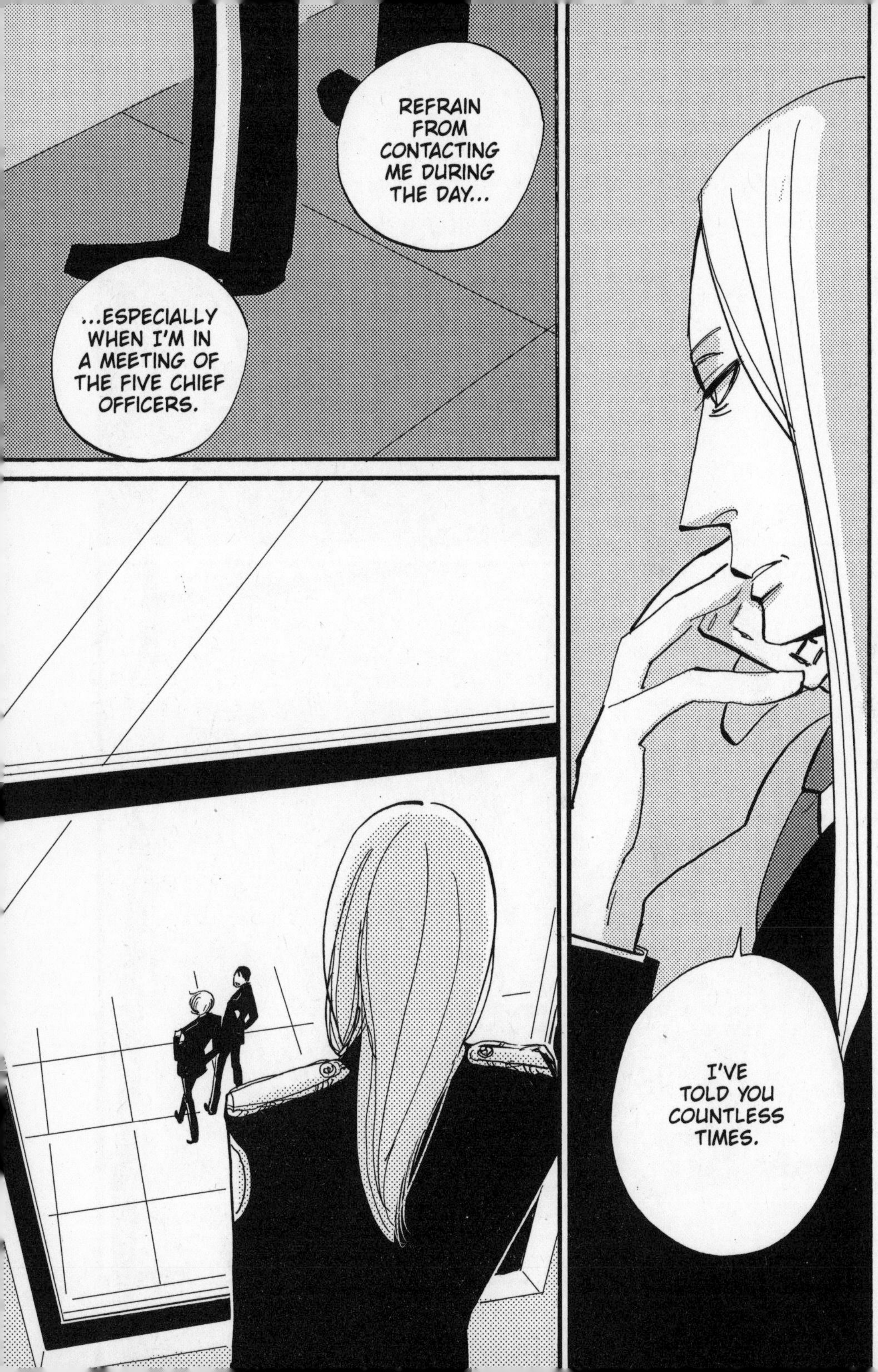
REFRAIN FROM CONTACTING ME DURING THE DAY...
...ESPECIALLY WHEN I'M IN A MEETING OF THE FIVE CHIEF OFFICERS.
I'VE TOLD YOU COUNTLESS TIMES.

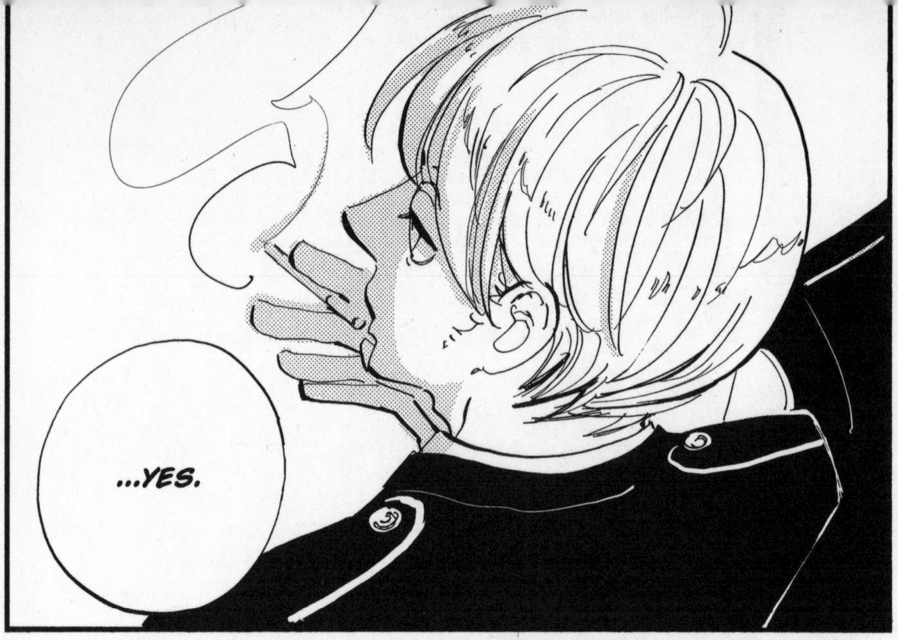
...YES.

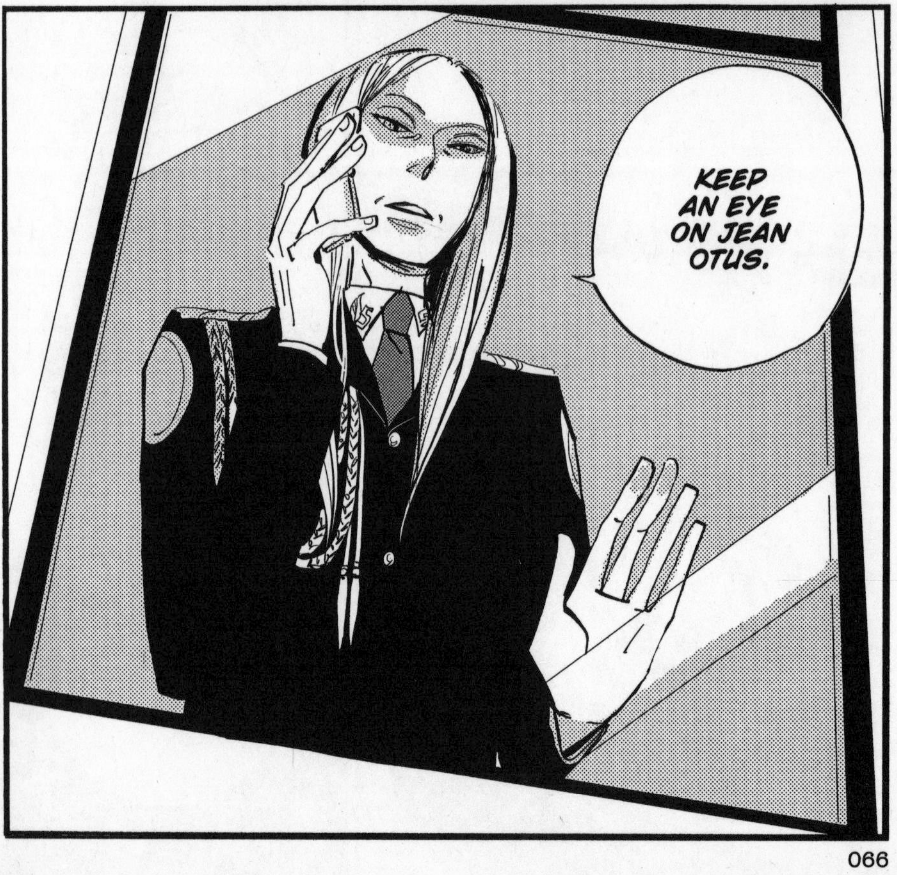
KEEP AN EYE ON JEAN OTUS.

ACCA Branch Uniforms | 1

Famasu District

As the foremost farming region of the thirteen districts, Famasu is made up of a vast territory and is responsible for 90% of the country's agricultural products. The branch staff dress in unrestrictive clothing, and they've also been known to help with the crops during harvest season.

CHAPTER 1

One More Cigarette in Famasu

CHAPTER 2

Watched in Badon

13

Eglinton Square 416-396-8920

Toronto Public Library

User ID: 2 ********* 4115

Date Format: DD/MM/YYYY

Number of Items: 3

Item ID:37131208107326
 Title:ACCA 13 Territory Inspection
Department. 1
 Date due:25/08/2018

Item ID:37131194012886
 Title:JoJo's bizarre adventure. Part 3,
Stardust crusaders. 07
 Date due:25/08/2018

Item ID:37131187934674
 Title:A study in emerald
 Date due:25/08/2018

Telephone Renewal# 416-395-5505
www.torontopubliclibrary.ca
 Saturday, August 4, 2018   12:55 PM

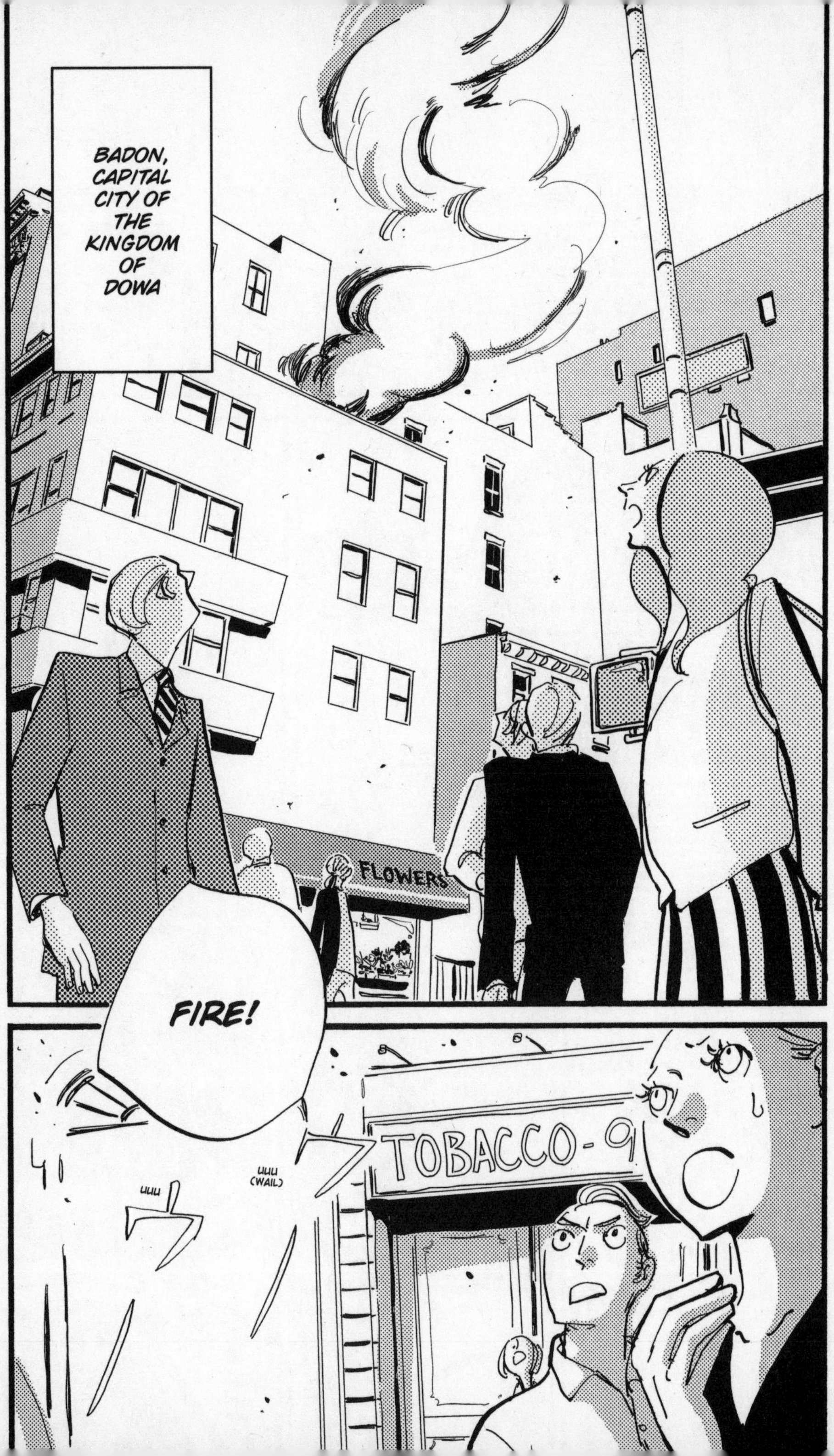
BADON, CAPITAL CITY OF THE KINGDOM OF DOWA
FLOWERS
FIRE!
TOBACCO-9
UUU (WAIL)
UUU

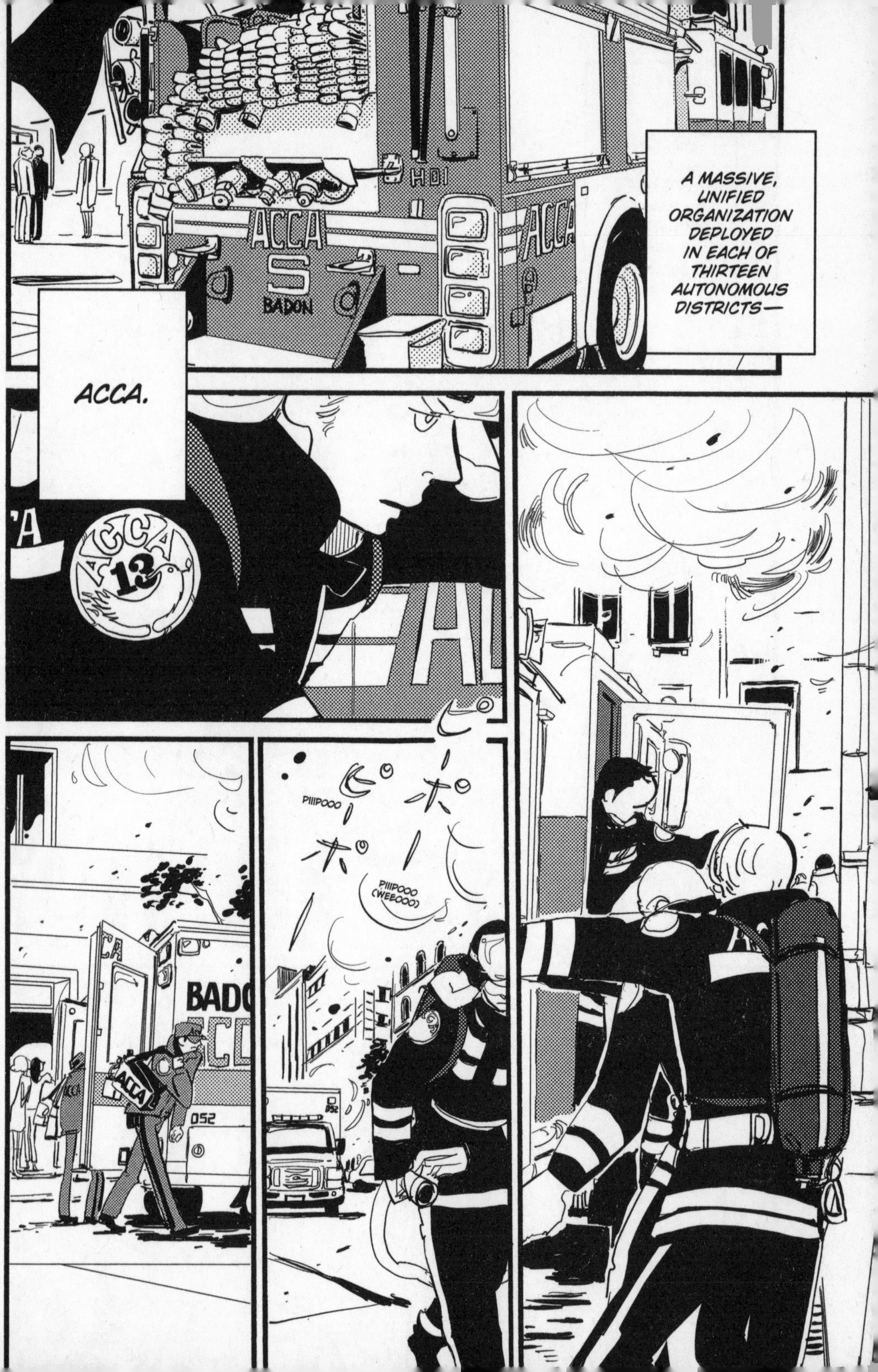
A MASSIVE, UNIFIED ORGANIZATION DEPLOYED IN EACH OF THIRTEEN AUTONOMOUS DISTRICTS—
ACCA.
PIIIPOOO
PIIIPOOO (WEEOOO)

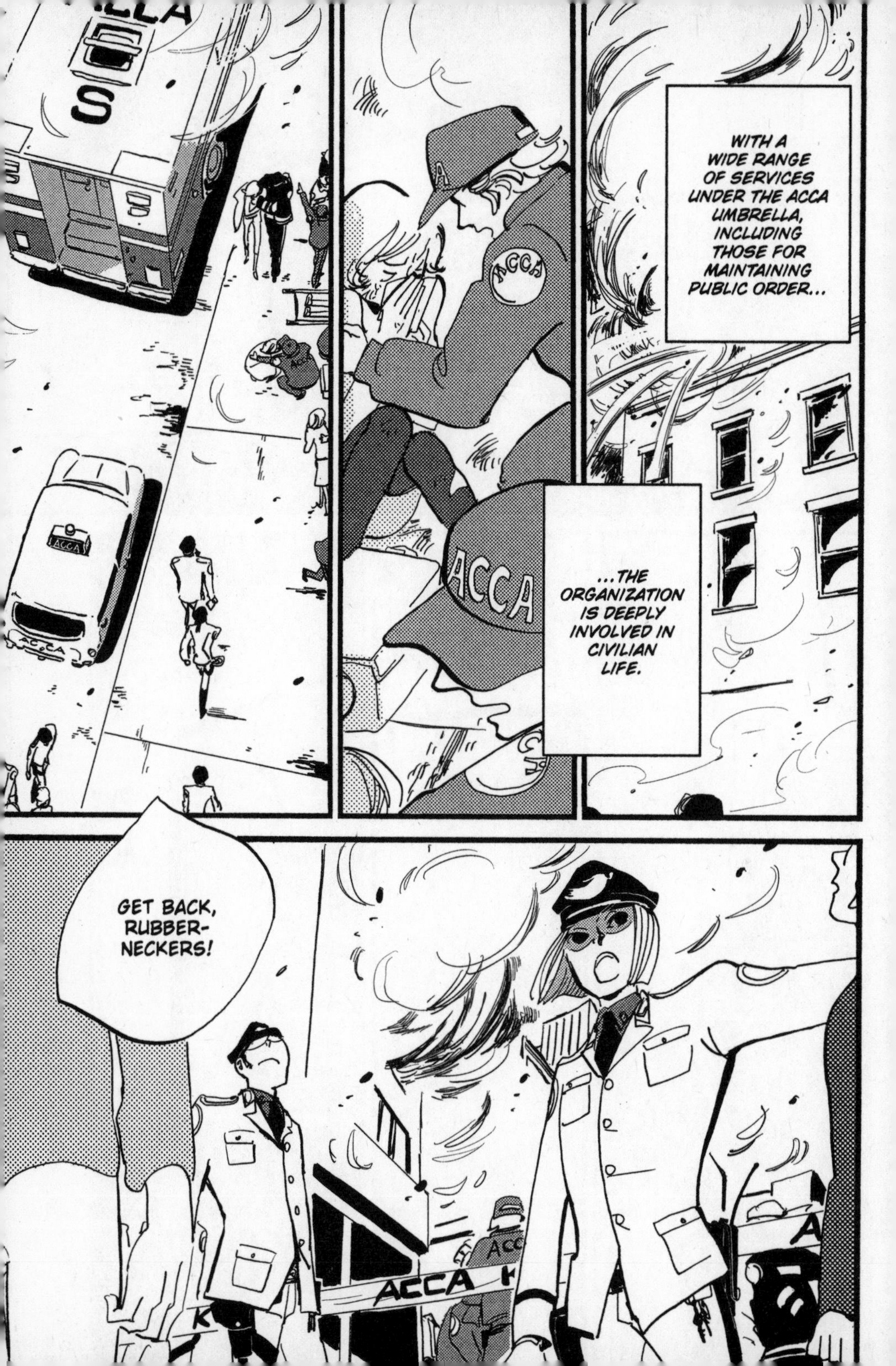
WITH A WIDE RANGE OF SERVICES UNDER THE ACCA UMBRELLA, INCLUDING THOSE FOR MAINTAINING PUBLIC ORDER...
...THE ORGANIZATION IS DEEPLY INVOLVED IN CIVILIAN LIFE.
GET BACK, RUBBER-NECKERS!
ACCA

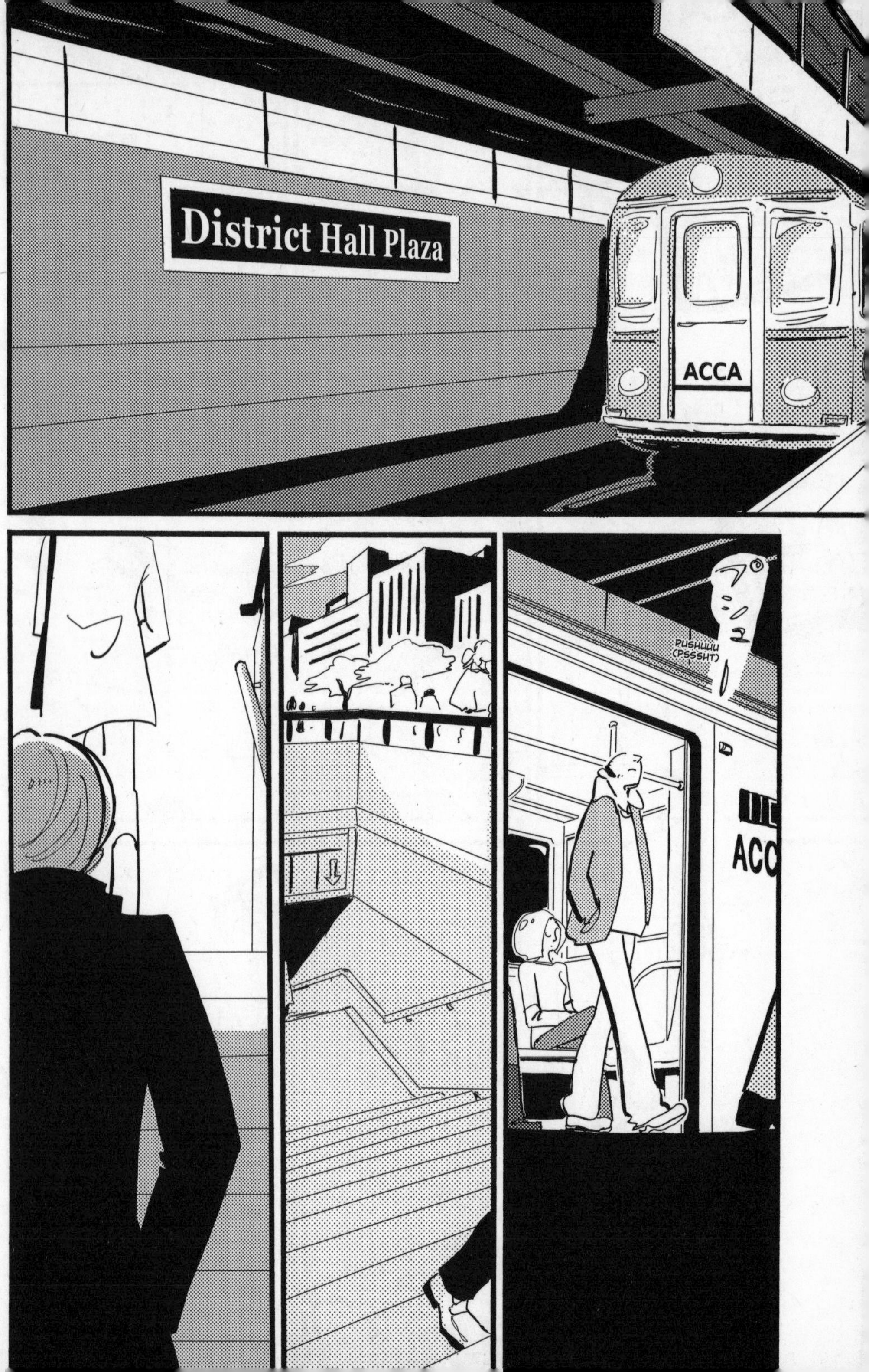
District Hall Plaza
ACCA
PUSHUUU (PSSSHT)
ACC

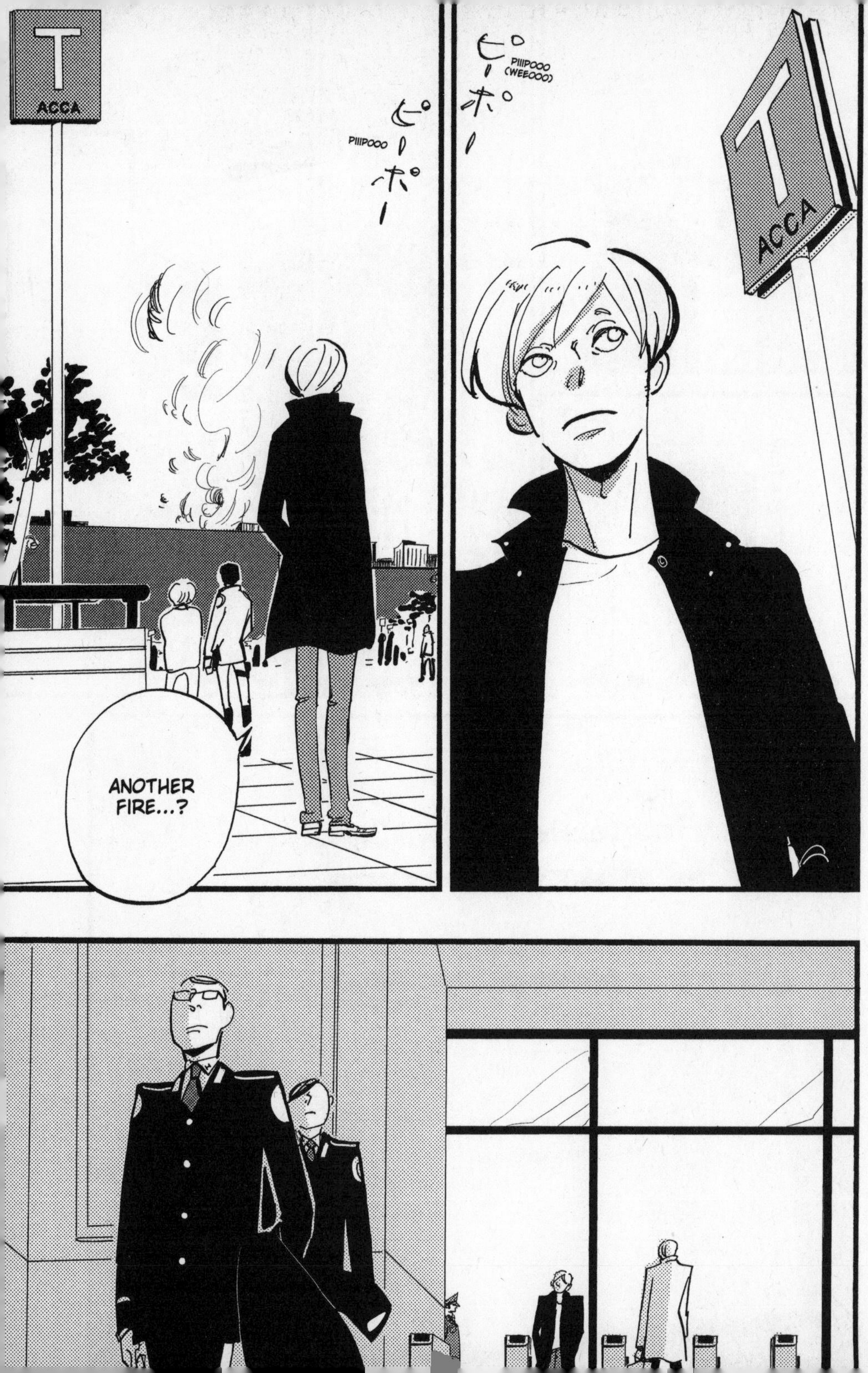
ピーポー
PIIPOOO (WEEOOO)
ピーポー
PIIPOOO
ACCA
ACCA
ANOTHER FIRE...?

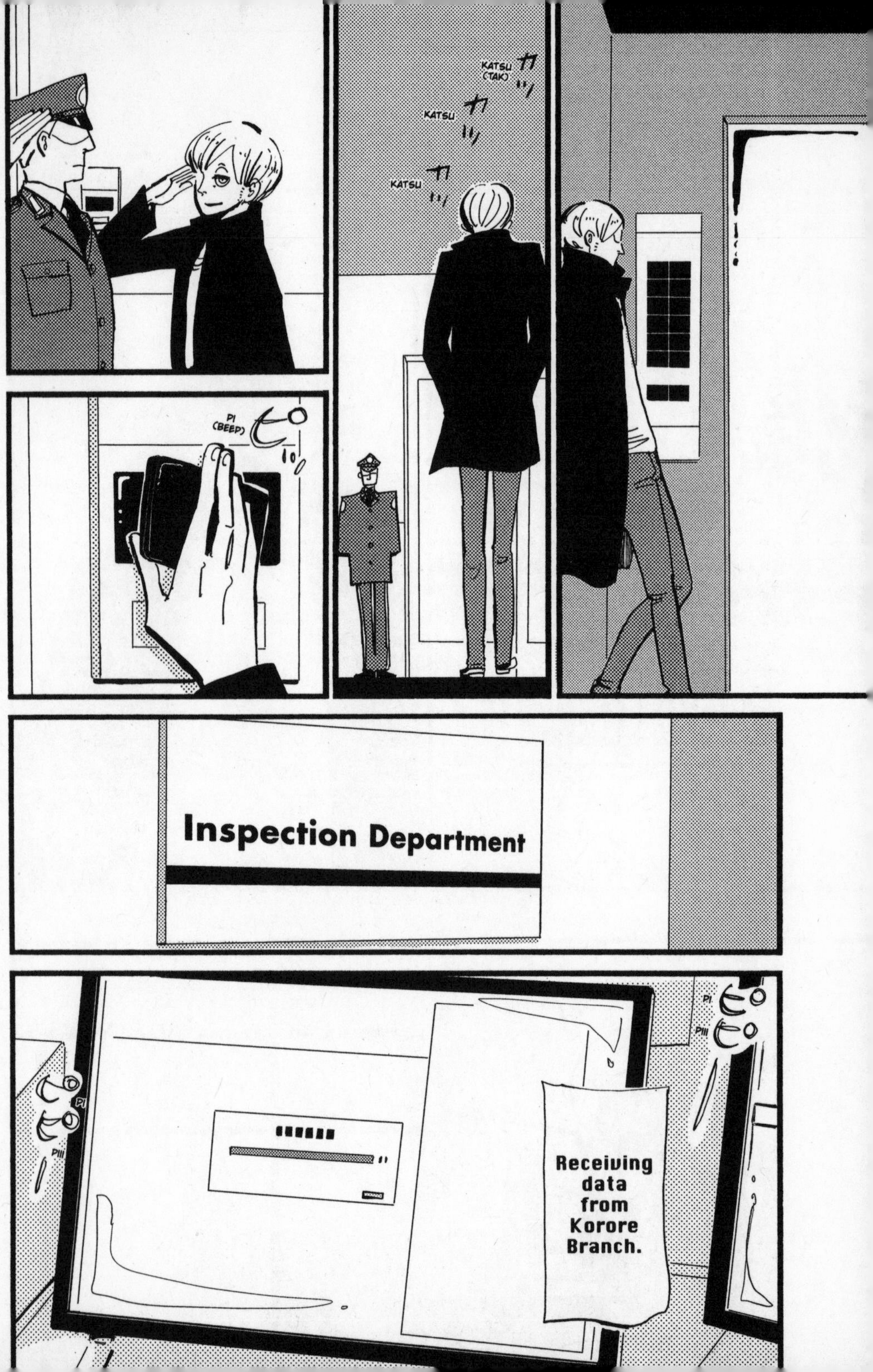
KATSU (TAK)
KATSU
KATSU
PI (BEEP)
Inspection Department
PI
PIII
Receiving data from Korore Branch.
PI
PIII

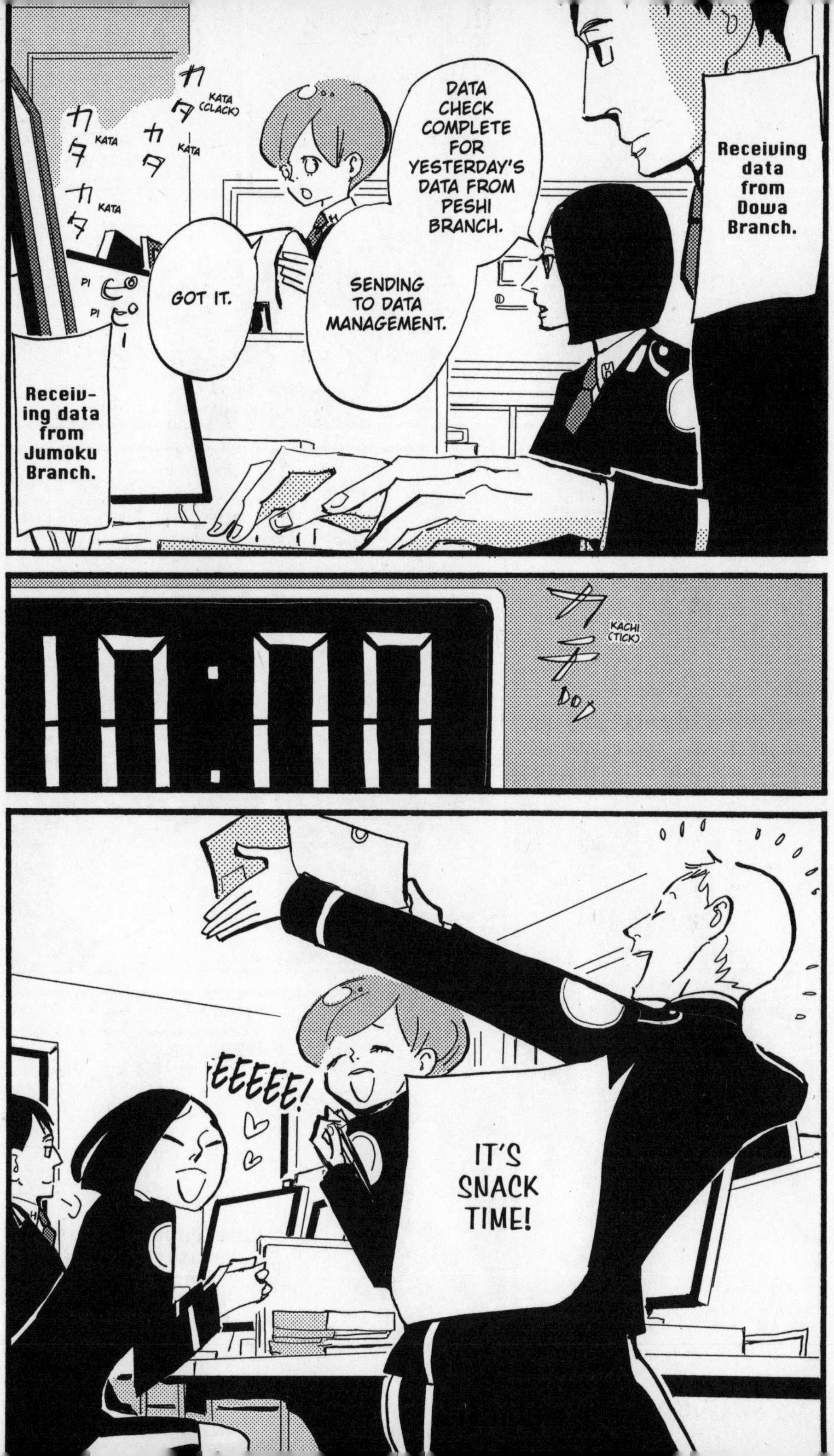
Receiving data from Dowa Branch.
DATA CHECK COMPLETE FOR YESTERDAY'S DATA FROM PESHI BRANCH.
SENDING TO DATA MANAGEMENT.
KATA (CLACK)
KATA
KATA
KATA
GOT IT.
PI
PI
Receiv-ing data from Jumoku Branch.
KACHI (TICK)
IT'S SNACK TIME!
EEEEE!

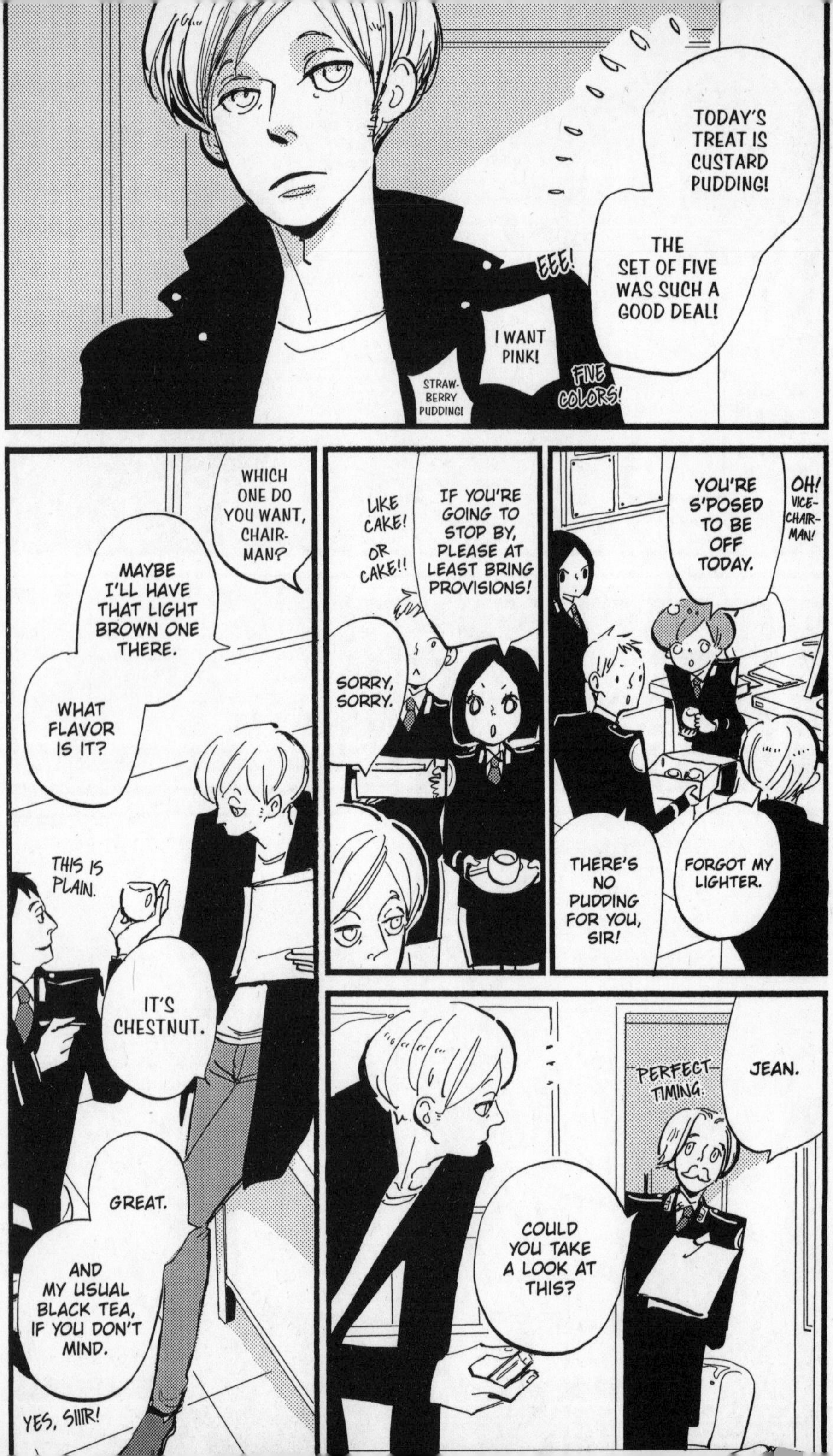

TODAY'S TREAT IS CUSTARD PUDDING!
THE SET OF FIVE WAS SUCH A GOOD DEAL!
EEE!
I WANT PINK!
FIVE COLORS!
STRAW-BERRY PUDDING!
OH! VICE-CHAIRMAN!
YOU'RE S'POSED TO BE OFF TODAY.
FORGOT MY LIGHTER.
THERE'S NO PUDDING FOR YOU, SIR!
IF YOU'RE GOING TO STOP BY, PLEASE AT LEAST BRING PROVISIONS!
LIKE CAKE!
OR CAKE!!
SORRY, SORRY.
JEAN.
PERFECT TIMING.
COULD YOU TAKE A LOOK AT THIS?
WHICH ONE DO YOU WANT, CHAIR-MAN?
MAYBE I'LL HAVE THAT LIGHT BROWN ONE THERE.
WHAT FLAVOR IS IT?
THIS IS PLAIN.
IT'S CHESTNUT.
GREAT.
AND MY USUAL BLACK TEA, IF YOU DON'T MIND.
YES, SIIR!

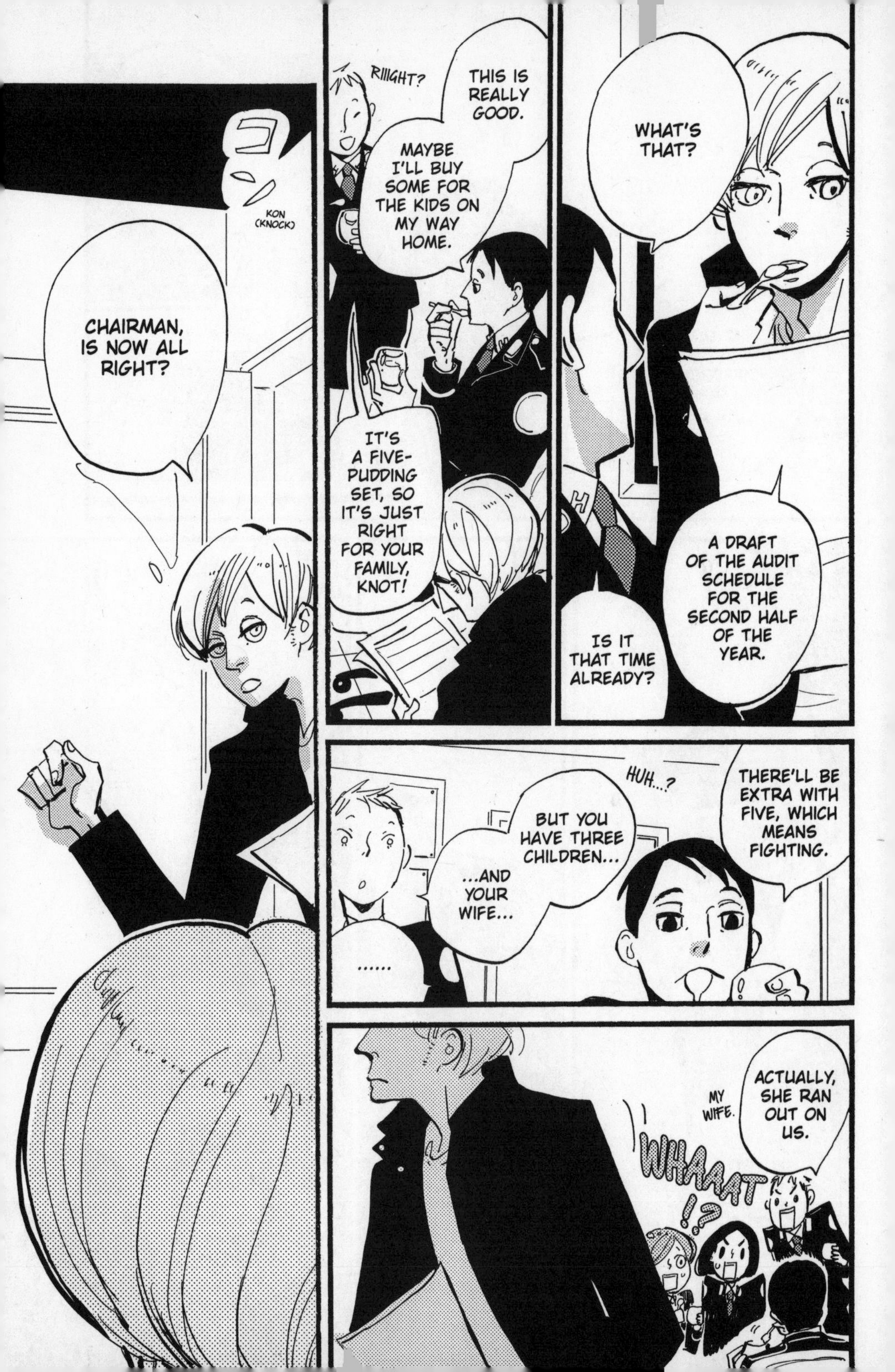
WHAT'S THAT?
A DRAFT OF THE AUDIT SCHEDULE FOR THE SECOND HALF OF THE YEAR.
IS IT THAT TIME ALREADY?
THIS IS REALLY GOOD.
RIIIGHT?
MAYBE I'LL BUY SOME FOR THE KIDS ON MY WAY HOME.
IT'S A FIVE-PUDDING SET, SO IT'S JUST RIGHT FOR YOUR FAMILY, KNOT!
THERE'LL BE EXTRA WITH FIVE, WHICH MEANS FIGHTING.
HUH...?
BUT YOU HAVE THREE CHILDREN...
...AND YOUR WIFE...
......
ACTUALLY, SHE RAN OUT ON US.
MY WIFE.
WHAAAT!?
KON (KNOCK)
CHAIRMAN, IS NOW ALL RIGHT?

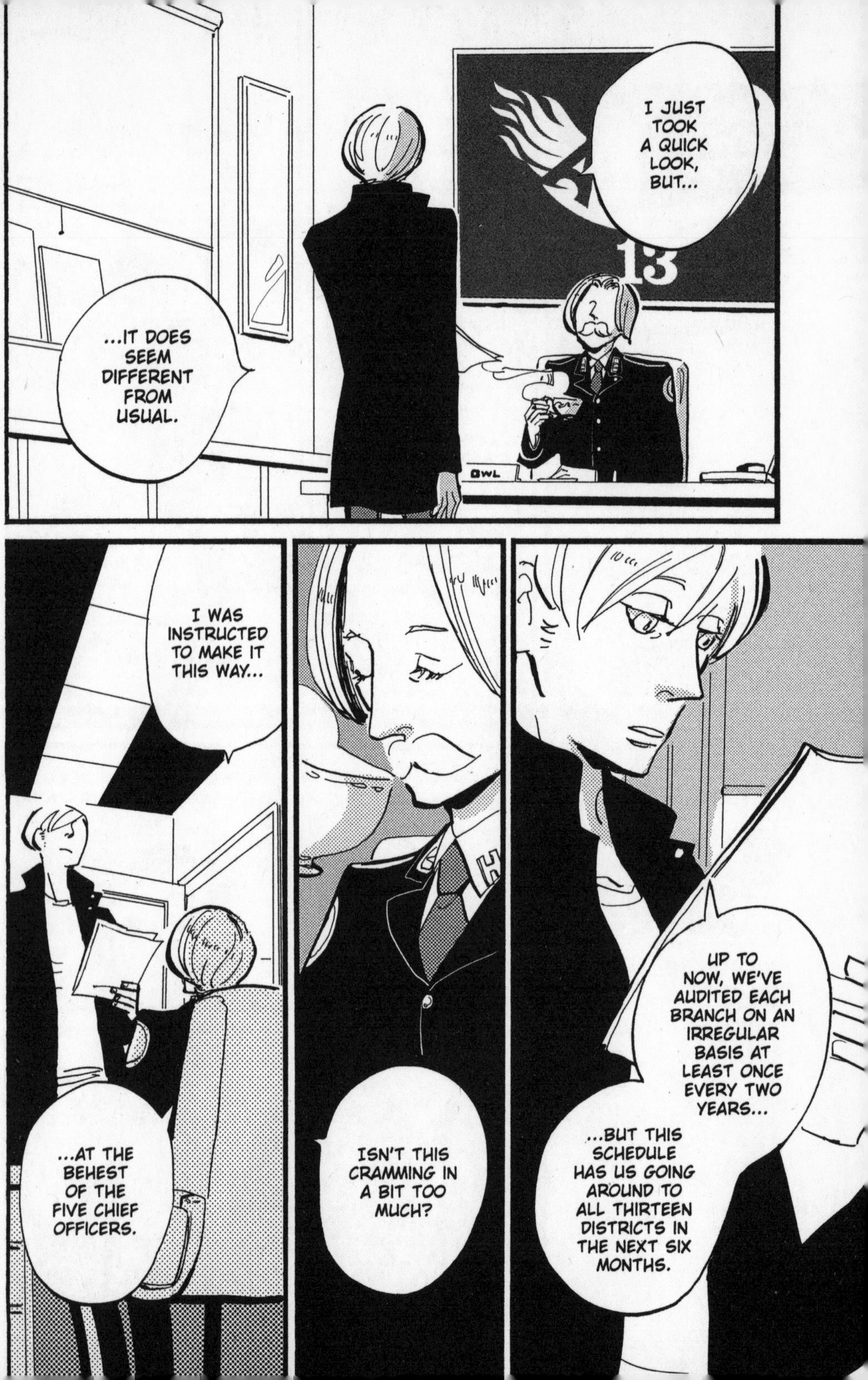
I JUST TOOK A QUICK LOOK, BUT...
13
...IT DOES SEEM DIFFERENT FROM USUAL.
OWL
UP TO NOW, WE'VE AUDITED EACH BRANCH ON AN IRREGULAR BASIS AT LEAST ONCE EVERY TWO YEARS...
...BUT THIS SCHEDULE HAS US GOING AROUND TO ALL THIRTEEN DISTRICTS IN THE NEXT SIX MONTHS.
ISN'T THIS CRAMMING IN A BIT TOO MUCH?
I WAS INSTRUCTED TO MAKE IT THIS WAY...
...AT THE BEHEST OF THE FIVE CHIEF OFFICERS.

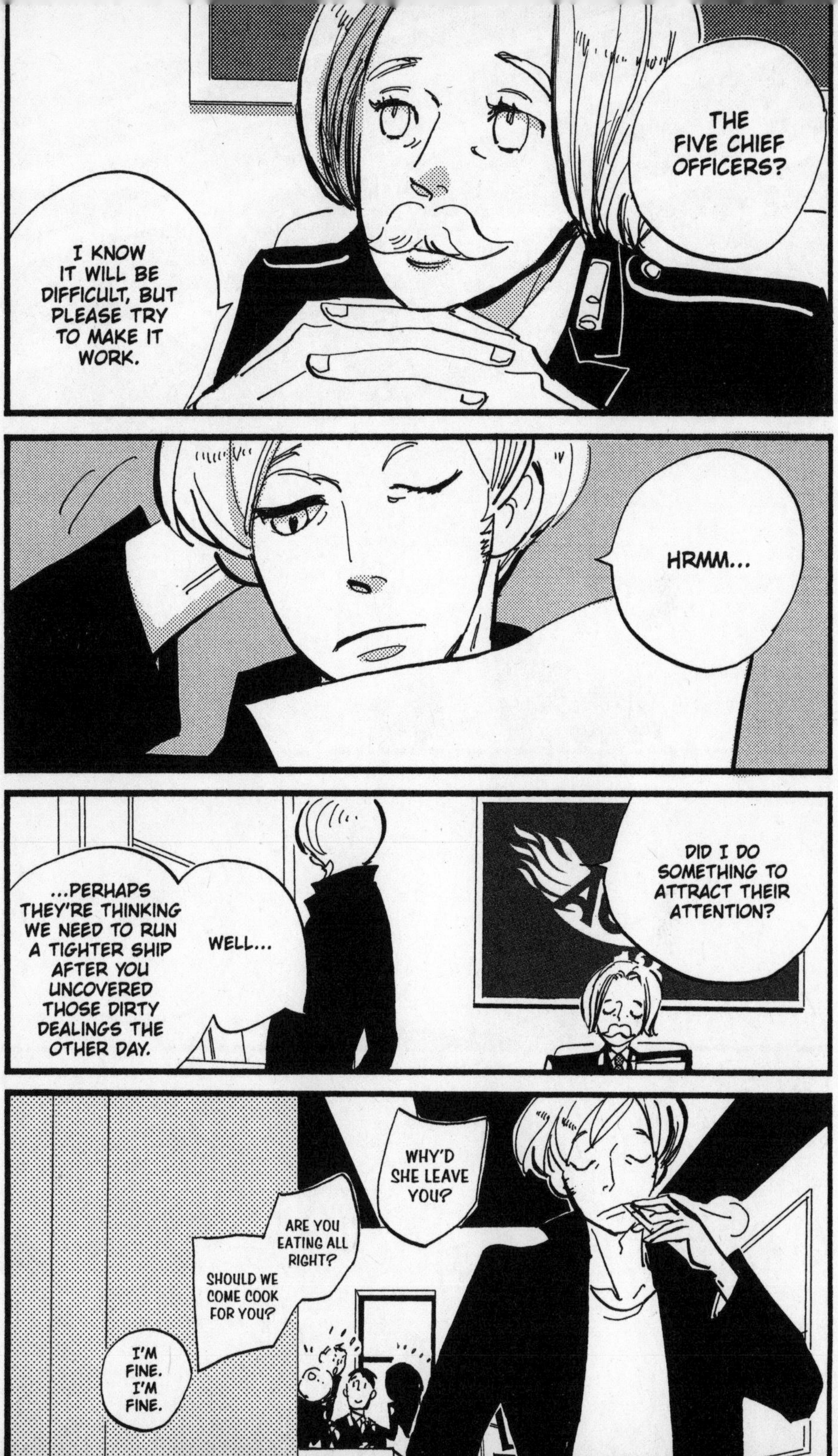

THE FIVE CHIEF OFFICERS?
I KNOW IT WILL BE DIFFICULT, BUT PLEASE TRY TO MAKE IT WORK.
HRMM...
DID I DO SOMETHING TO ATTRACT THEIR ATTENTION?
WELL...
...PERHAPS THEY'RE THINKING WE NEED TO RUN A TIGHTER SHIP AFTER YOU UNCOVERED THOSE DIRTY DEALINGS THE OTHER DAY.
WHY'D SHE LEAVE YOU?
ARE YOU EATING ALL RIGHT?
SHOULD WE COME COOK FOR YOU?
I'M FINE. I'M FINE.

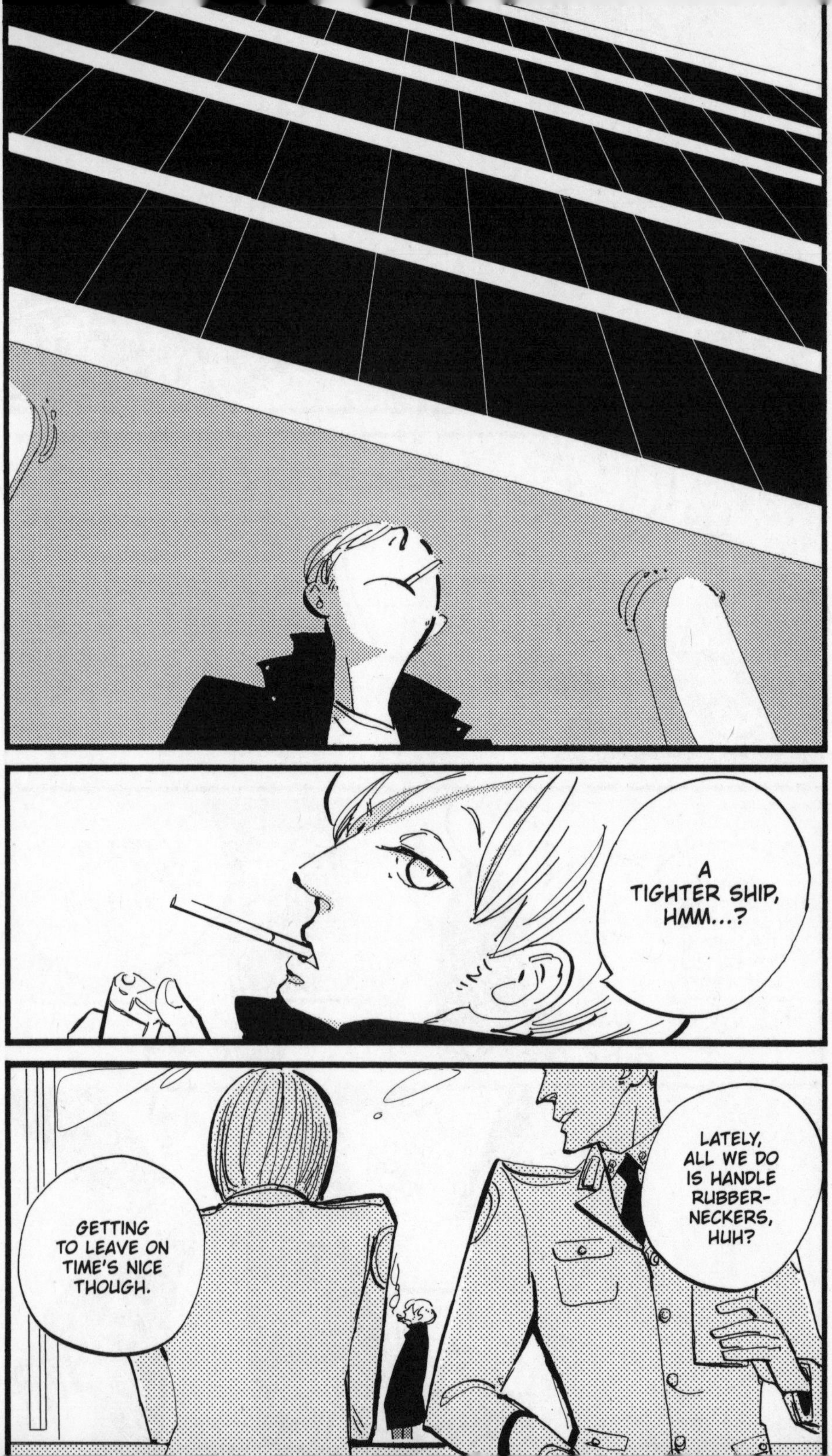
A TIGHTER SHIP, HMM...?
LATELY, ALL WE DO IS HANDLE RUBBER-NECKERS, HUH?
GETTING TO LEAVE ON TIME'S NICE THOUGH.

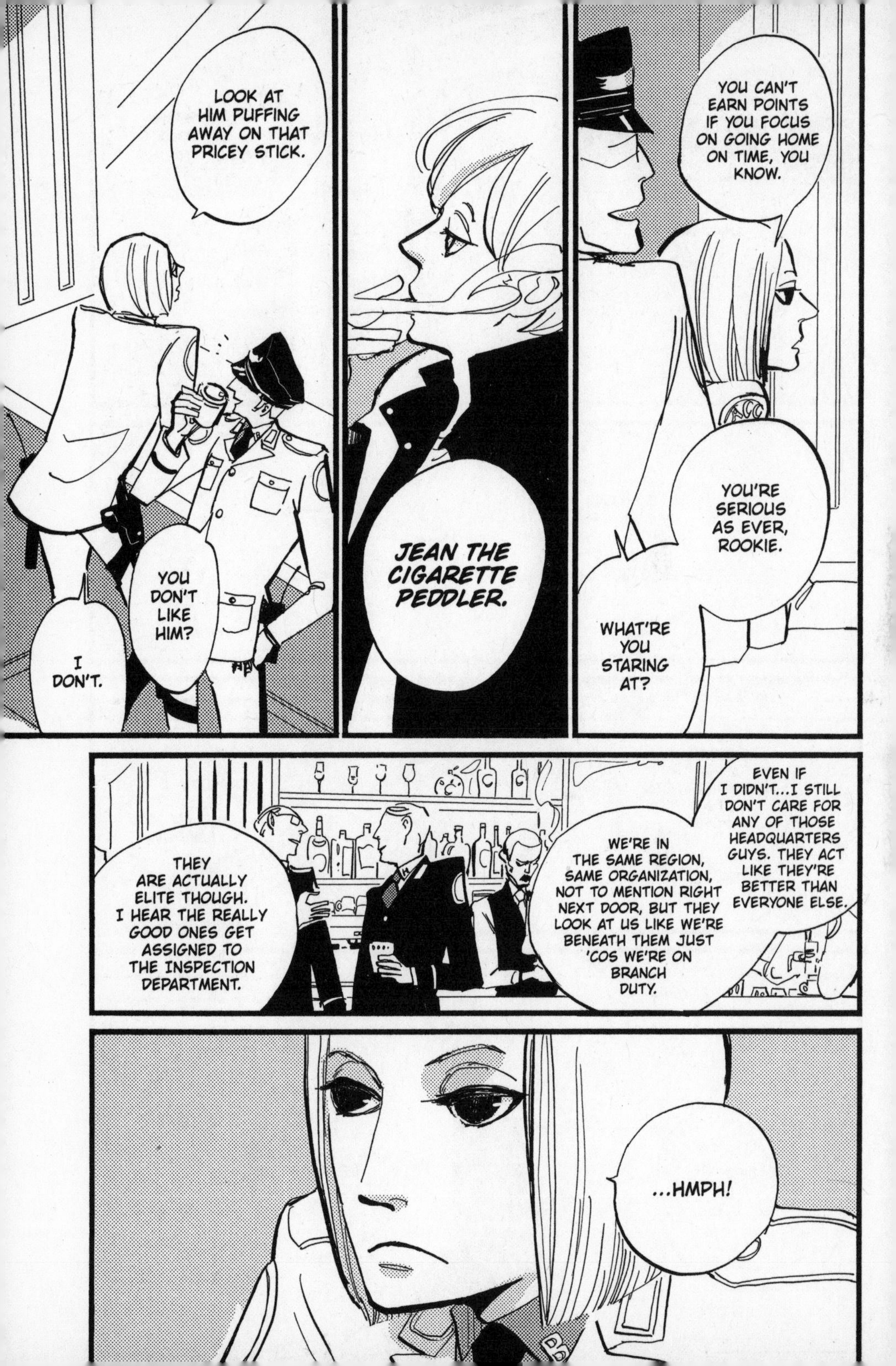
LOOK AT HIM PUFFING AWAY ON THAT PRICEY STICK.
YOU DON'T LIKE HIM?
I DON'T.
JEAN THE CIGARETTE PEDDLER.
YOU CAN'T EARN POINTS IF YOU FOCUS ON GOING HOME ON TIME, YOU KNOW.
YOU'RE SERIOUS AS EVER, ROOKIE.
WHAT'RE YOU STARING AT?
THEY ARE ACTUALLY ELITE THOUGH. I HEAR THE REALLY GOOD ONES GET ASSIGNED TO THE INSPECTION DEPARTMENT.
WE'RE IN THE SAME REGION, SAME ORGANIZATION, NOT TO MENTION RIGHT NEXT DOOR, BUT THEY LOOK AT US LIKE WE'RE BENEATH THEM JUST 'COS WE'RE ON BRANCH DUTY.
EVEN IF I DIDN'T...I STILL DON'T CARE FOR ANY OF THOSE HEADQUARTERS GUYS. THEY ACT LIKE THEY'RE BETTER THAN EVERYONE ELSE.
...HMPH!

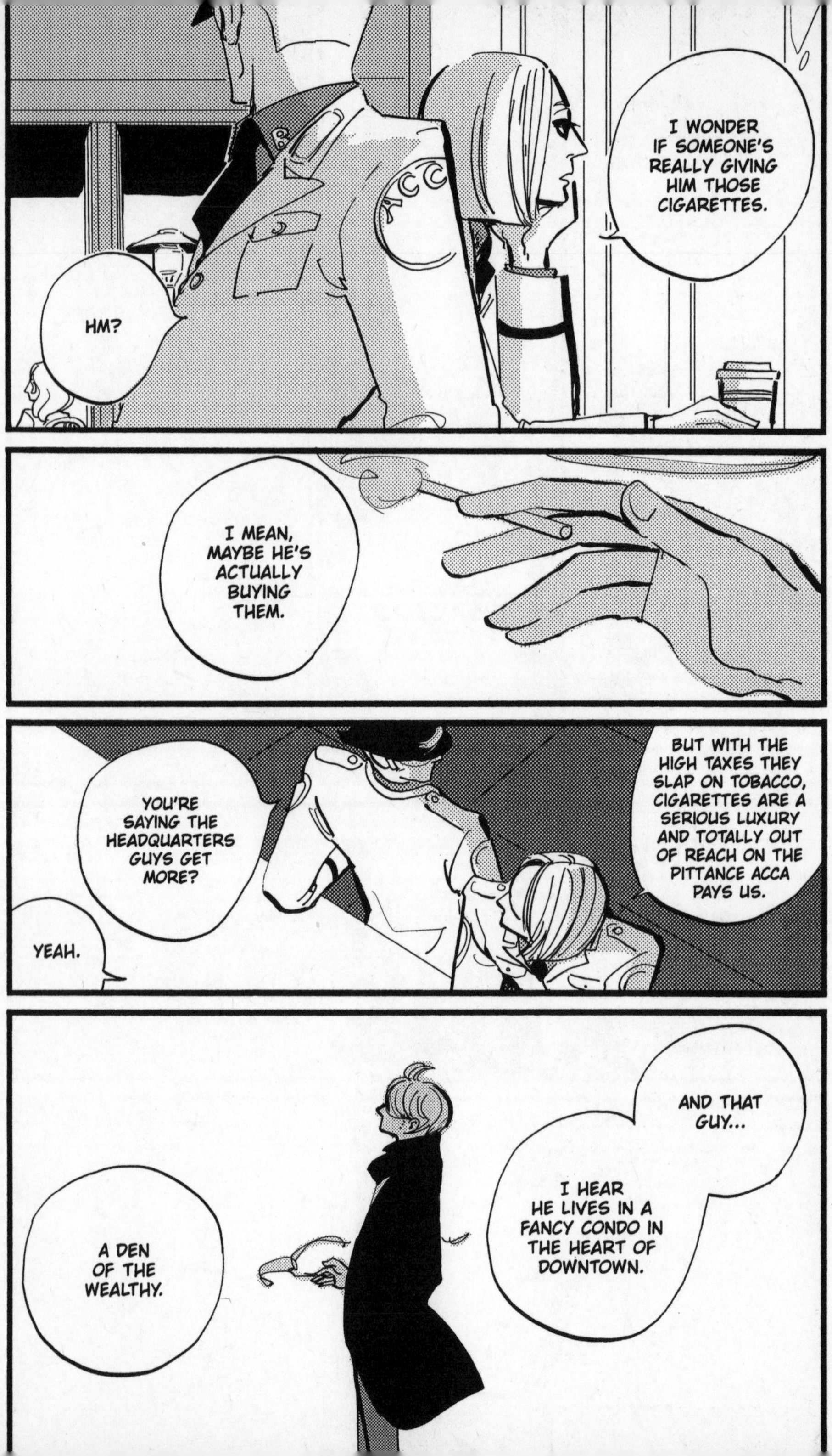
I WONDER IF SOMEONE'S REALLY GIVING HIM THOSE CIGARETTES.
HM?
I MEAN, MAYBE HE'S ACTUALLY BUYING THEM.
BUT WITH THE HIGH TAXES THEY SLAP ON TOBACCO, CIGARETTES ARE A SERIOUS LUXURY AND TOTALLY OUT OF REACH ON THE PITTANCE ACCA PAYS US.
YOU'RE SAYING THE HEADQUARTERS GUYS GET MORE?
YEAH.
AND THAT GUY...
I HEAR HE LIVES IN A FANCY CONDO IN THE HEART OF DOWNTOWN.
A DEN OF THE WEALTHY.

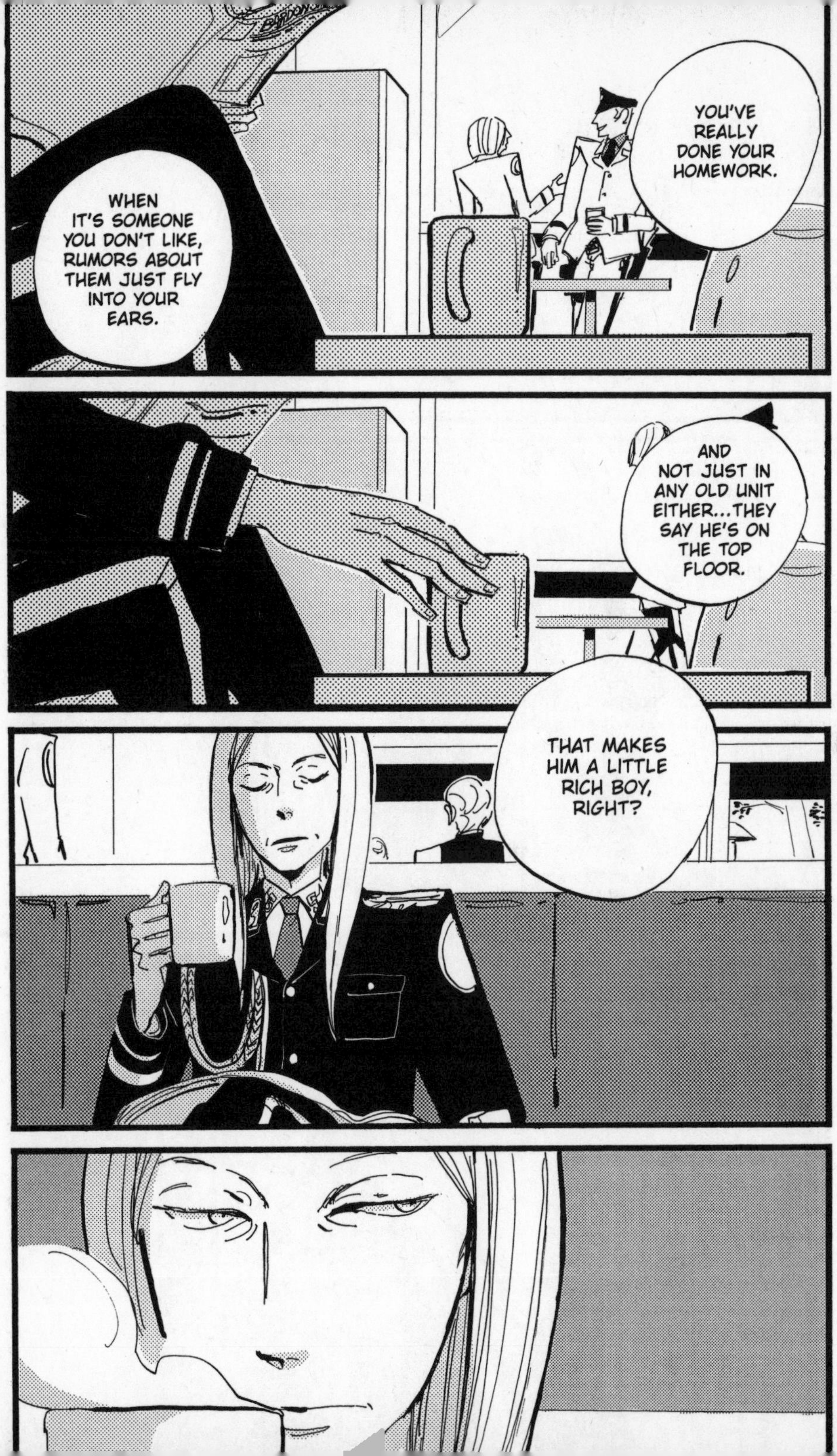
YOU'VE REALLY DONE YOUR HOMEWORK.
WHEN IT'S SOMEONE YOU DON'T LIKE, RUMORS ABOUT THEM JUST FLY INTO YOUR EARS.
AND NOT JUST IN ANY OLD UNIT EITHER...THEY SAY HE'S ON THE TOP FLOOR.
THAT MAKES HIM A LITTLE RICH BOY, RIGHT?

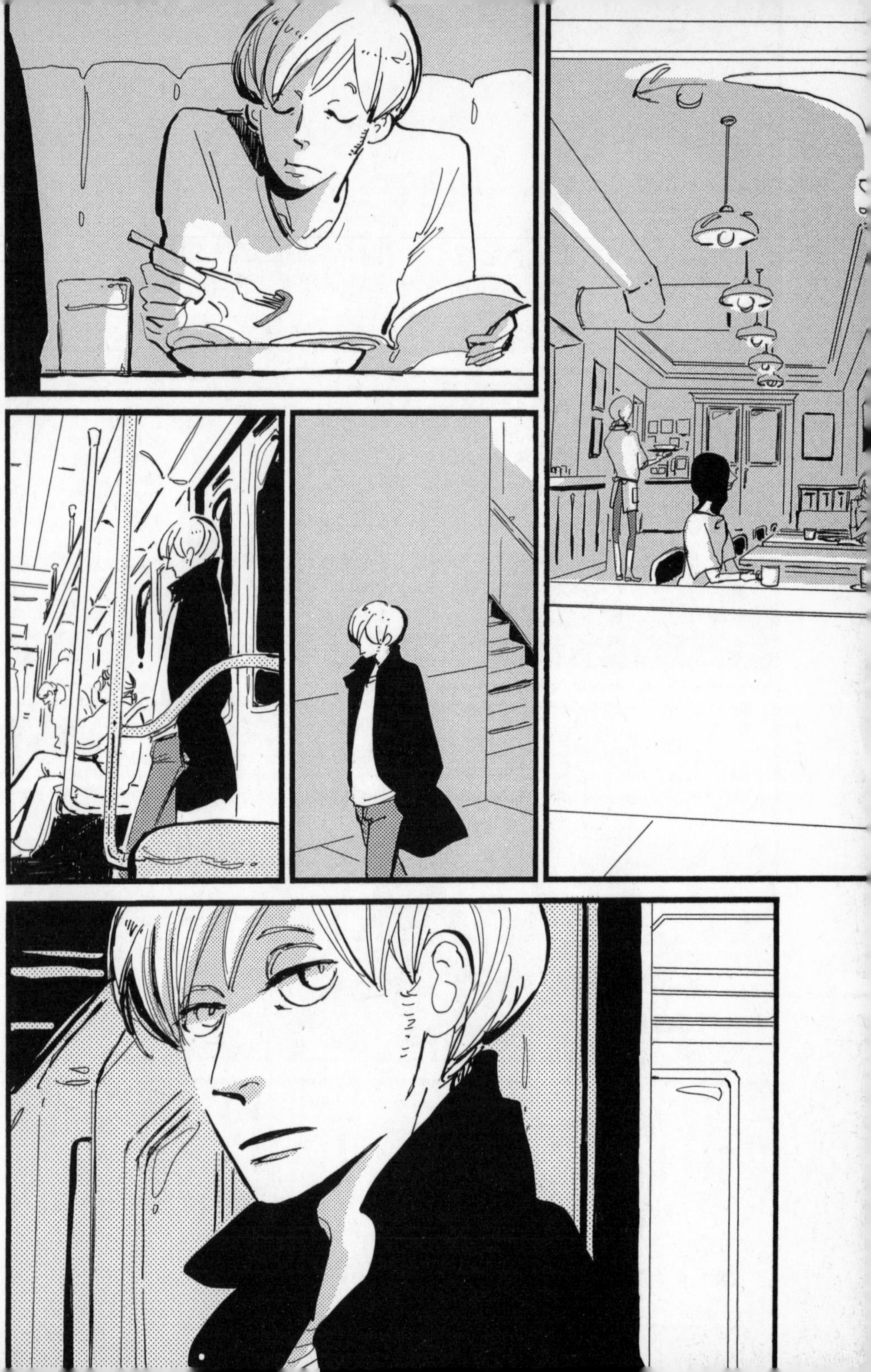

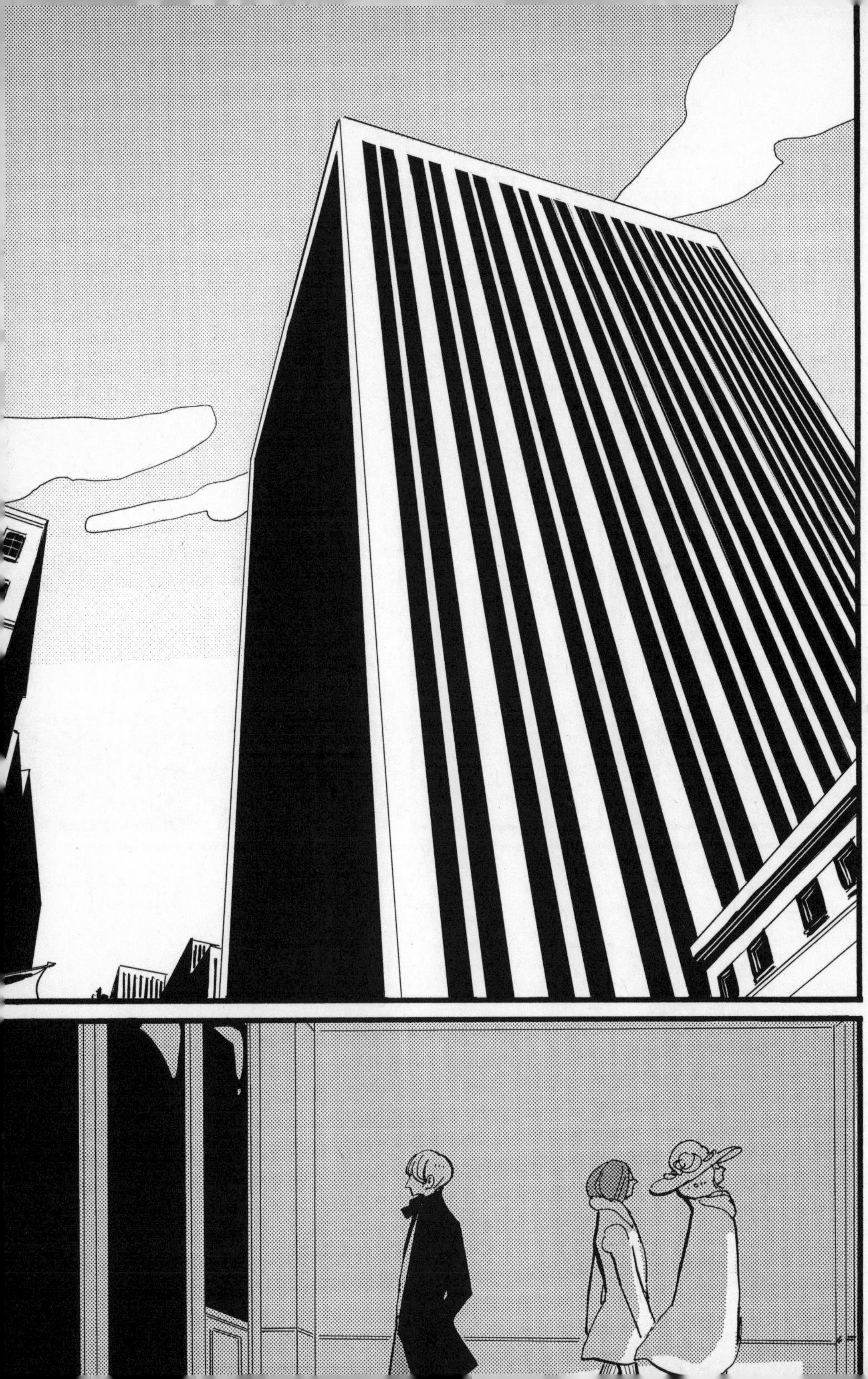

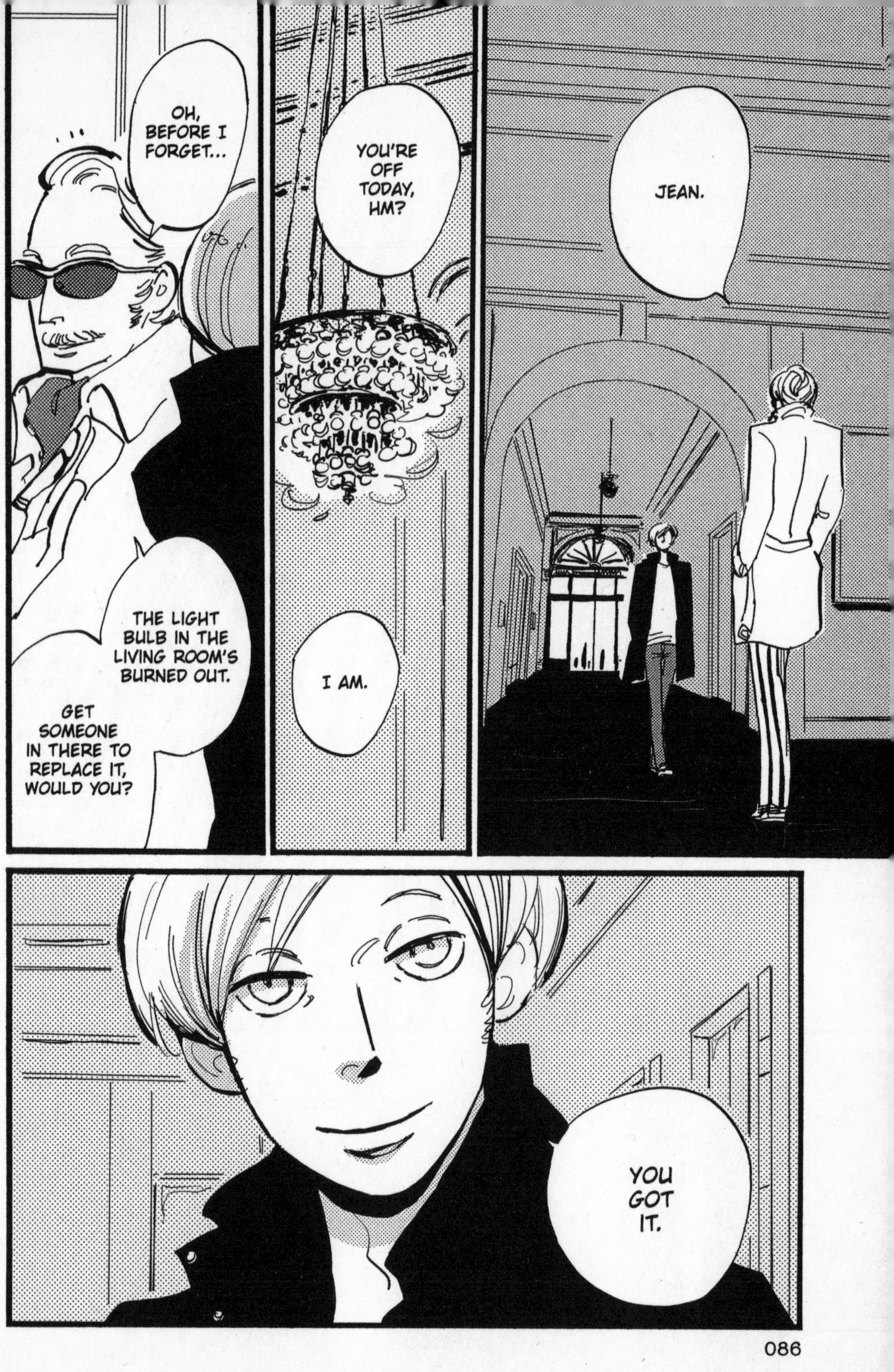
JEAN.
YOU'RE OFF TODAY, HM?
I AM.
OH, BEFORE I FORGET...
THE LIGHT BULB IN THE LIVING ROOM'S BURNED OUT.
GET SOMEONE IN THERE TO REPLACE IT, WOULD YOU?
YOU GOT IT.

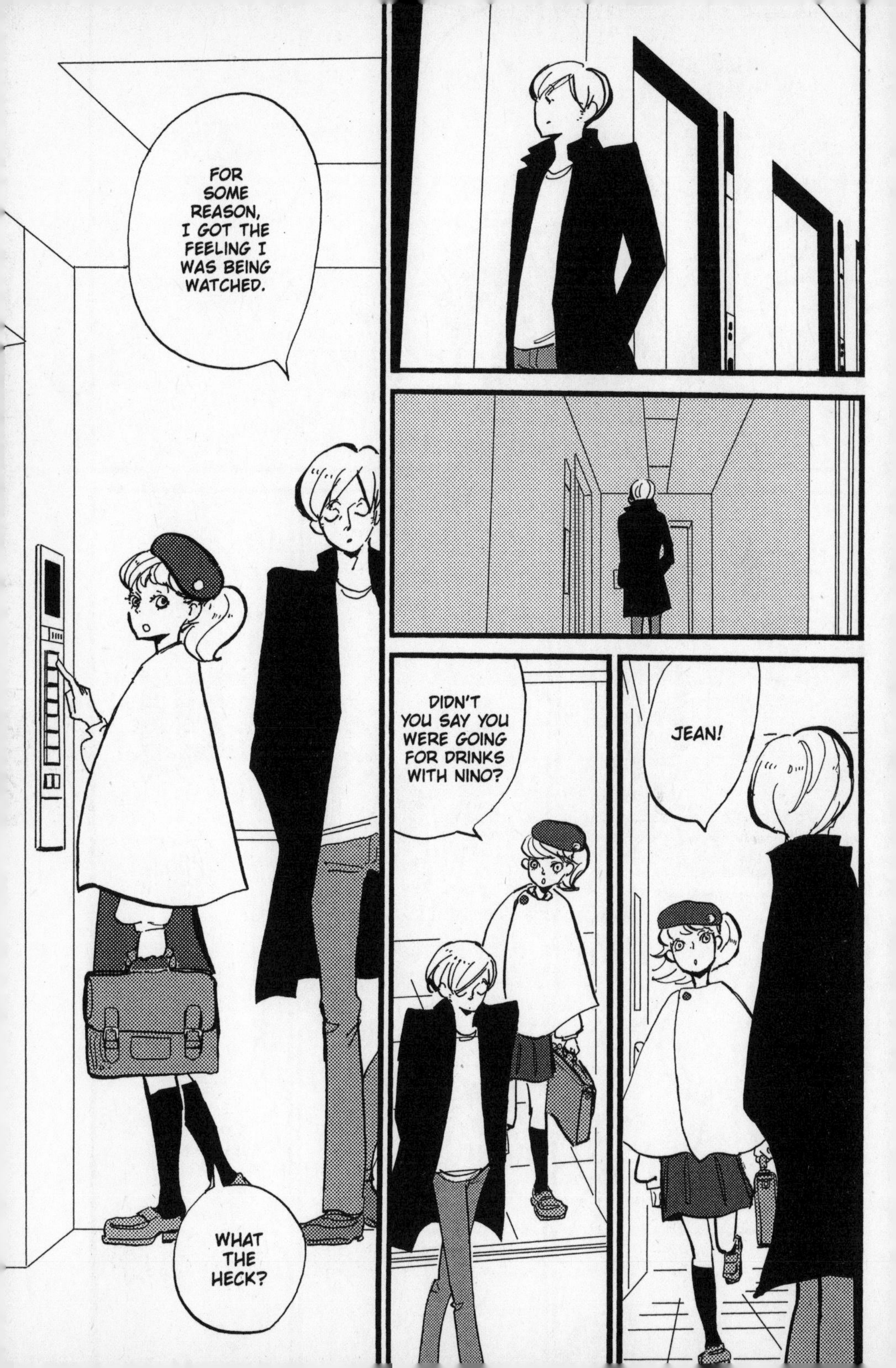
FOR SOME REASON, I GOT THE FEELING I WAS BEING WATCHED.
WHAT THE HECK?
JEAN!
DIDN'T YOU SAY YOU WERE GOING FOR DRINKS WITH NINO?

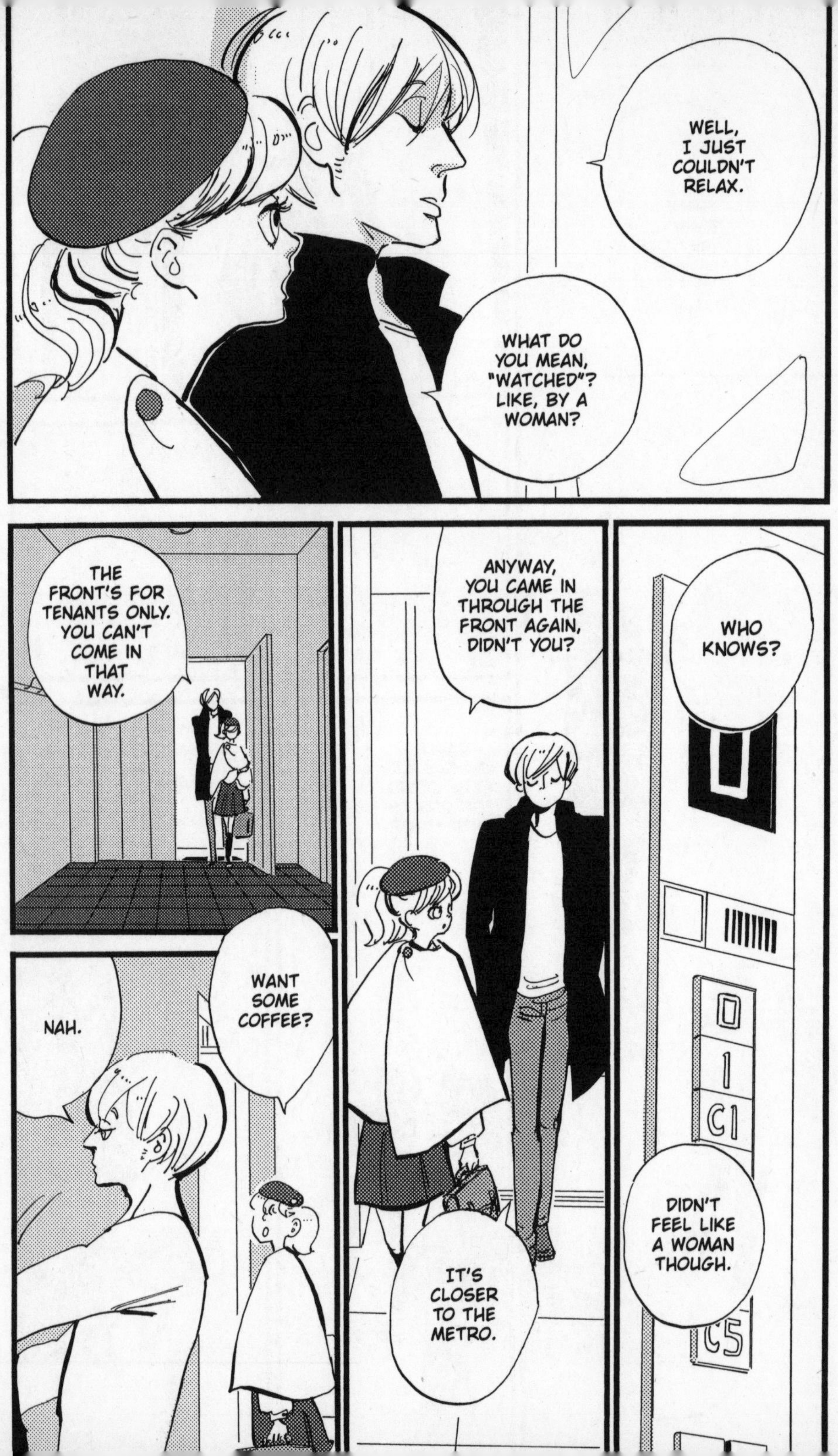

WELL, I JUST COULDN'T RELAX.
WHAT DO YOU MEAN, "WATCHED"? LIKE, BY A WOMAN?
WHO KNOWS?
DIDN'T FEEL LIKE A WOMAN THOUGH.
ANYWAY, YOU CAME IN THROUGH THE FRONT AGAIN, DIDN'T YOU?
IT'S CLOSER TO THE METRO.
THE FRONT'S FOR TENANTS ONLY. YOU CAN'T COME IN THAT WAY.
WANT SOME COFFEE?
NAH.

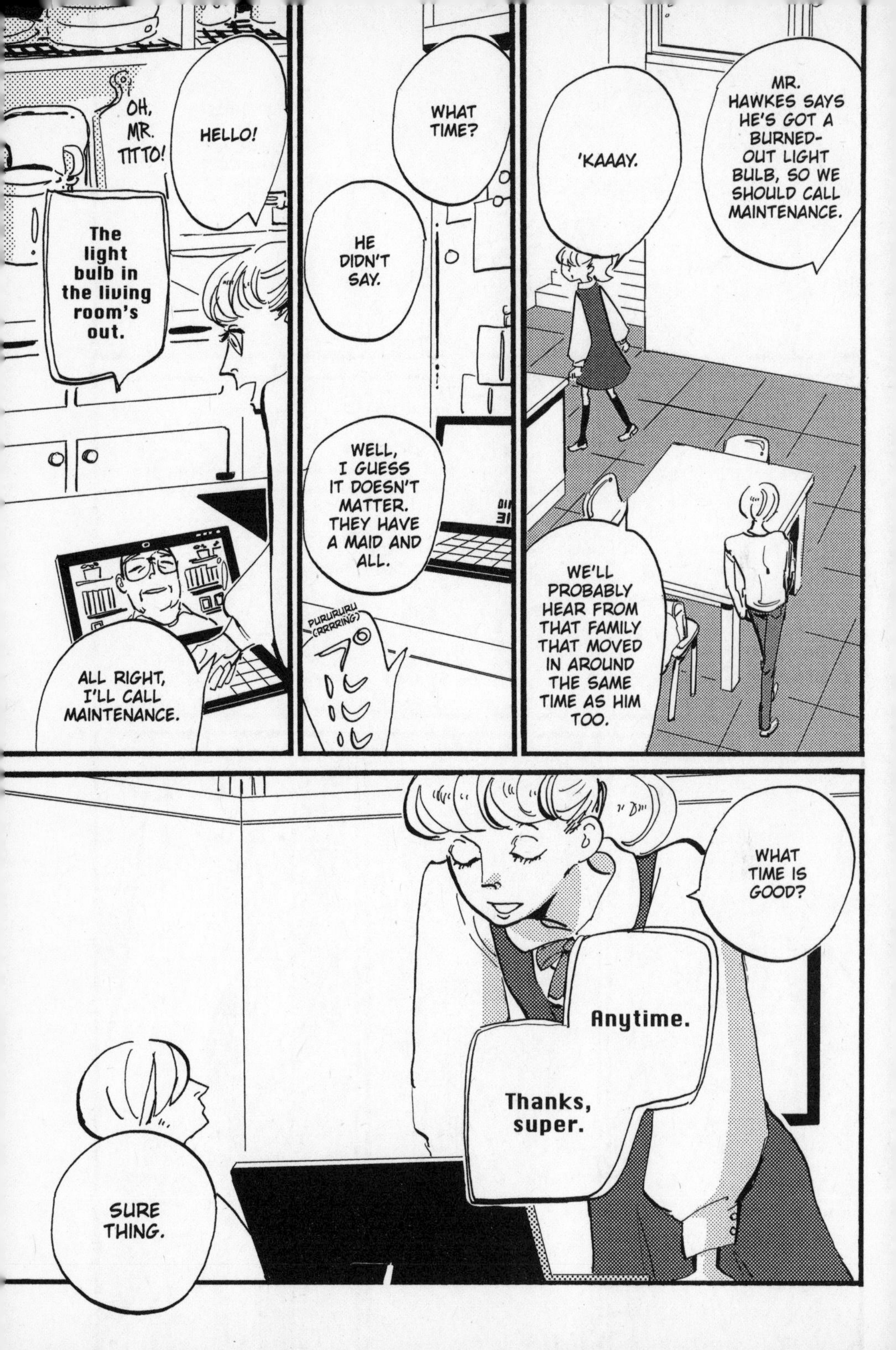
MR. HAWKES SAYS HE'S GOT A BURNED-OUT LIGHT BULB, SO WE SHOULD CALL MAINTENANCE.
'KAAAY.
WE'LL PROBABLY HEAR FROM THAT FAMILY THAT MOVED IN AROUND THE SAME TIME AS HIM TOO.
WHAT TIME?
HE DIDN'T SAY.
WELL, I GUESS IT DOESN'T MATTER. THEY HAVE A MAID AND ALL.
PURURURU (RRRRING)
OH, MR. TITTO!
HELLO!
The light bulb in the living room's out.
ALL RIGHT, I'LL CALL MAINTENANCE.
WHAT TIME IS GOOD?
Anytime.
Thanks, super.
SURE THING.

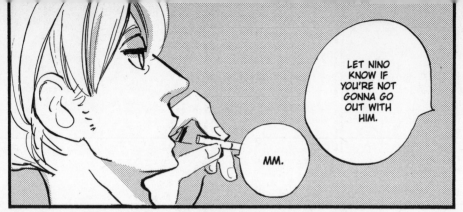

LET NINO KNOW IF YOU'RE NOT GONNA GO OUT WITH HIM.

MM.

YEAH, YEAH.

AND SMOKE OUTSIDE, JEAN!

KACHI (CLICK)

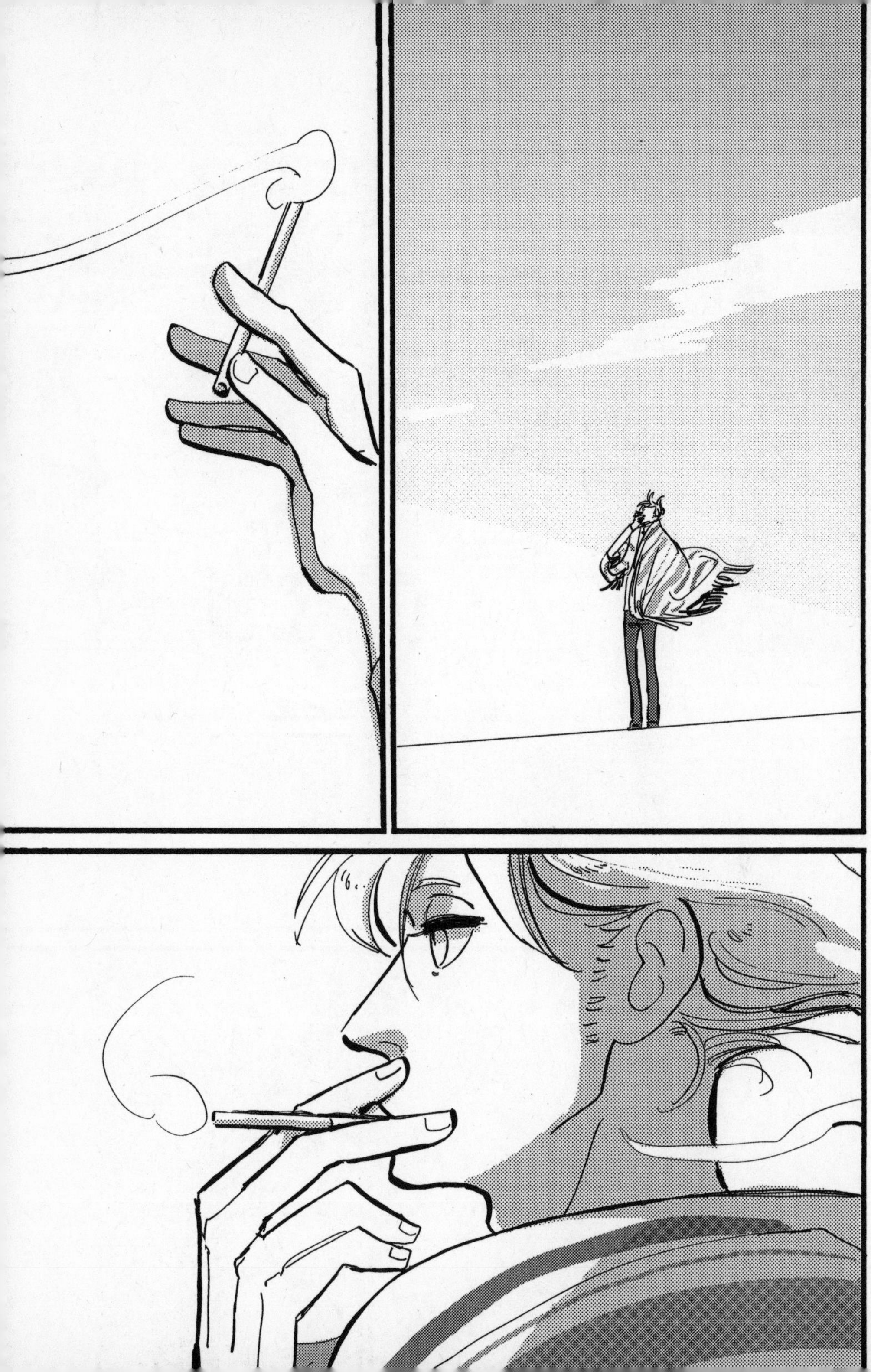

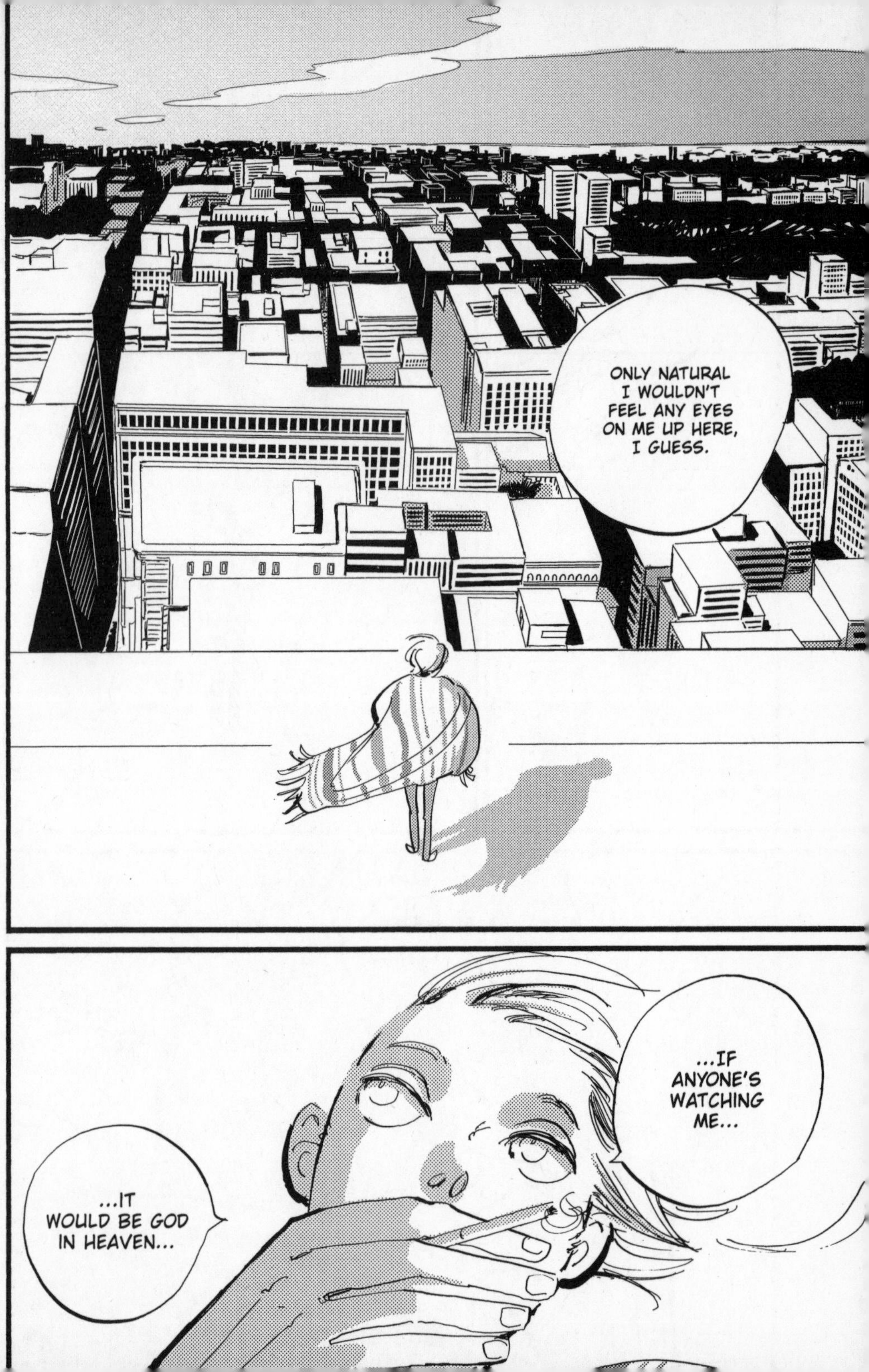
ONLY NATURAL I WOULDN'T FEEL ANY EYES ON ME UP HERE, I GUESS.
...IF ANYONE'S WATCHING ME...
...IT WOULD BE GOD IN HEAVEN...

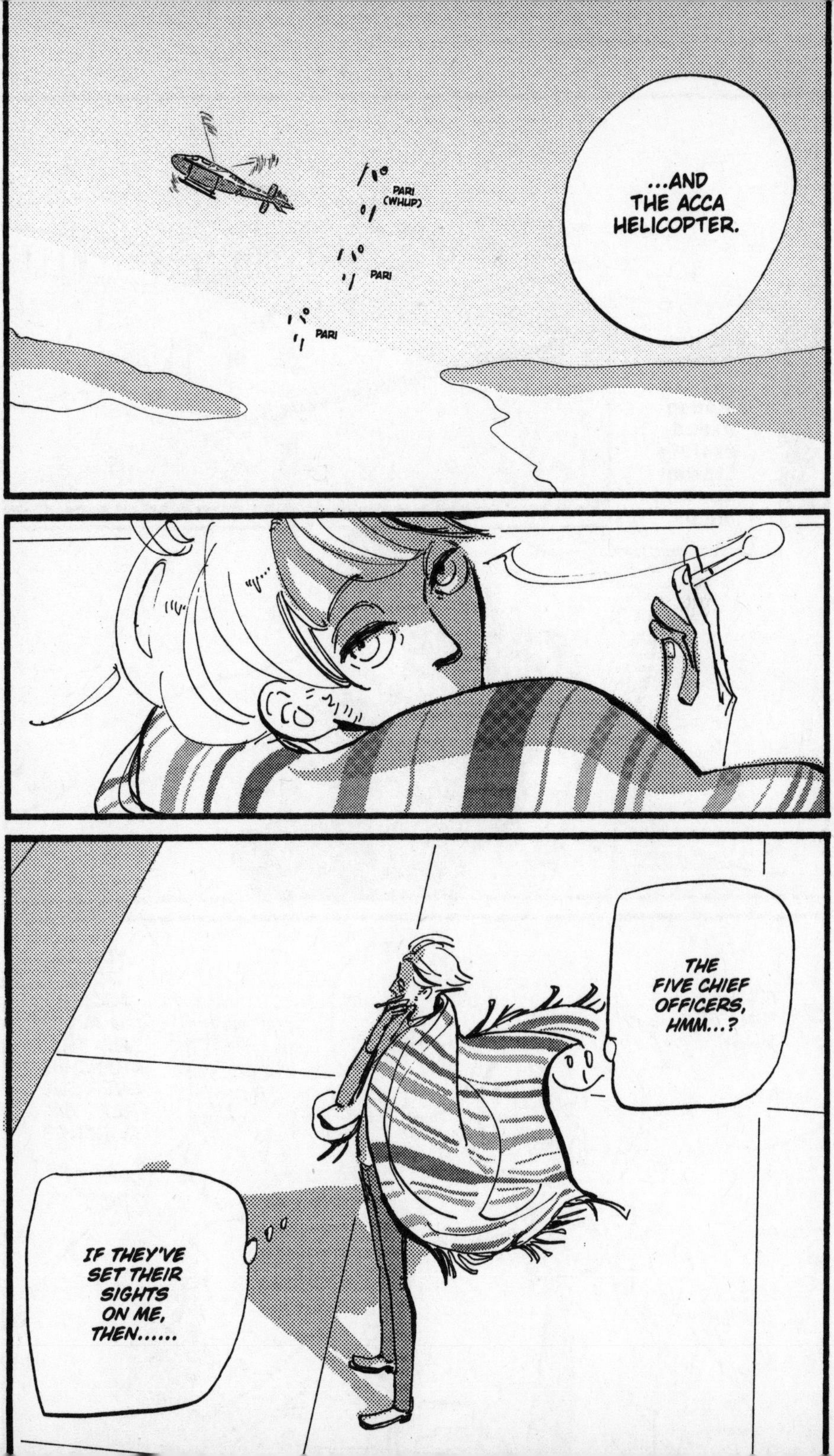
...AND THE ACCA HELICOPTER.
PARI (WHUP)
PARI
PARI
THE FIVE CHIEF OFFICERS, HMM...?
IF THEY'VE SET THEIR SIGHTS ON ME, THEN......

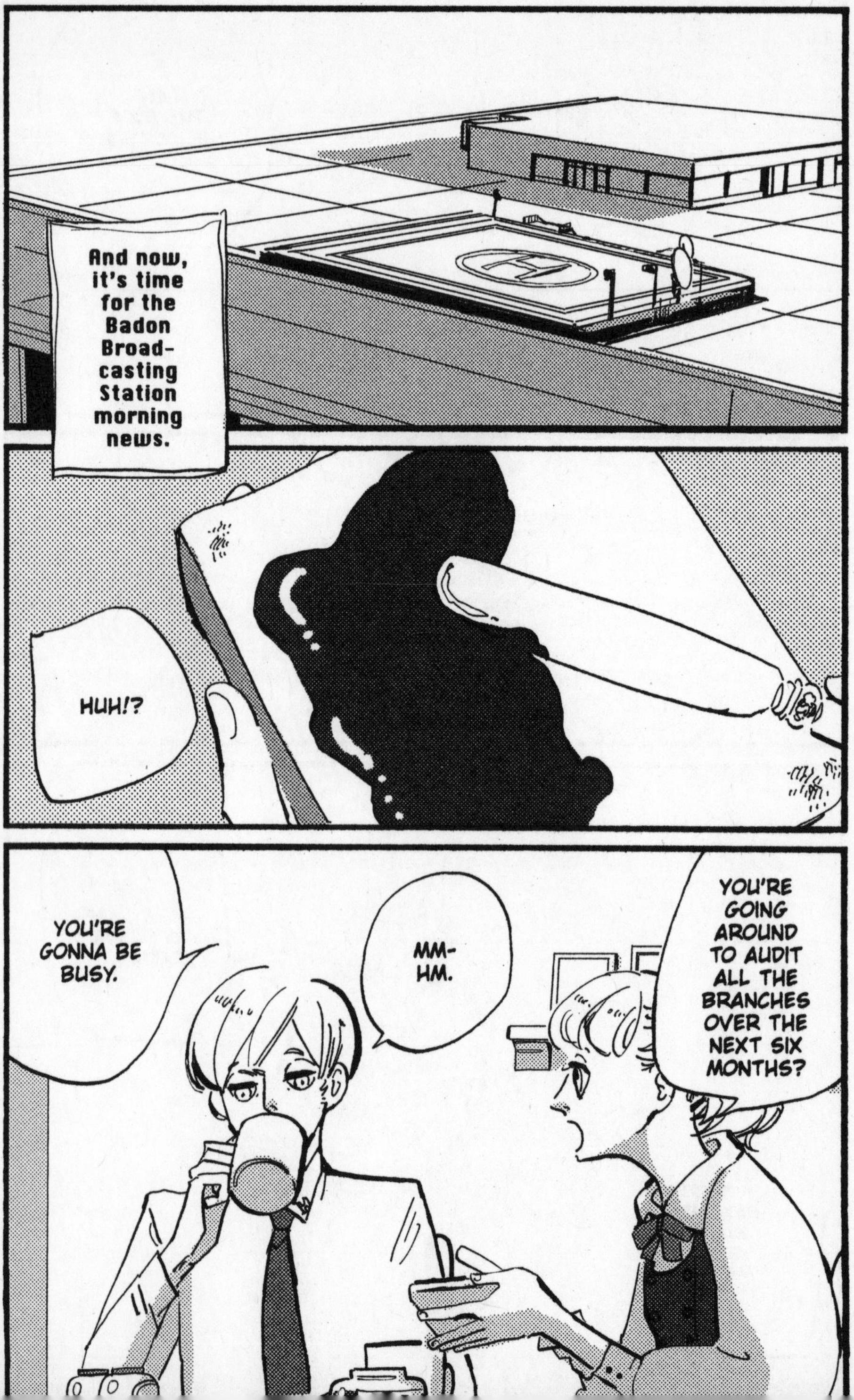
And now, it's time for the Badon Broad-casting Station morning news.
HUH!?
YOU'RE GOING AROUND TO AUDIT ALL THE BRANCHES OVER THE NEXT SIX MONTHS?
MM-HM.
YOU'RE GONNA BE BUSY.

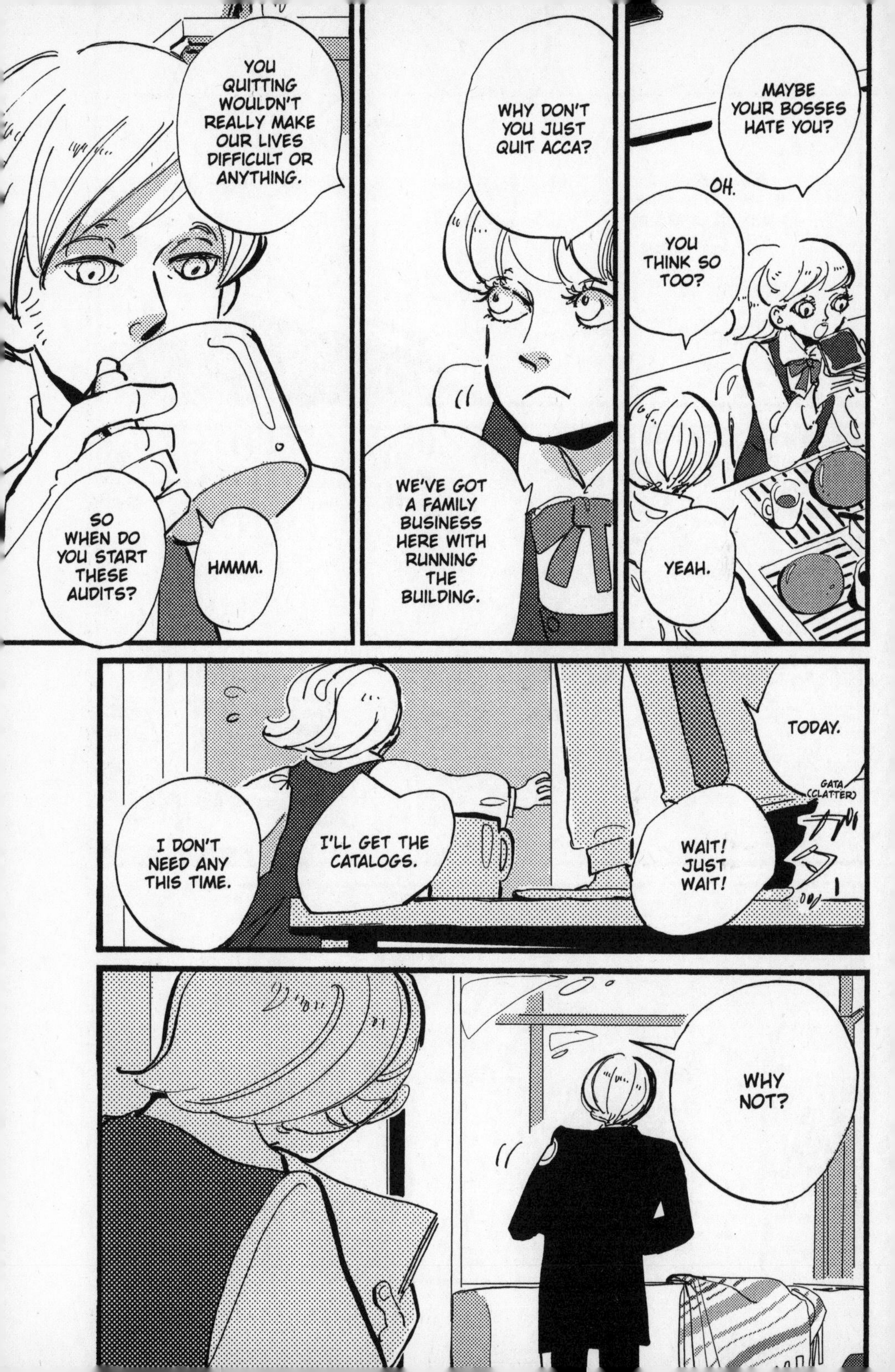
MAYBE YOUR BOSSES HATE YOU?
OH.
YOU THINK SO TOO?
YEAH.
WHY DON'T YOU JUST QUIT ACCA?
WE'VE GOT A FAMILY BUSINESS HERE WITH RUNNING THE BUILDING.
YOU QUITTING WOULDN'T REALLY MAKE OUR LIVES DIFFICULT OR ANYTHING.
HMMM.
SO WHEN DO YOU START THESE AUDITS?
TODAY.
GATA (CLATTER)
WAIT! JUST WAIT!
I'LL GET THE CATALOGS.
I DON'T NEED ANY THIS TIME.
WHY NOT?

BECAUSE I'M INSPECTING THE BRANCH HERE IN THE CAPITAL.

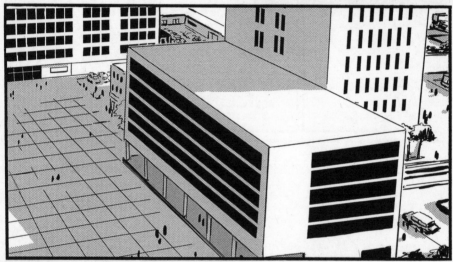

WELL, GOOD LUCK ON YOUR *BUSINESS TRIP.*

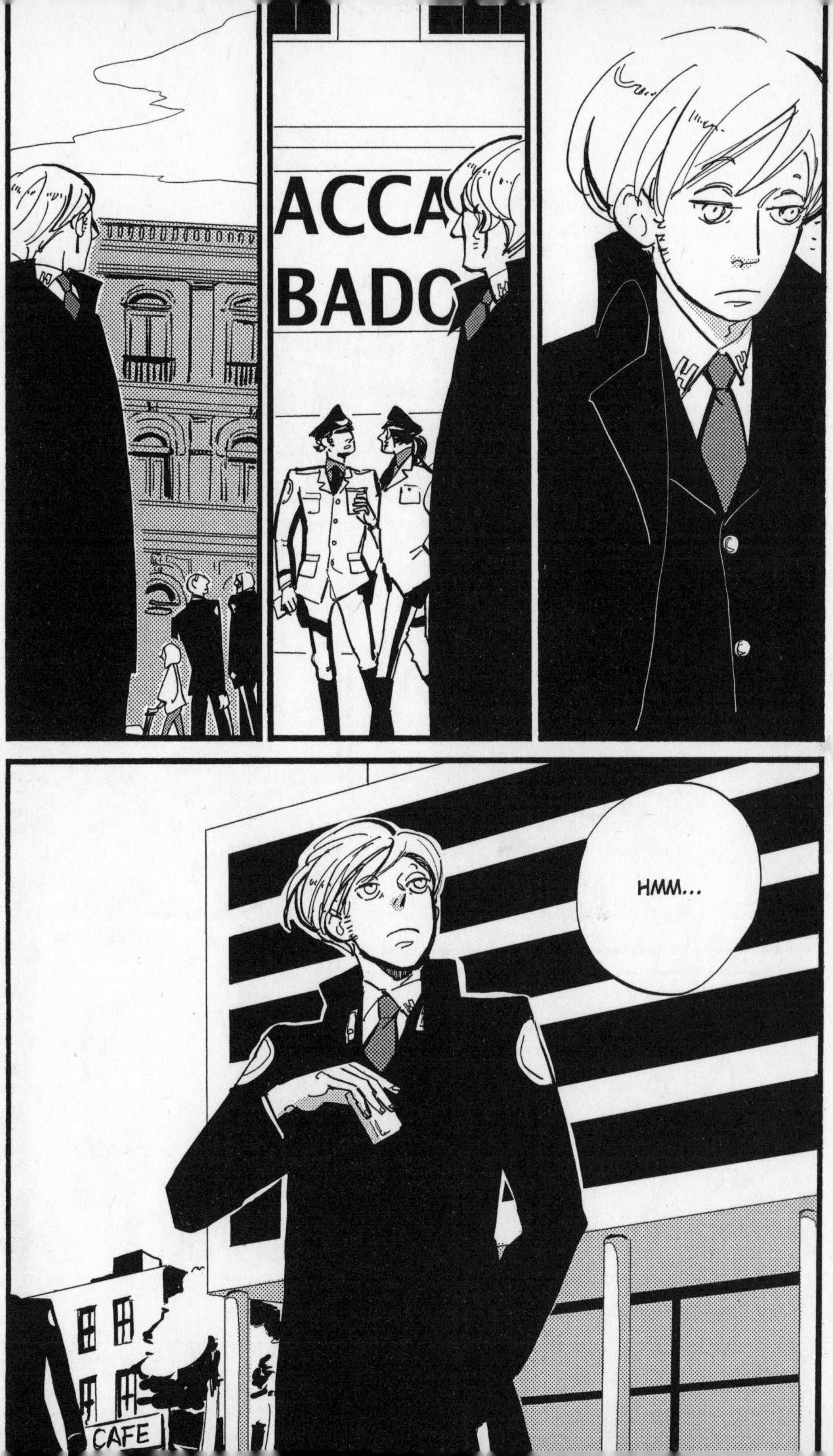
ACCA
BADO
HMM...
CAFE

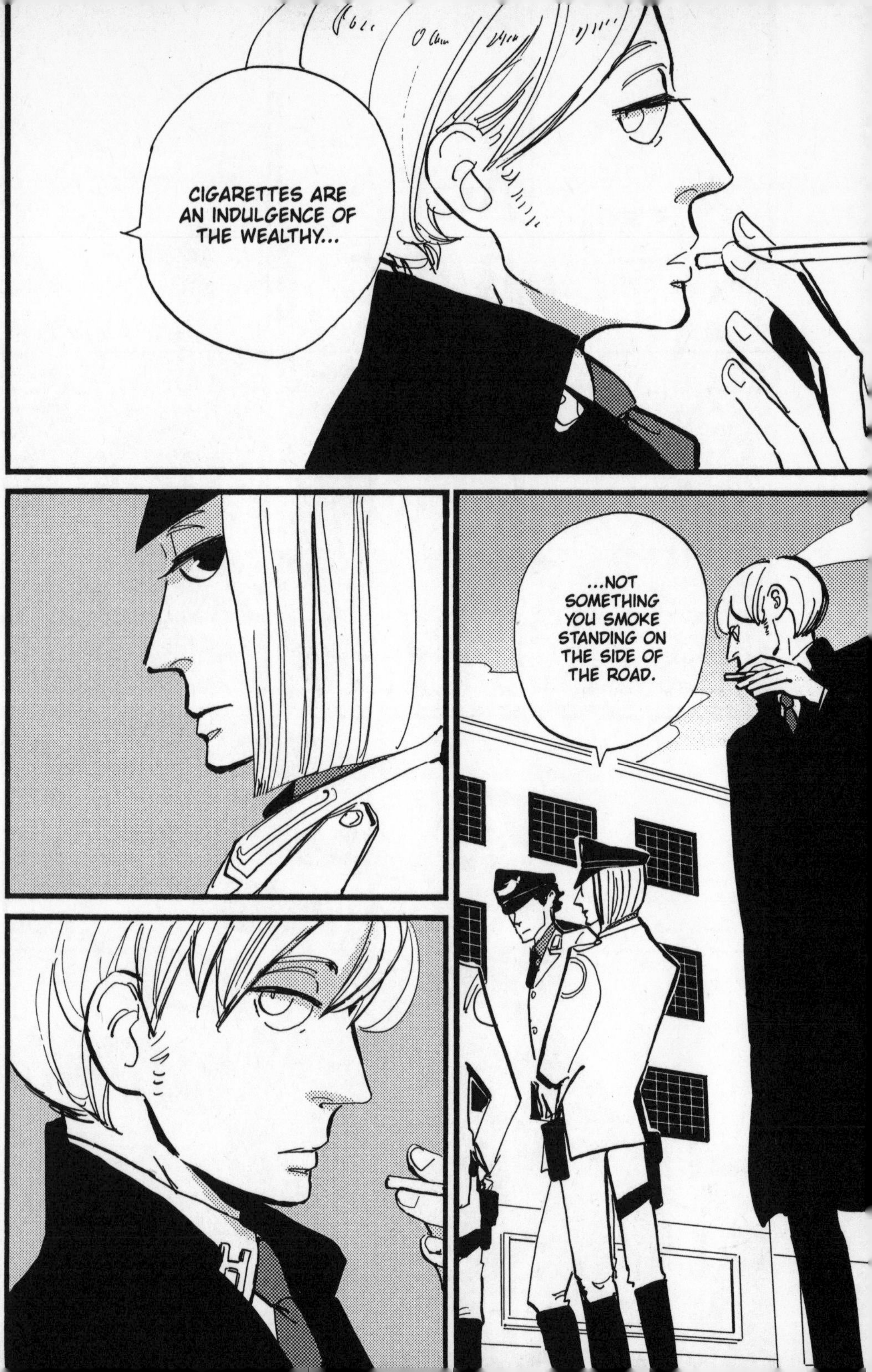
CIGARETTES ARE AN INDULGENCE OF THE WEALTHY...
...NOT SOMETHING YOU SMOKE STANDING ON THE SIDE OF THE ROAD.

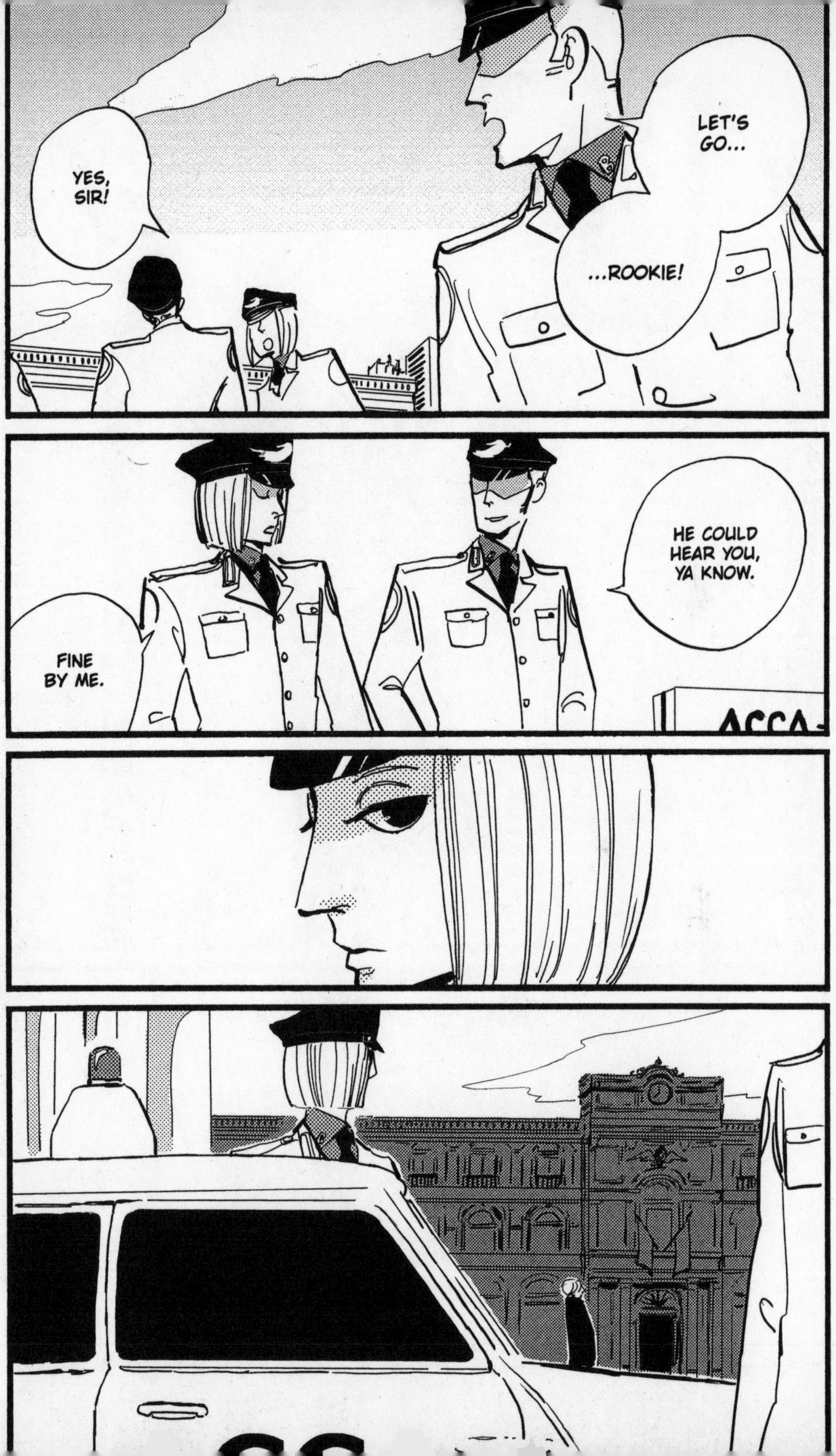
LET'S GO...
...ROOKIE!
YES, SIR!
HE COULD HEAR YOU, YA KNOW.
FINE BY ME.

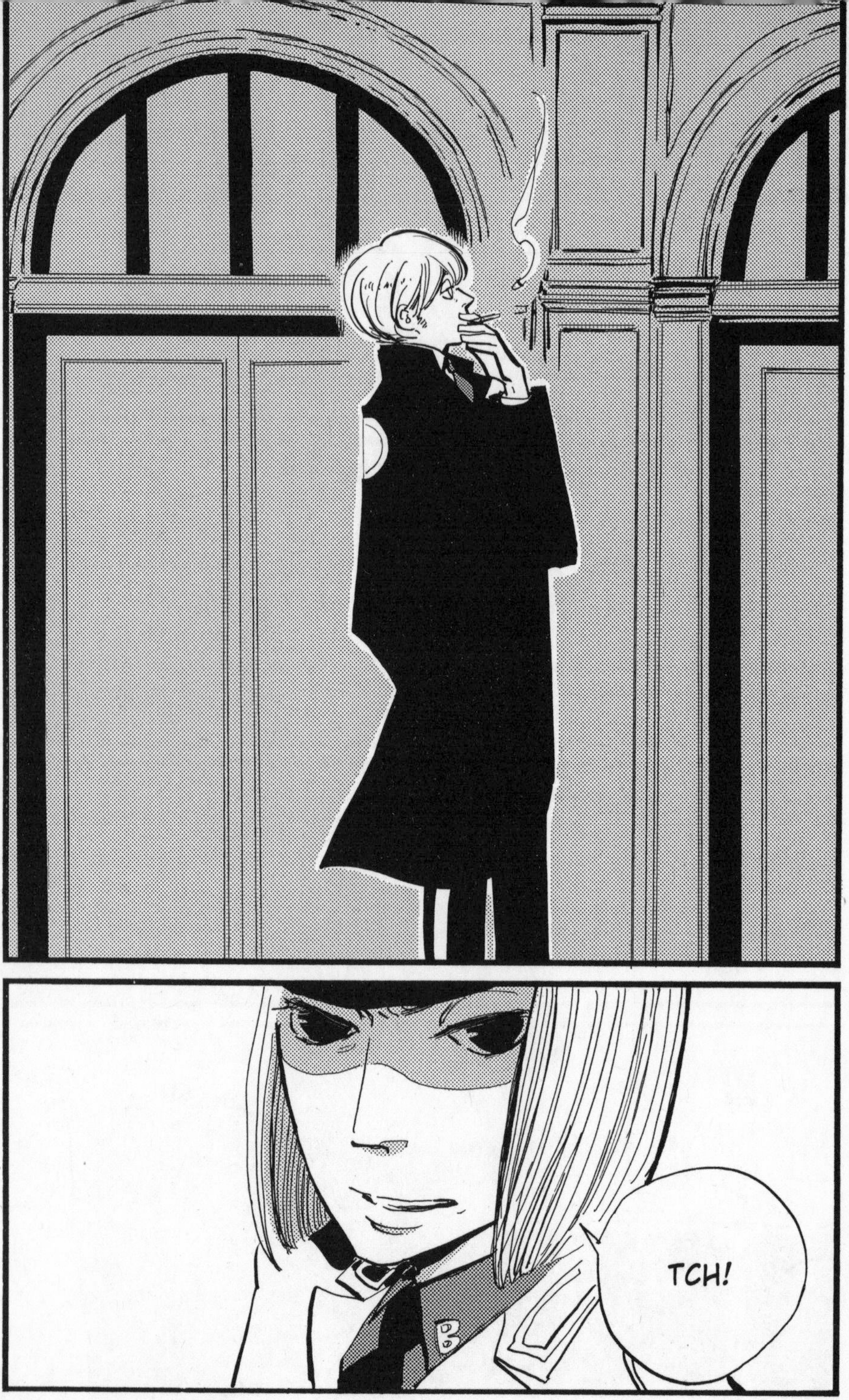
TCH!

CHAPTER 2

Watched in Badon

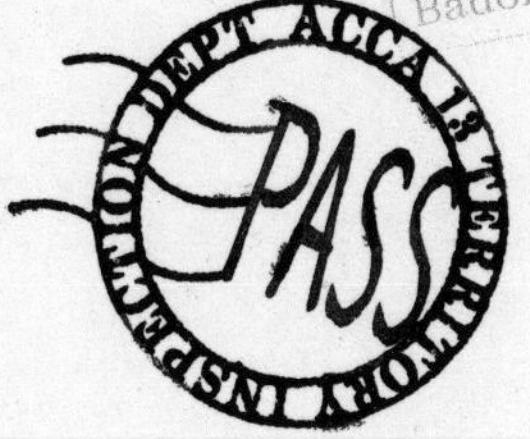
INSPECTION DEPT ACCA 13 TERRITORY
PASS

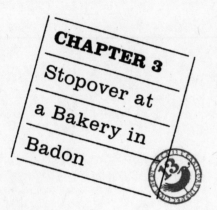

CHAPTER 3

Stopover at a Bakery in Badon

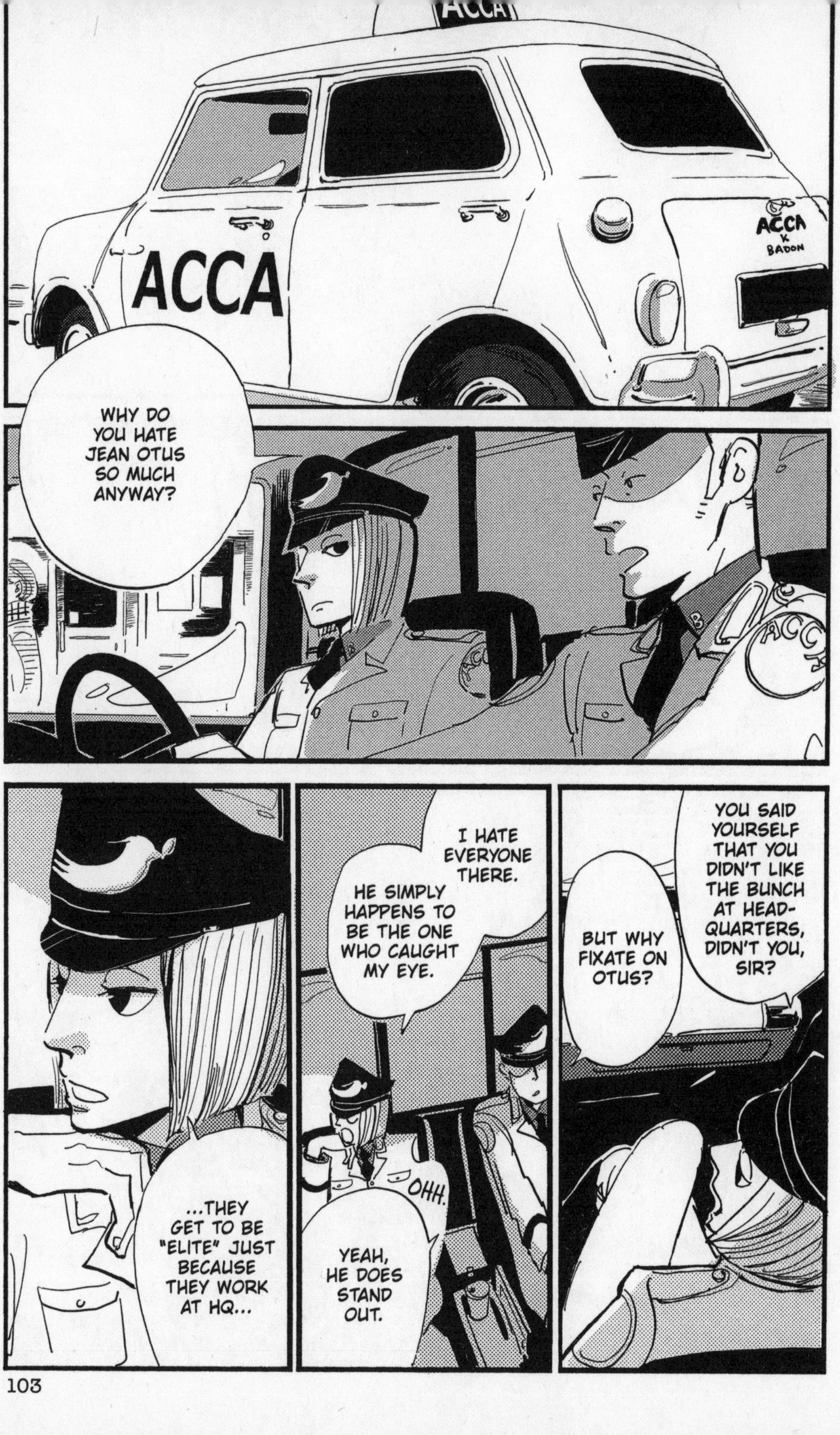
ACCA
ACCA
ACCA
BADON
WHY DO YOU HATE JEAN OTUS SO MUCH ANYWAY?
YOU SAID YOURSELF THAT YOU DIDN'T LIKE THE BUNCH AT HEAD-QUARTERS, DIDN'T YOU, SIR?
BUT WHY FIXATE ON OTUS?
I HATE EVERYONE THERE.
HE SIMPLY HAPPENS TO BE THE ONE WHO CAUGHT MY EYE.
OHH.
YEAH, HE DOES STAND OUT.
...THEY GET TO BE "ELITE" JUST BECAUSE THEY WORK AT HQ...

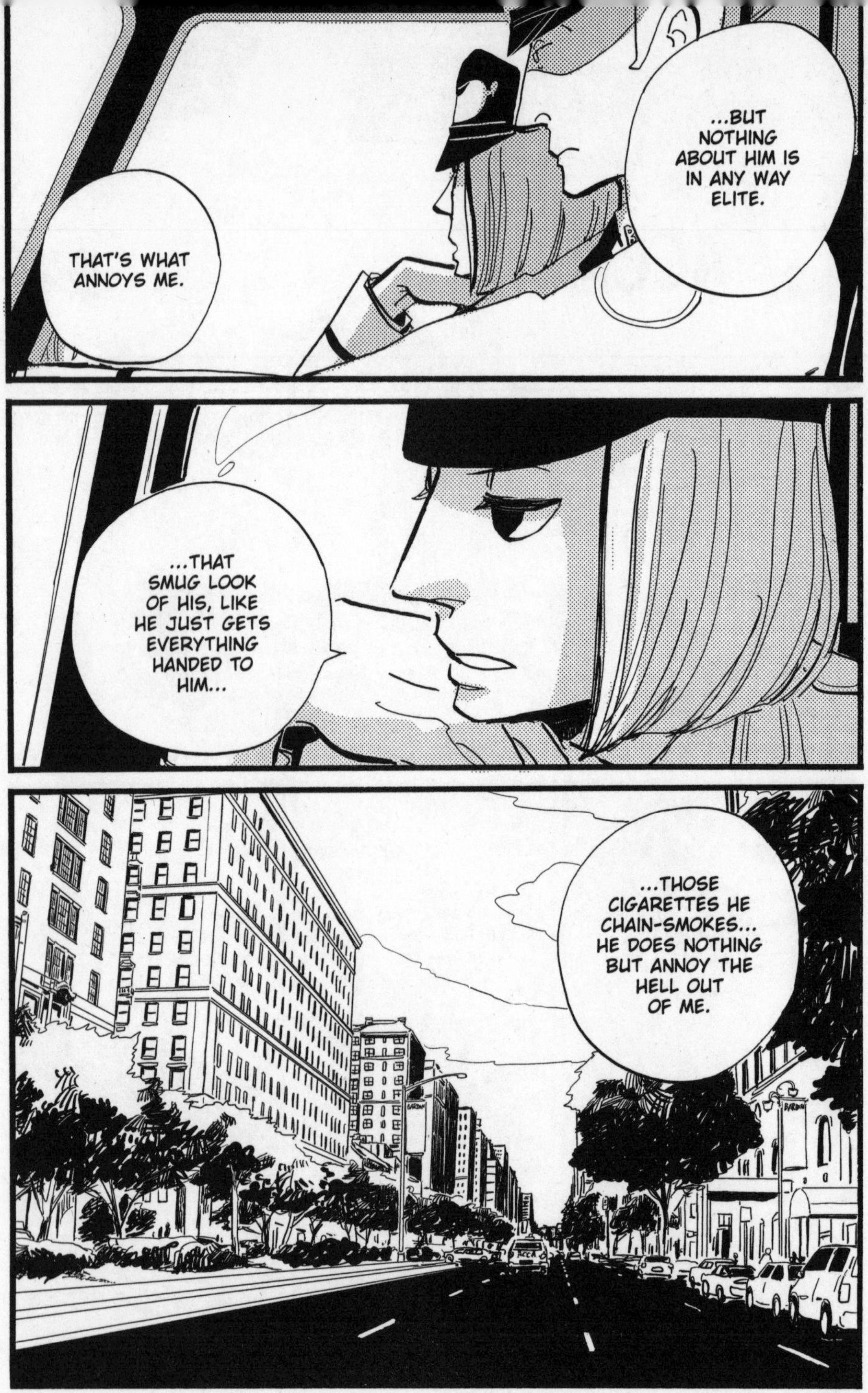
...BUT NOTHING ABOUT HIM IS IN ANY WAY ELITE.
THAT'S WHAT ANNOYS ME.
...THAT SMUG LOOK OF HIS, LIKE HE JUST GETS EVERYTHING HANDED TO HIM...
...THOSE CIGARETTES HE CHAIN-SMOKES... HE DOES NOTHING BUT ANNOY THE HELL OUT OF ME.

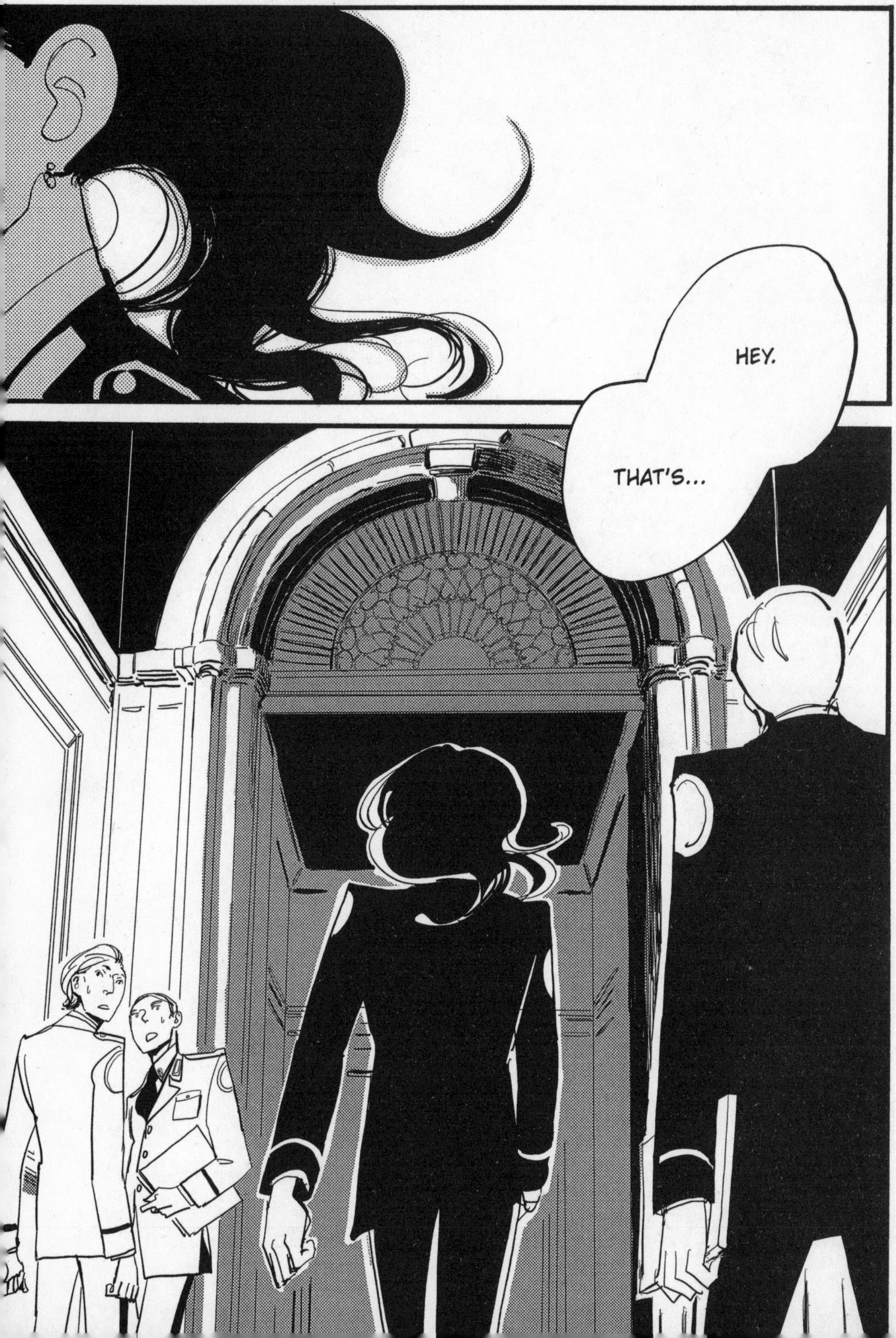
HEY.
THAT'S...

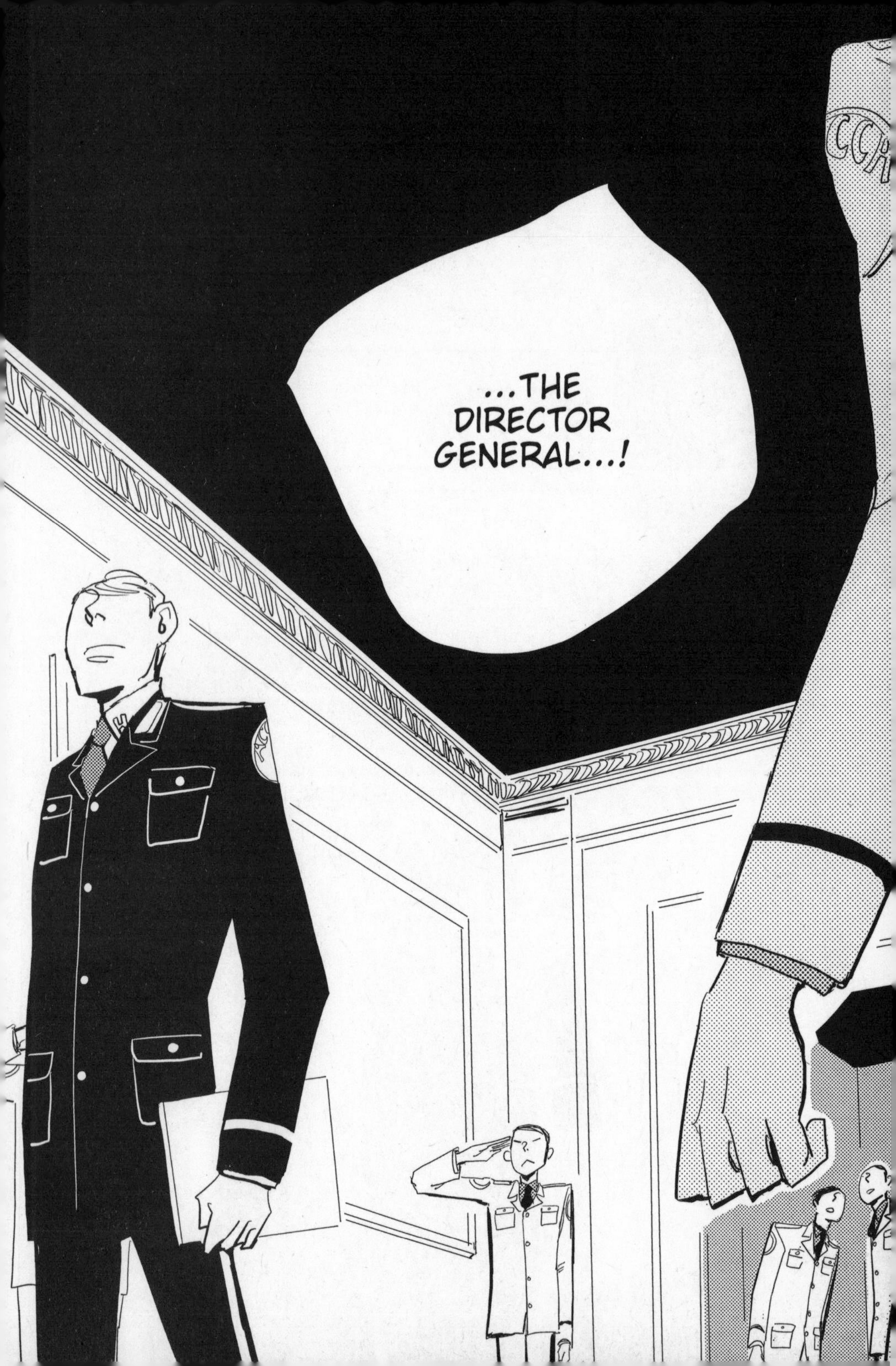
...THE DIRECTOR GENERAL...!

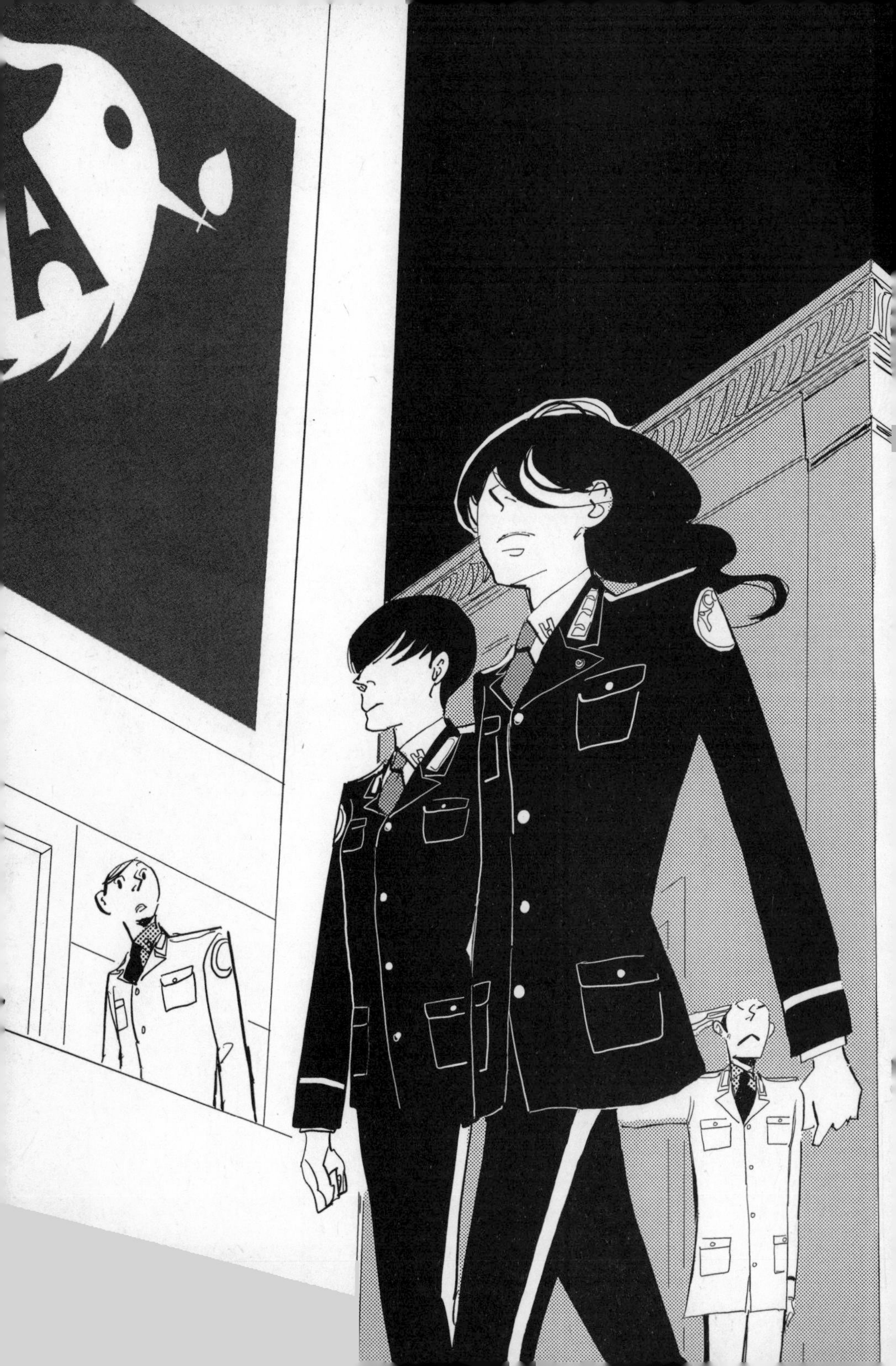

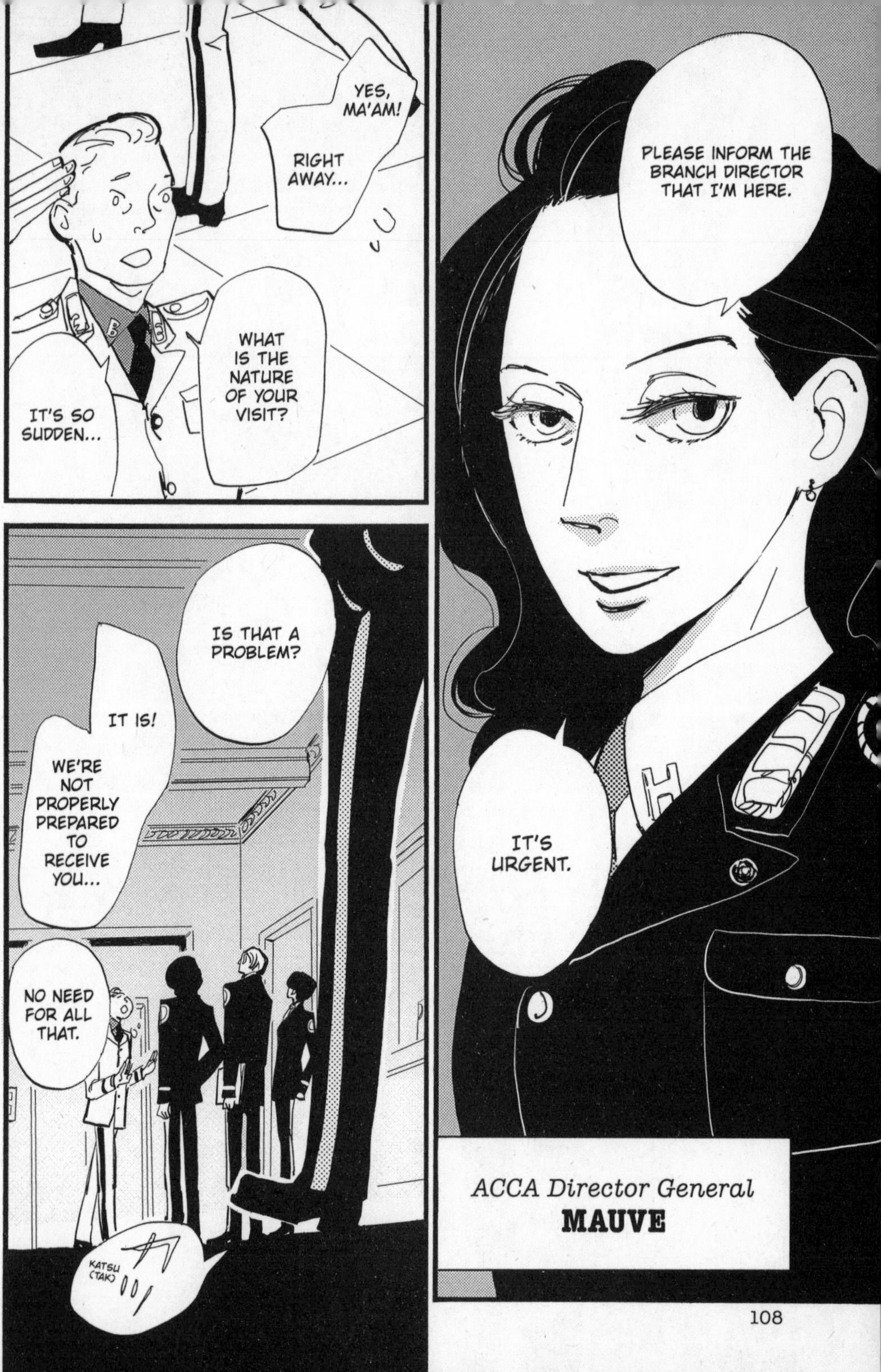
YES, MA'AM!
RIGHT AWAY...
WHAT IS THE NATURE OF YOUR VISIT?
IT'S SO SUDDEN...
IS THAT A PROBLEM?
IT IS!
WE'RE NOT PROPERLY PREPARED TO RECEIVE YOU...
NO NEED FOR ALL THAT.
KATSU (TAK)
PLEASE INFORM THE BRANCH DIRECTOR THAT I'M HERE.
IT'S URGENT.
ACCA Director General
MAUVE

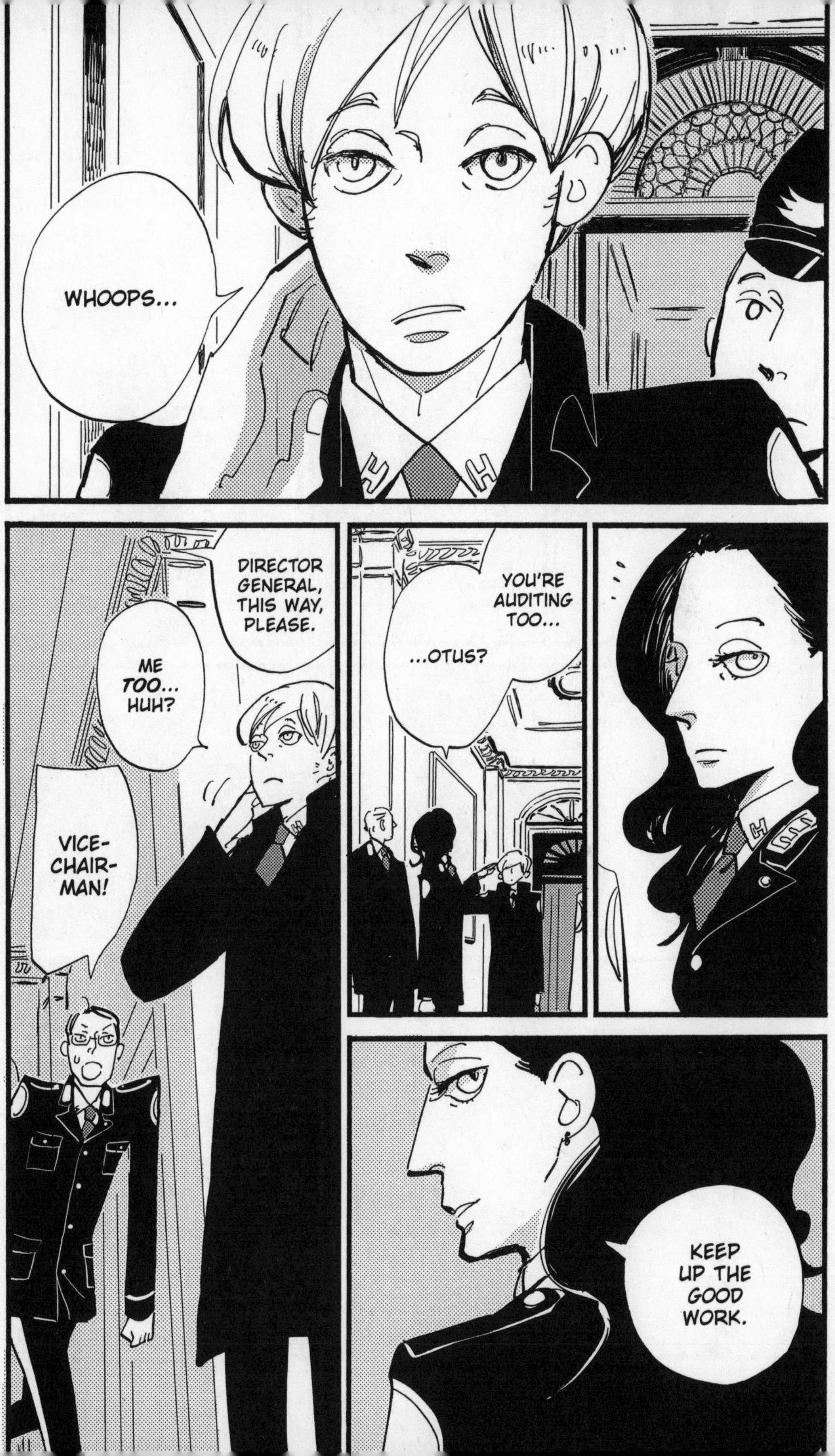
WHOOPS...
YOU'RE AUDITING TOO...
...OTUS?
KEEP UP THE GOOD WORK.
DIRECTOR GENERAL, THIS WAY, PLEASE.
ME *TOO*... HUH?
VICE-CHAIRMAN!

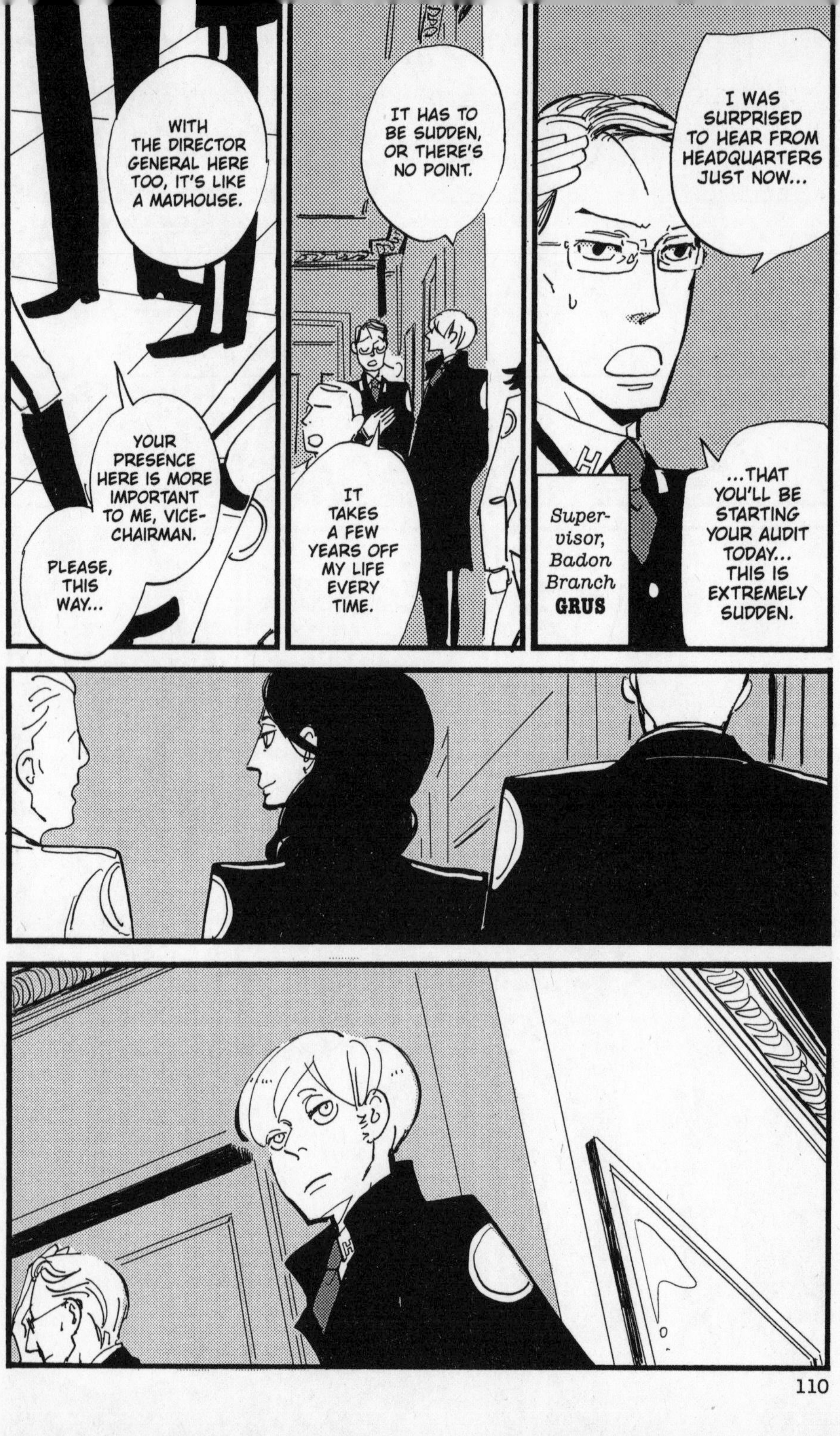
I WAS SURPRISED TO HEAR FROM HEADQUARTERS JUST NOW...
...THAT YOU'LL BE STARTING YOUR AUDIT TODAY... THIS IS EXTREMELY SUDDEN.
Supervisor, Badon Branch **GRUS**
IT HAS TO BE SUDDEN, OR THERE'S NO POINT.
IT TAKES A FEW YEARS OFF MY LIFE EVERY TIME.
WITH THE DIRECTOR GENERAL HERE TOO, IT'S LIKE A MADHOUSE.
YOUR PRESENCE HERE IS MORE IMPORTANT TO ME, VICE-CHAIRMAN.
PLEASE, THIS WAY...

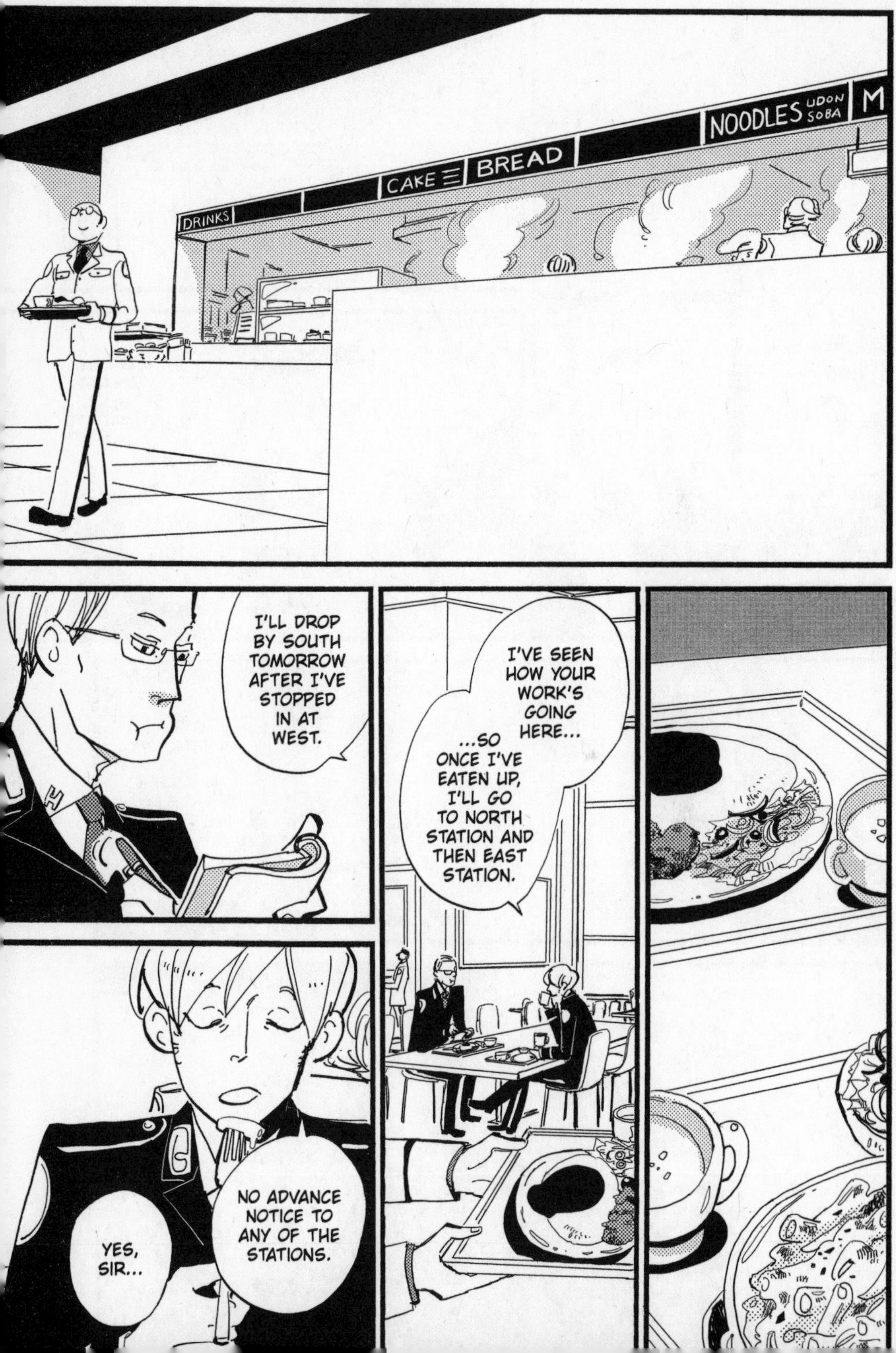
M
NOODLES UDON SOBA
BREAD
CAKE
DRINKS
I'VE SEEN HOW YOUR WORK'S GOING HERE...
...SO ONCE I'VE EATEN UP, I'LL GO TO NORTH STATION AND THEN EAST STATION.
I'LL DROP BY SOUTH TOMORROW AFTER I'VE STOPPED IN AT WEST.
...
NO ADVANCE NOTICE TO ANY OF THE STATIONS.
YES, SIR...

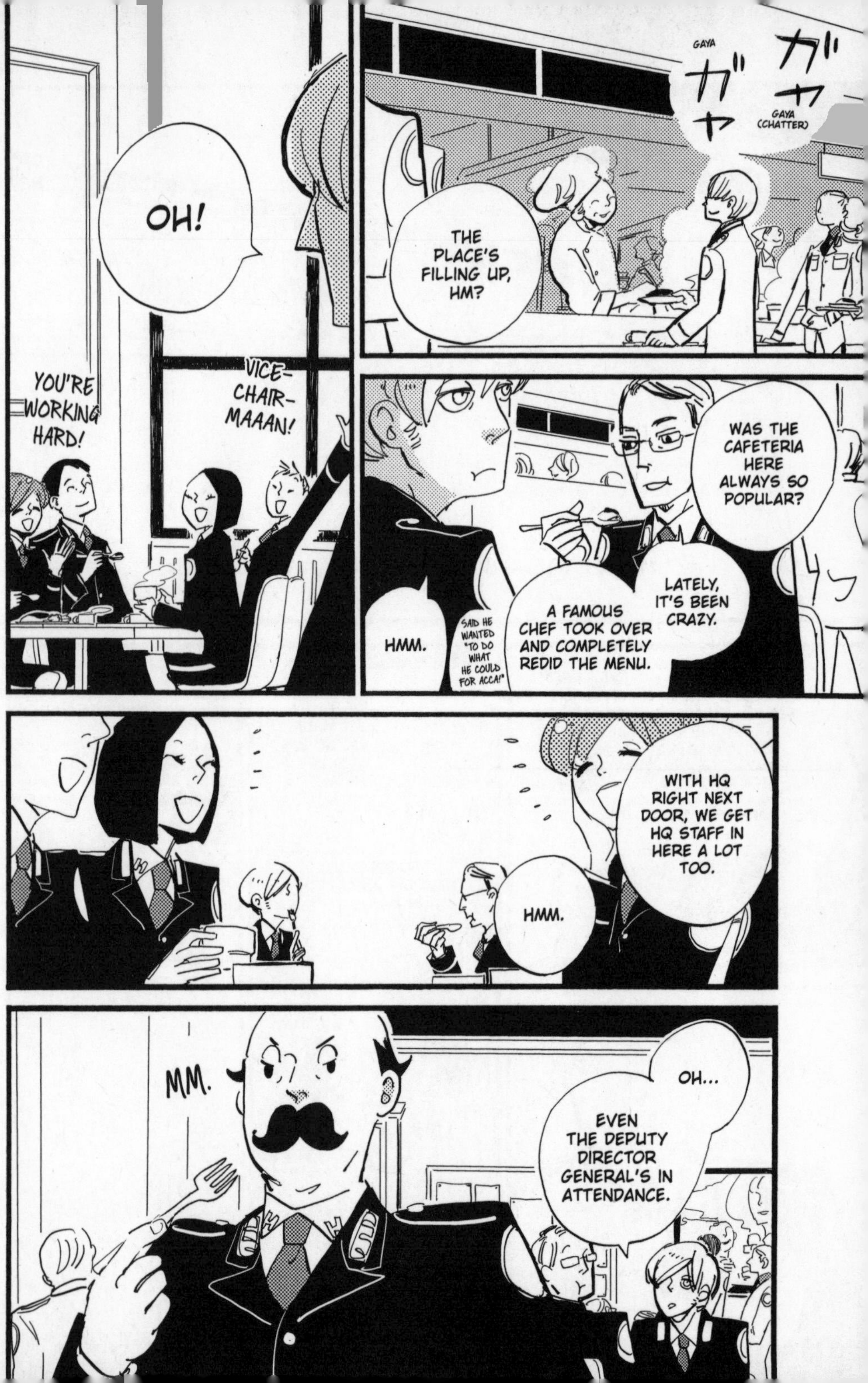
GAYA
ガヤ
ガヤ
GAYA (CHATTER)
THE PLACE'S FILLING UP, HM?
OH!
VICE-CHAIR-MAAAN!
YOU'RE WORKING HARD!
WAS THE CAFETERIA HERE ALWAYS SO POPULAR?
LATELY, IT'S BEEN CRAZY.
A FAMOUS CHEF TOOK OVER AND COMPLETELY REDID THE MENU.
SAID HE WANTED "TO DO WHAT HE COULD FOR ACCA!"
HMM.
WITH HQ RIGHT NEXT DOOR, WE GET HQ STAFF IN HERE A LOT TOO.
HMM.
OH...
EVEN THE DEPUTY DIRECTOR GENERAL'S IN ATTENDANCE.
MM.

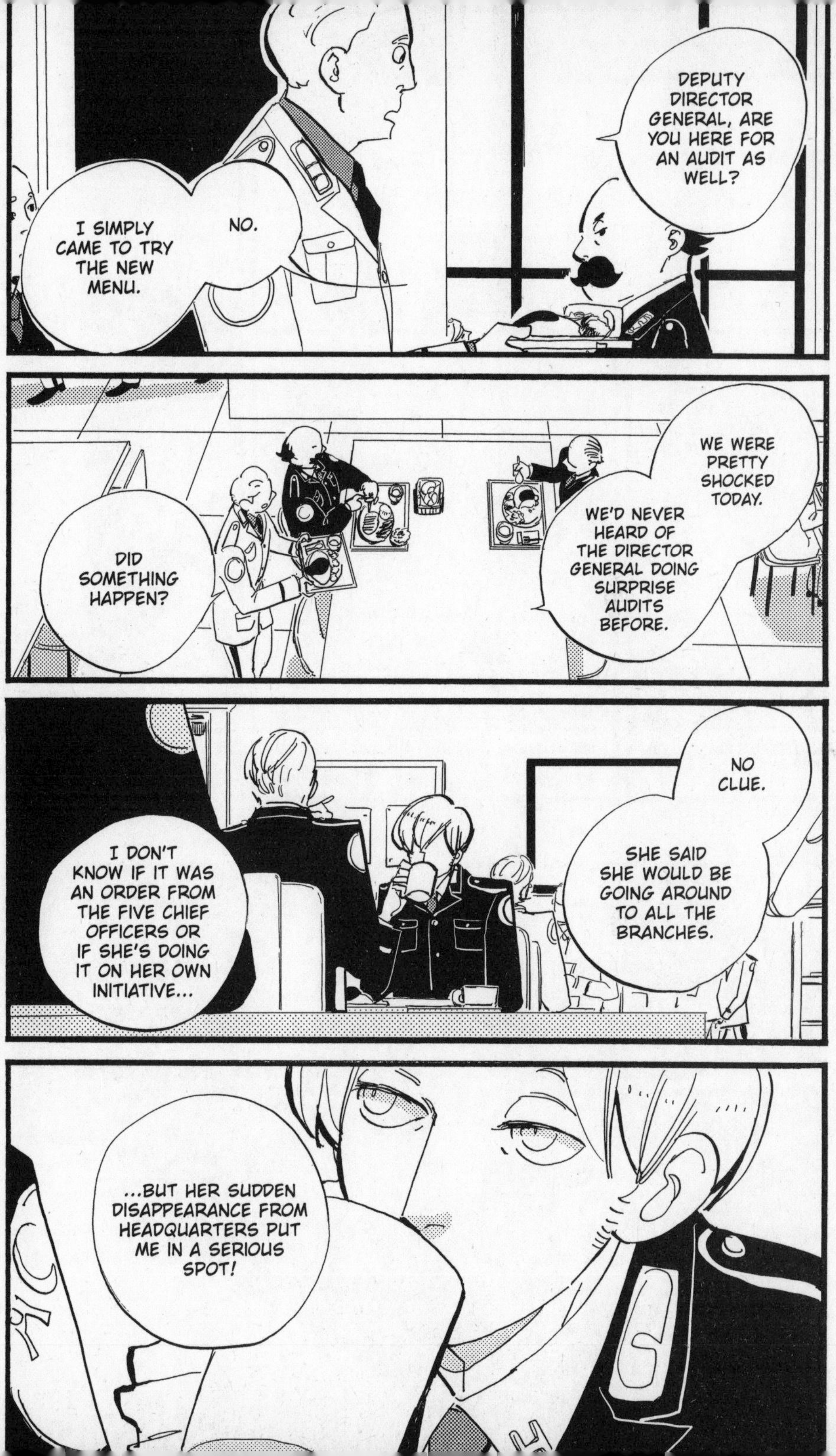
DEPUTY DIRECTOR GENERAL, ARE YOU HERE FOR AN AUDIT AS WELL?
NO.
I SIMPLY CAME TO TRY THE NEW MENU.
WE WERE PRETTY SHOCKED TODAY.
WE'D NEVER HEARD OF THE DIRECTOR GENERAL DOING SURPRISE AUDITS BEFORE.
DID SOMETHING HAPPEN?
NO CLUE.
SHE SAID SHE WOULD BE GOING AROUND TO ALL THE BRANCHES.
I DON'T KNOW IF IT WAS AN ORDER FROM THE FIVE CHIEF OFFICERS OR IF SHE'S DOING IT ON HER OWN INITIATIVE...
...BUT HER SUDDEN DISAPPEARANCE FROM HEADQUARTERS PUT ME IN A SERIOUS SPOT!

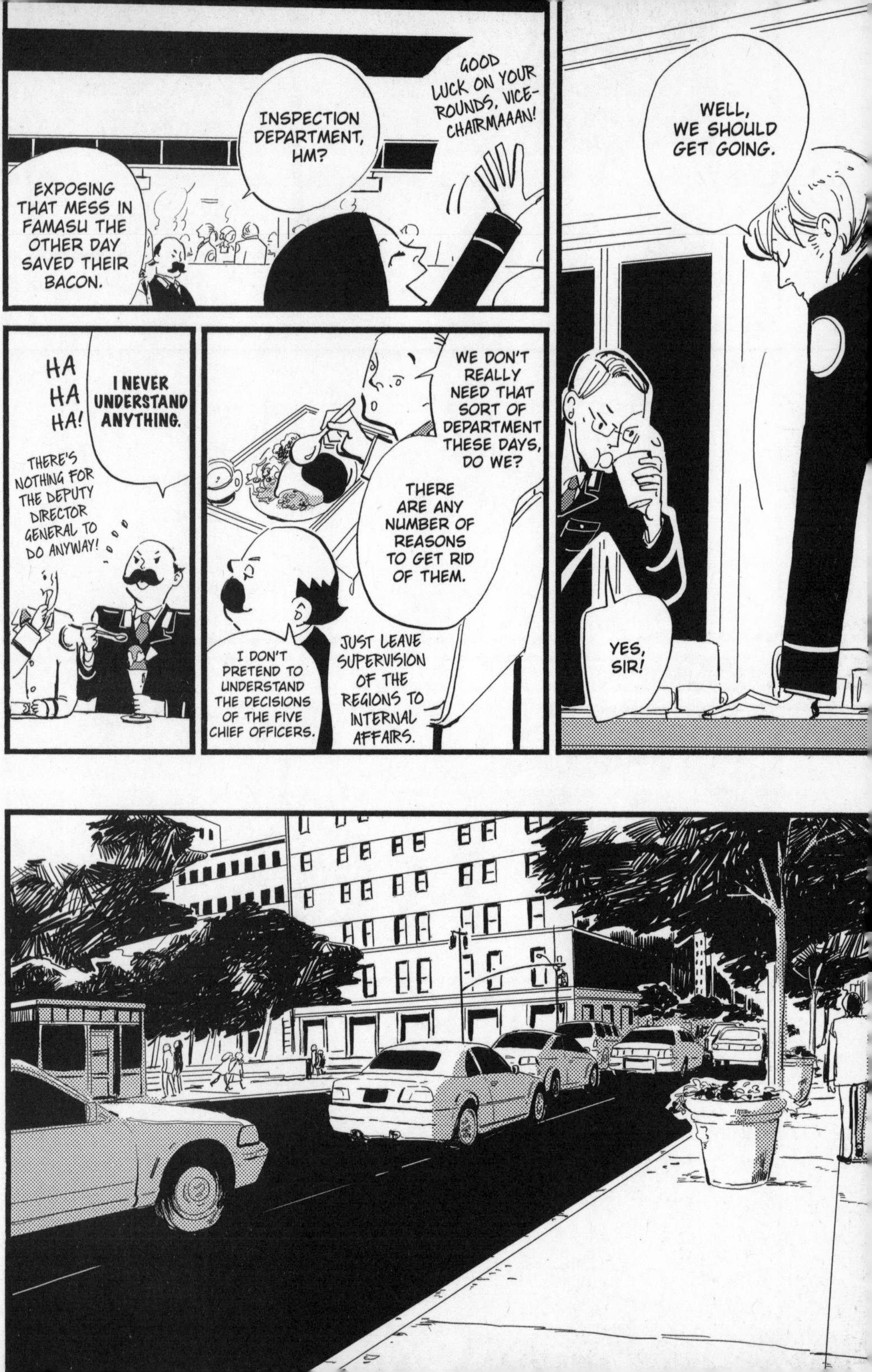
WELL, WE SHOULD GET GOING.
GOOD LUCK ON YOUR ROUNDS, VICE-CHAIRMAAAN!
INSPECTION DEPARTMENT, HM?
EXPOSING THAT MESS IN FAMASU THE OTHER DAY SAVED THEIR BACON.
YES, SIR!
WE DON'T REALLY NEED THAT SORT OF DEPARTMENT THESE DAYS, DO WE?
THERE ARE ANY NUMBER OF REASONS TO GET RID OF THEM.
JUST LEAVE SUPERVISION OF THE REGIONS TO INTERNAL AFFAIRS.
I DON'T PRETEND TO UNDERSTAND THE DECISIONS OF THE FIVE CHIEF OFFICERS.
I NEVER UNDERSTAND ANYTHING.
HA HA HA!
THERE'S NOTHING FOR THE DEPUTY DIRECTOR GENERAL TO DO ANYWAY!

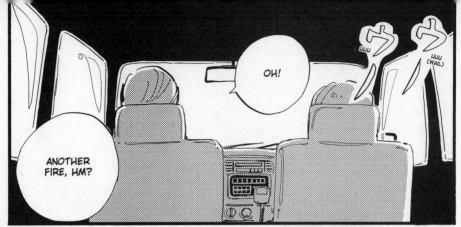

OH!

ウ (WAIL)

ウ (WAIL)

ANOTHER FIRE, HM?

MORE AND MORE OF THE DATA BEING SENT IN FROM THE STATIONS INVOLVES ARSON.

SCARY.

STILL NO IDEA WHO'S STARTING THEM OR WHY?

INDEED.

IF THIS KEEPS UP, IT'LL MAKE ACCA LOOK BAD.

NO, NOT THAT.

I'D BE IN A REAL PINCH IF MY BUILDING WAS SET ON FIRE.

SEEMS NOT.

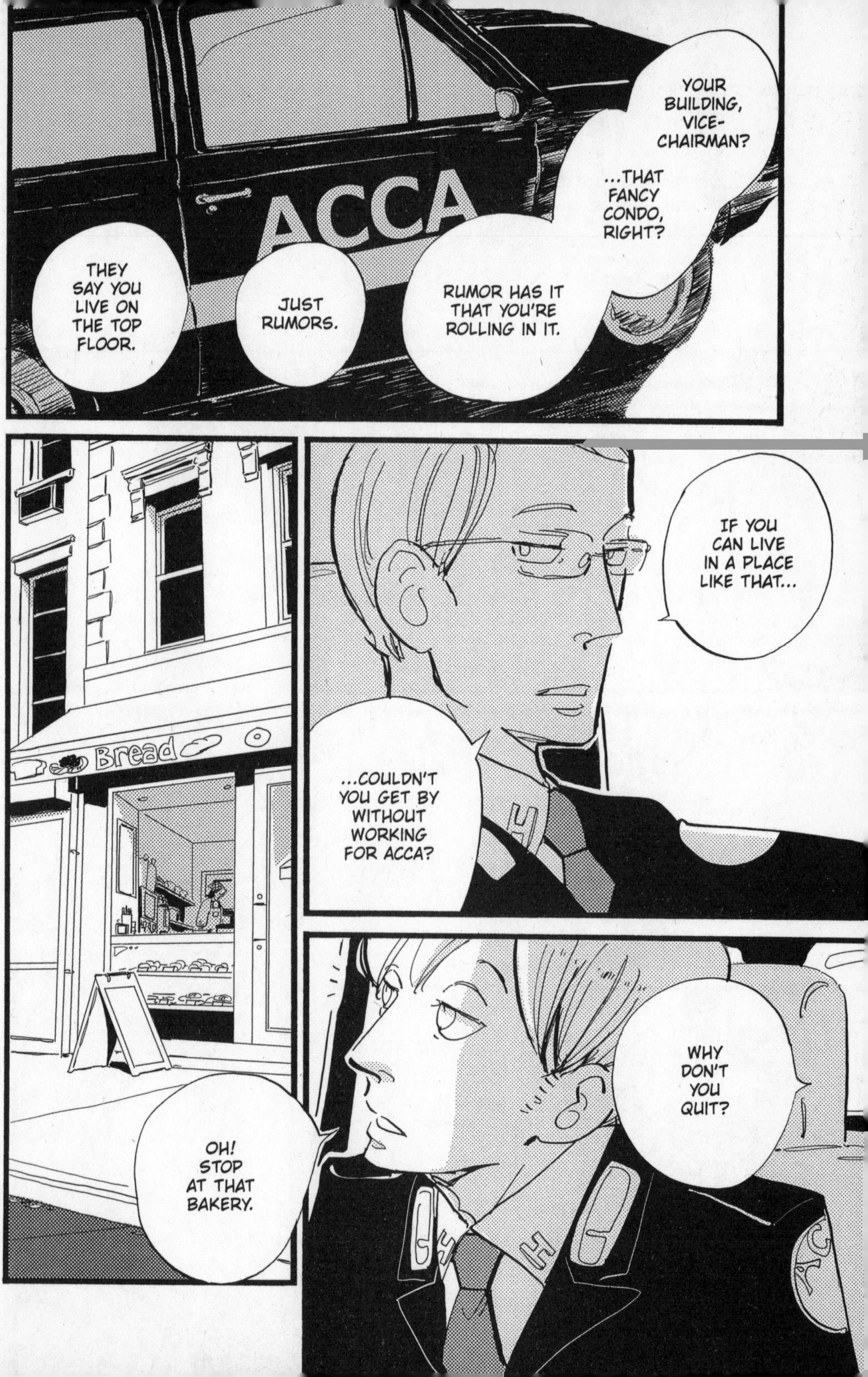

YOUR BUILDING, VICE-CHAIRMAN?
...THAT FANCY CONDO, RIGHT?
RUMOR HAS IT THAT YOU'RE ROLLING IN IT.
JUST RUMORS.
THEY SAY YOU LIVE ON THE TOP FLOOR.
ACCA
IF YOU CAN LIVE IN A PLACE LIKE THAT...
...COULDN'T YOU GET BY WITHOUT WORKING FOR ACCA?
WHY DON'T YOU QUIT?
OH! STOP AT THAT BAKERY.
Bread

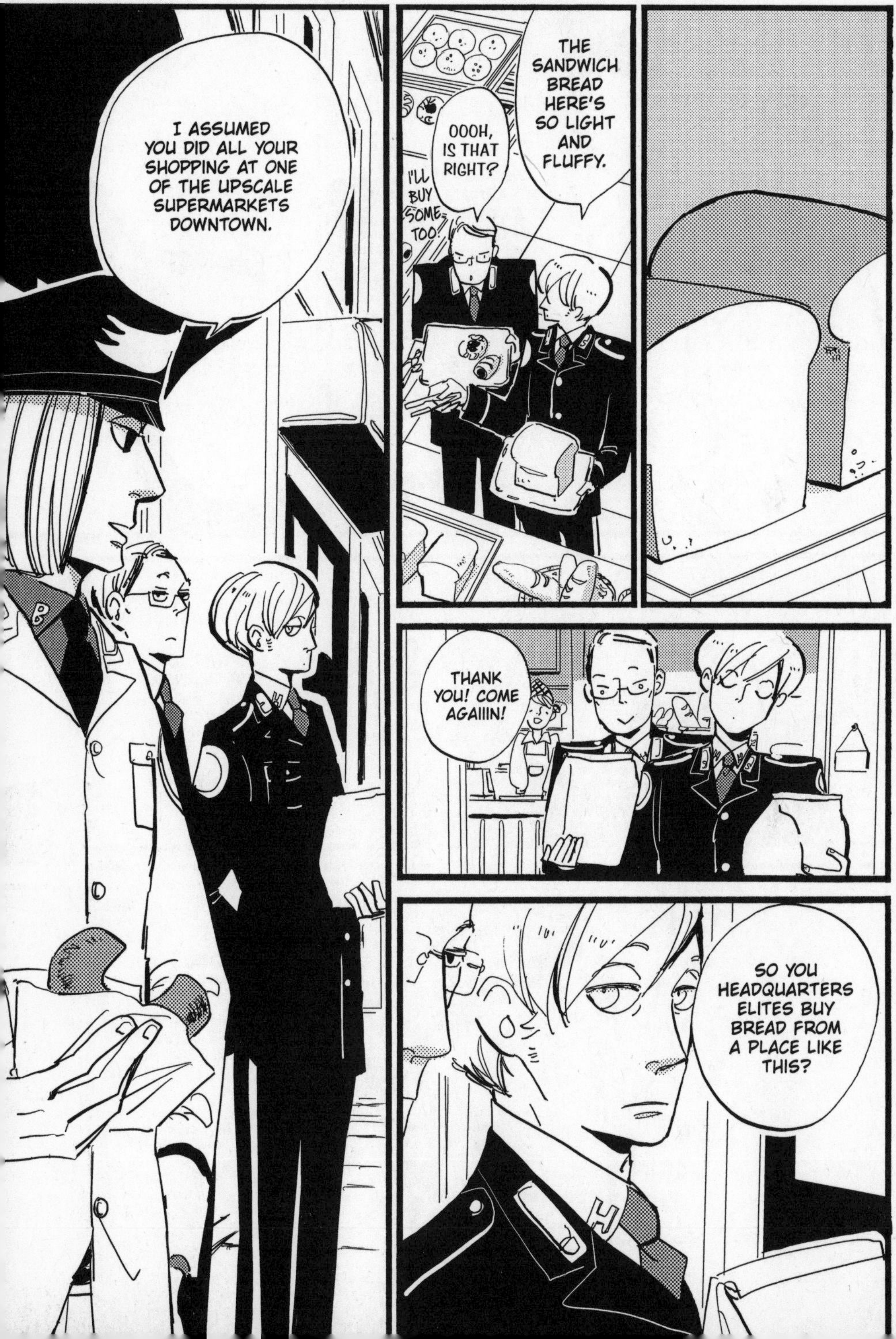
I ASSUMED YOU DID ALL YOUR SHOPPING AT ONE OF THE UPSCALE SUPERMARKETS DOWNTOWN.
THE SANDWICH BREAD HERE'S SO LIGHT AND FLUFFY.
OOOH, IS THAT RIGHT?
I'LL BUY SOME TOO.
THANK YOU! COME AGAIIIN!
SO YOU HEADQUARTERS ELITES BUY BREAD FROM A PLACE LIKE THIS?

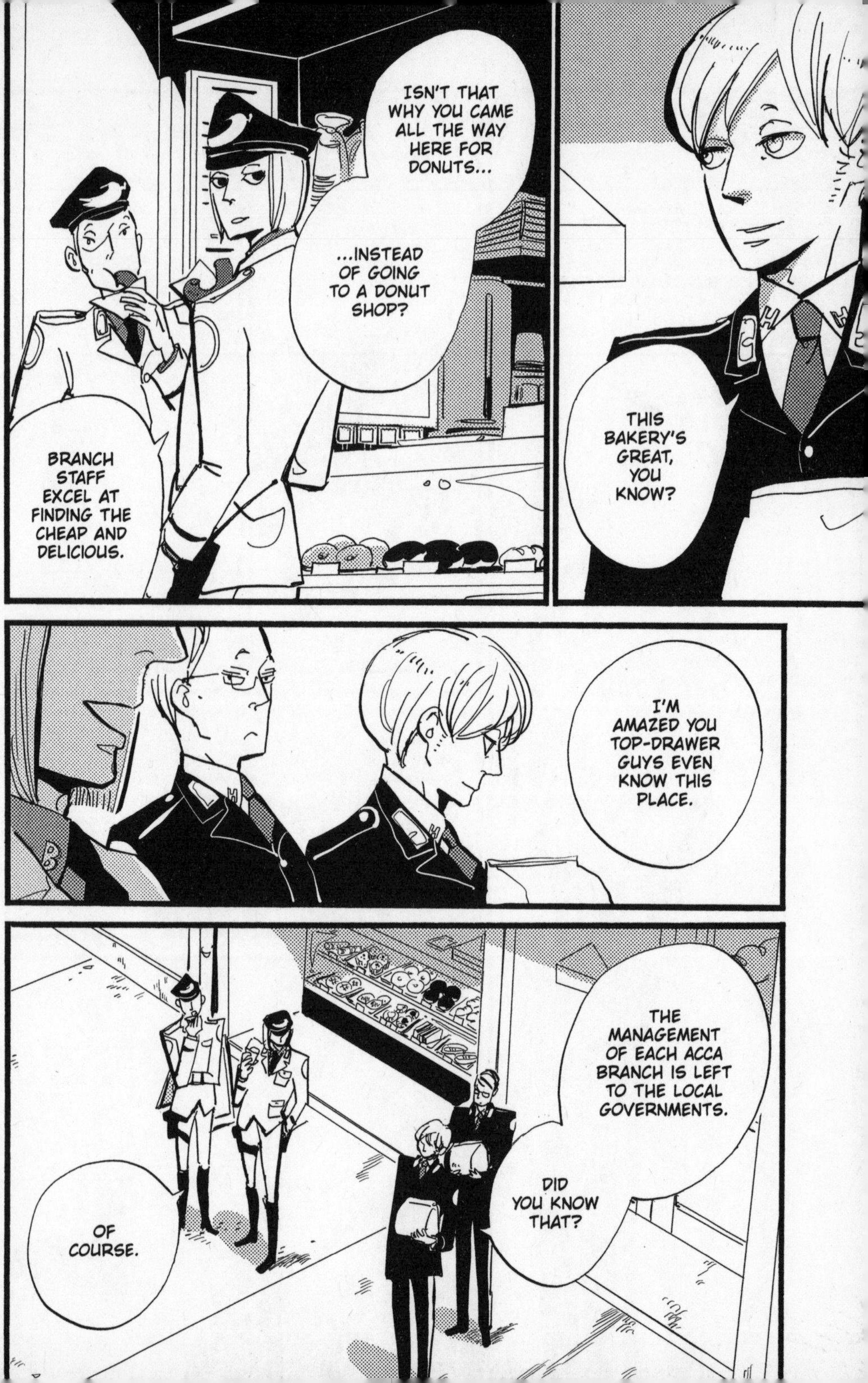
THIS BAKERY'S GREAT, YOU KNOW?
ISN'T THAT WHY YOU CAME ALL THE WAY HERE FOR DONUTS...
...INSTEAD OF GOING TO A DONUT SHOP?
BRANCH STAFF EXCEL AT FINDING THE CHEAP AND DELICIOUS.
I'M AMAZED YOU TOP-DRAWER GUYS EVEN KNOW THIS PLACE.
THE MANAGEMENT OF EACH ACCA BRANCH IS LEFT TO THE LOCAL GOVERNMENTS.
DID YOU KNOW THAT?
OF COURSE.

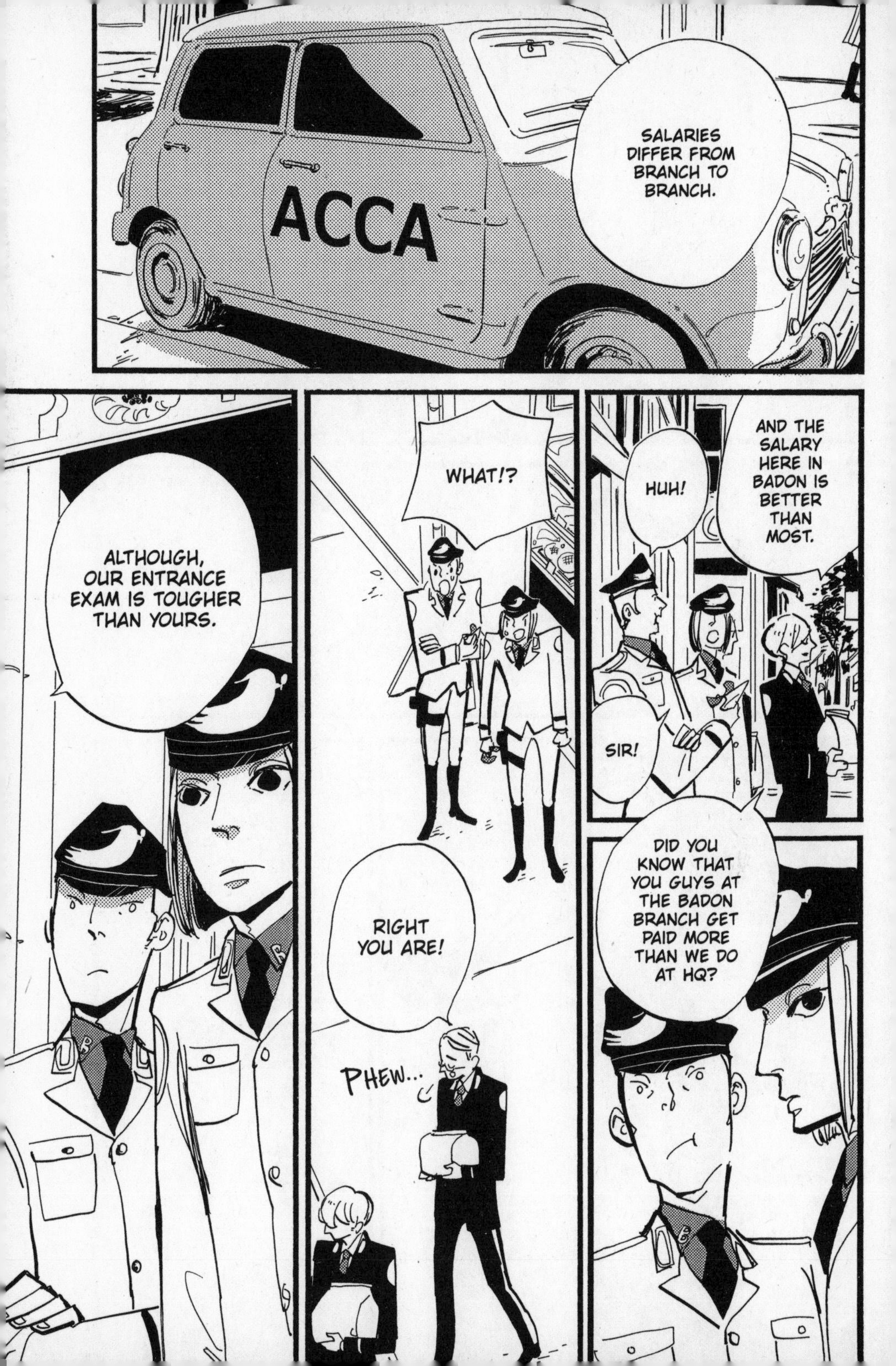
ACCA
SALARIES DIFFER FROM BRANCH TO BRANCH.
AND THE SALARY HERE IN BADON IS BETTER THAN MOST.
HUH!
SIR!
DID YOU KNOW THAT YOU GUYS AT THE BADON BRANCH GET PAID MORE THAN WE DO AT HQ?
WHAT!?
RIGHT YOU ARE!
PHEW...
ALTHOUGH, OUR ENTRANCE EXAM IS TOUGHER THAN YOURS.

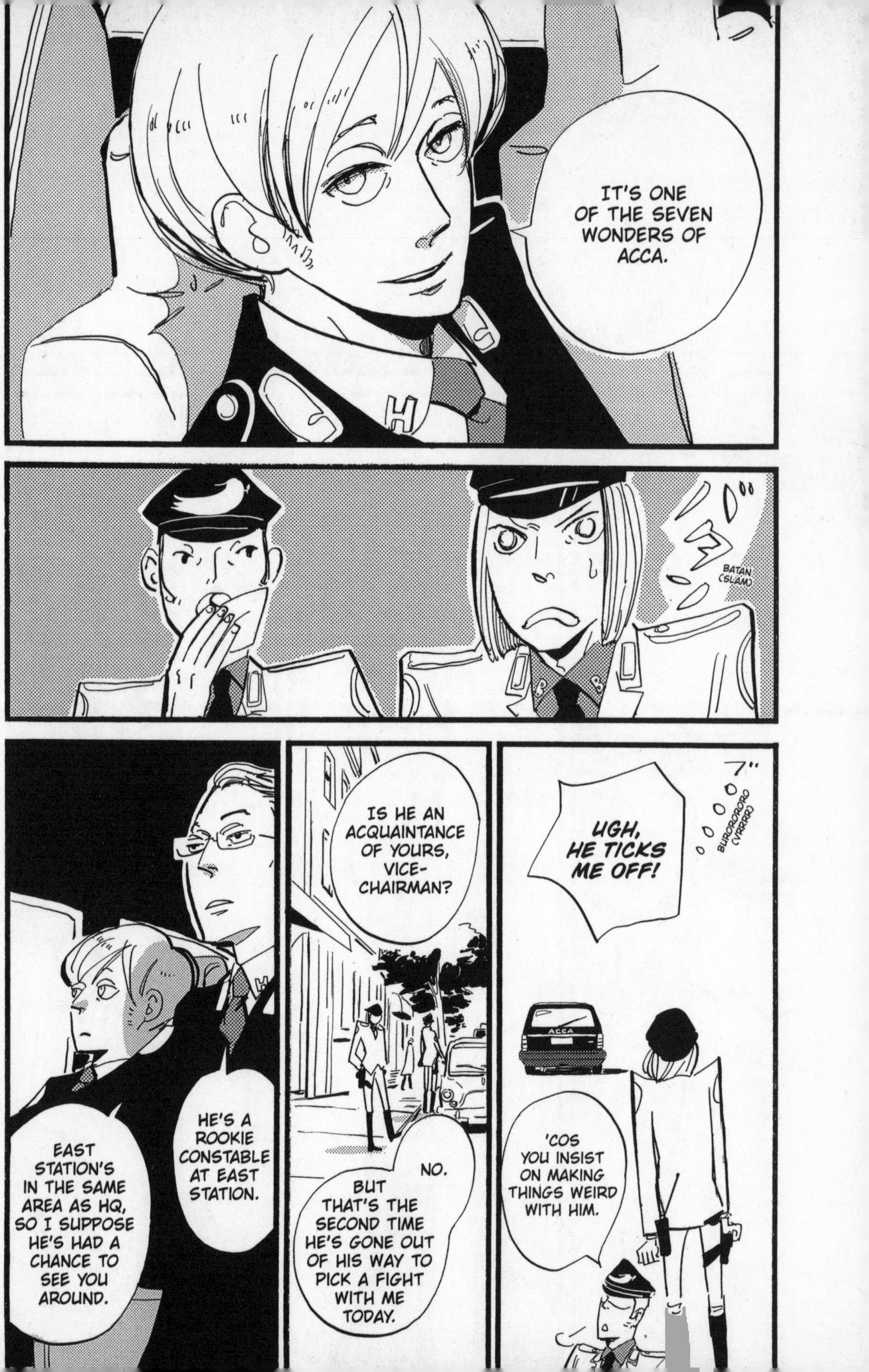
IT'S ONE OF THE SEVEN WONDERS OF ACCA.
BATAN (SLAM)
UGH, HE TICKS ME OFF!
BUROROROROR (VRRRR)
IS HE AN ACQUAINTANCE OF YOURS, VICE-CHAIRMAN?
NO.
BUT THAT'S THE SECOND TIME HE'S GONE OUT OF HIS WAY TO PICK A FIGHT WITH ME TODAY.
'COS YOU INSIST ON MAKING THINGS WEIRD WITH HIM.
HE'S A ROOKIE CONSTABLE AT EAST STATION.
EAST STATION'S IN THE SAME AREA AS HQ, SO I SUPPOSE HE'S HAD A CHANCE TO SEE YOU AROUND.
ACCA

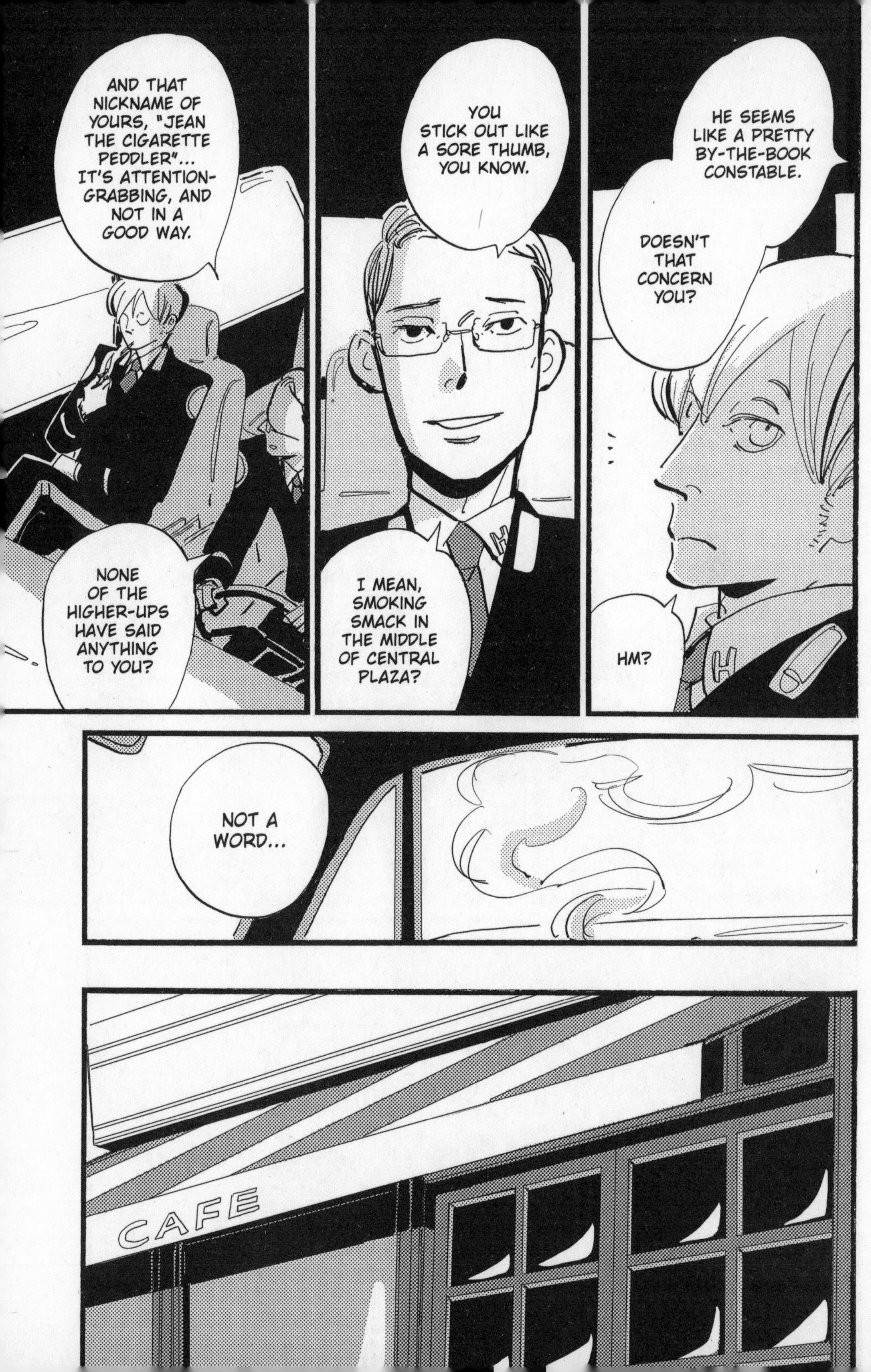
HE SEEMS LIKE A PRETTY BY-THE-BOOK CONSTABLE.
DOESN'T THAT CONCERN YOU?
HM?
YOU STICK OUT LIKE A SORE THUMB, YOU KNOW.
I MEAN, SMOKING SMACK IN THE MIDDLE OF CENTRAL PLAZA?
AND THAT NICKNAME OF YOURS, "JEAN THE CIGARETTE PEDDLER"... IT'S ATTENTION-GRABBING, AND NOT IN A GOOD WAY.
NONE OF THE HIGHER-UPS HAVE SAID ANYTHING TO YOU?
NOT A WORD...
CAFE

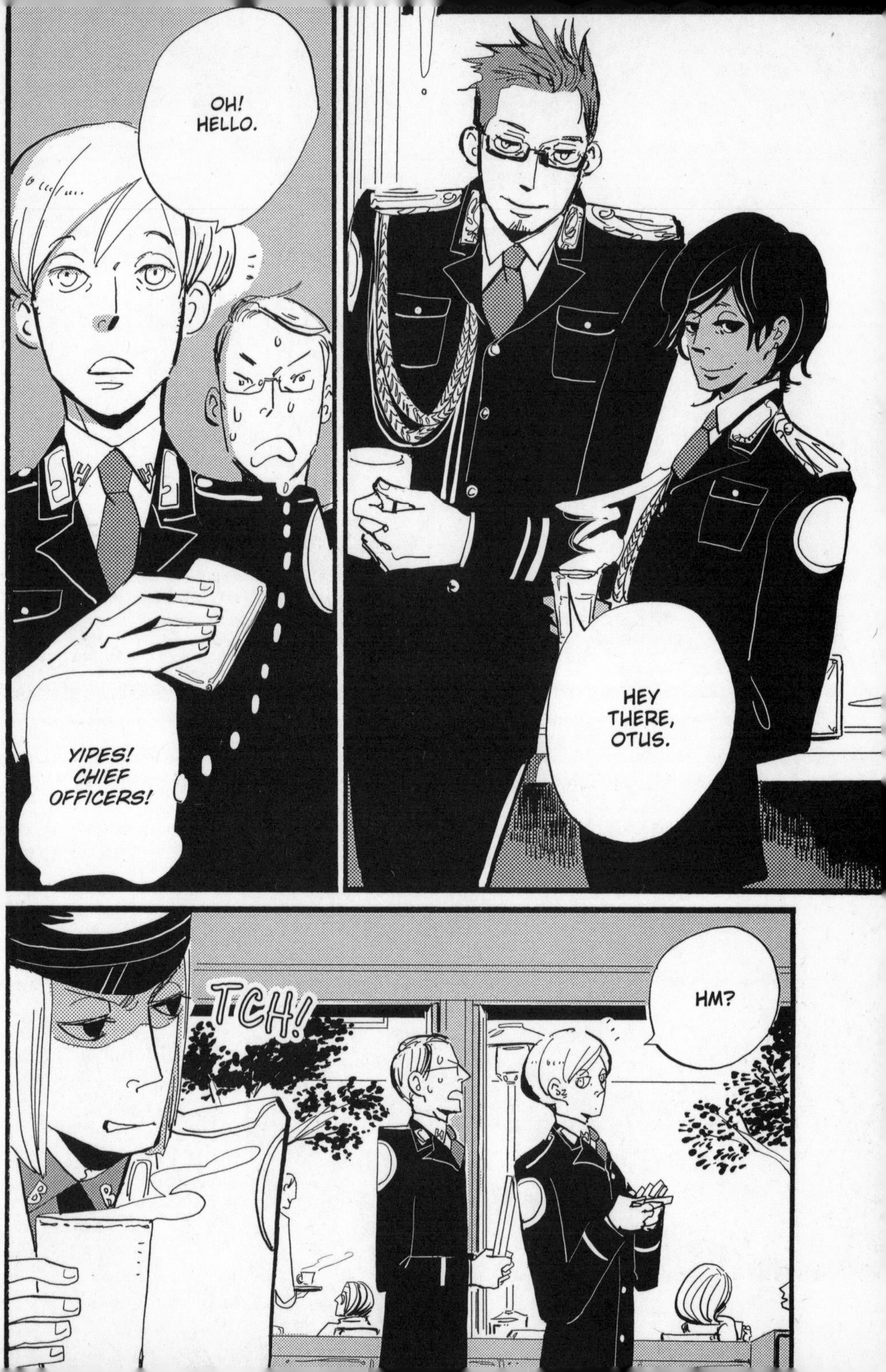
HEY THERE, OTUS.
OH! HELLO.
YIPES! CHIEF OFFICERS!
HM?
TCH!

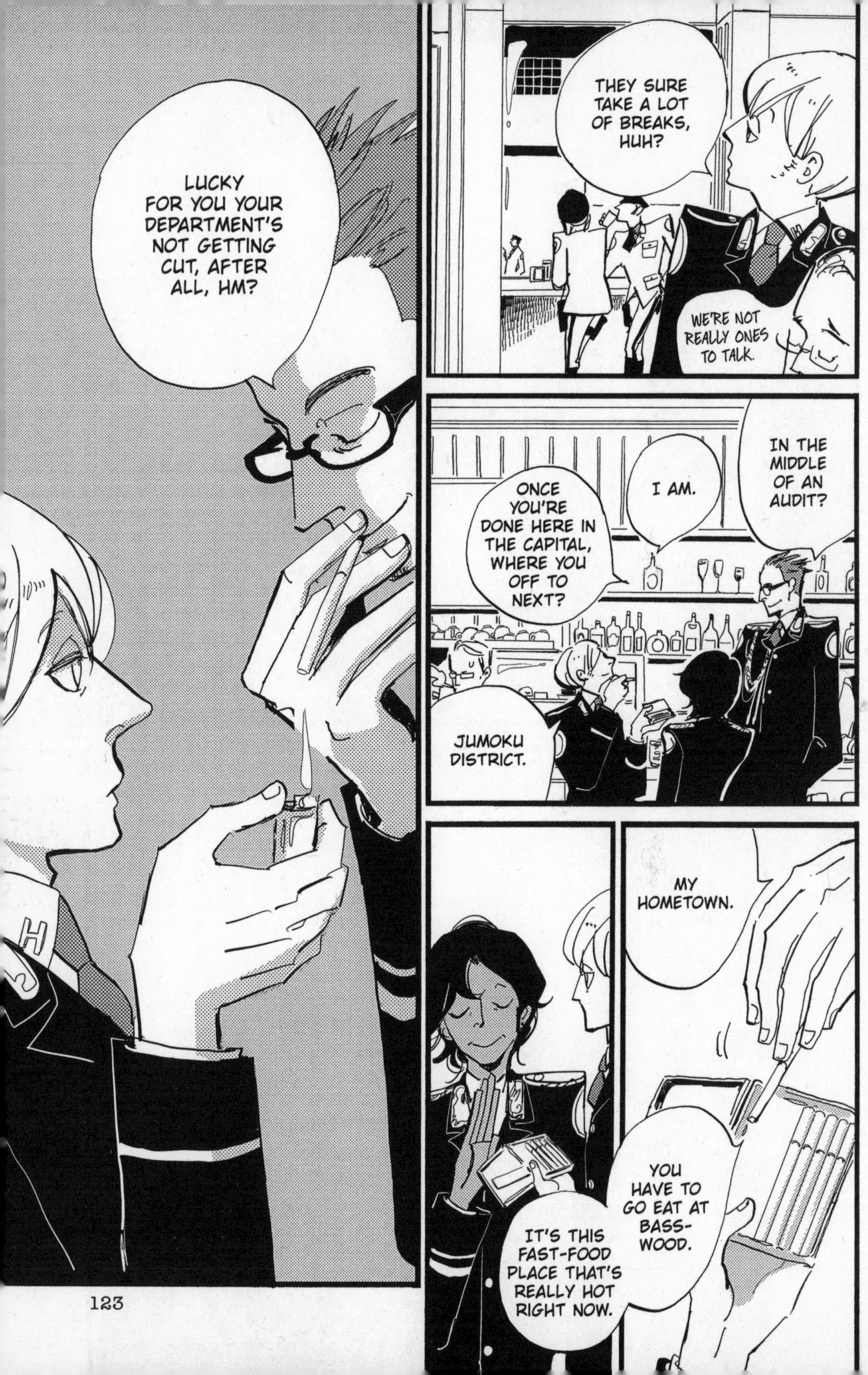
THEY SURE TAKE A LOT OF BREAKS, HUH?
WE'RE NOT REALLY ONES TO TALK.
IN THE MIDDLE OF AN AUDIT?
I AM.
ONCE YOU'RE DONE HERE IN THE CAPITAL, WHERE YOU OFF TO NEXT?
JUMOKU DISTRICT.
MY HOMETOWN.
YOU HAVE TO GO EAT AT BASS-WOOD.
IT'S THIS FAST-FOOD PLACE THAT'S REALLY HOT RIGHT NOW.
LUCKY FOR YOU YOUR DEPARTMENT'S NOT GETTING CUT, AFTER ALL, HM?

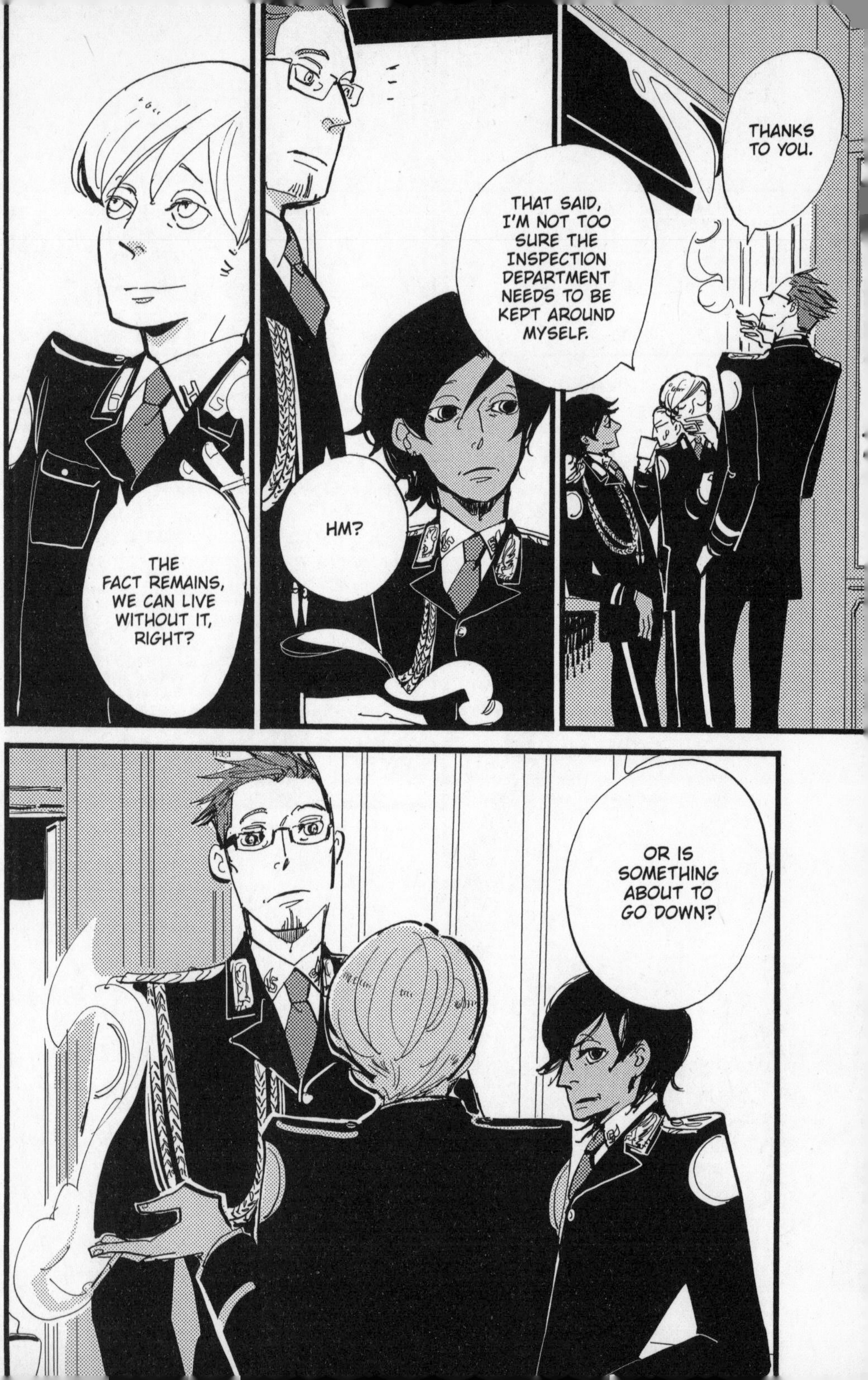
THANKS TO YOU.
THAT SAID, I'M NOT TOO SURE THE INSPECTION DEPARTMENT NEEDS TO BE KEPT AROUND MYSELF.
HM?
THE FACT REMAINS, WE CAN LIVE WITHOUT IT, RIGHT?
OR IS SOMETHING ABOUT TO GO DOWN?

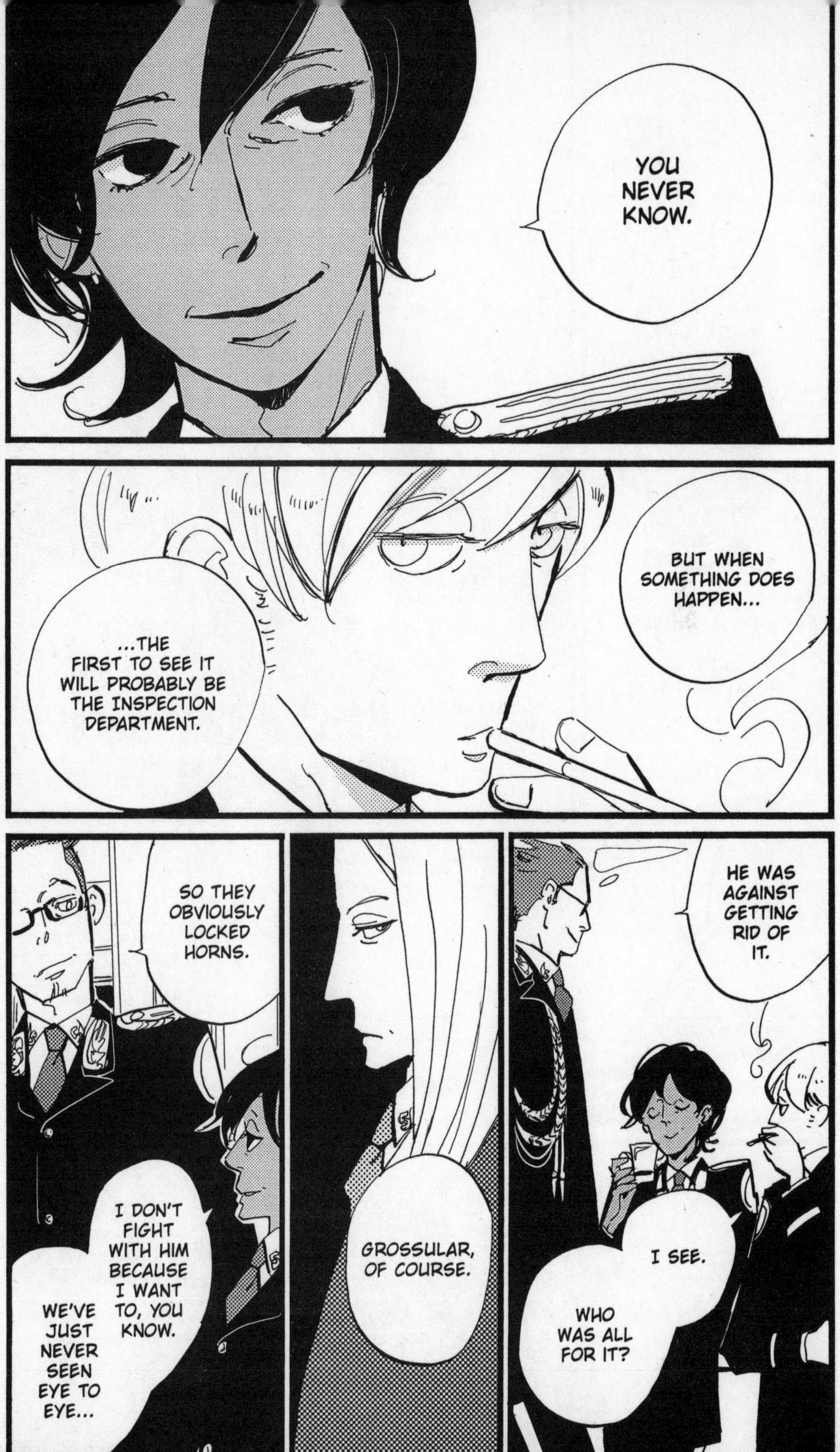
YOU NEVER KNOW.
BUT WHEN SOMETHING DOES HAPPEN...
...THE FIRST TO SEE IT WILL PROBABLY BE THE INSPECTION DEPARTMENT.
HE WAS AGAINST GETTING RID OF IT.
I SEE.
WHO WAS ALL FOR IT?
GROSSULAR, OF COURSE.
SO THEY OBVIOUSLY LOCKED HORNS.
I DON'T FIGHT WITH HIM BECAUSE I WANT TO, YOU KNOW.
WE'VE JUST NEVER SEEN EYE TO EYE...

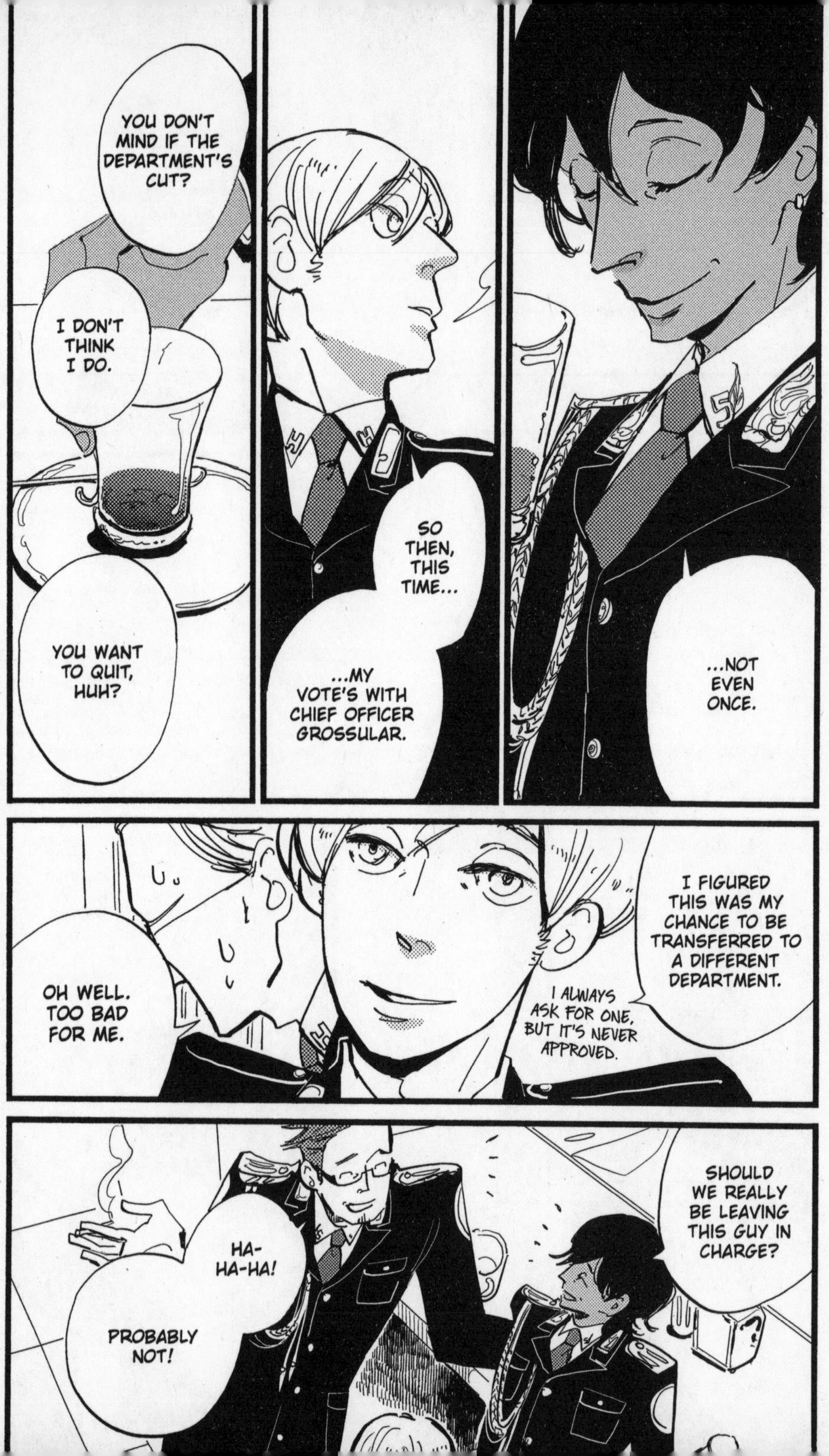
YOU DON'T MIND IF THE DEPARTMENT'S CUT?
I DON'T THINK I DO.
YOU WANT TO QUIT, HUH?
SO THEN, THIS TIME...
...MY VOTE'S WITH CHIEF OFFICER GROSSULAR.
...NOT EVEN ONCE.
I FIGURED THIS WAS MY CHANCE TO BE TRANSFERRED TO A DIFFERENT DEPARTMENT.
I ALWAYS ASK FOR ONE, BUT IT'S NEVER APPROVED.
OH WELL. TOO BAD FOR ME.
SHOULD WE REALLY BE LEAVING THIS GUY IN CHARGE?
HA-HA-HA!
PROBABLY NOT!

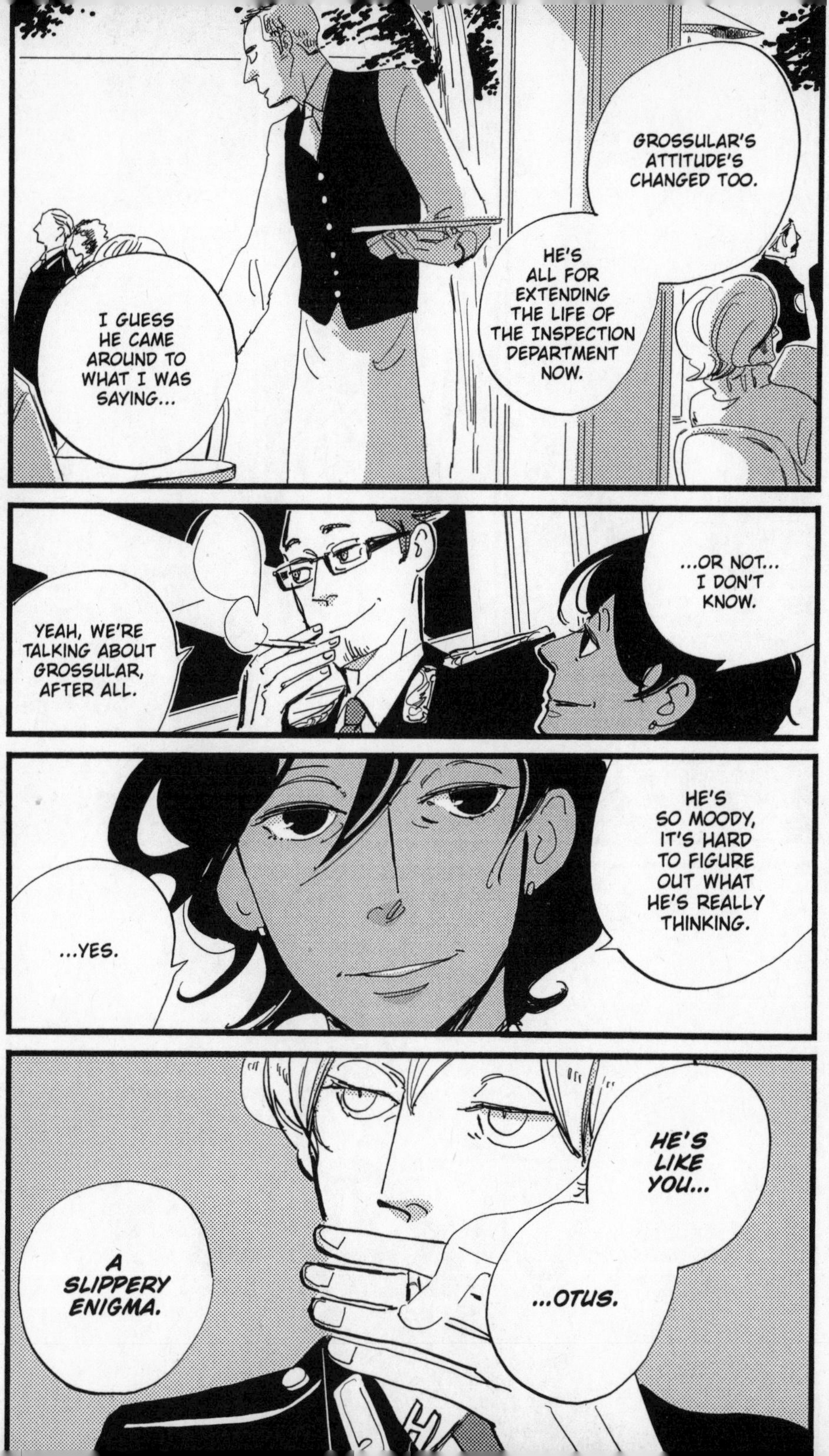
GROSSULAR'S ATTITUDE'S CHANGED TOO.
HE'S ALL FOR EXTENDING THE LIFE OF THE INSPECTION DEPARTMENT NOW.
I GUESS HE CAME AROUND TO WHAT I WAS SAYING...
...OR NOT... I DON'T KNOW.
YEAH, WE'RE TALKING ABOUT GROSSULAR, AFTER ALL.
HE'S SO MOODY, IT'S HARD TO FIGURE OUT WHAT HE'S REALLY THINKING.
...YES.
HE'S LIKE YOU...
...OTUS.
A SLIPPERY ENIGMA.

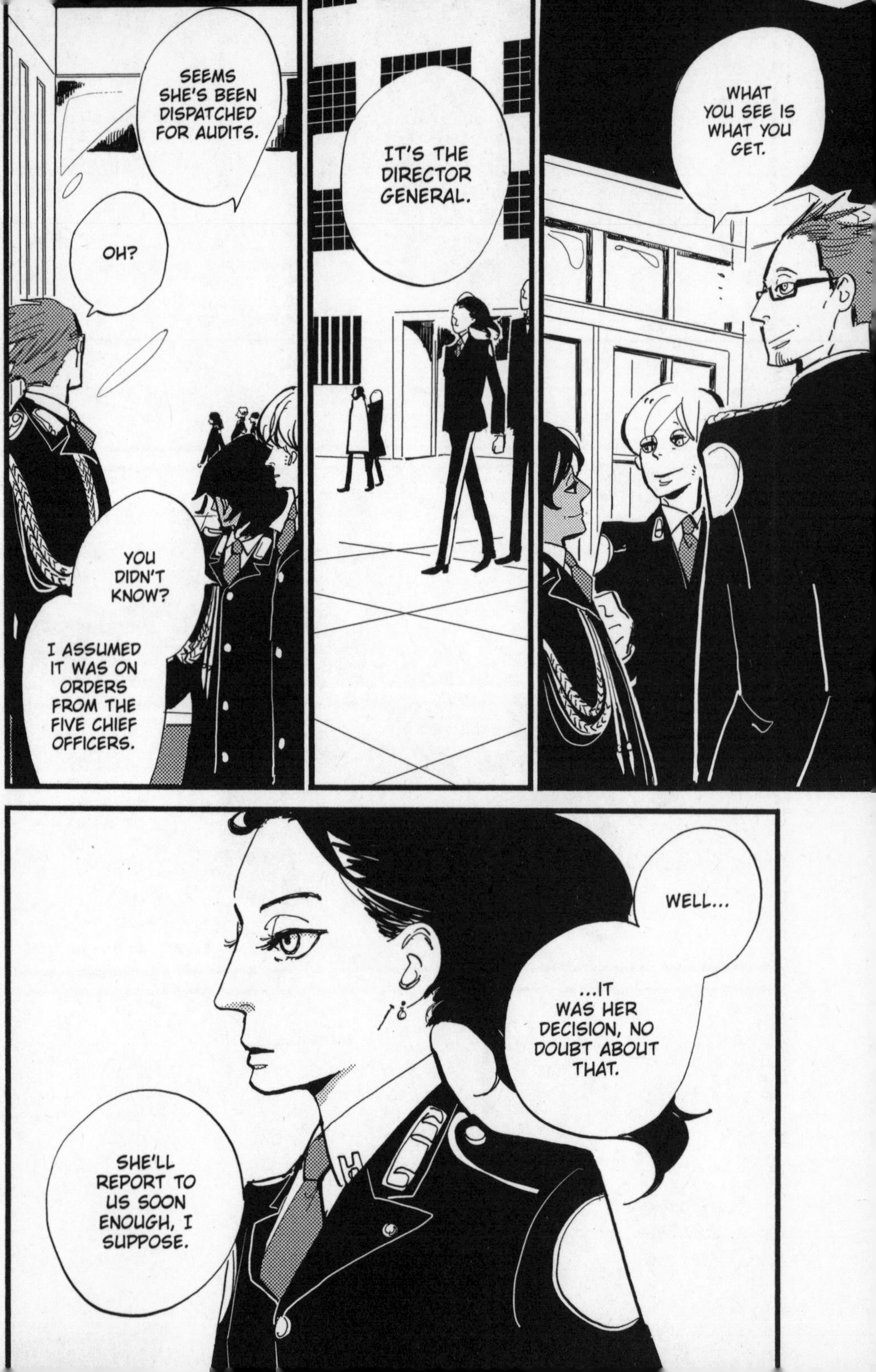
WHAT YOU SEE IS WHAT YOU GET.
IT'S THE DIRECTOR GENERAL.
SEEMS SHE'S BEEN DISPATCHED FOR AUDITS.
OH?
YOU DIDN'T KNOW?
I ASSUMED IT WAS ON ORDERS FROM THE FIVE CHIEF OFFICERS.
WELL...
...IT WAS HER DECISION, NO DOUBT ABOUT THAT.
SHE'LL REPORT TO US SOON ENOUGH, I SUPPOSE.

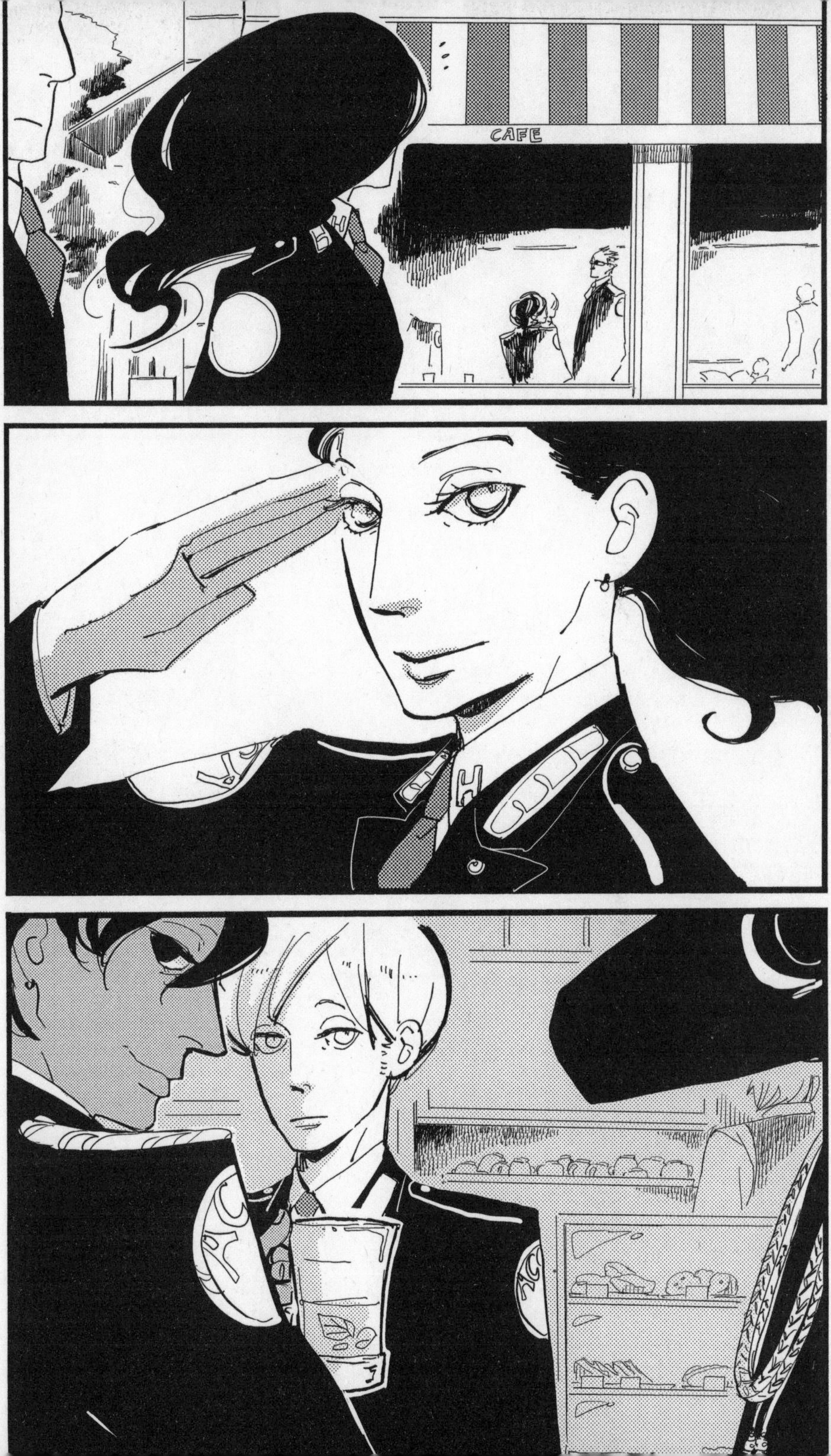
CAFE

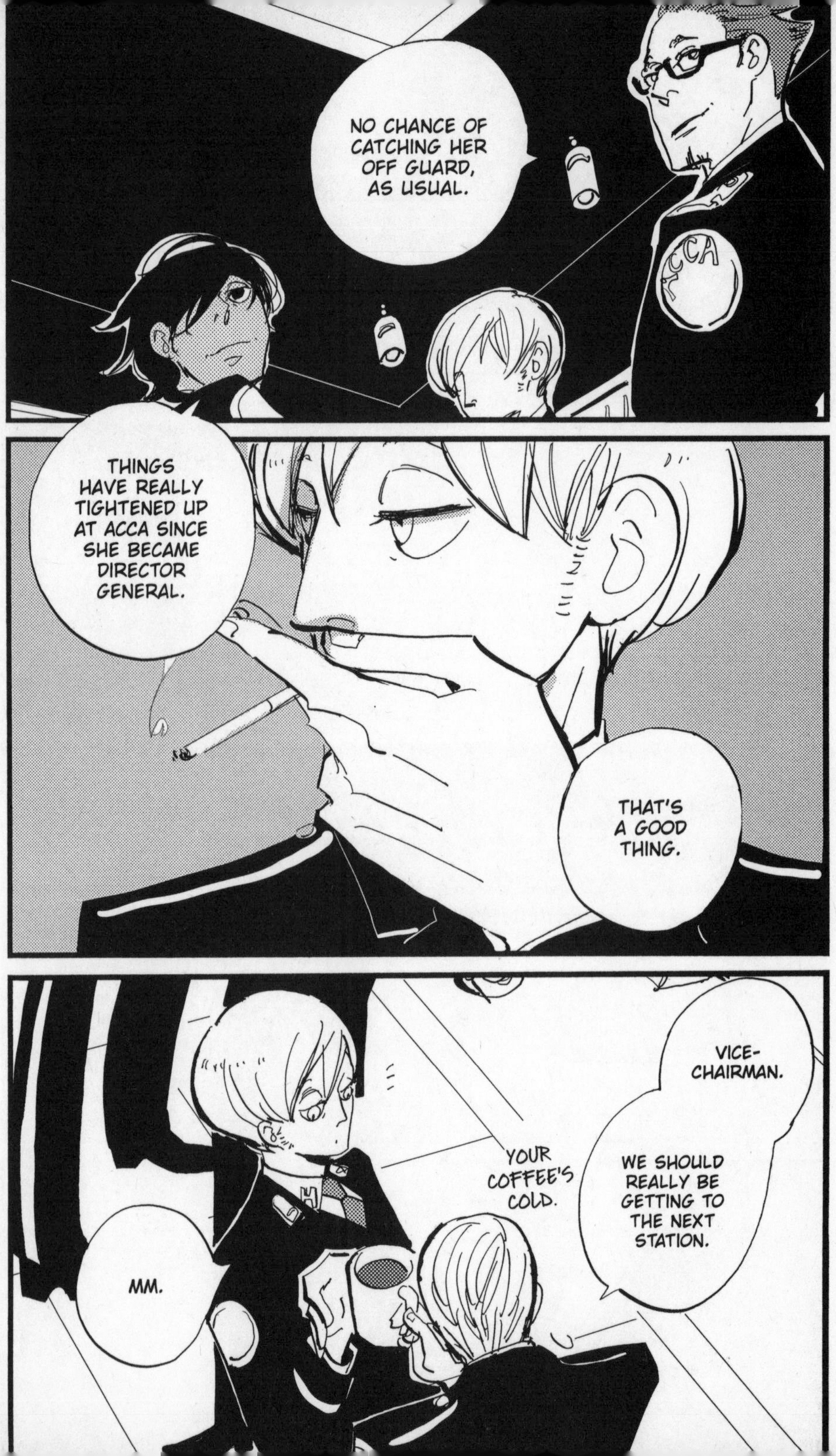
NO CHANCE OF CATCHING HER OFF GUARD, AS USUAL.
THINGS HAVE REALLY TIGHTENED UP AT ACCA SINCE SHE BECAME DIRECTOR GENERAL.
THAT'S A GOOD THING.
VICE-CHAIRMAN.
WE SHOULD REALLY BE GETTING TO THE NEXT STATION.
YOUR COFFEE'S COLD.
MM.

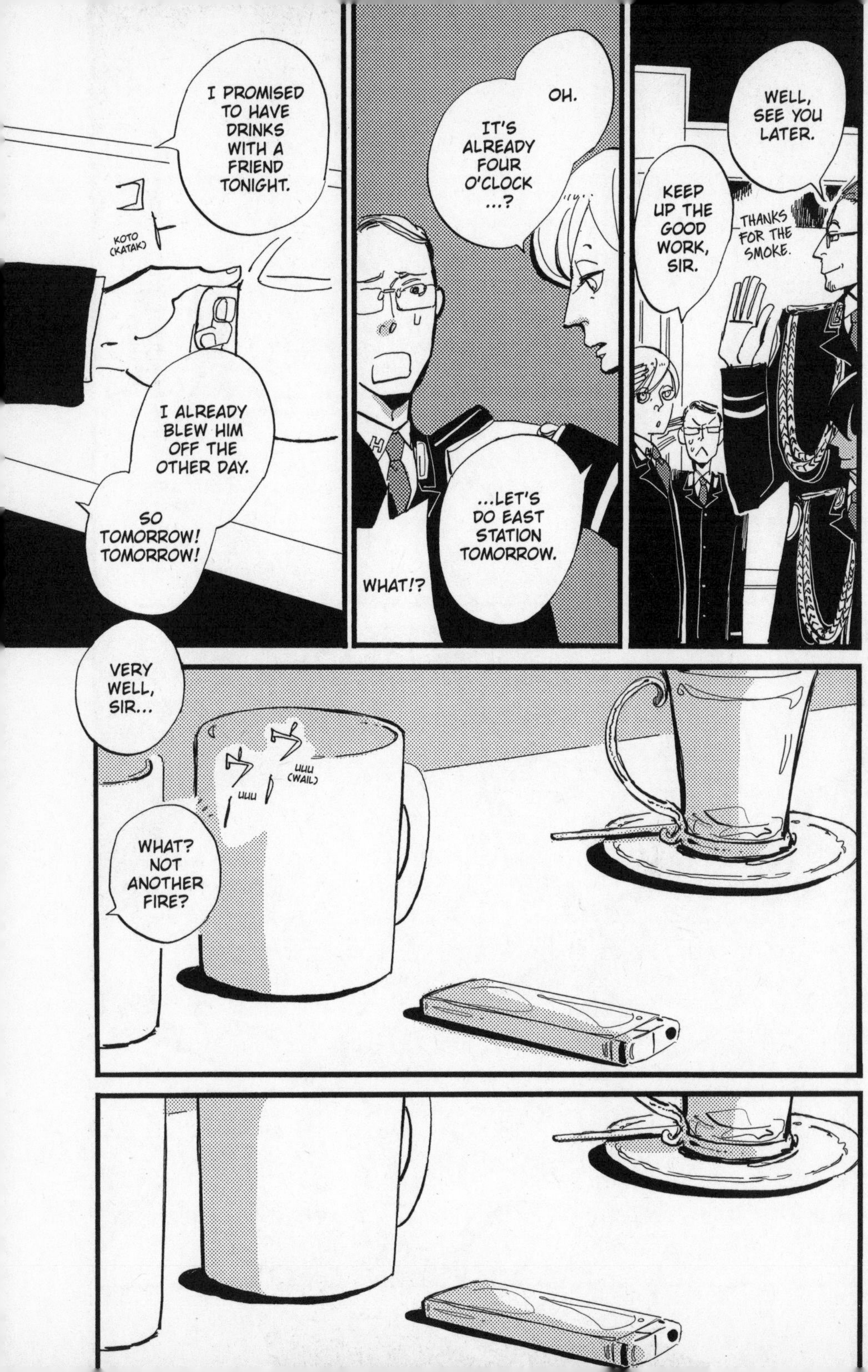
WELL, SEE YOU LATER.
THANKS FOR THE SMOKE.
KEEP UP THE GOOD WORK, SIR.
OH.
IT'S ALREADY FOUR O'CLOCK ...?
...LET'S DO EAST STATION TOMORROW.
WHAT!?
I PROMISED TO HAVE DRINKS WITH A FRIEND TONIGHT.
KOTO (KATAK)
I ALREADY BLEW HIM OFF THE OTHER DAY.
SO TOMORROW! TOMORROW!
VERY WELL, SIR...
uuu (WAIL)
uuu
WHAT? NOT ANOTHER FIRE?

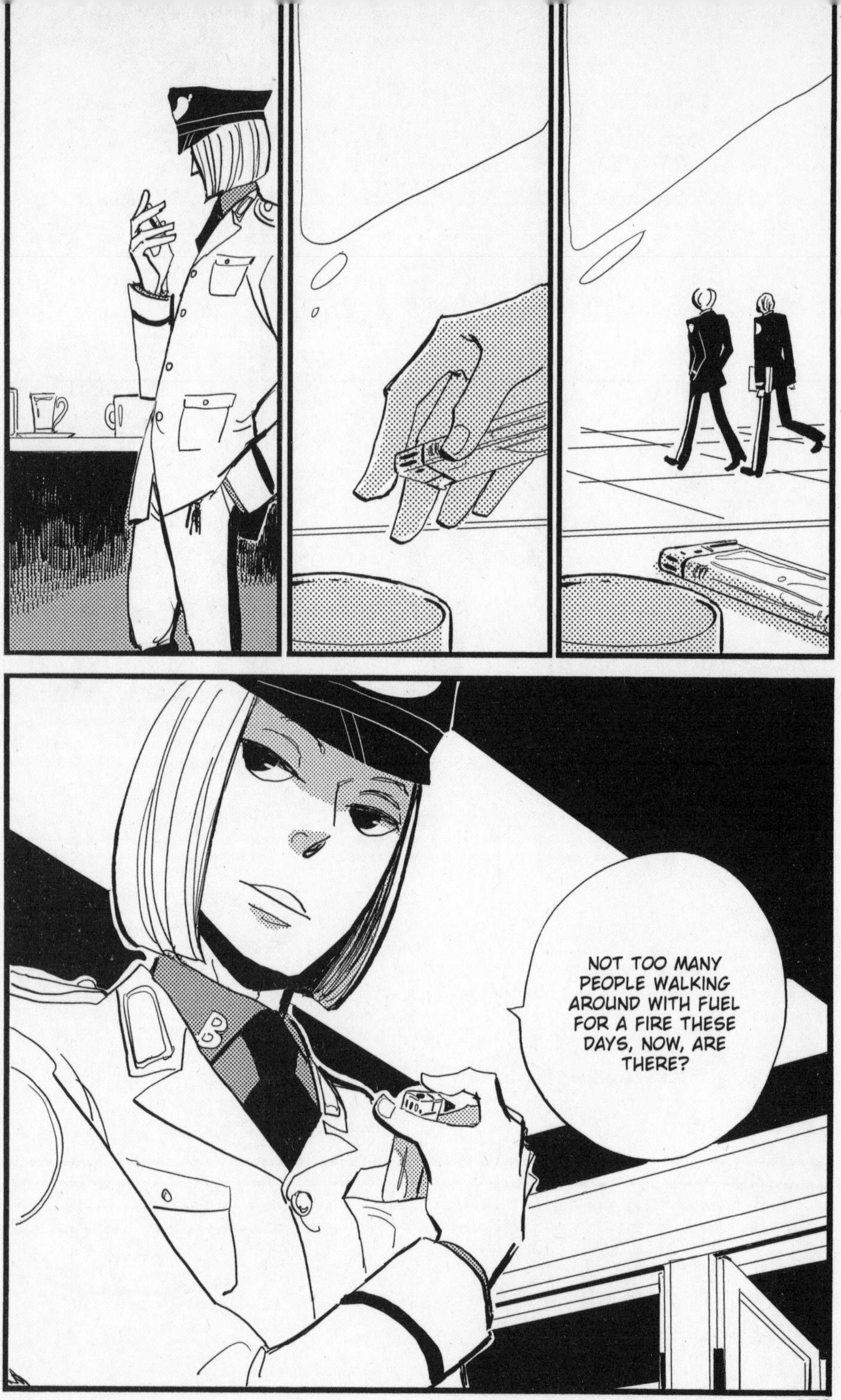
NOT TOO MANY PEOPLE WALKING AROUND WITH FUEL FOR A FIRE THESE DAYS, NOW, ARE THERE?

CHAPTER 3

Stopover at a Bakery in Badon

DEPT. ACCA 13 TERRITORY INSPECTION
PASS

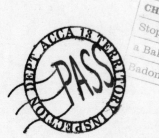

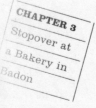

CHAPTER 4

Lighter Thief
in Badon

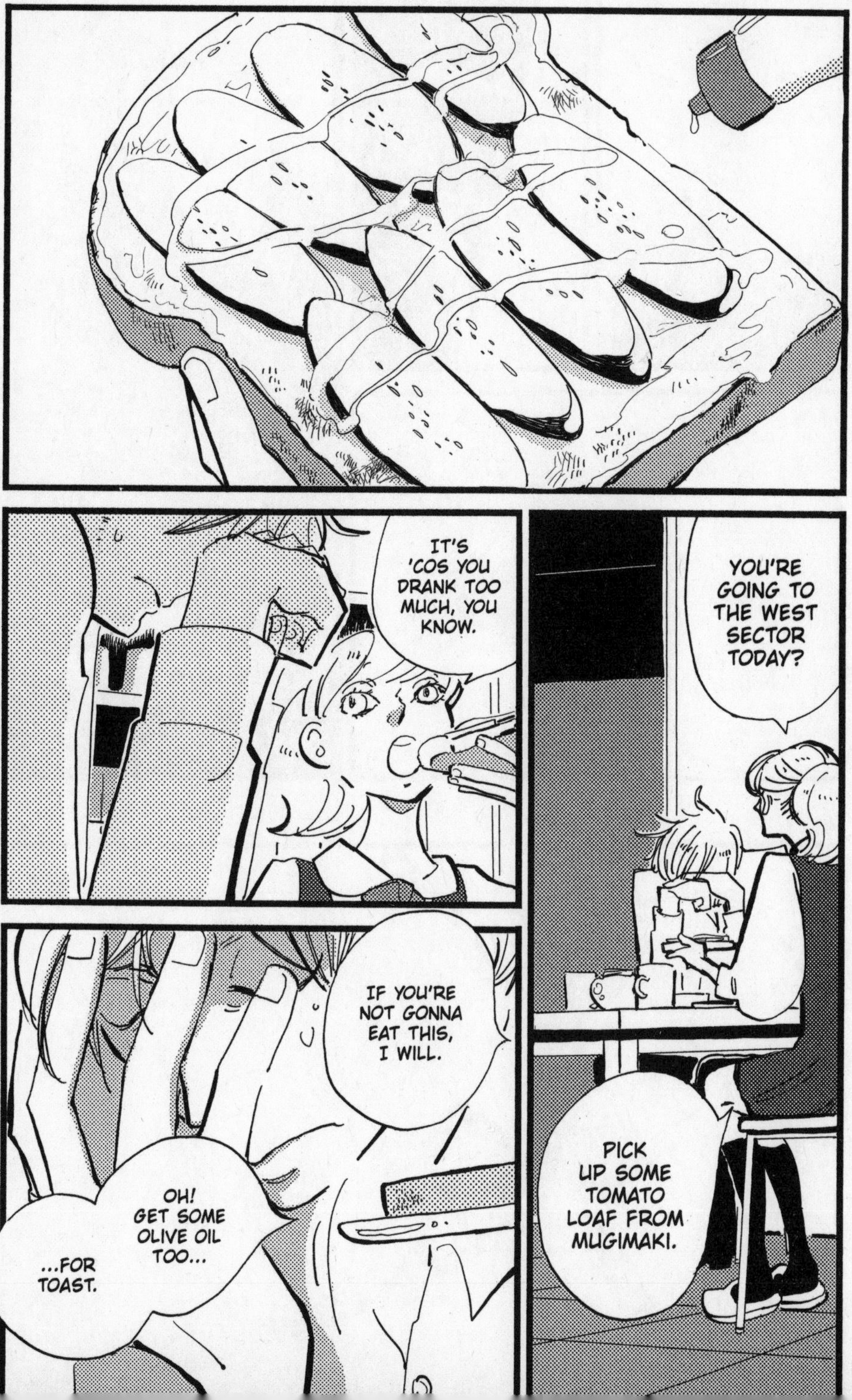
YOU'RE GOING TO THE WEST SECTOR TODAY?
PICK UP SOME TOMATO LOAF FROM MUGIMAKI.
IT'S 'COS YOU DRANK TOO MUCH, YOU KNOW.
IF YOU'RE NOT GONNA EAT THIS, I WILL.
OH! GET SOME OLIVE OIL TOO...
...FOR TOAST.

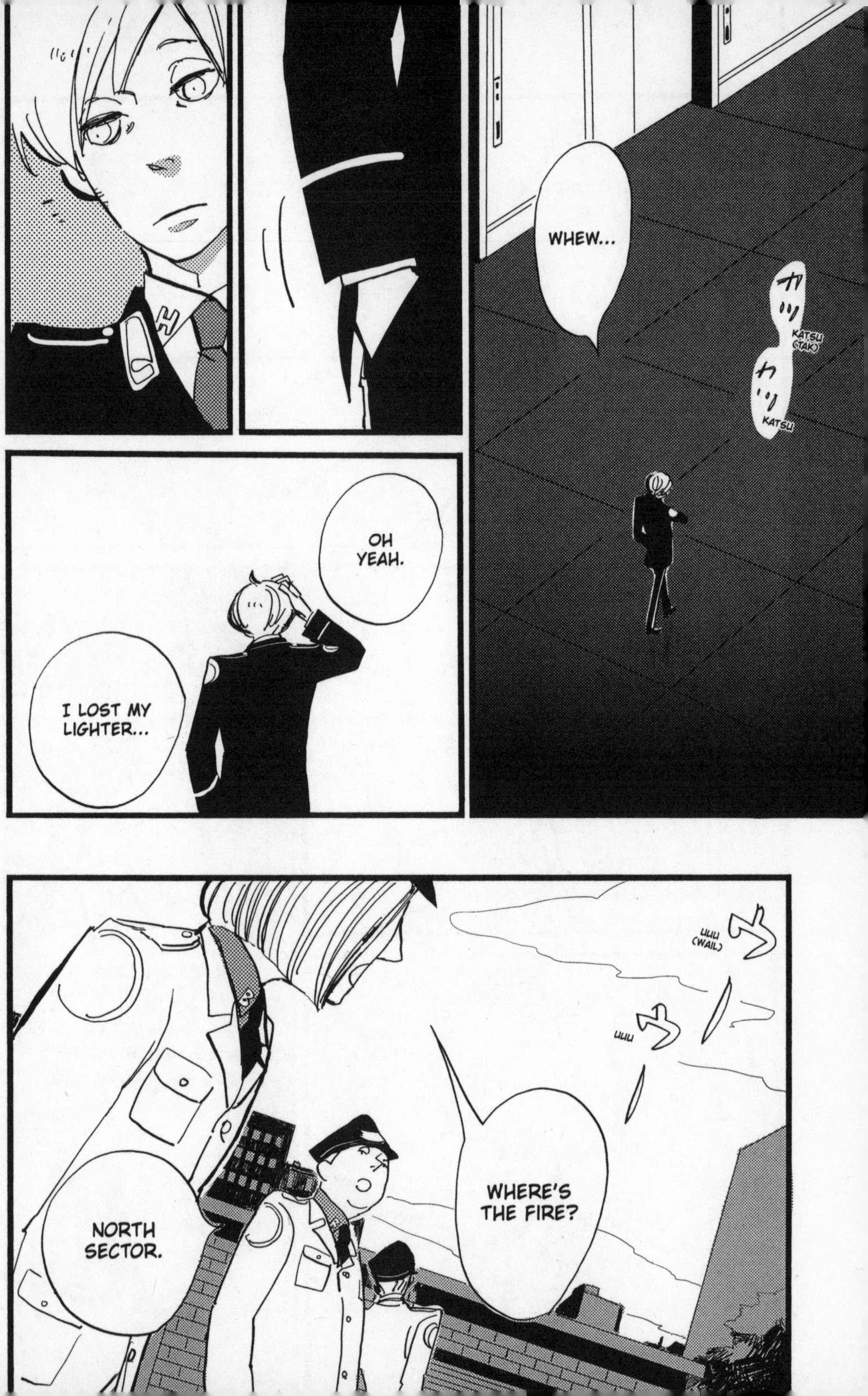
WHEW...
KATSU (TAK)
KATSU
OH YEAH.
I LOST MY LIGHTER...
UUU (WAIL)
UUU
WHERE'S THE FIRE?
NORTH SECTOR.

NORTH IS TOO FAR...

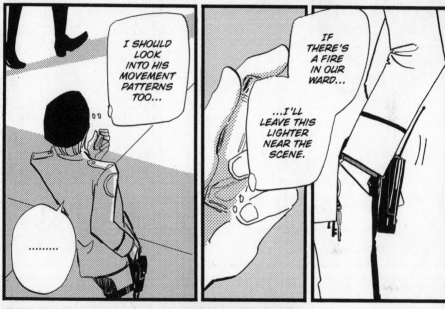

I SHOULD LOOK INTO HIS MOVEMENT PATTERNS TOO...

....

IF THERE'S A FIRE IN OUR WARD...

...I'LL LEAVE THIS LIGHTER NEAR THE SCENE.

...MAYBE IT'D BE FASTER TO START A FIRE WITH THIS WHEREVER HE'S HANGING AROUND?

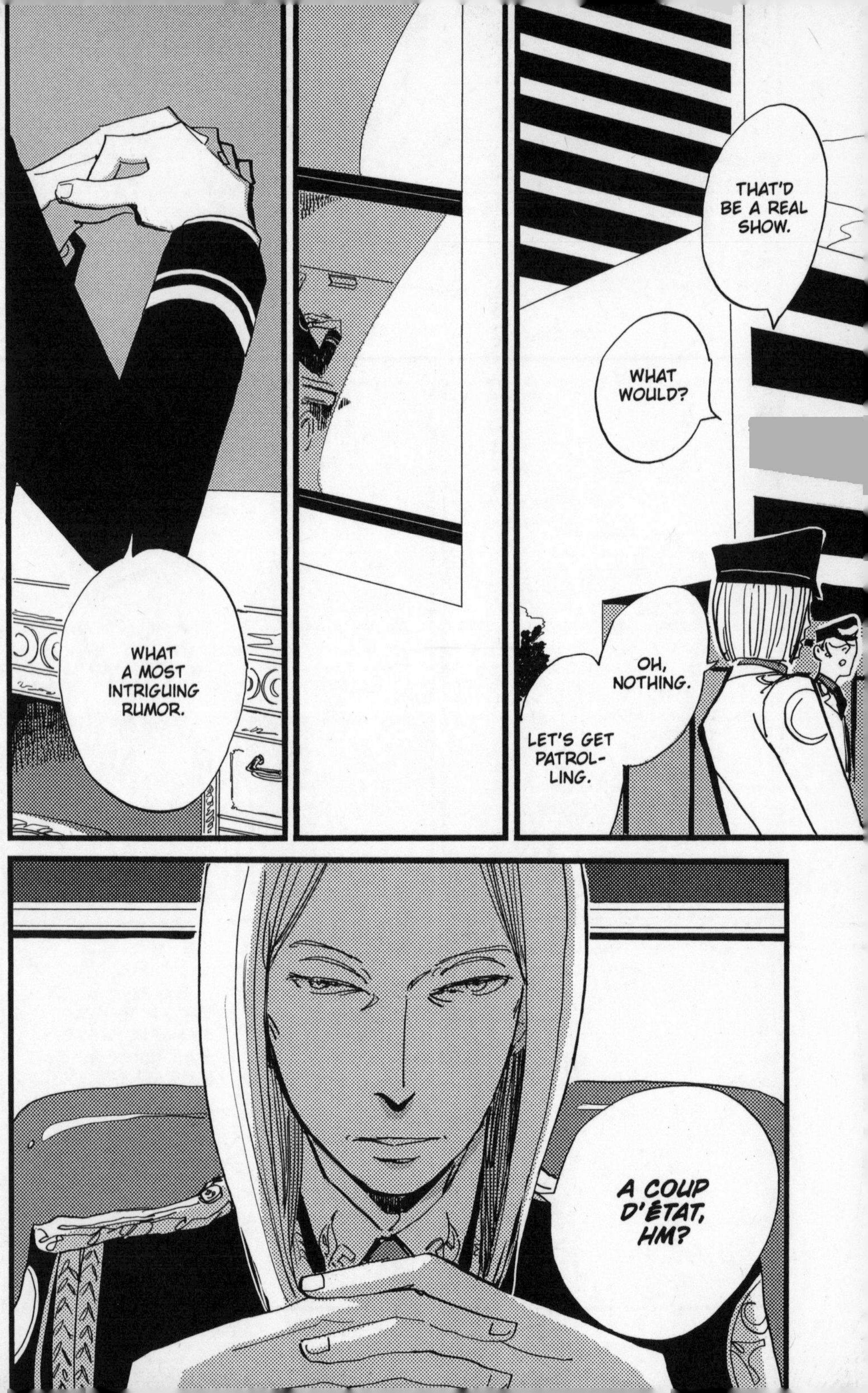
THAT'D BE A REAL SHOW.
WHAT WOULD?
OH, NOTHING.
LET'S GET PATROL-LING.
WHAT A MOST INTRIGUING RUMOR.
A COUP D'ÉTAT, HM?

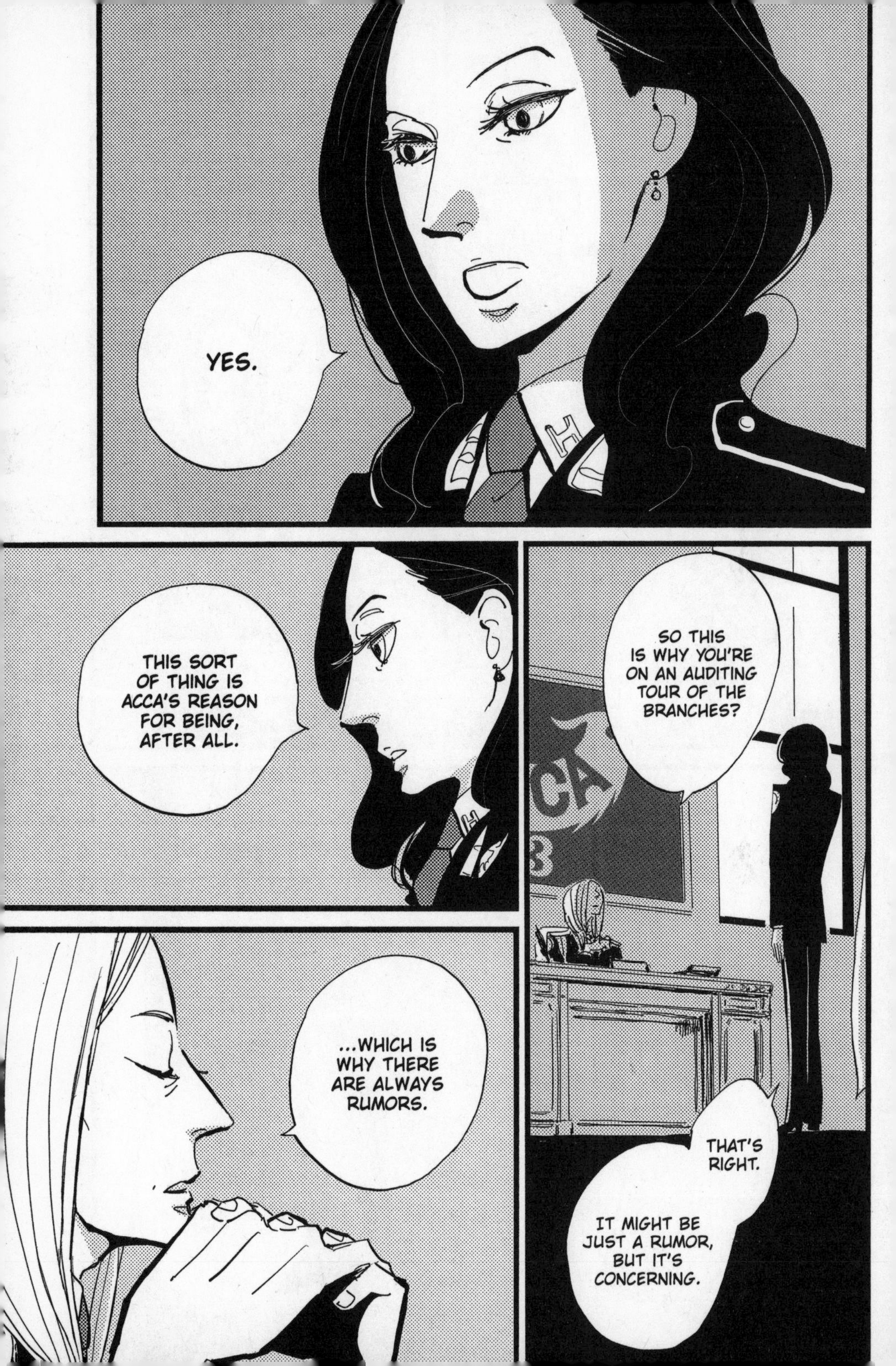
YES.
THIS SORT OF THING IS ACCA'S REASON FOR BEING, AFTER ALL.
SO THIS IS WHY YOU'RE ON AN AUDITING TOUR OF THE BRANCHES?
...WHICH IS WHY THERE ARE ALWAYS RUMORS.
THAT'S RIGHT.
IT MIGHT BE JUST A RUMOR, BUT IT'S CONCERNING.

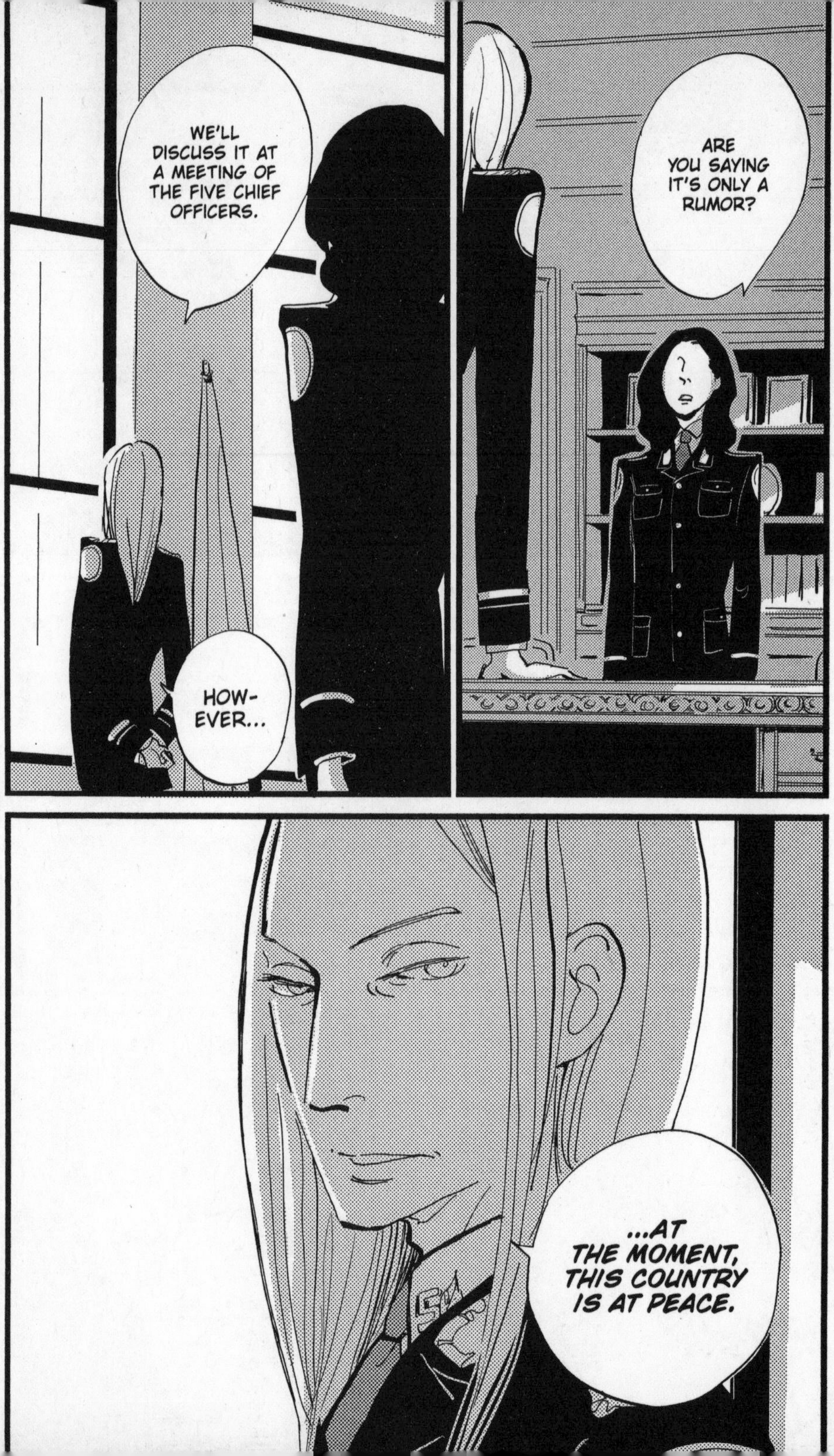
ARE YOU SAYING IT'S ONLY A RUMOR?
WE'LL DISCUSS IT AT A MEETING OF THE FIVE CHIEF OFFICERS.
HOW-EVER...
...AT THE MOMENT, THIS COUNTRY IS AT PEACE.

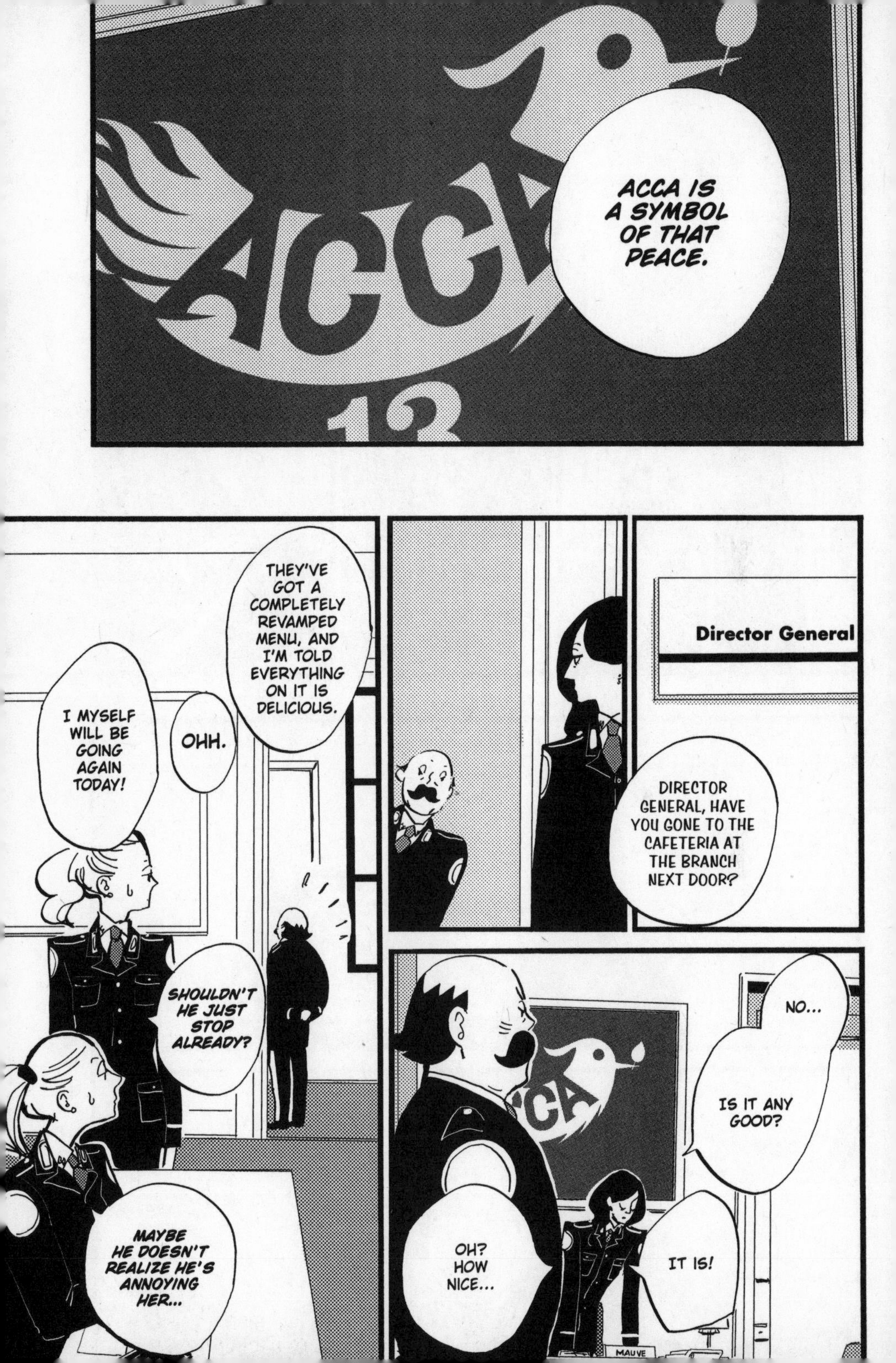
ACCA
13
ACCA IS A SYMBOL OF THAT PEACE.
Director General
DIRECTOR GENERAL, HAVE YOU GONE TO THE CAFETERIA AT THE BRANCH NEXT DOOR?
NO...
IS IT ANY GOOD?
IT IS!
OH? HOW NICE...
MAUVE
THEY'VE GOT A COMPLETELY REVAMPED MENU, AND I'M TOLD EVERYTHING ON IT IS DELICIOUS.
OHH.
I MYSELF WILL BE GOING AGAIN TODAY!
SHOULDN'T HE JUST STOP ALREADY?
MAYBE HE DOESN'T REALIZE HE'S ANNOYING HER...

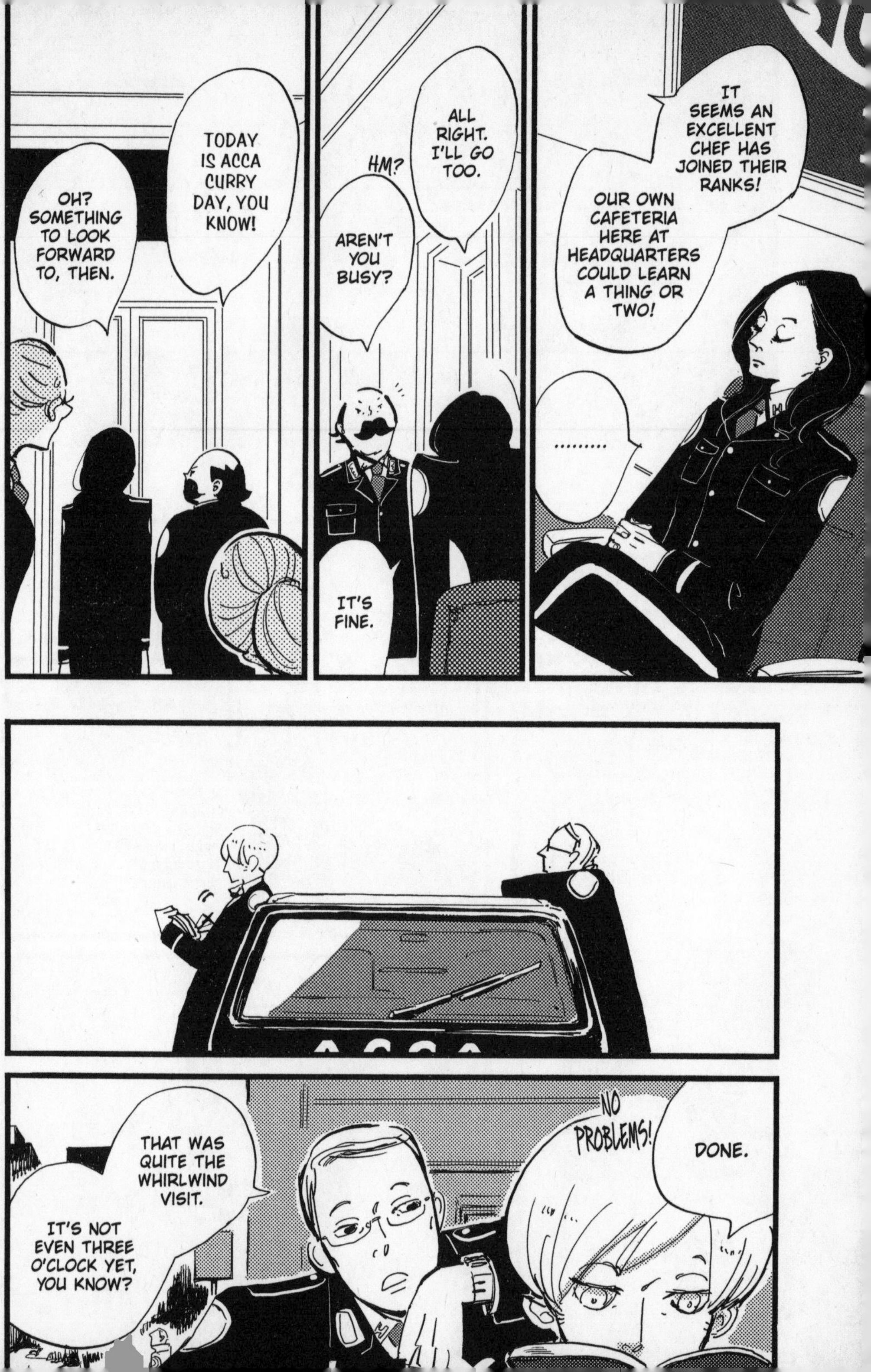

TODAY IS ACCA CURRY DAY, YOU KNOW!
OH? SOMETHING TO LOOK FORWARD TO, THEN.
ALL RIGHT. I'LL GO TOO.
HM?
AREN'T YOU BUSY?
IT'S FINE.
IT SEEMS AN EXCELLENT CHEF HAS JOINED THEIR RANKS!
OUR OWN CAFETERIA HERE AT HEADQUARTERS COULD LEARN A THING OR TWO!
....
ACCA
THAT WAS QUITE THE WHIRLWIND VISIT.
IT'S NOT EVEN THREE O'CLOCK YET, YOU KNOW?
NO PROBLEMS!
DONE.

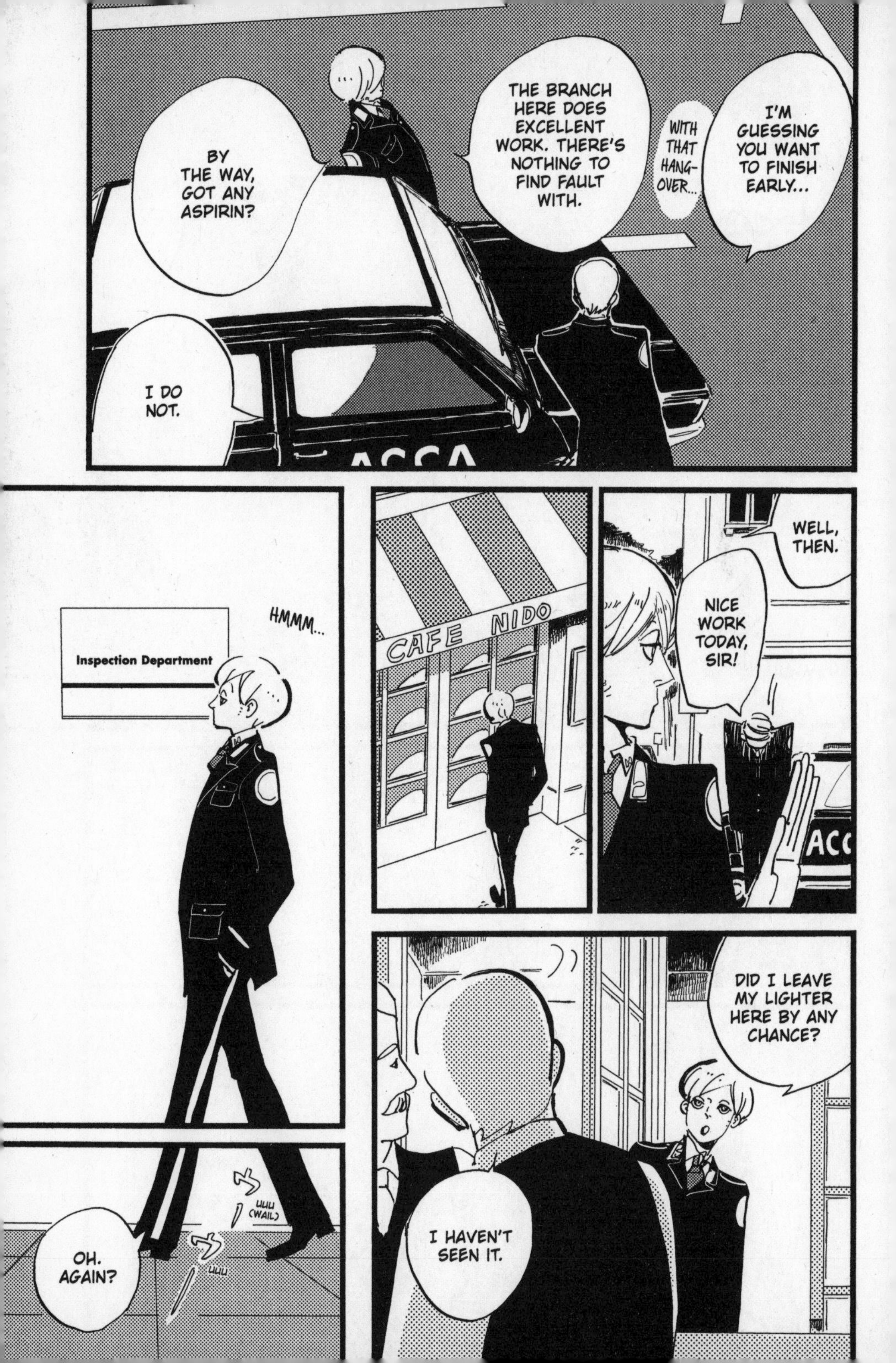
I'M GUESSING YOU WANT TO FINISH EARLY...
WITH THAT HANG-OVER...
THE BRANCH HERE DOES EXCELLENT WORK. THERE'S NOTHING TO FIND FAULT WITH.
...
BY THE WAY, GOT ANY ASPIRIN?
I DO NOT.
ACCA
WELL, THEN.
NICE WORK TODAY, SIR!
ACC
CAFE NIDO
HMMM...
Inspection Department
DID I LEAVE MY LIGHTER HERE BY ANY CHANCE?
I HAVEN'T SEEN IT.
UUU (WAIL)
UUU
OH. AGAIN?

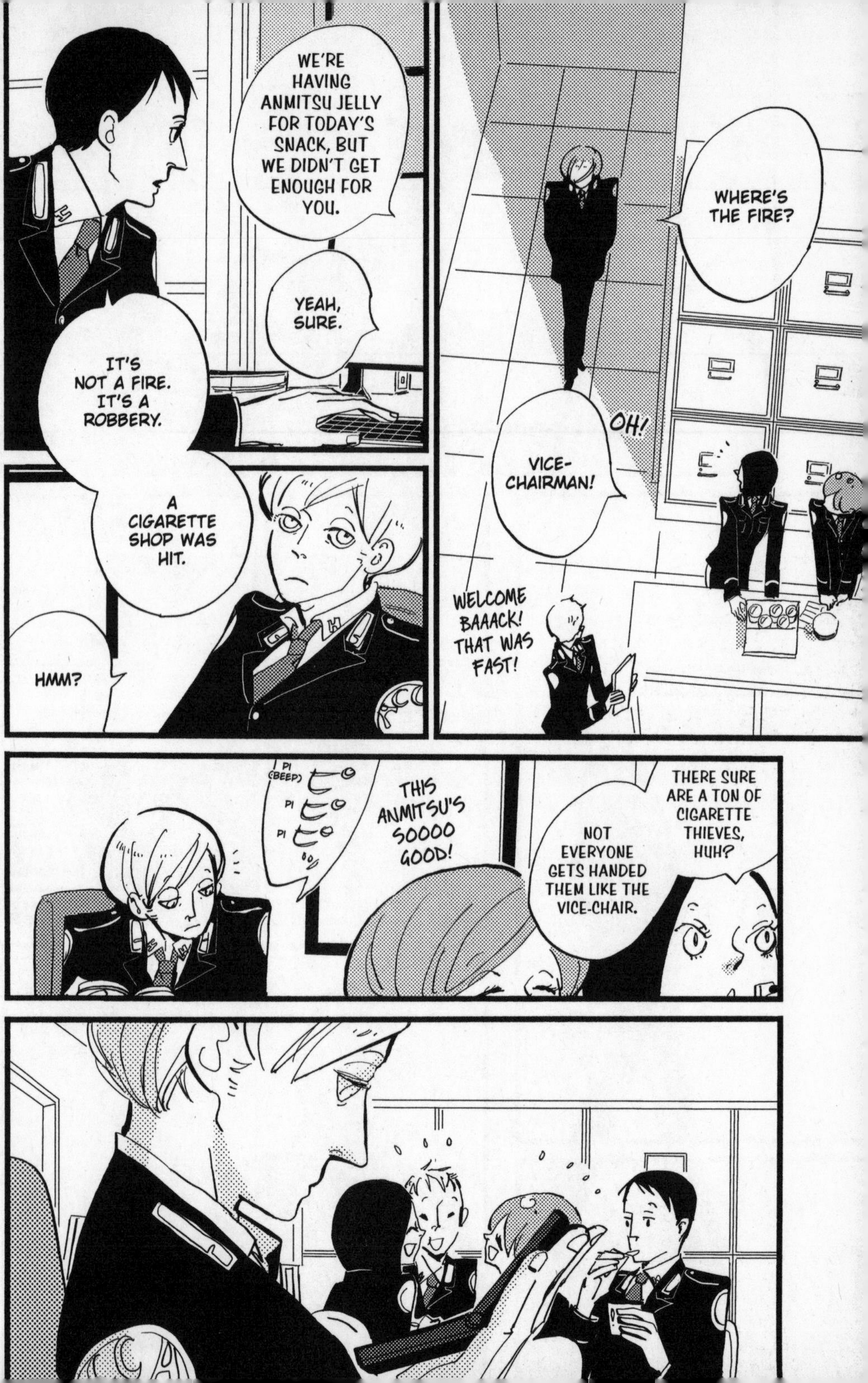

OH!
VICE-CHAIRMAN!
WELCOME BAAACK! THAT WAS FAST!
WHERE'S THE FIRE?
WE'RE HAVING ANMITSU JELLY FOR TODAY'S SNACK, BUT WE DIDN'T GET ENOUGH FOR YOU.
YEAH, SURE.
IT'S NOT A FIRE. IT'S A ROBBERY.
A CIGARETTE SHOP WAS HIT.
HMM?
THERE SURE ARE A TON OF CIGARETTE THIEVES, HUH?
NOT EVERYONE GETS HANDED THEM LIKE THE VICE-CHAIR.
THIS ANMITSU'S SOOOO GOOD!
PI (BEEP)
PI
PI

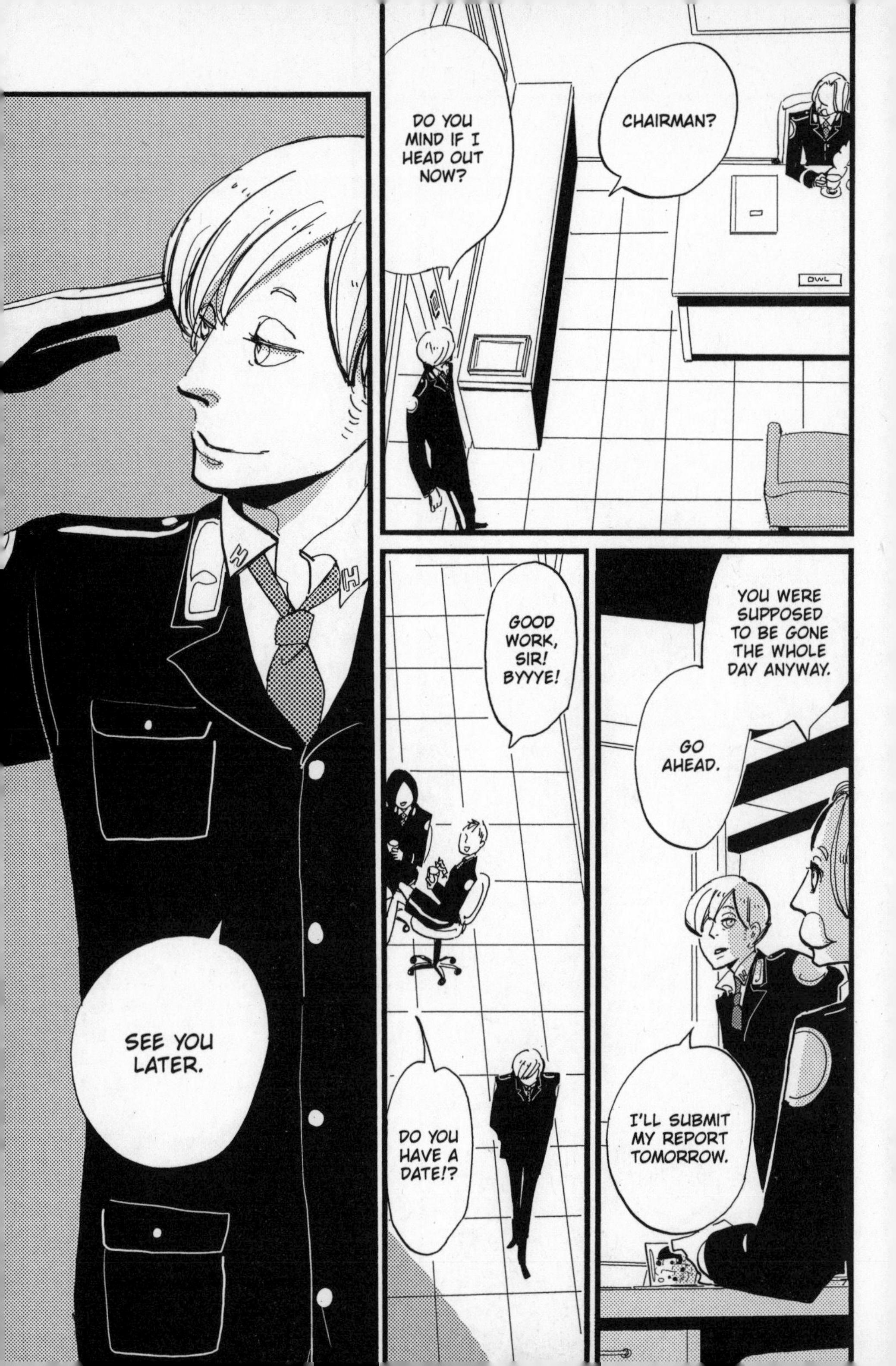
CHAIRMAN?
DO YOU MIND IF I HEAD OUT NOW?
OWL
YOU WERE SUPPOSED TO BE GONE THE WHOLE DAY ANYWAY.
GO AHEAD.
I'LL SUBMIT MY REPORT TOMORROW.
GOOD WORK, SIR! BYYYE!
DO YOU HAVE A DATE!?
SEE YOU LATER.

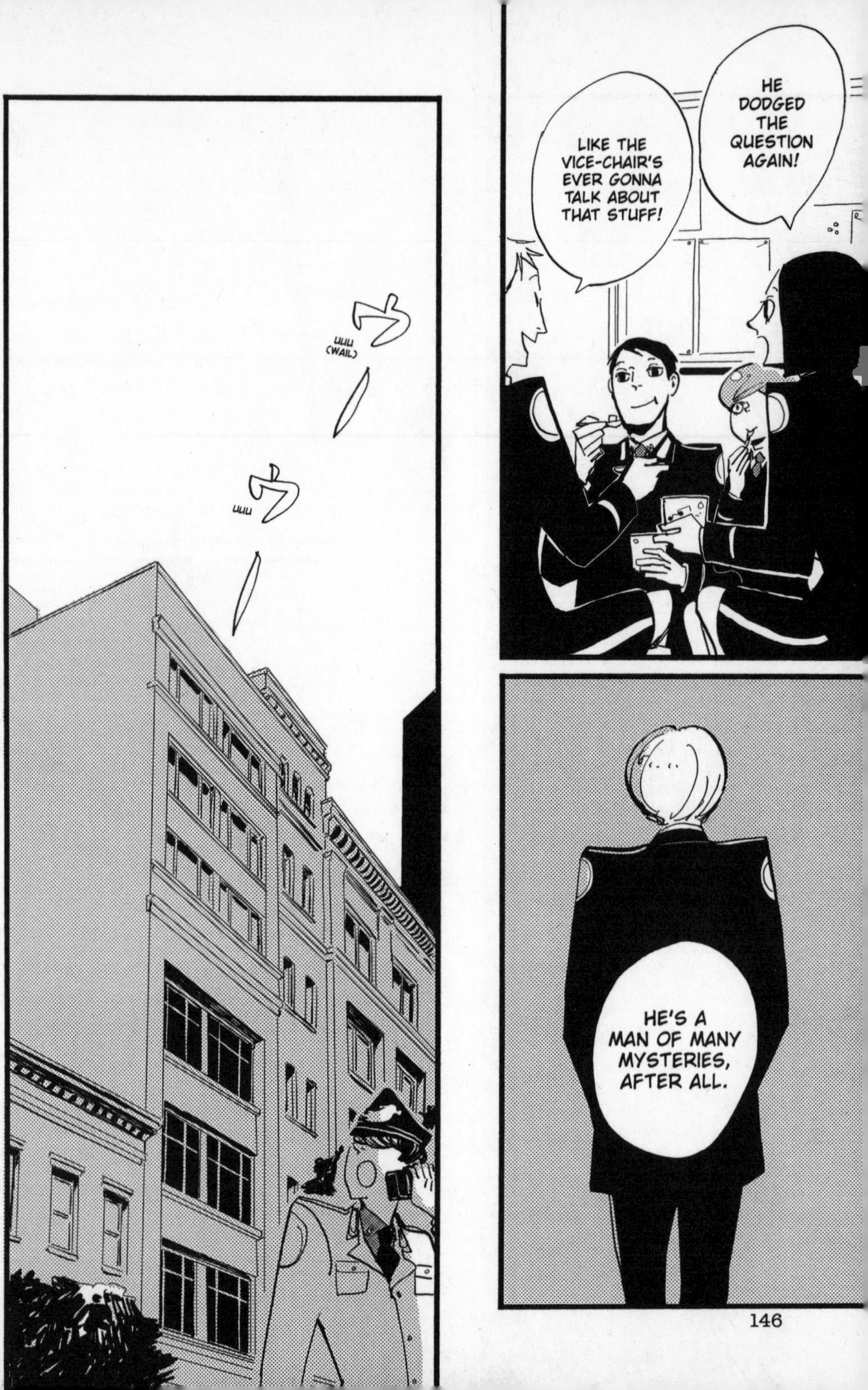
HE DODGED THE QUESTION AGAIN!
LIKE THE VICE-CHAIR'S EVER GONNA TALK ABOUT THAT STUFF!
HE'S A MAN OF MANY MYSTERIES, AFTER ALL.
UUU (WAIL)
UUU

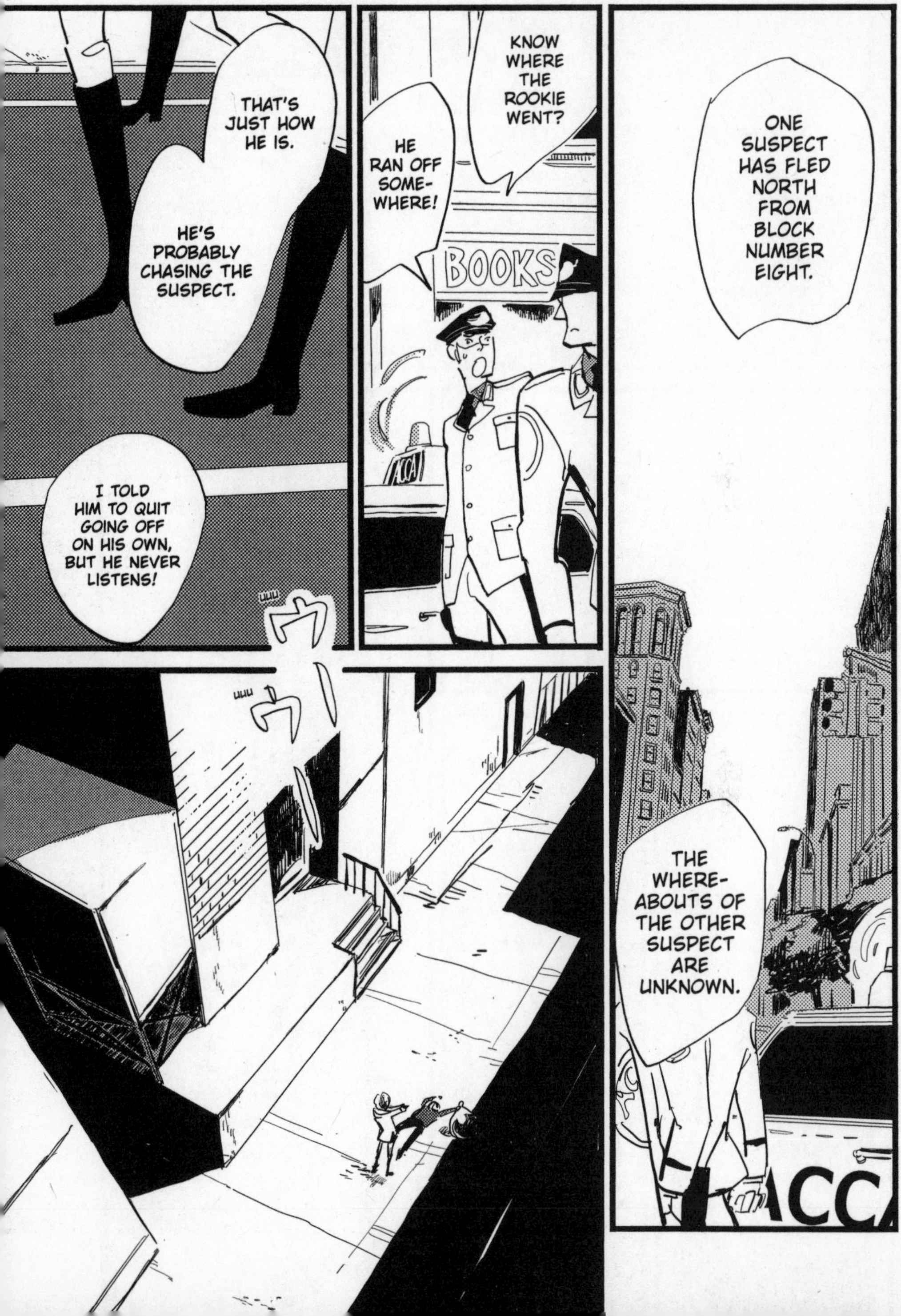
ONE SUSPECT HAS FLED NORTH FROM BLOCK NUMBER EIGHT.
THE WHERE-ABOUTS OF THE OTHER SUSPECT ARE UNKNOWN.
ACCA
KNOW WHERE THE ROOKIE WENT?
HE RAN OFF SOME-WHERE!
BOOKS
ACCA
THAT'S JUST HOW HE IS.
HE'S PROBABLY CHASING THE SUSPECT.
I TOLD HIM TO QUIT GOING OFF ON HIS OWN, BUT HE NEVER LISTENS!
UUU
ウー
UUU
ウー

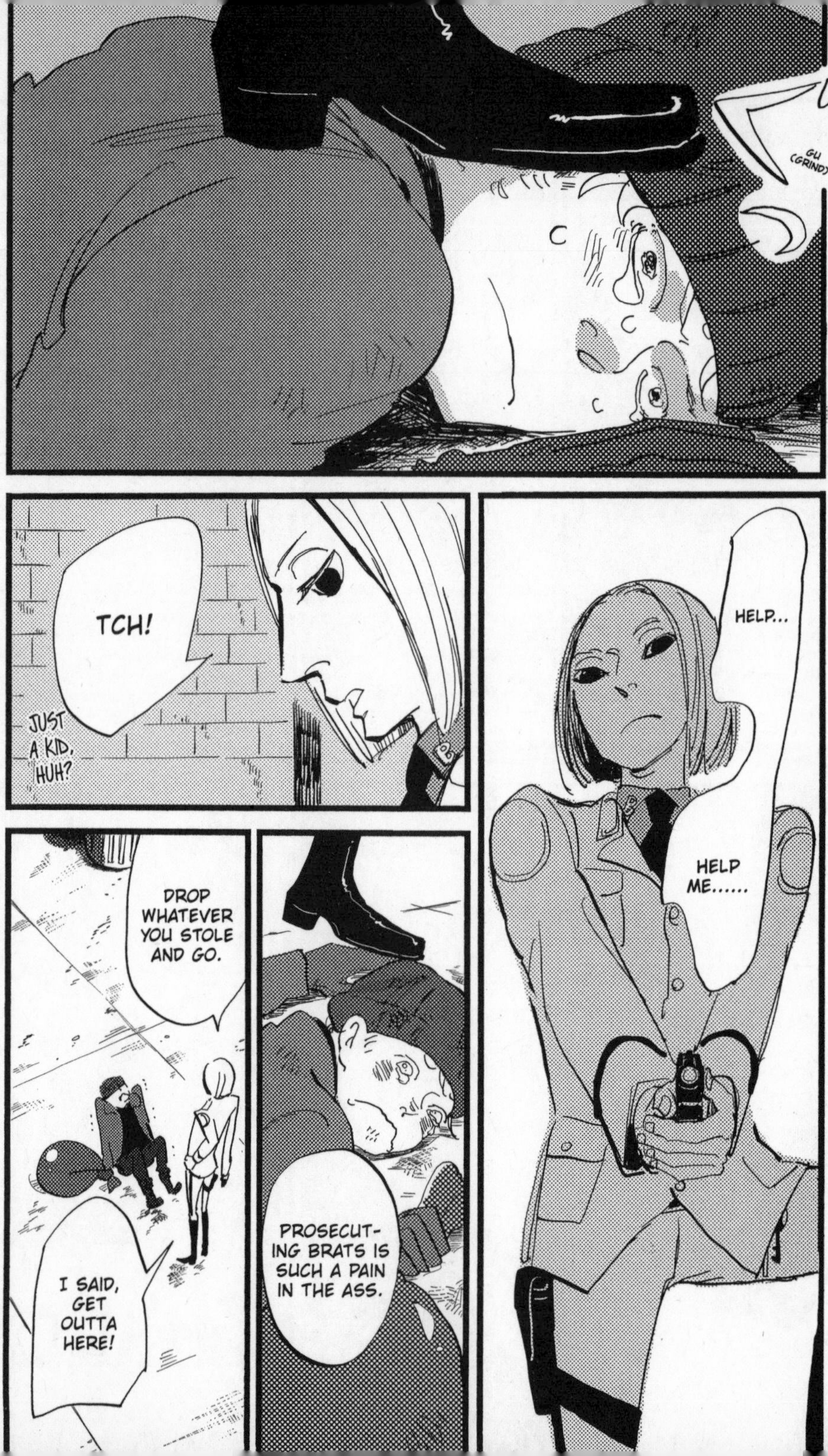
GU (GRIND)
HELP...
HELP ME......
TCH!
JUST A KID, HUH?
PROSECUT-ING BRATS IS SUCH A PAIN IN THE ASS.
DROP WHATEVER YOU STOLE AND GO.
I SAID, GET OUTTA HERE!

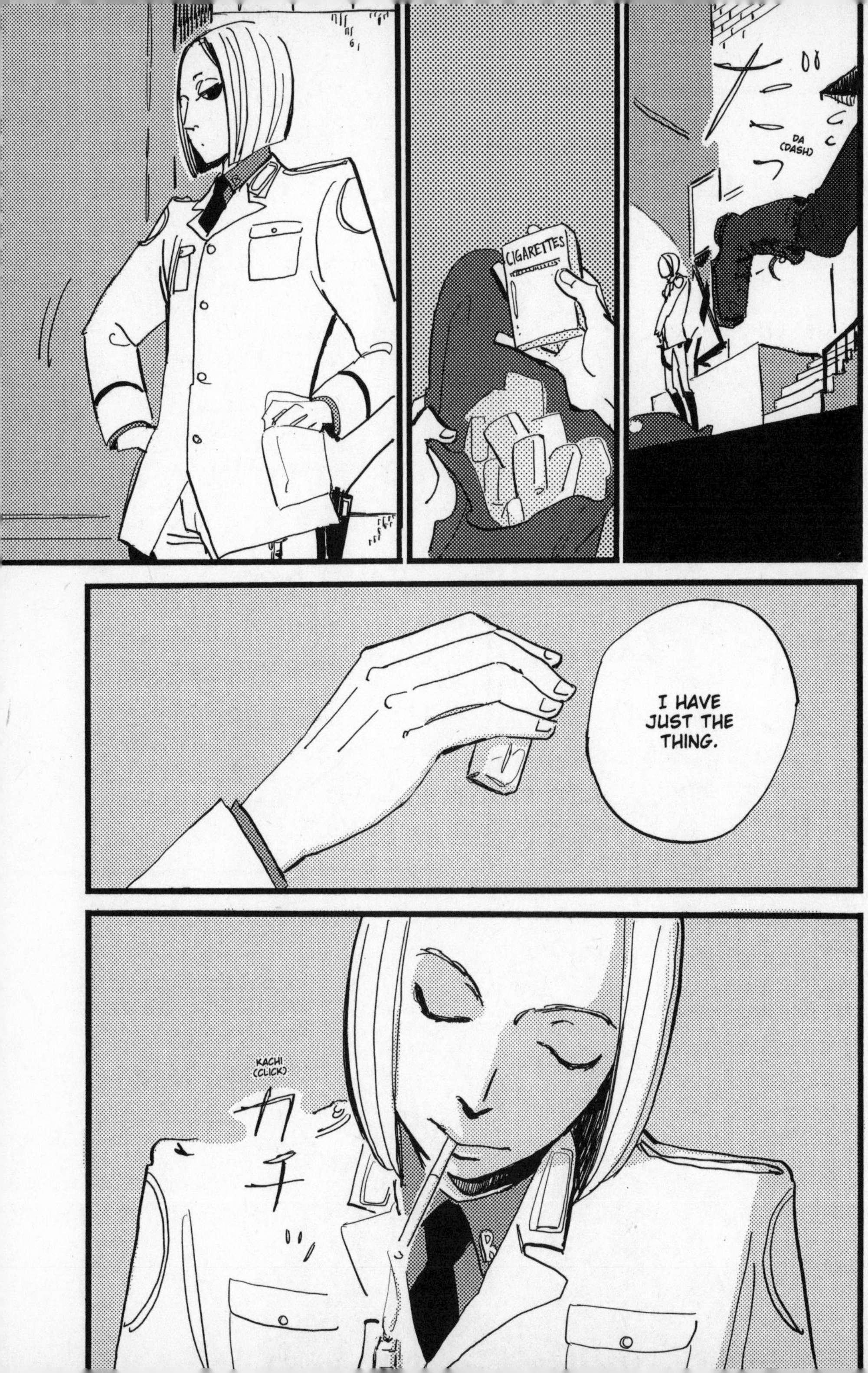
DA
(DASH)
CIGARETTES
I HAVE JUST THE THING.
KACHI
(CLICK)

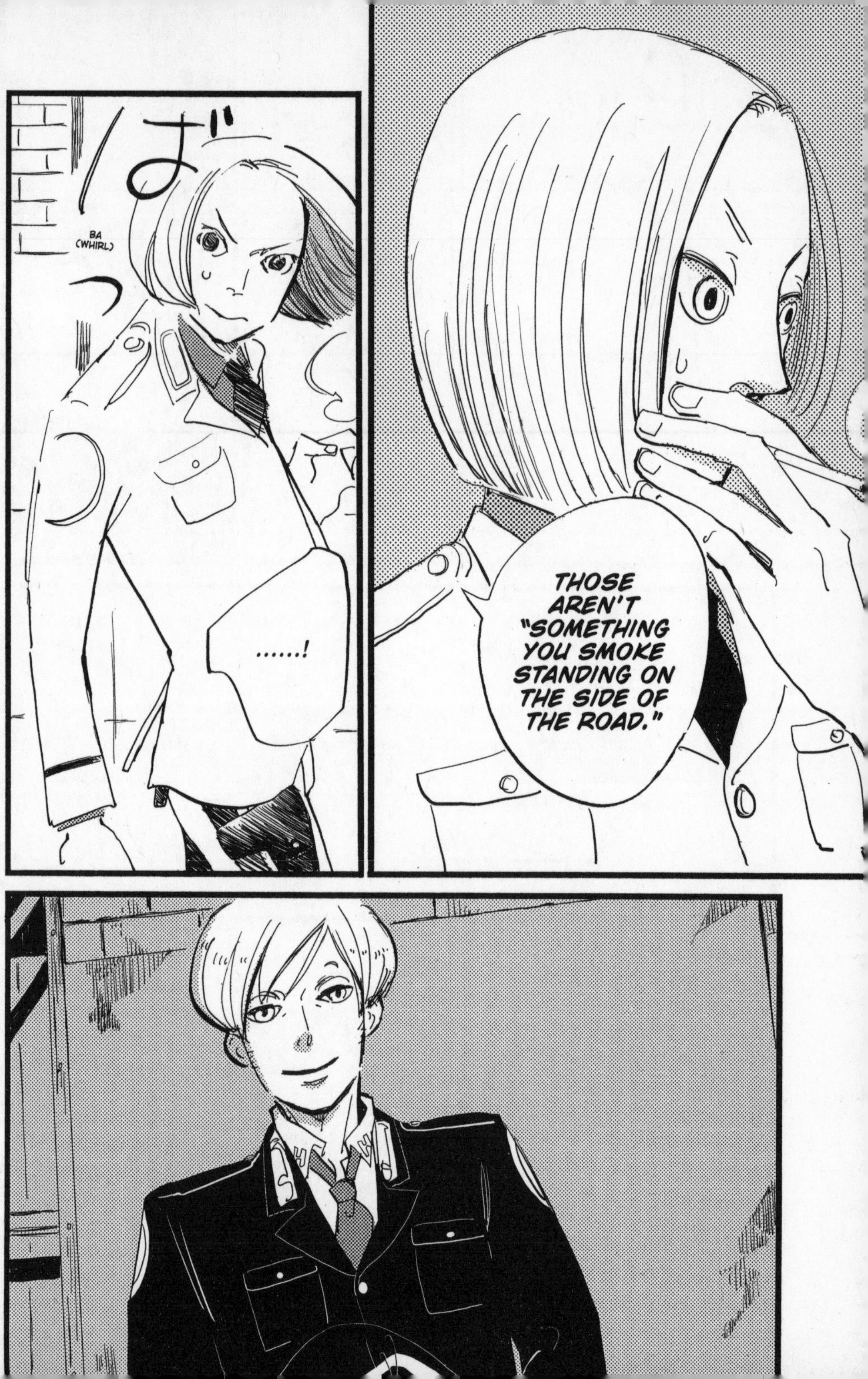
THOSE AREN'T "SOMETHING YOU SMOKE STANDING ON THE SIDE OF THE ROAD."
ばっ
BA (WHIRL)
......!

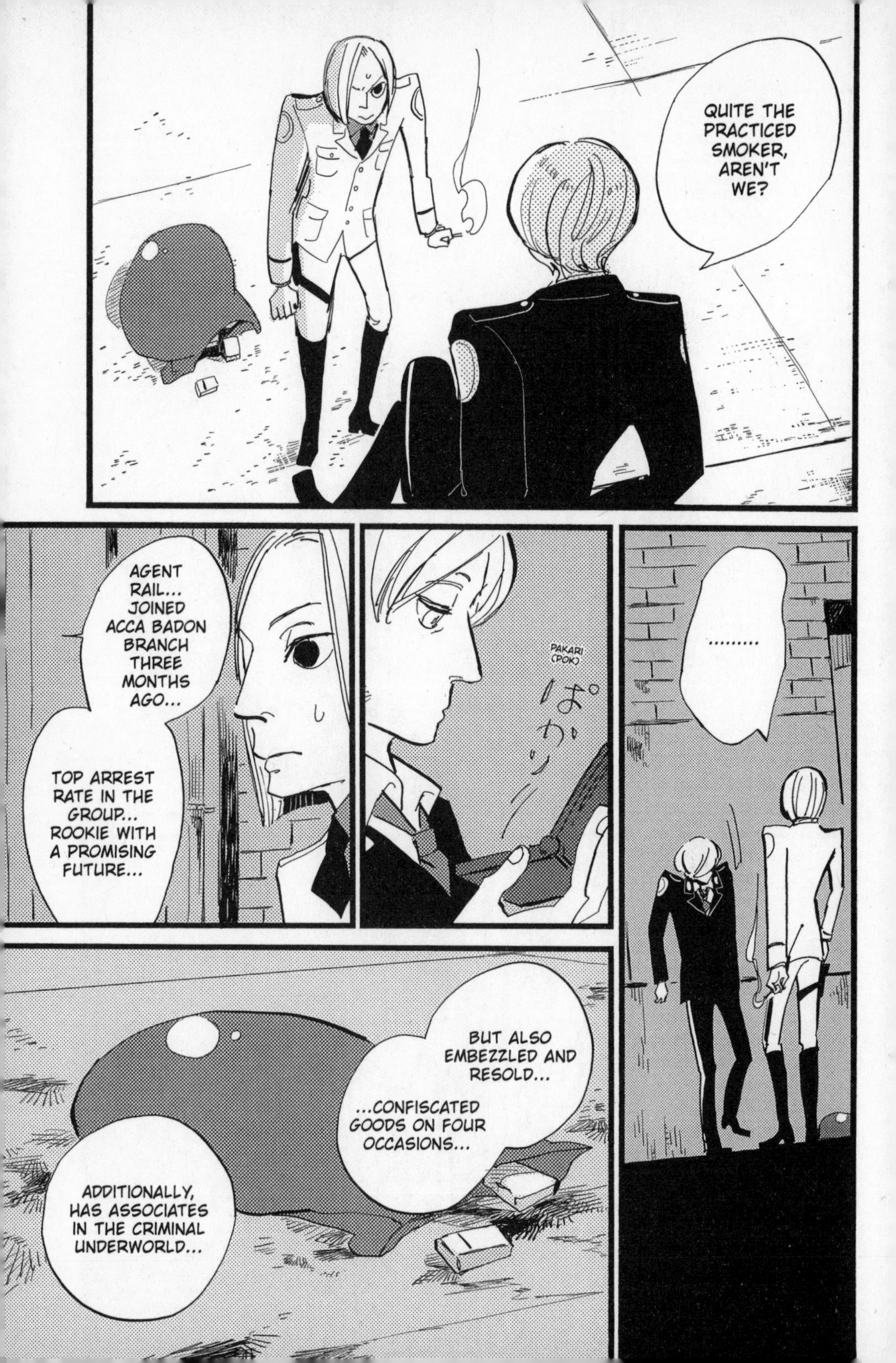
QUITE THE PRACTICED SMOKER, AREN'T WE?
....
PAKARI (POK)
AGENT RAIL... JOINED ACCA BADON BRANCH THREE MONTHS AGO...
TOP ARREST RATE IN THE GROUP... ROOKIE WITH A PROMISING FUTURE...
BUT ALSO EMBEZZLED AND RESOLD...
...CONFISCATED GOODS ON FOUR OCCASIONS...
ADDITIONALLY, HAS ASSOCIATES IN THE CRIMINAL UNDERWORLD...

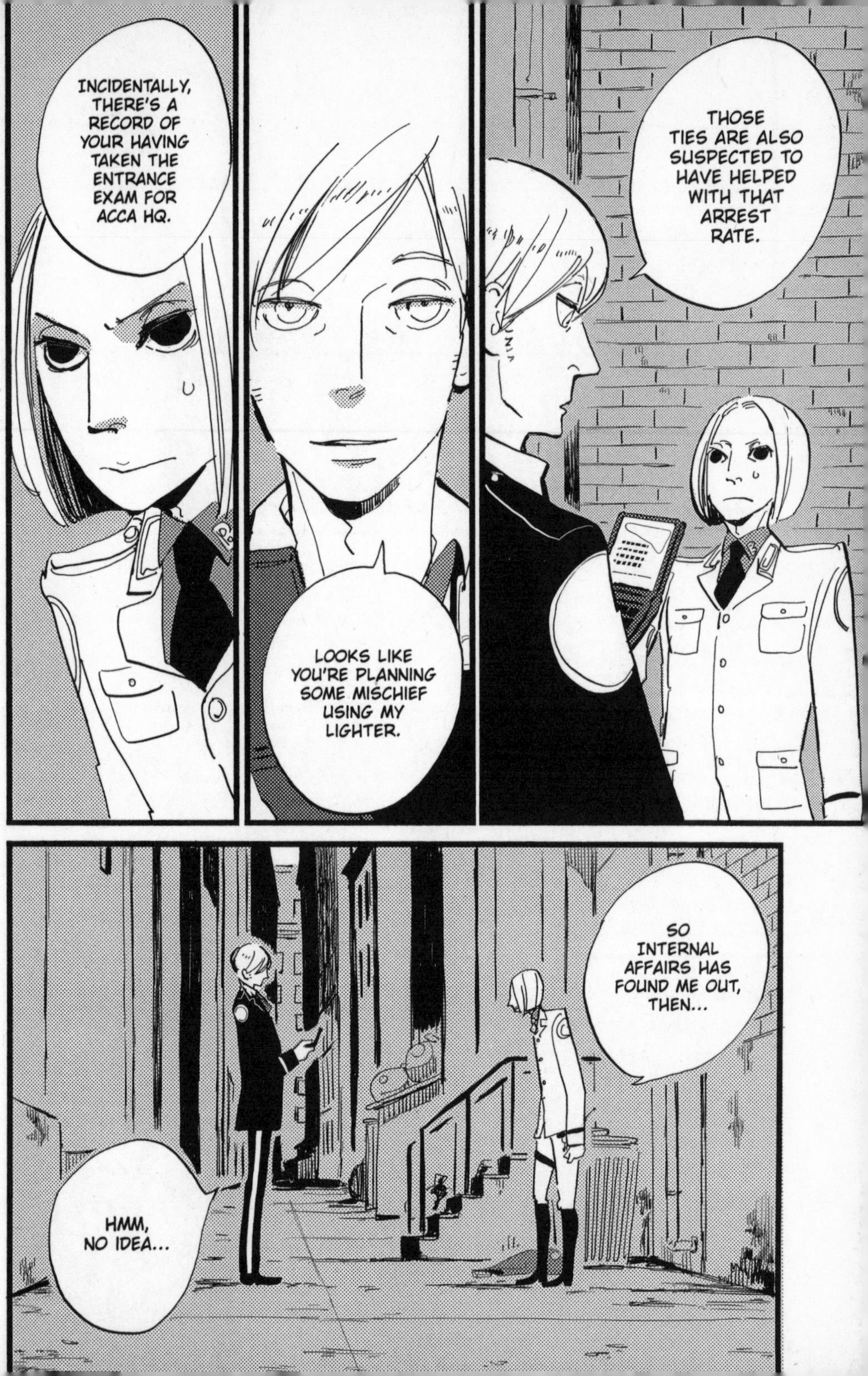
INCIDENTALLY, THERE'S A RECORD OF YOUR HAVING TAKEN THE ENTRANCE EXAM FOR ACCA HQ.
LOOKS LIKE YOU'RE PLANNING SOME MISCHIEF USING MY LIGHTER.
THOSE TIES ARE ALSO SUSPECTED TO HAVE HELPED WITH THAT ARREST RATE.
SO INTERNAL AFFAIRS HAS FOUND ME OUT, THEN...
HMM, NO IDEA...

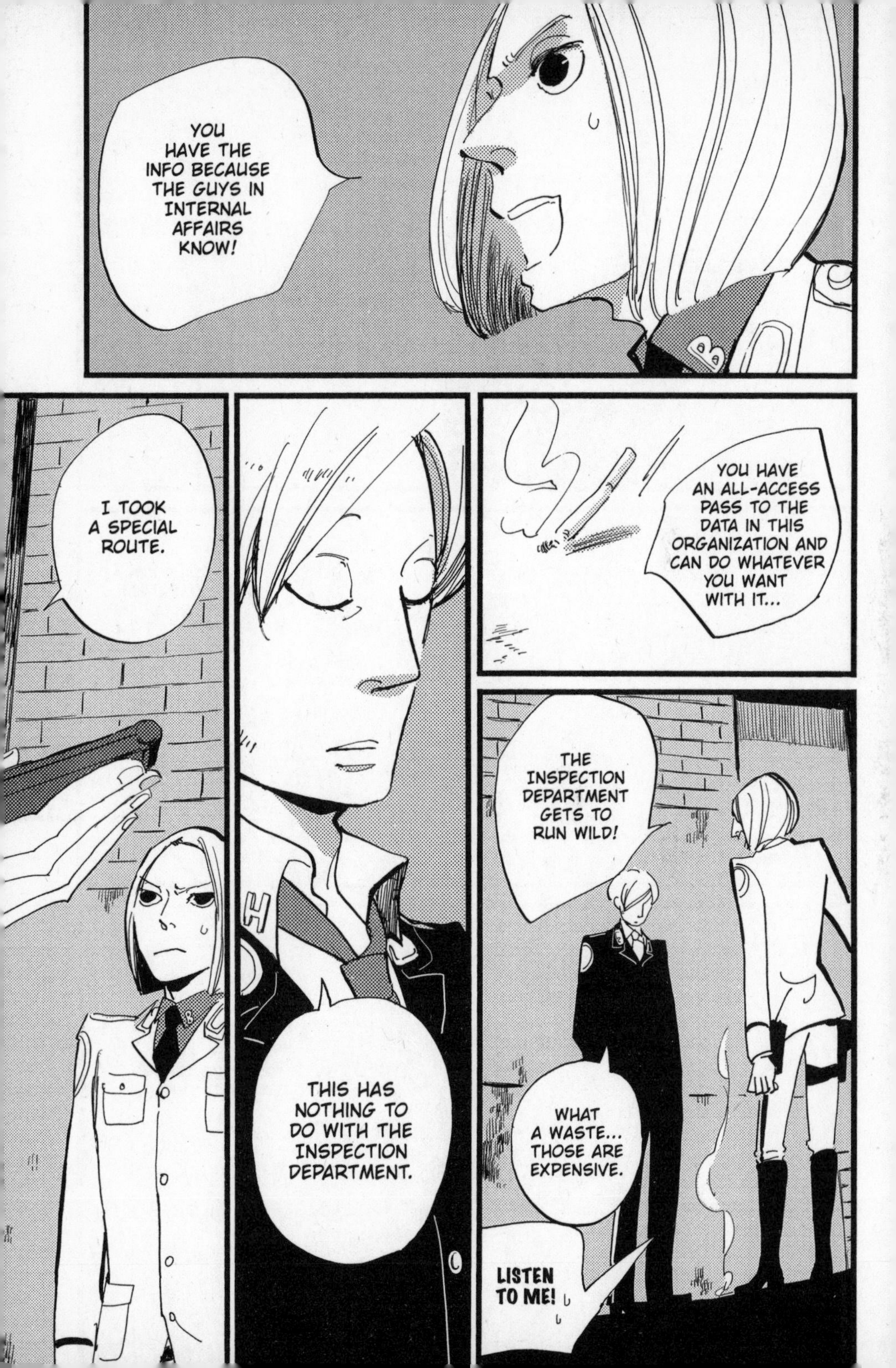
YOU HAVE THE INFO BECAUSE THE GUYS IN INTERNAL AFFAIRS KNOW!
YOU HAVE AN ALL-ACCESS PASS TO THE DATA IN THIS ORGANIZATION AND CAN DO WHATEVER YOU WANT WITH IT...
I TOOK A SPECIAL ROUTE.
THE INSPECTION DEPARTMENT GETS TO RUN WILD!
THIS HAS NOTHING TO DO WITH THE INSPECTION DEPARTMENT.
WHAT A WASTE... THOSE ARE EXPENSIVE.
LISTEN TO ME!

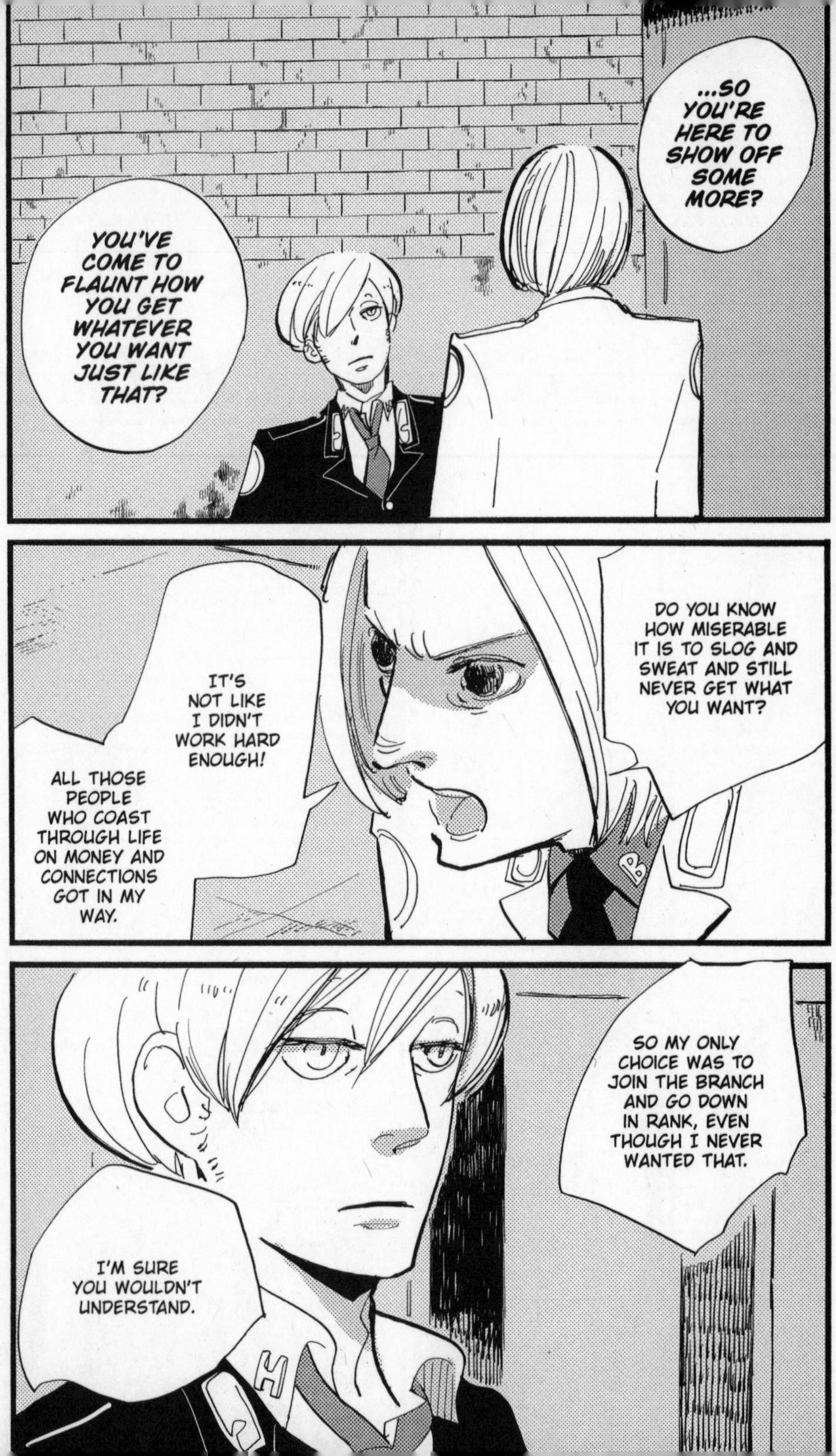
...SO YOU'RE HERE TO SHOW OFF SOME MORE?
YOU'VE COME TO FLAUNT HOW YOU GET WHATEVER YOU WANT JUST LIKE THAT?
DO YOU KNOW HOW MISERABLE IT IS TO SLOG AND SWEAT AND STILL NEVER GET WHAT YOU WANT?
IT'S NOT LIKE I DIDN'T WORK HARD ENOUGH!
ALL THOSE PEOPLE WHO COAST THROUGH LIFE ON MONEY AND CONNECTIONS GOT IN MY WAY.
SO MY ONLY CHOICE WAS TO JOIN THE BRANCH AND GO DOWN IN RANK, EVEN THOUGH I NEVER WANTED THAT.
I'M SURE YOU WOULDN'T UNDERSTAND.

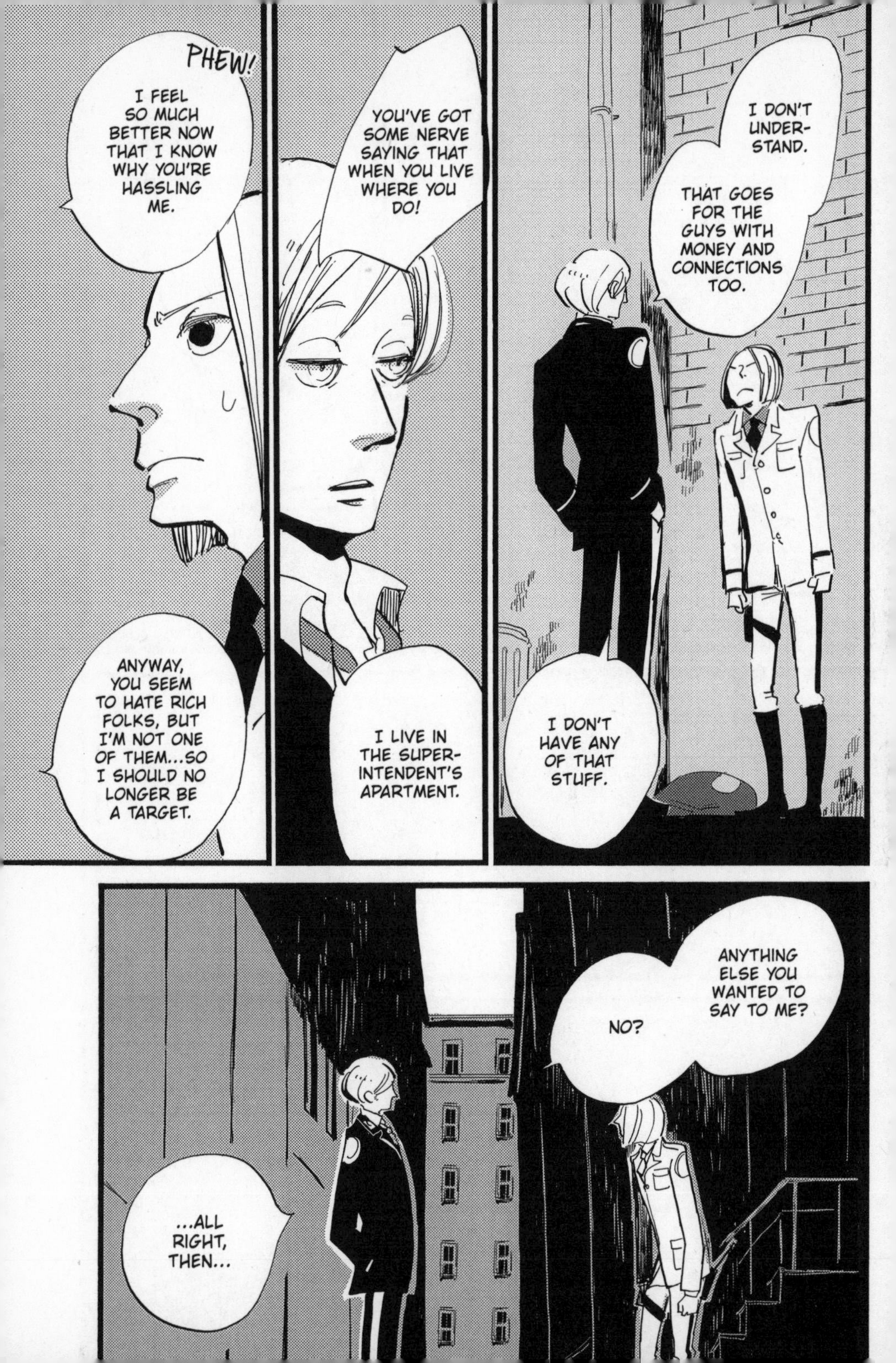
I DON'T UNDER-STAND.
THAT GOES FOR THE GUYS WITH MONEY AND CONNECTIONS TOO.
I DON'T HAVE ANY OF THAT STUFF.
YOU'VE GOT SOME NERVE SAYING THAT WHEN YOU LIVE WHERE YOU DO!
I LIVE IN THE SUPER-INTENDENT'S APARTMENT.
PHEW!
I FEEL SO MUCH BETTER NOW THAT I KNOW WHY YOU'RE HASSLING ME.
ANYWAY, YOU SEEM TO HATE RICH FOLKS, BUT I'M NOT ONE OF THEM...SO I SHOULD NO LONGER BE A TARGET.
ANYTHING ELSE YOU WANTED TO SAY TO ME?
NO?
...ALL RIGHT, THEN...

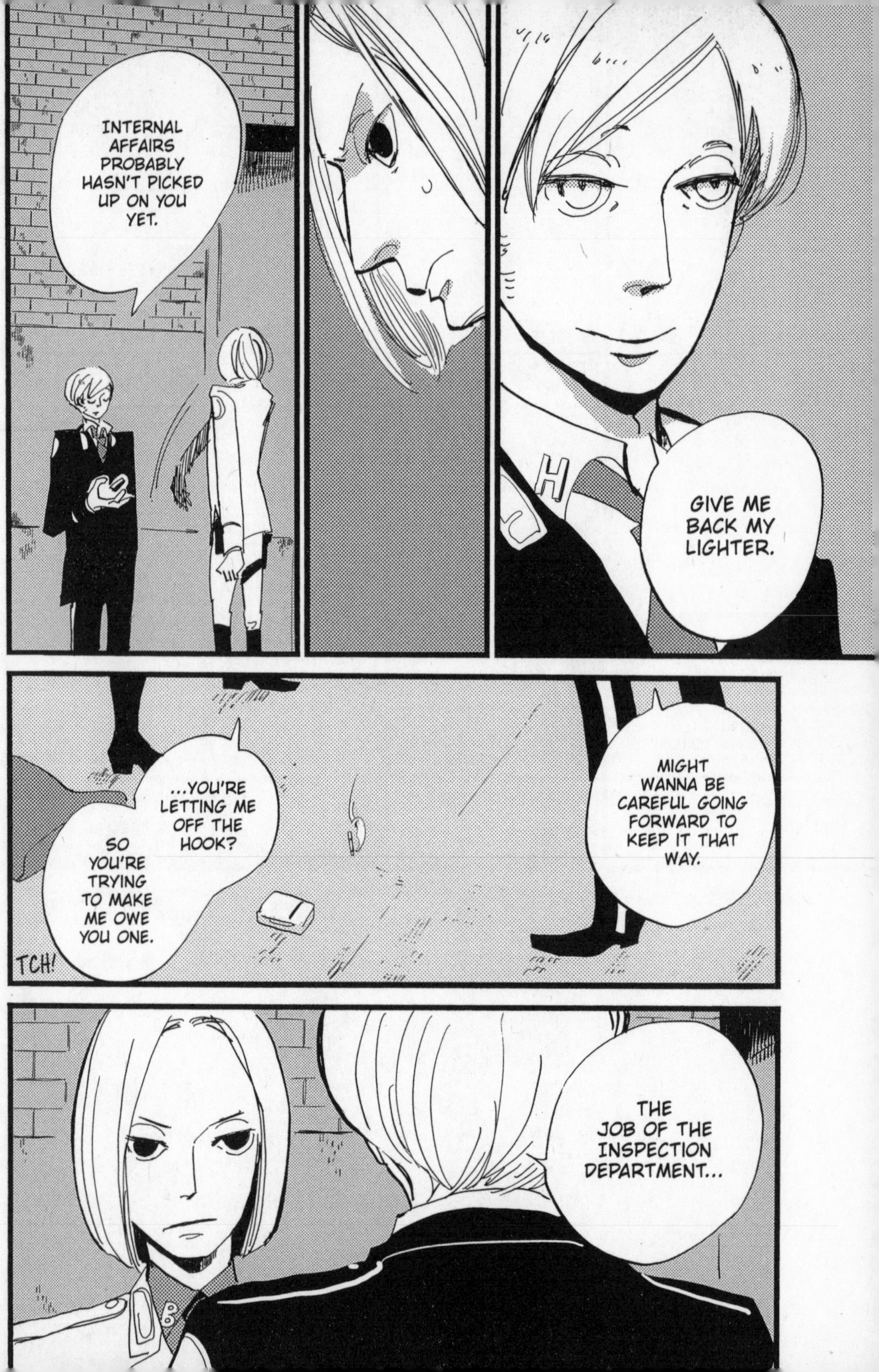
GIVE ME BACK MY LIGHTER.
INTERNAL AFFAIRS PROBABLY HASN'T PICKED UP ON YOU YET.
MIGHT WANNA BE CAREFUL GOING FORWARD TO KEEP IT THAT WAY.
...YOU'RE LETTING ME OFF THE HOOK?
SO YOU'RE TRYING TO MAKE ME OWE YOU ONE.
TCH!
THE JOB OF THE INSPECTION DEPARTMENT...

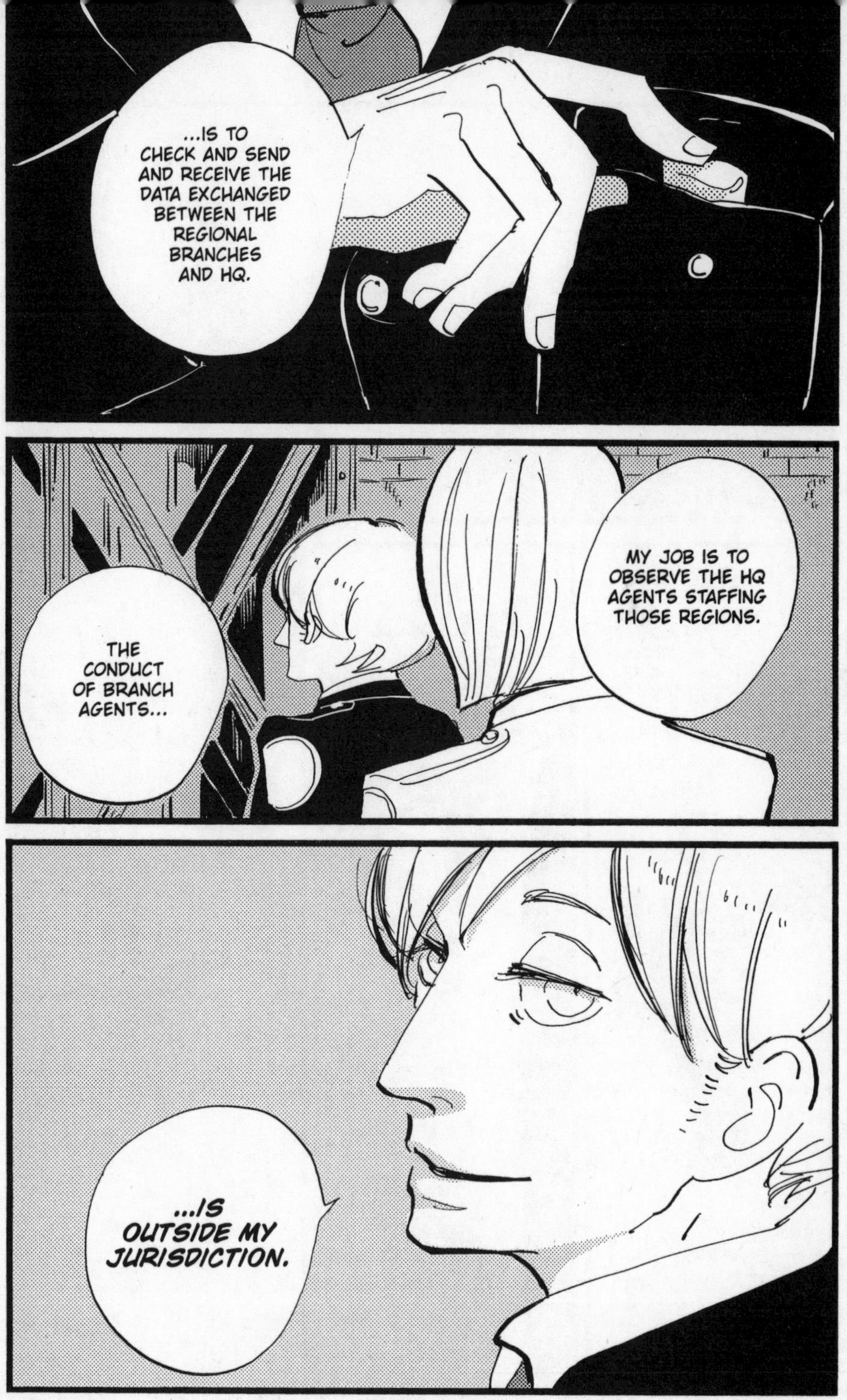
...IS TO CHECK AND SEND AND RECEIVE THE DATA EXCHANGED BETWEEN THE REGIONAL BRANCHES AND HQ.
MY JOB IS TO OBSERVE THE HQ AGENTS STAFFING THOSE REGIONS.
THE CONDUCT OF BRANCH AGENTS...
...IS OUTSIDE MY JURISDICTION.

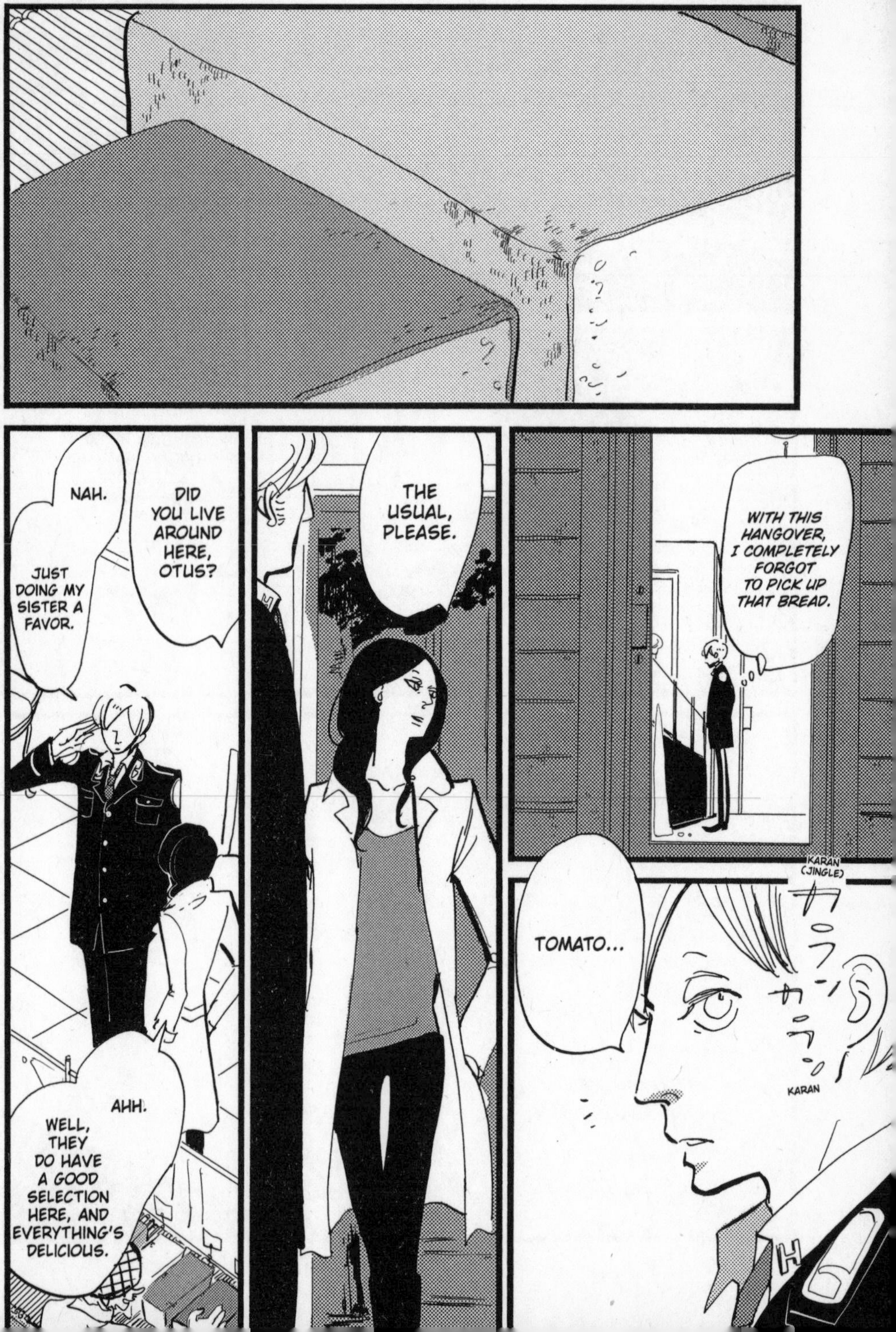
WITH THIS HANGOVER, I COMPLETELY FORGOT TO PICK UP THAT BREAD.
KARAN (JINGLE)
KARAN
TOMATO...
THE USUAL, PLEASE.
DID YOU LIVE AROUND HERE, OTUS?
NAH.
JUST DOING MY SISTER A FAVOR.
AHH.
WELL, THEY DO HAVE A GOOD SELECTION HERE, AND EVERYTHING'S DELICIOUS.

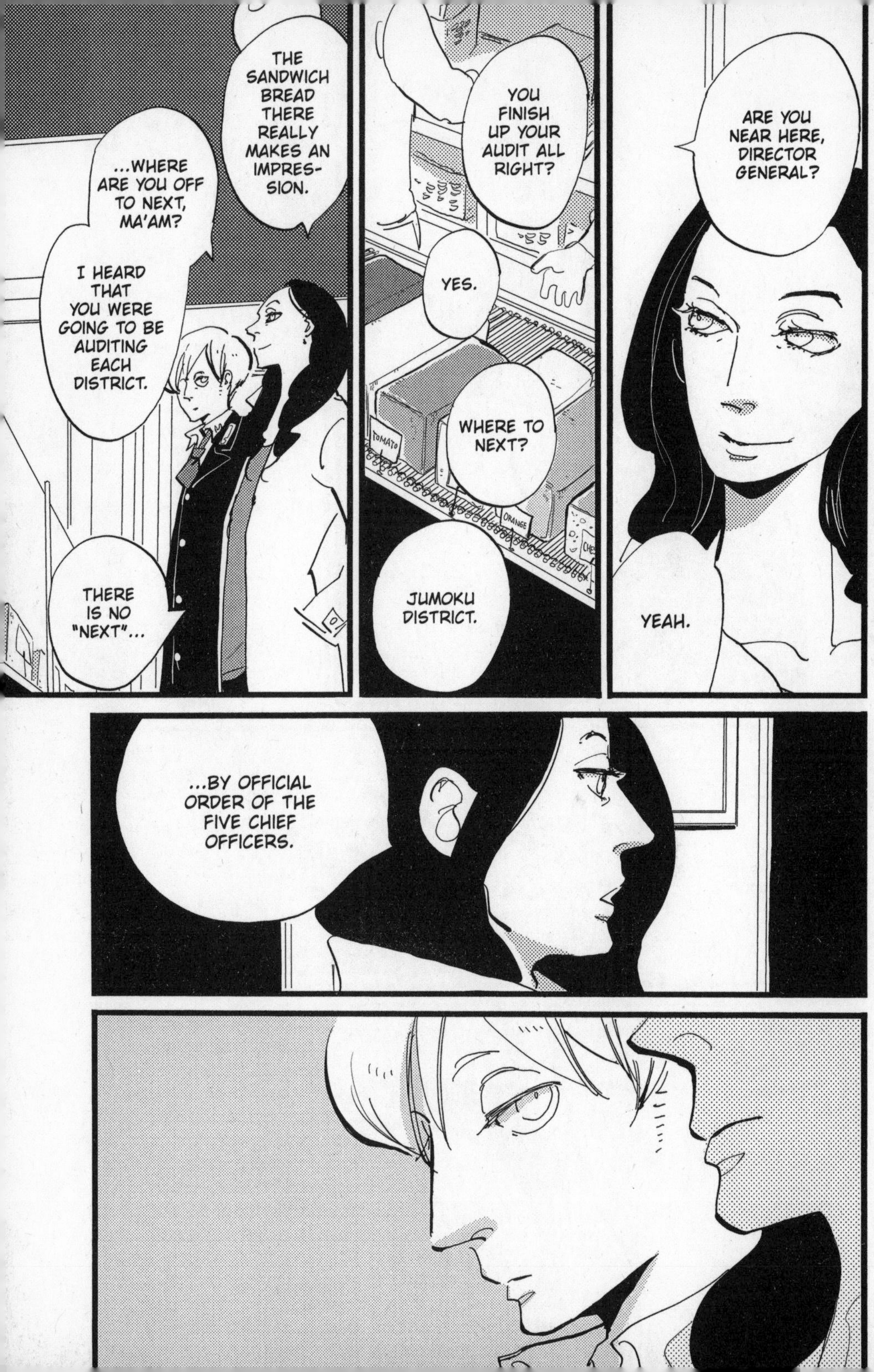
ARE YOU NEAR HERE, DIRECTOR GENERAL?
YEAH.
YOU FINISH UP YOUR AUDIT ALL RIGHT?
YES.
WHERE TO NEXT?
JUMOKU DISTRICT.
TOMATO
ORANGE
THE SANDWICH BREAD THERE REALLY MAKES AN IMPRES-SION.
...WHERE ARE YOU OFF TO NEXT, MA'AM?
I HEARD THAT YOU WERE GOING TO BE AUDITING EACH DISTRICT.
THERE IS NO "NEXT"...
...BY OFFICIAL ORDER OF THE FIVE CHIEF OFFICERS.

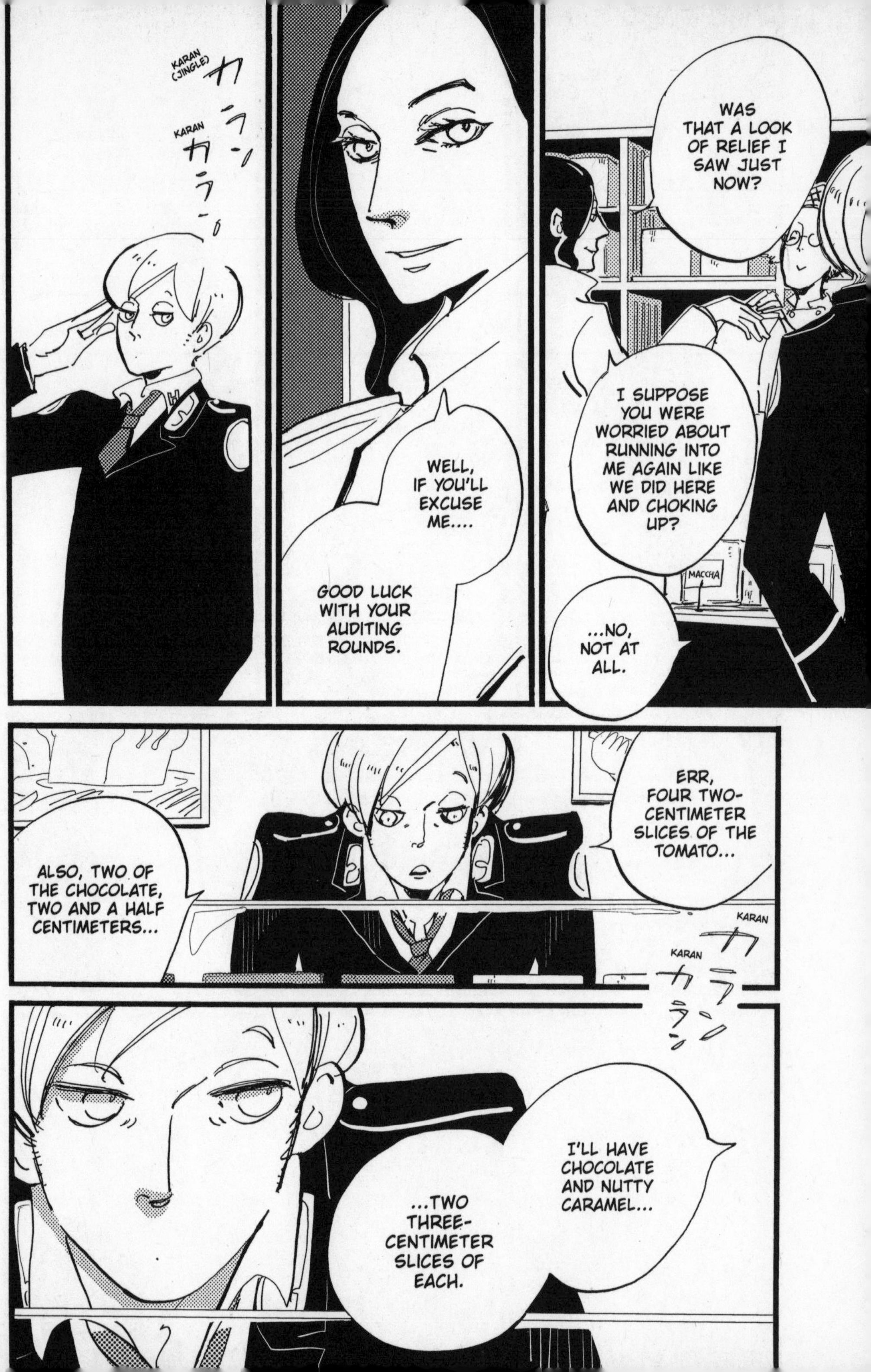
WAS THAT A LOOK OF RELIEF I SAW JUST NOW?
I SUPPOSE YOU WERE WORRIED ABOUT RUNNING INTO ME AGAIN LIKE WE DID HERE AND CHOKING UP?
MACCHA
...NO, NOT AT ALL.
WELL, IF YOU'LL EXCUSE ME....
GOOD LUCK WITH YOUR AUDITING ROUNDS.
KARAN (JINGLE)
カラン
KARAN
カラン
ERR, FOUR TWO-CENTIMETER SLICES OF THE TOMATO...
ALSO, TWO OF THE CHOCOLATE, TWO AND A HALF CENTIMETERS...
KARAN
カラン
KARAN
カラン
I'LL HAVE CHOCOLATE AND NUTTY CARAMEL...
...TWO THREE-CENTIMETER SLICES OF EACH.

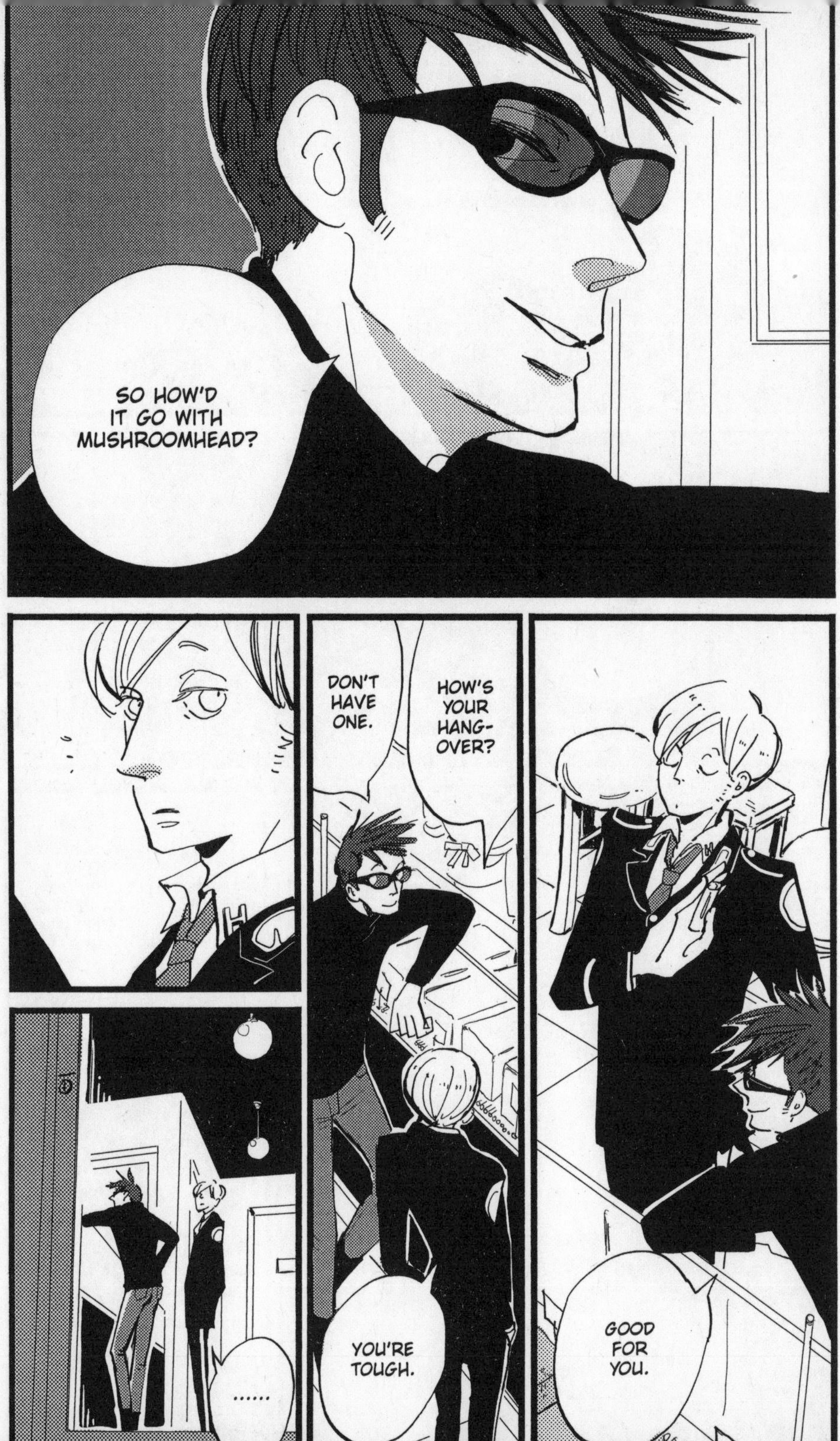
SO HOW'D IT GO WITH MUSHROOMHEAD?
HOW'S YOUR HANG-OVER?
DON'T HAVE ONE.
GOOD FOR YOU.
YOU'RE TOUGH.
......

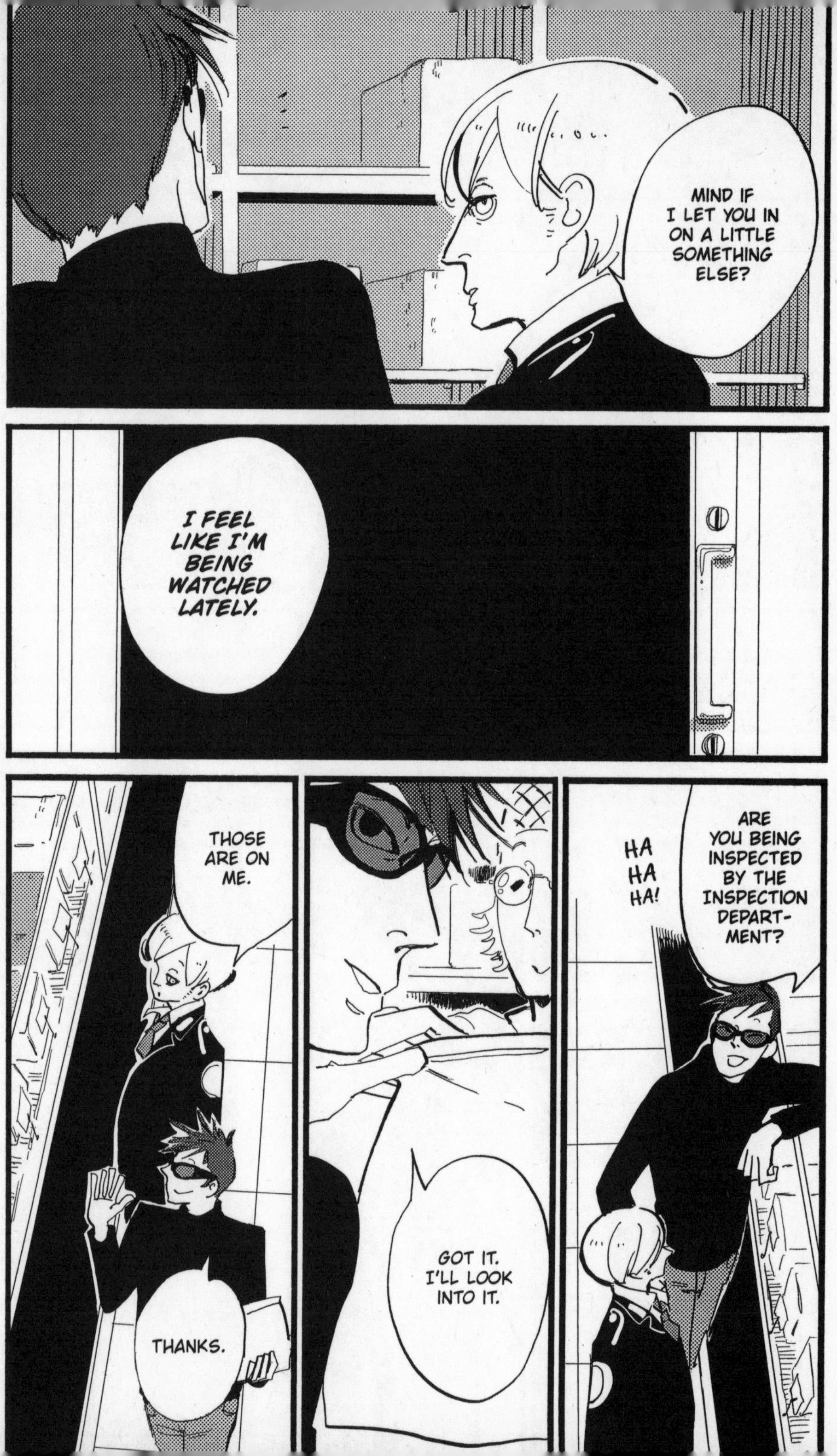
MIND IF I LET YOU IN ON A LITTLE SOMETHING ELSE?
I FEEL LIKE I'M BEING WATCHED LATELY.
ARE YOU BEING INSPECTED BY THE INSPECTION DEPARTMENT?
HA HA HA!
GOT IT. I'LL LOOK INTO IT.
THOSE ARE ON ME.
THANKS.

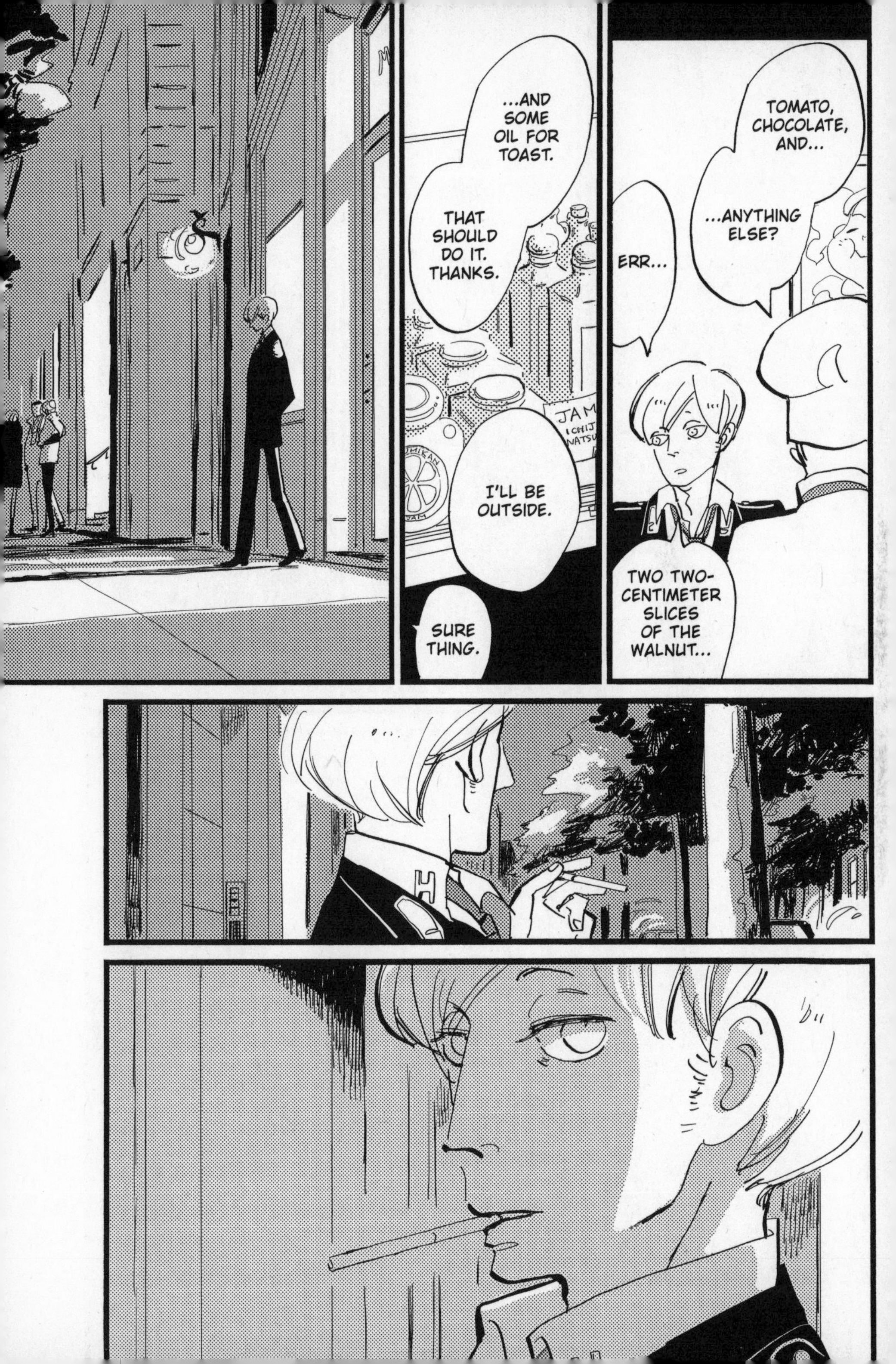
TOMATO, CHOCOLATE, AND...
...ANYTHING ELSE?
ERR...
TWO TWO-CENTIMETER SLICES OF THE WALNUT...
...AND SOME OIL FOR TOAST.
THAT SHOULD DO IT. THANKS.
I'LL BE OUTSIDE.
SURE THING.
JAM
...

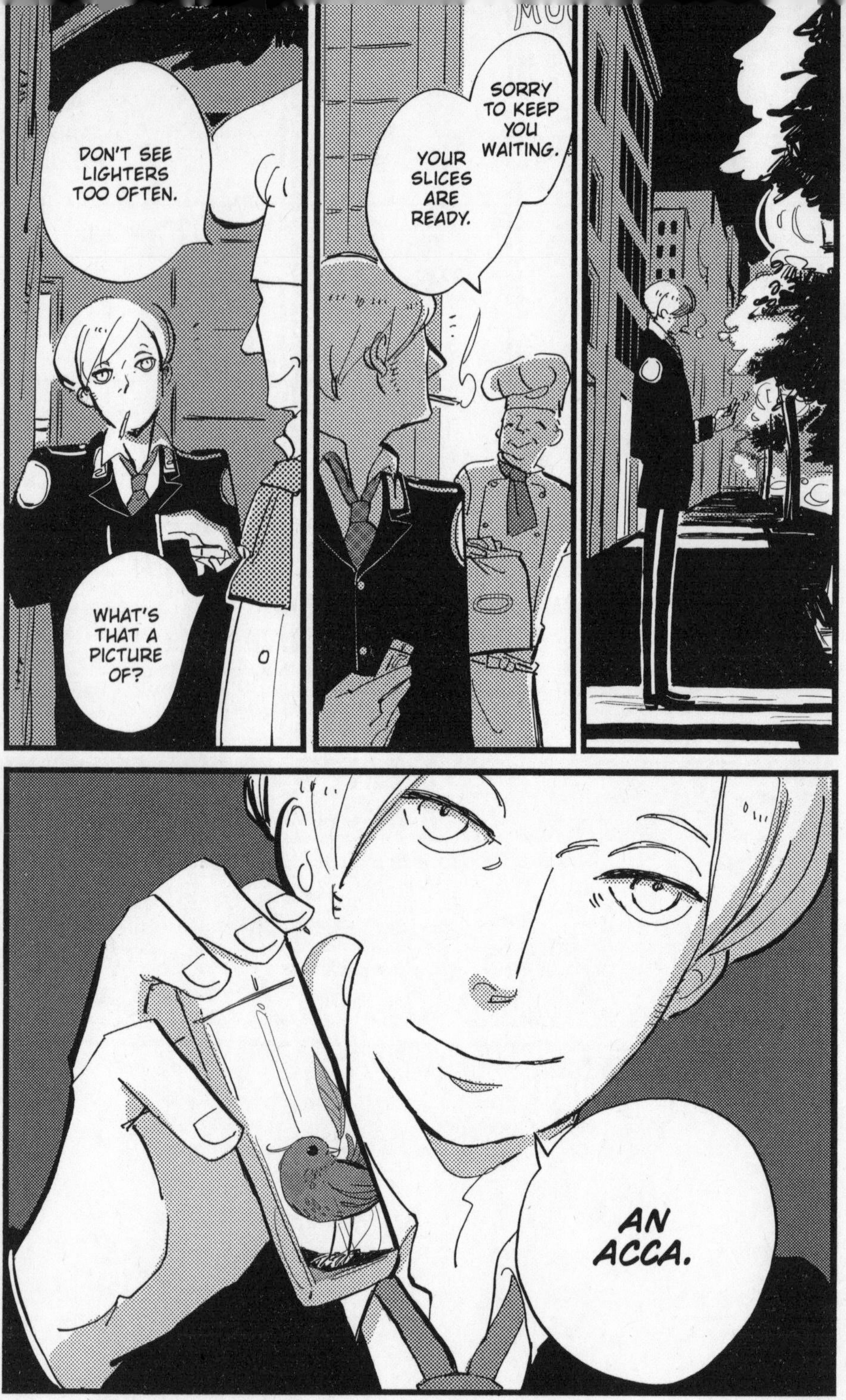
DON'T SEE LIGHTERS TOO OFTEN.
WHAT'S THAT A PICTURE OF?
SORRY TO KEEP YOU WAITING.
YOUR SLICES ARE READY.
AN ACCA.

ACCA Branch Uniforms 2

Badon (Capital) District

The Badon Branch is located right next to ACCA HQ in the capital. In contrast with the black uniforms of HQ, this branch is known for the urban look of its white uniforms. The police wear knee-high boots.

CHAPTER 4

Lighter Thief in Badon

PASS
INSPECTION DEPT. ACCA 13 TERRITORY

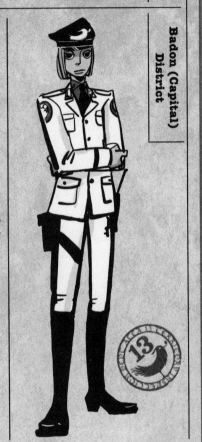

CHAPTER 5
Famed Smoker
in Badon

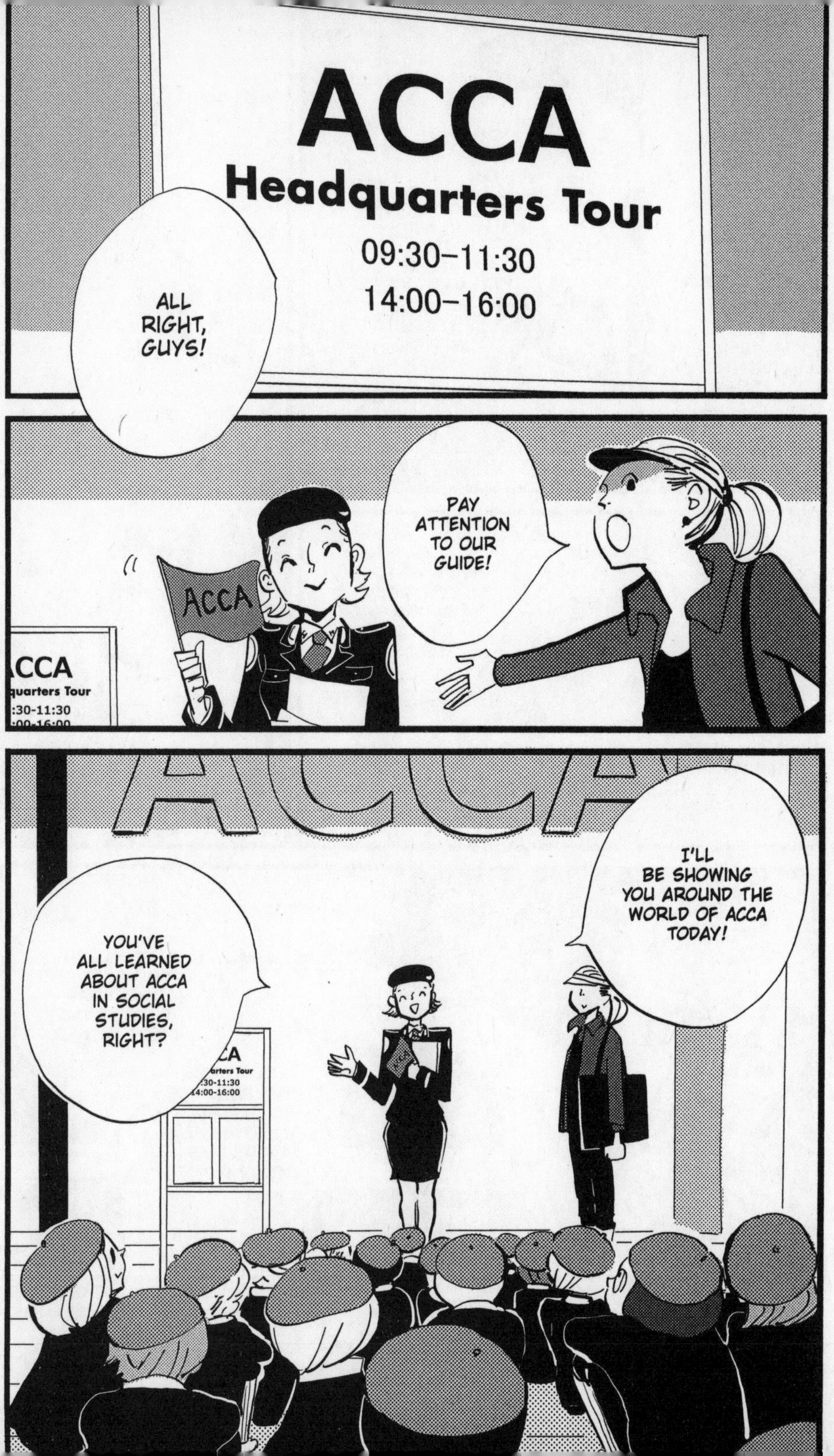
ACCA
Headquarters Tour
09:30–11:30
14:00–16:00
ALL RIGHT, GUYS!
PAY ATTENTION TO OUR GUIDE!
ACCA
ACCA
Headquarters Tour
ACCA
I'LL BE SHOWING YOU AROUND THE WORLD OF ACCA TODAY!
YOU'VE ALL LEARNED ABOUT ACCA IN SOCIAL STUDIES, RIGHT?

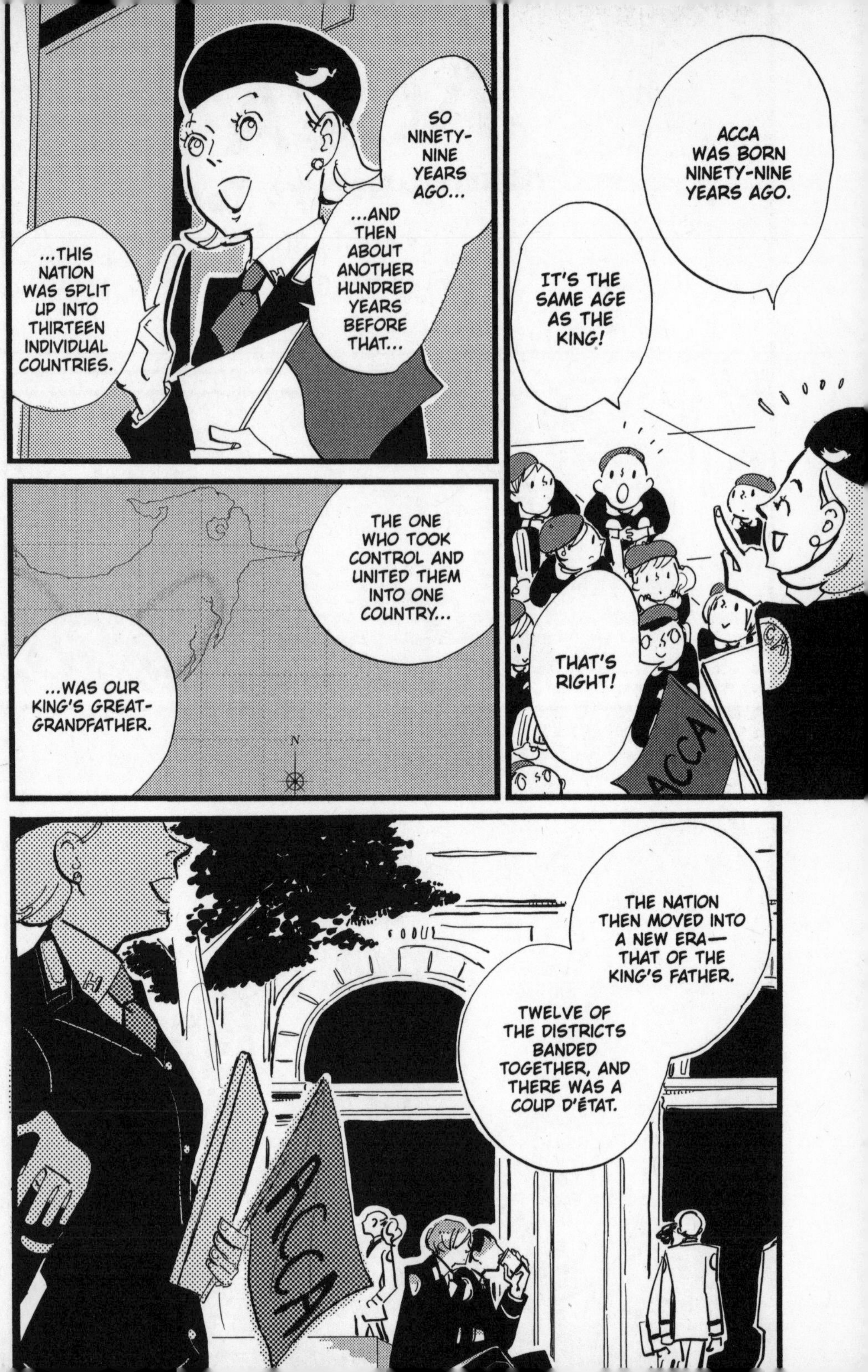
ACCA WAS BORN NINETY-NINE YEARS AGO.
IT'S THE SAME AGE AS THE KING!
THAT'S RIGHT!
SO NINETY-NINE YEARS AGO...
...AND THEN ABOUT ANOTHER HUNDRED YEARS BEFORE THAT...
...THIS NATION WAS SPLIT UP INTO THIRTEEN INDIVIDUAL COUNTRIES.
THE ONE WHO TOOK CONTROL AND UNITED THEM INTO ONE COUNTRY...
...WAS OUR KING'S GREAT-GRANDFATHER.
N
ACCA
THE NATION THEN MOVED INTO A NEW ERA—THAT OF THE KING'S FATHER.
TWELVE OF THE DISTRICTS BANDED TOGETHER, AND THERE WAS A COUP D'ÉTAT.
ACCA

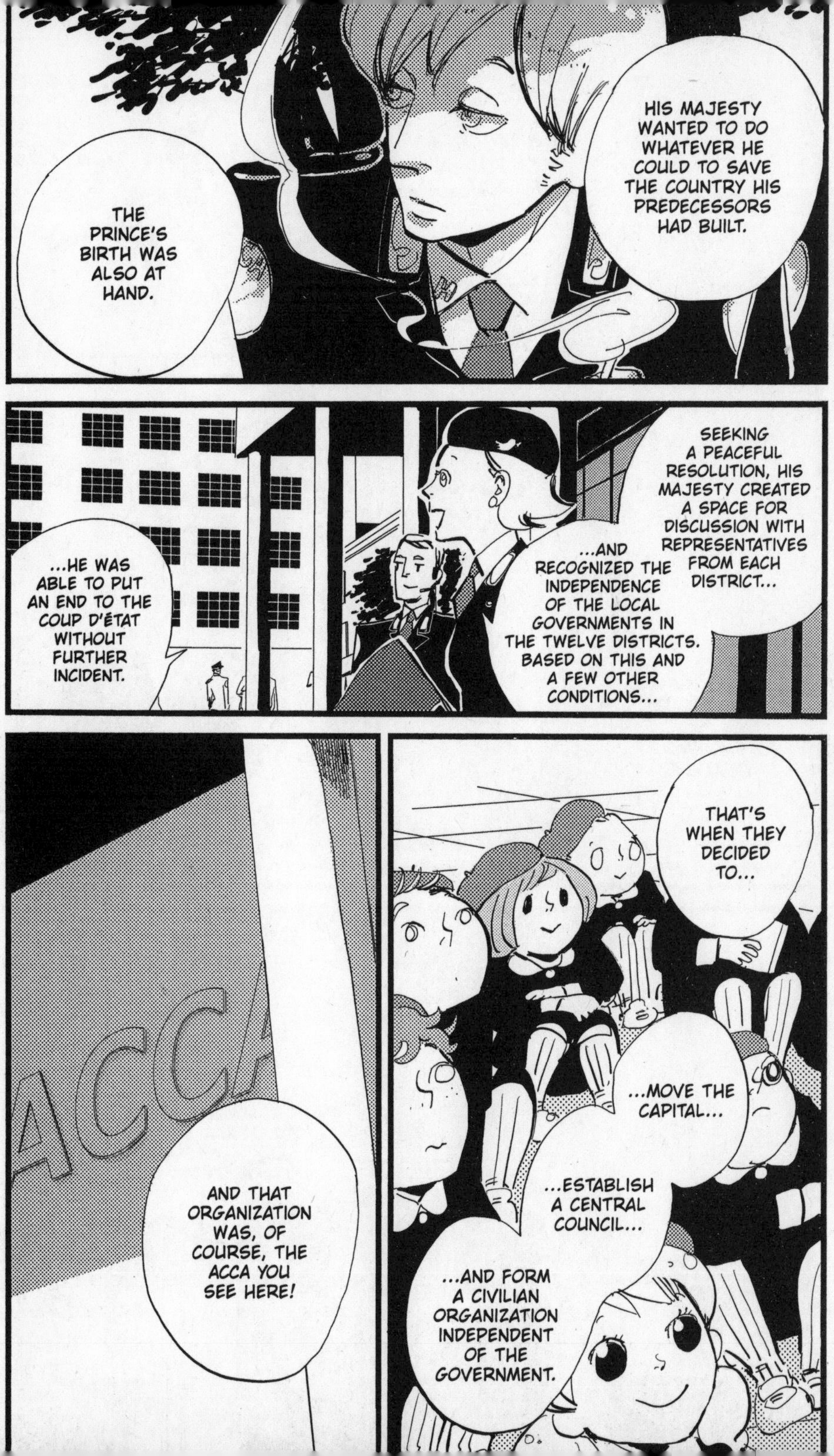
HIS MAJESTY WANTED TO DO WHATEVER HE COULD TO SAVE THE COUNTRY HIS PREDECESSORS HAD BUILT.
THE PRINCE'S BIRTH WAS ALSO AT HAND.
SEEKING A PEACEFUL RESOLUTION, HIS MAJESTY CREATED A SPACE FOR DISCUSSION WITH REPRESENTATIVES FROM EACH DISTRICT...
...AND RECOGNIZED THE INDEPENDENCE OF THE LOCAL GOVERNMENTS IN THE TWELVE DISTRICTS. BASED ON THIS AND A FEW OTHER CONDITIONS...
...HE WAS ABLE TO PUT AN END TO THE COUP D'ÉTAT WITHOUT FURTHER INCIDENT.
THAT'S WHEN THEY DECIDED TO...
...MOVE THE CAPITAL...
...ESTABLISH A CENTRAL COUNCIL...
...AND FORM A CIVILIAN ORGANIZATION INDEPENDENT OF THE GOVERNMENT.
ACCA
AND THAT ORGANIZATION WAS, OF COURSE, THE ACCA YOU SEE HERE!

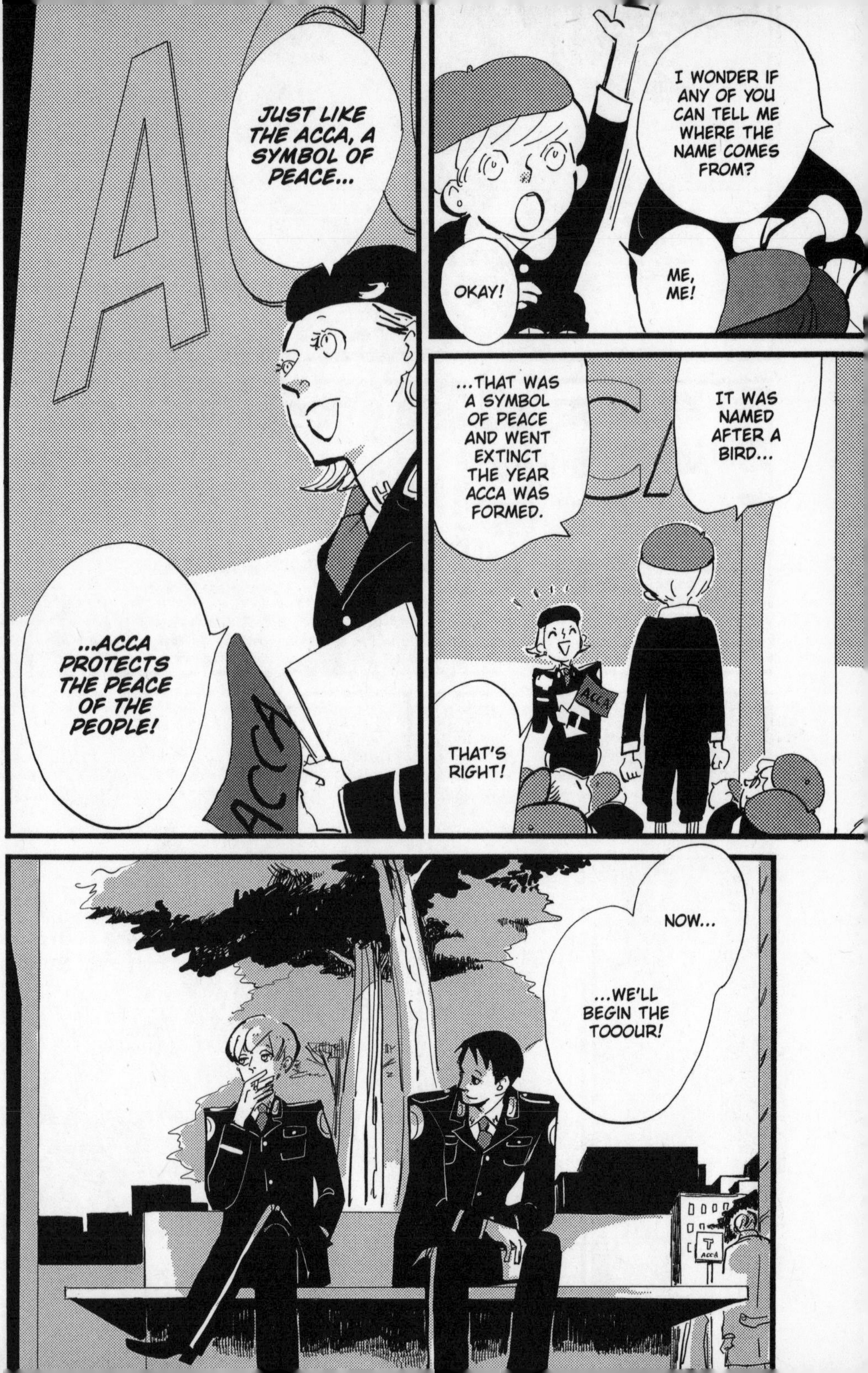
I WONDER IF ANY OF YOU CAN TELL ME WHERE THE NAME COMES FROM?
ME, ME!
OKAY!
IT WAS NAMED AFTER A BIRD...
...THAT WAS A SYMBOL OF PEACE AND WENT EXTINCT THE YEAR ACCA WAS FORMED.
THAT'S RIGHT!
JUST LIKE THE ACCA, A SYMBOL OF PEACE...
...ACCA PROTECTS THE PEACE OF THE PEOPLE!
NOW...
...WE'LL BEGIN THE TOOOUR!

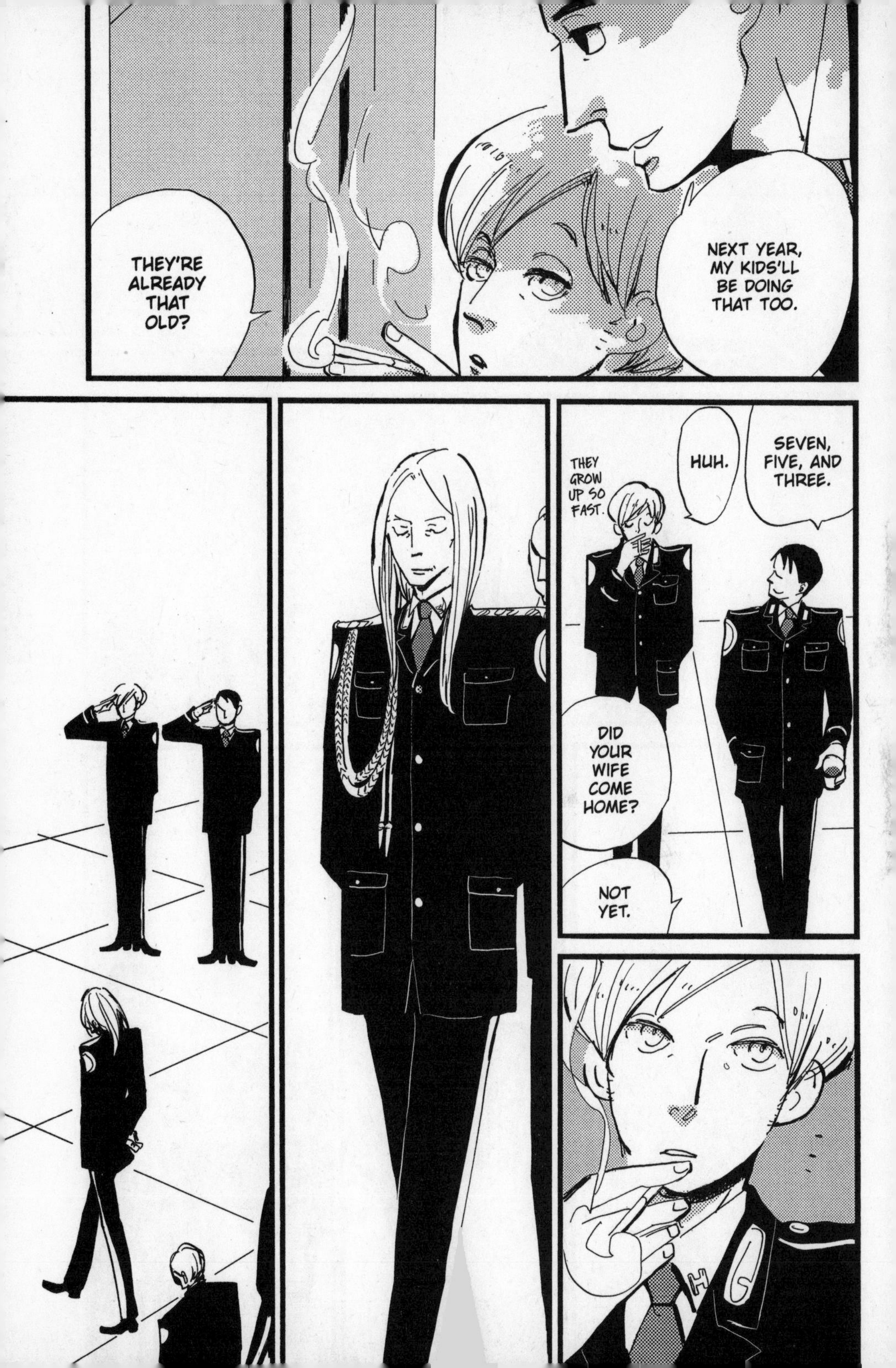
NEXT YEAR, MY KIDS'LL BE DOING THAT TOO.
THEY'RE ALREADY THAT OLD?
SEVEN, FIVE, AND THREE.
HUH.
THEY GROW UP SO FAST.
DID YOUR WIFE COME HOME?
NOT YET.

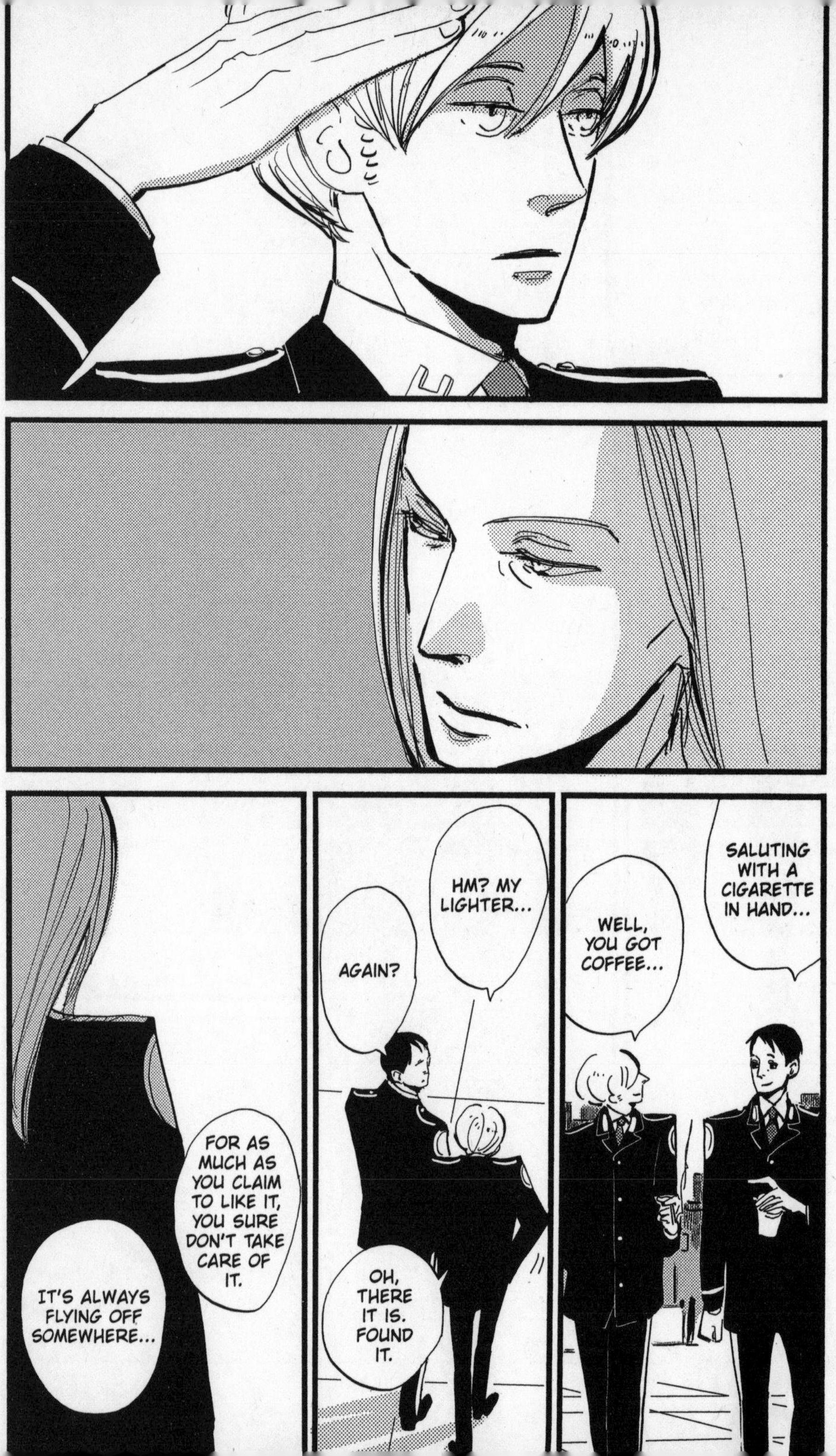
SALUTING WITH A CIGARETTE IN HAND...
WELL, YOU GOT COFFEE...
HM? MY LIGHTER...
AGAIN?
OH, THERE IT IS. FOUND IT.
FOR AS MUCH AS YOU CLAIM TO LIKE IT, YOU SURE DON'T TAKE CARE OF IT.
IT'S ALWAYS FLYING OFF SOMEWHERE...

...THAT
"SYMBOL OF
PEACE"...

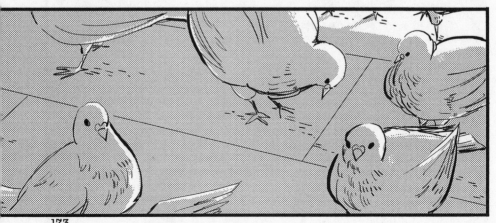

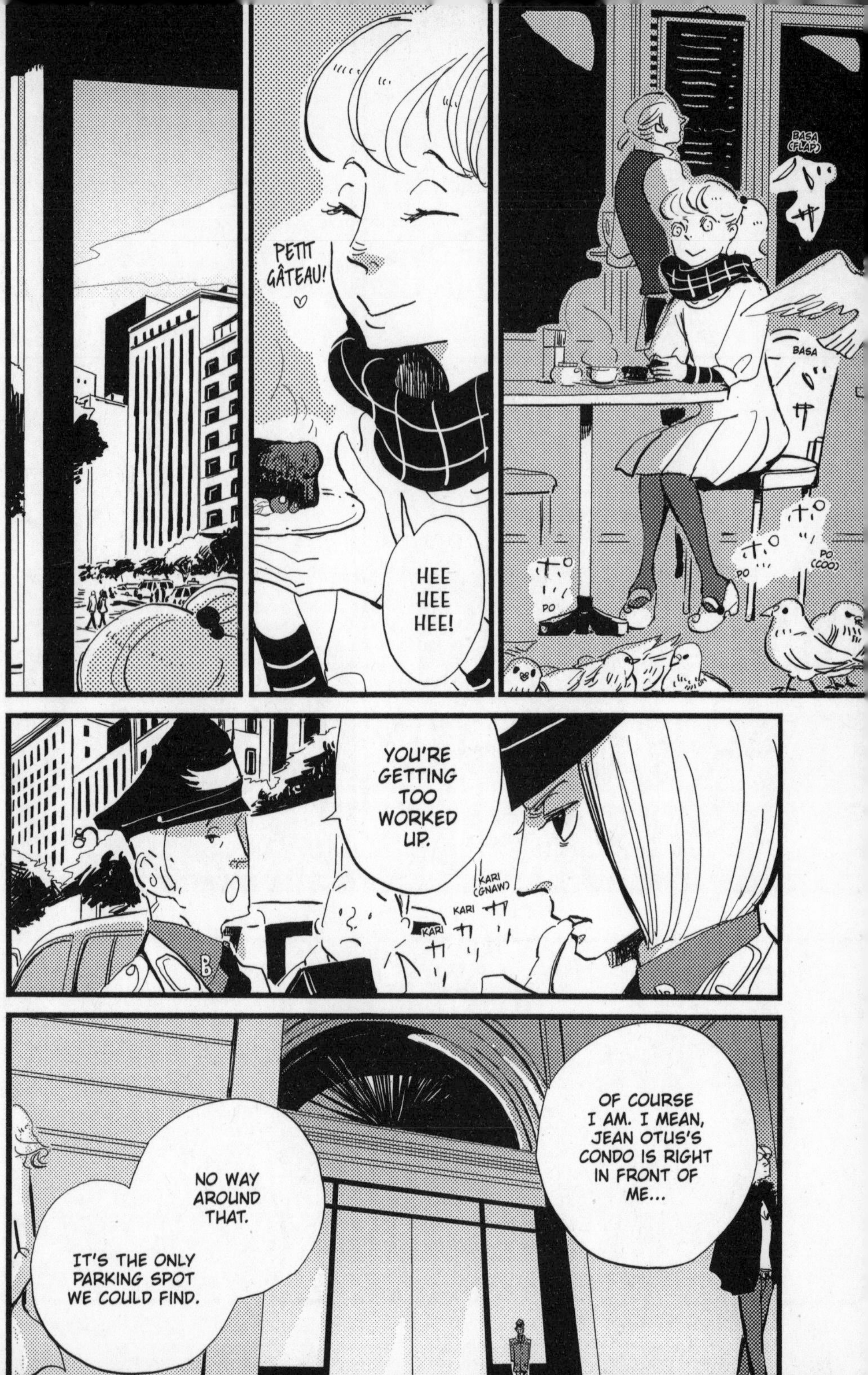

PETIT GÂTEAU!
HEE HEE HEE!
BASA (FLAP)
BASA
PO (COO)
PO
PO
YOU'RE GETTING TOO WORKED UP.
KARI (GNAW)
KARI
KARI
OF COURSE I AM. I MEAN, JEAN OTUS'S CONDO IS RIGHT IN FRONT OF ME...
NO WAY AROUND THAT.
IT'S THE ONLY PARKING SPOT WE COULD FIND.

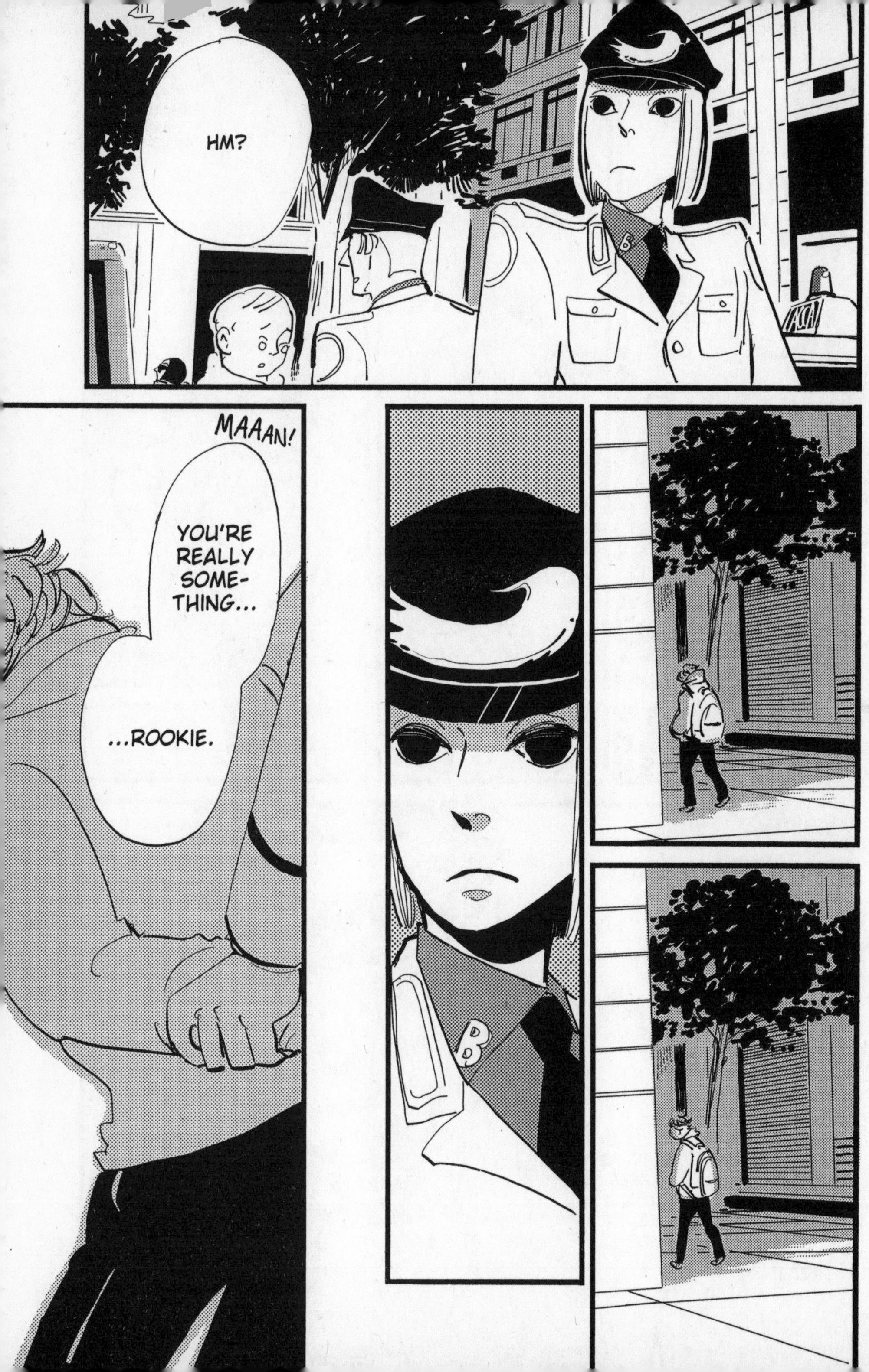
HM?
MAAAN!
YOU'RE REALLY SOMETHING...
...ROOKIE.

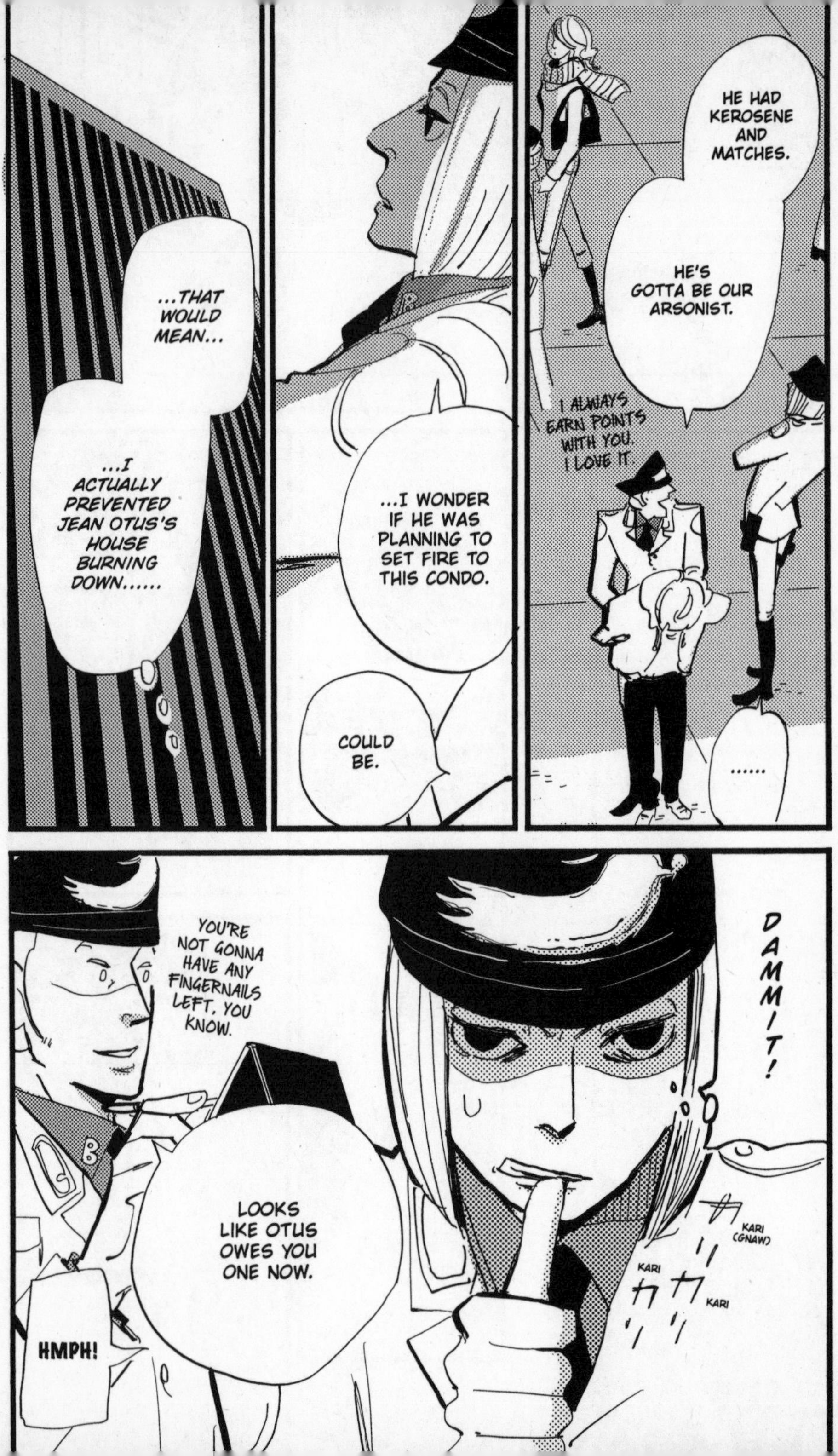
HE HAD KEROSENE AND MATCHES.
HE'S GOTTA BE OUR ARSONIST.
I ALWAYS EARN POINTS WITH YOU. I LOVE IT.
......
...I WONDER IF HE WAS PLANNING TO SET FIRE TO THIS CONDO.
COULD BE.
...THAT WOULD MEAN...
...I ACTUALLY PREVENTED JEAN OTUS'S HOUSE BURNING DOWN......
DAMMIT!
KARI (GNAW)
KARI
KARI
YOU'RE NOT GONNA HAVE ANY FINGERNAILS LEFT, YOU KNOW.
LOOKS LIKE OTUS OWES YOU ONE NOW.
HMPH!

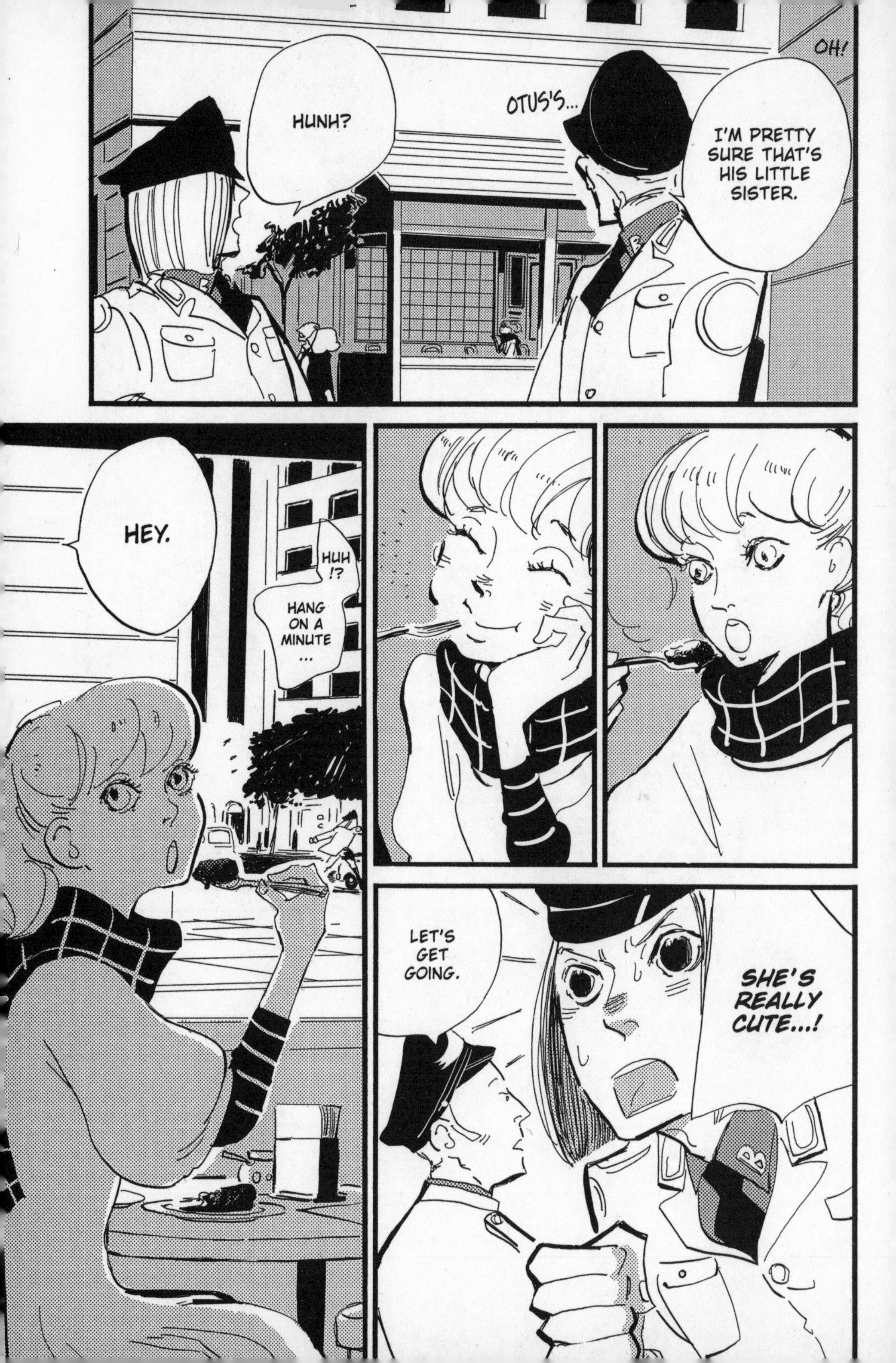
OH!
I'M PRETTY SURE THAT'S HIS LITTLE SISTER.
OTUS'S...
HUNH?
HEY.
HUH !?
HANG ON A MINUTE ...
SHE'S REALLY CUTE...!
LET'S GET GOING.

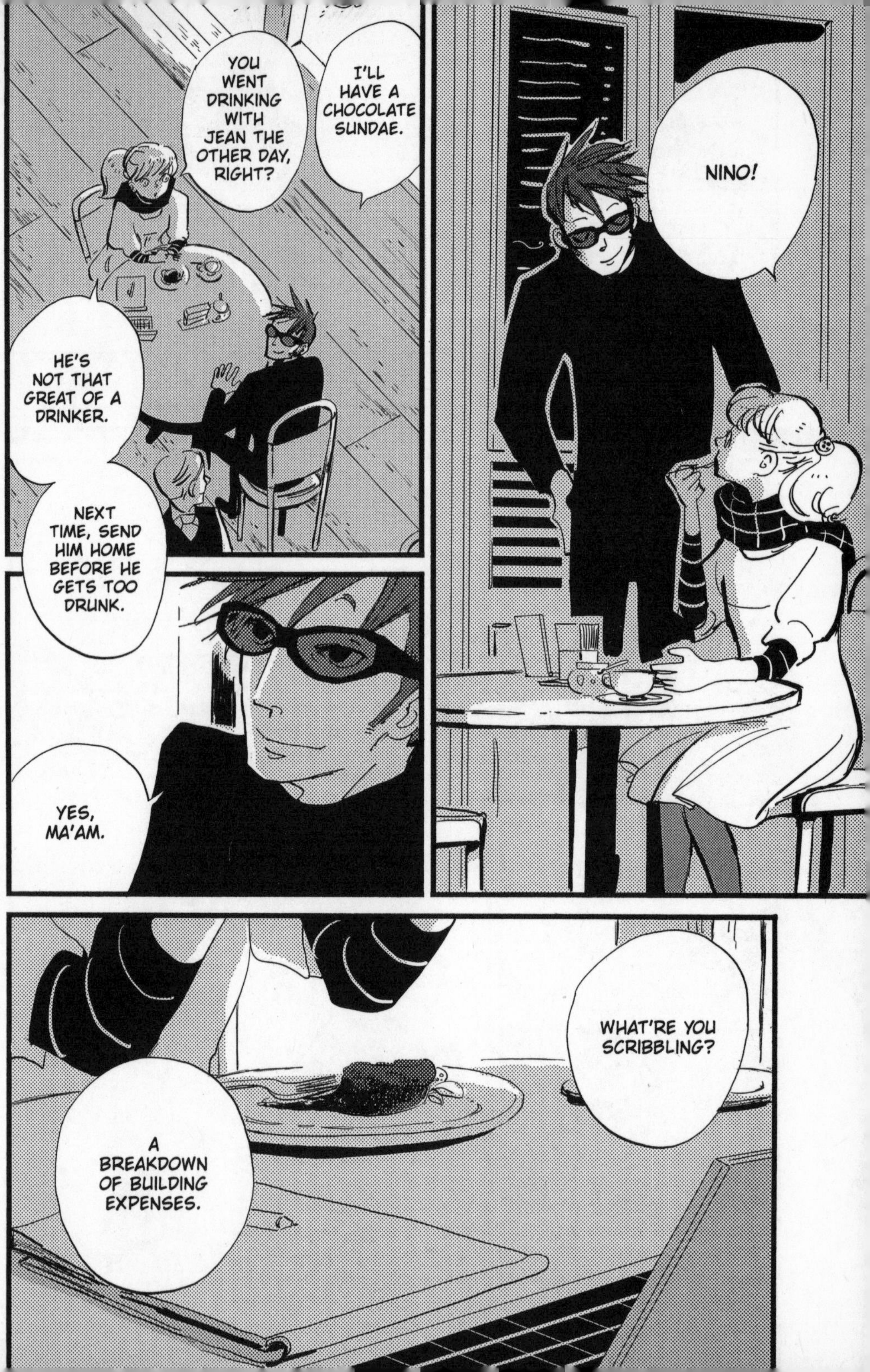
NINO!
I'LL HAVE A CHOCOLATE SUNDAE.
YOU WENT DRINKING WITH JEAN THE OTHER DAY, RIGHT?
HE'S NOT THAT GREAT OF A DRINKER.
NEXT TIME, SEND HIM HOME BEFORE HE GETS TOO DRUNK.
YES, MA'AM.
WHAT'RE YOU SCRIBBLING?
A BREAKDOWN OF BUILDING EXPENSES.

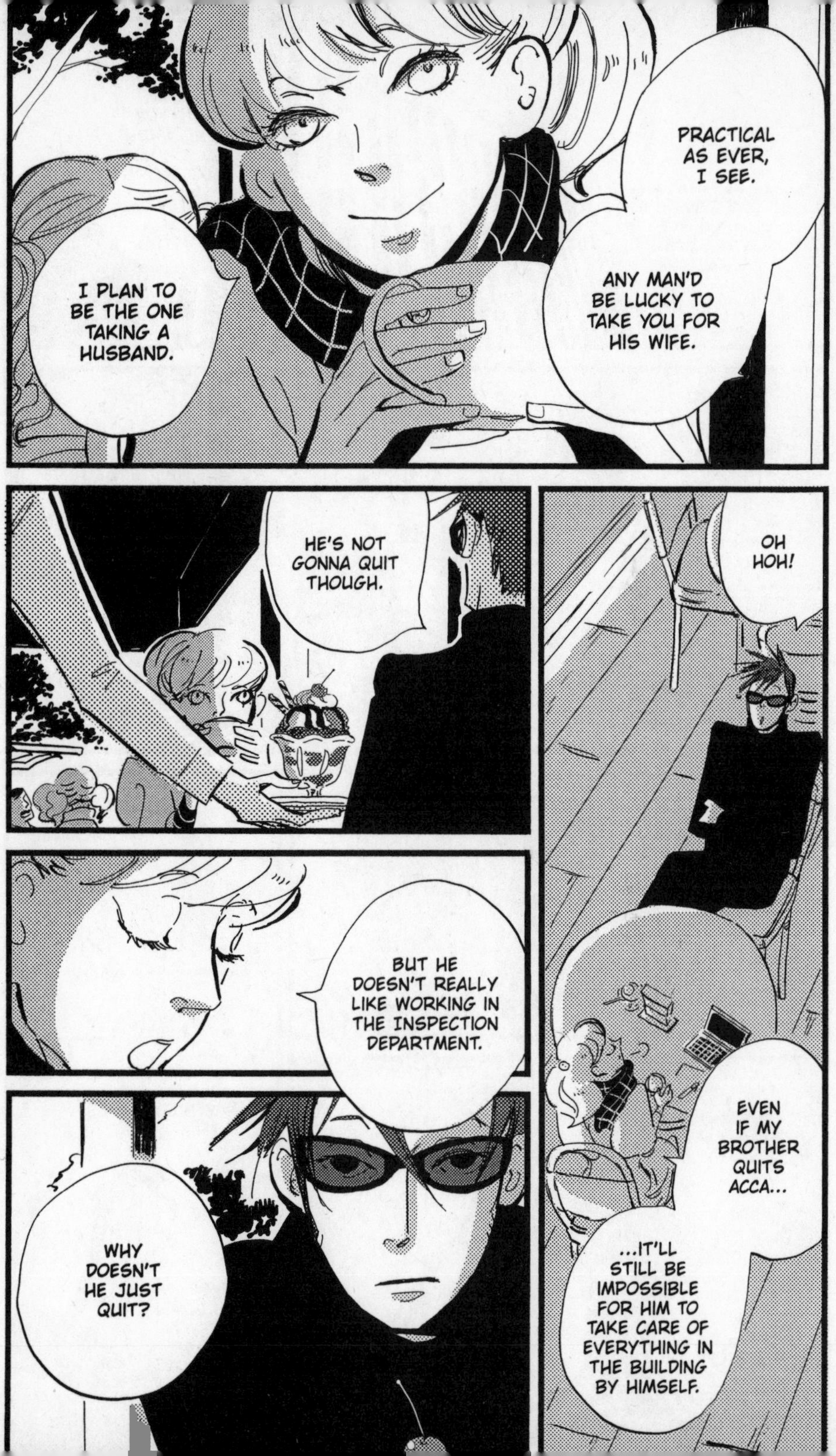
PRACTICAL AS EVER, I SEE.
ANY MAN'D BE LUCKY TO TAKE YOU FOR HIS WIFE.
I PLAN TO BE THE ONE TAKING A HUSBAND.
OH HOH!
HE'S NOT GONNA QUIT THOUGH.
BUT HE DOESN'T REALLY LIKE WORKING IN THE INSPECTION DEPARTMENT.
WHY DOESN'T HE JUST QUIT?
EVEN IF MY BROTHER QUITS ACCA...
...IT'LL STILL BE IMPOSSIBLE FOR HIM TO TAKE CARE OF EVERYTHING IN THE BUILDING BY HIMSELF.

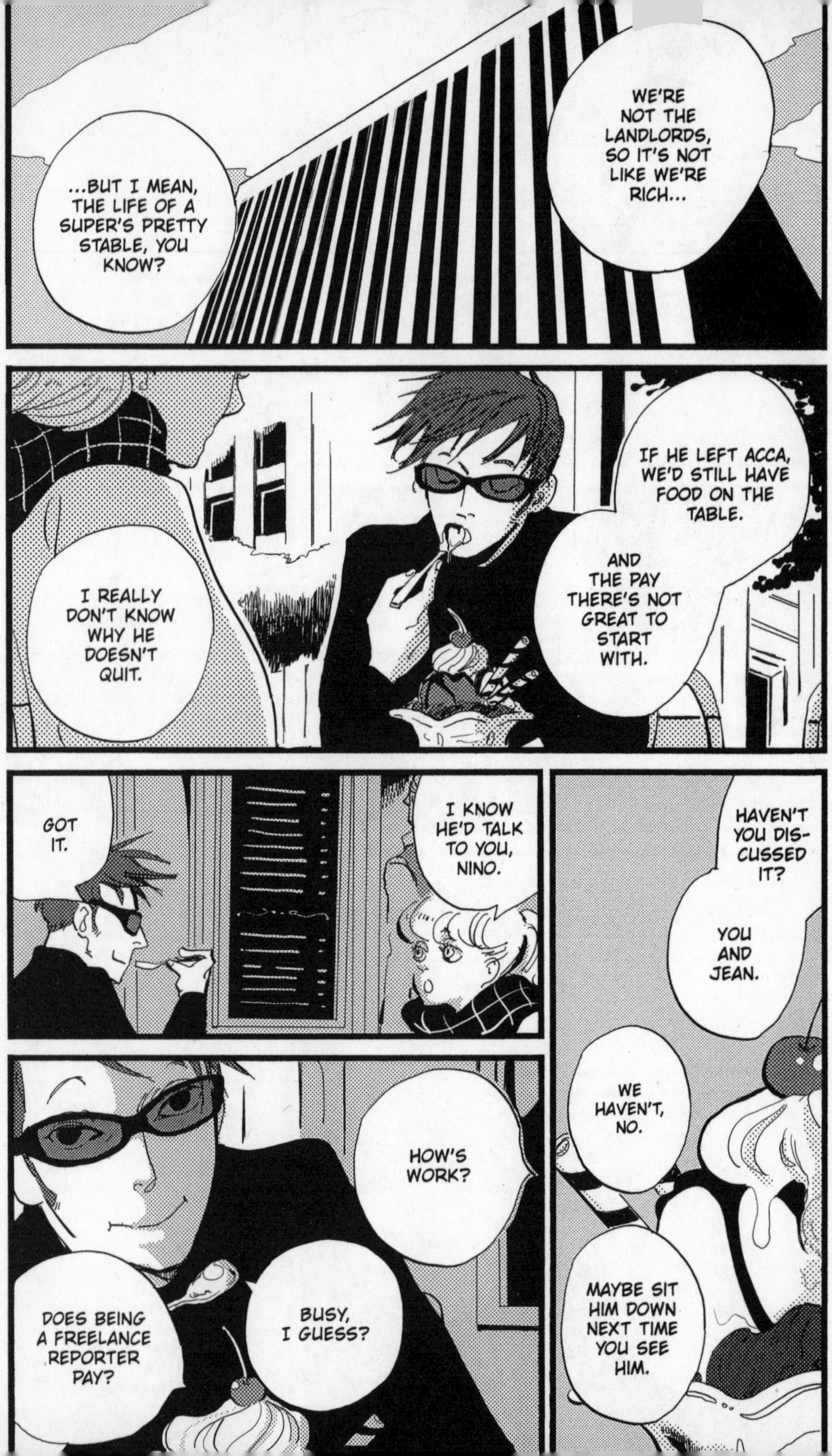
WE'RE NOT THE LANDLORDS, SO IT'S NOT LIKE WE'RE RICH...
...BUT I MEAN, THE LIFE OF A SUPER'S PRETTY STABLE, YOU KNOW?
IF HE LEFT ACCA, WE'D STILL HAVE FOOD ON THE TABLE.
AND THE PAY THERE'S NOT GREAT TO START WITH.
I REALLY DON'T KNOW WHY HE DOESN'T QUIT.
HAVEN'T YOU DIS-CUSSED IT?
YOU AND JEAN.
WE HAVEN'T, NO.
MAYBE SIT HIM DOWN NEXT TIME YOU SEE HIM.
I KNOW HE'D TALK TO YOU, NINO.
GOT IT.
HOW'S WORK?
BUSY, I GUESS?
DOES BEING A FREELANCE REPORTER PAY?

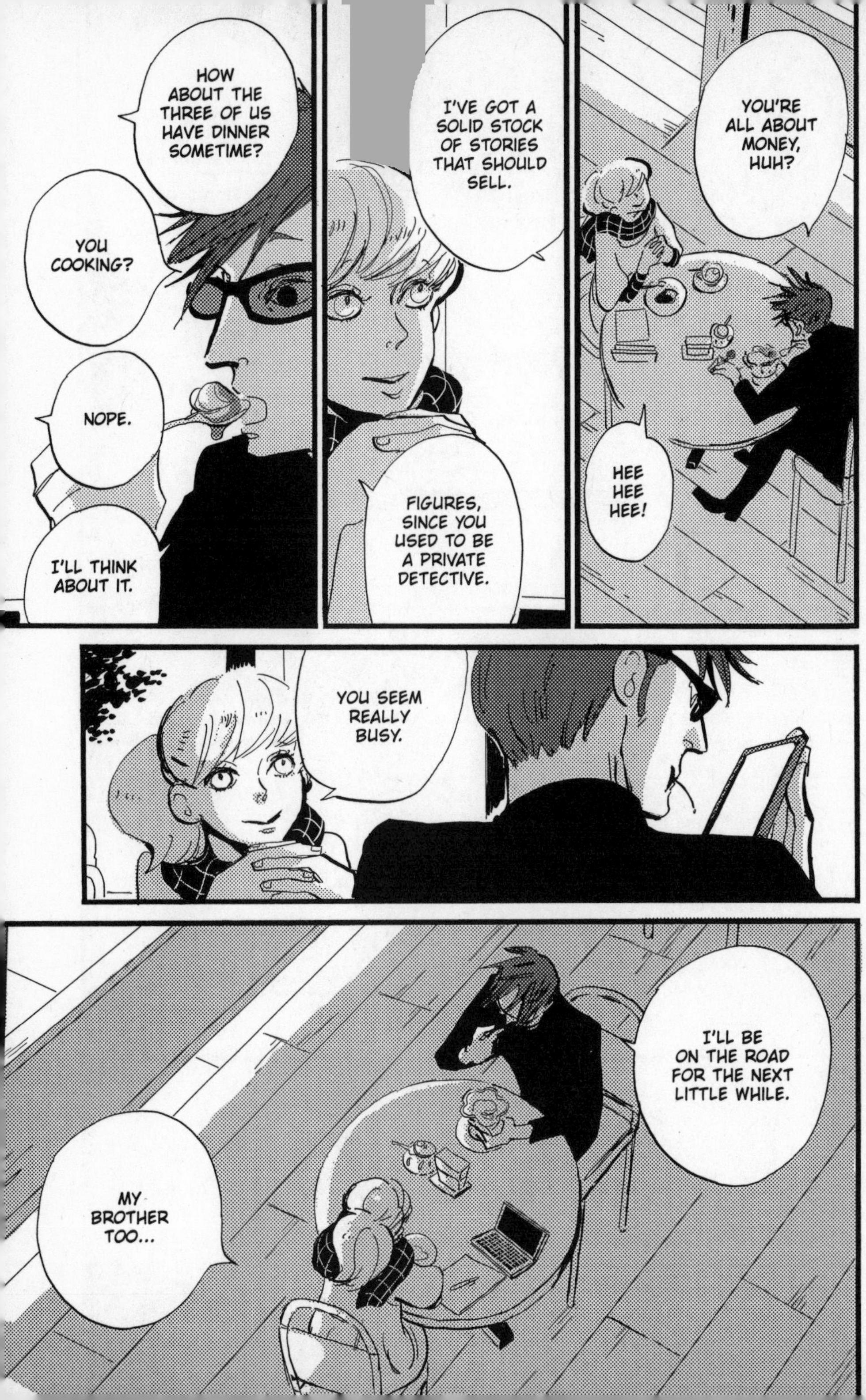
YOU'RE ALL ABOUT MONEY, HUH?
HEE HEE HEE!
I'VE GOT A SOLID STOCK OF STORIES THAT SHOULD SELL.
FIGURES, SINCE YOU USED TO BE A PRIVATE DETECTIVE.
HOW ABOUT THE THREE OF US HAVE DINNER SOMETIME?
YOU COOKING?
NOPE.
I'LL THINK ABOUT IT.
YOU SEEM REALLY BUSY.
I'LL BE ON THE ROAD FOR THE NEXT LITTLE WHILE.
MY BROTHER TOO...

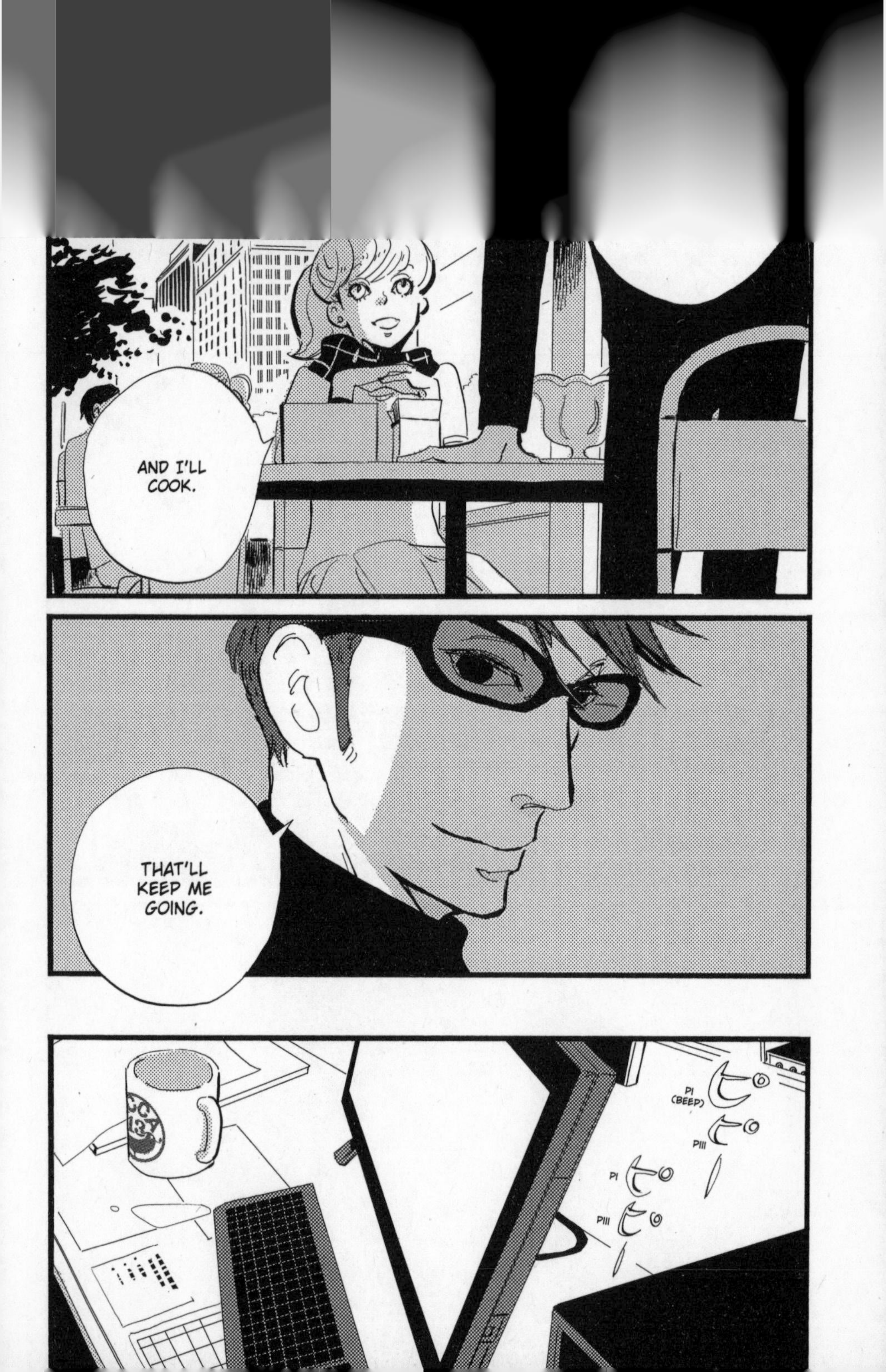
AND I'LL COOK.
THAT'LL KEEP ME GOING.
PI (BEEP)
PIII
PI
PIII

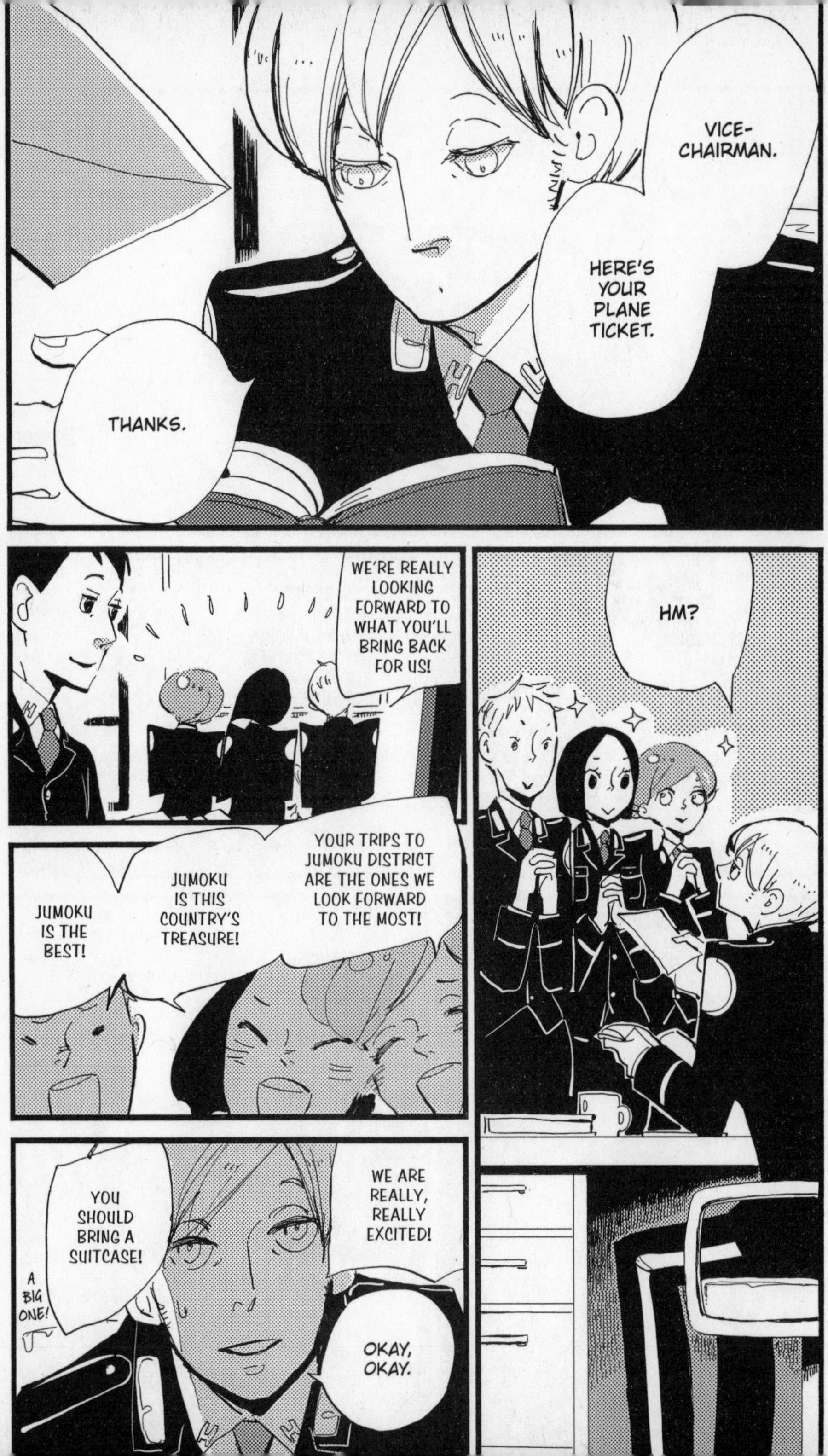
VICE-CHAIRMAN.
HERE'S YOUR PLANE TICKET.
THANKS.
HM?
WE'RE REALLY LOOKING FORWARD TO WHAT YOU'LL BRING BACK FOR US!
YOUR TRIPS TO JUMOKU DISTRICT ARE THE ONES WE LOOK FORWARD TO THE MOST!
JUMOKU IS THIS COUNTRY'S TREASURE!
JUMOKU IS THE BEST!
WE ARE REALLY, REALLY EXCITED!
YOU SHOULD BRING A SUITCASE!
A BIG ONE!
OKAY, OKAY.

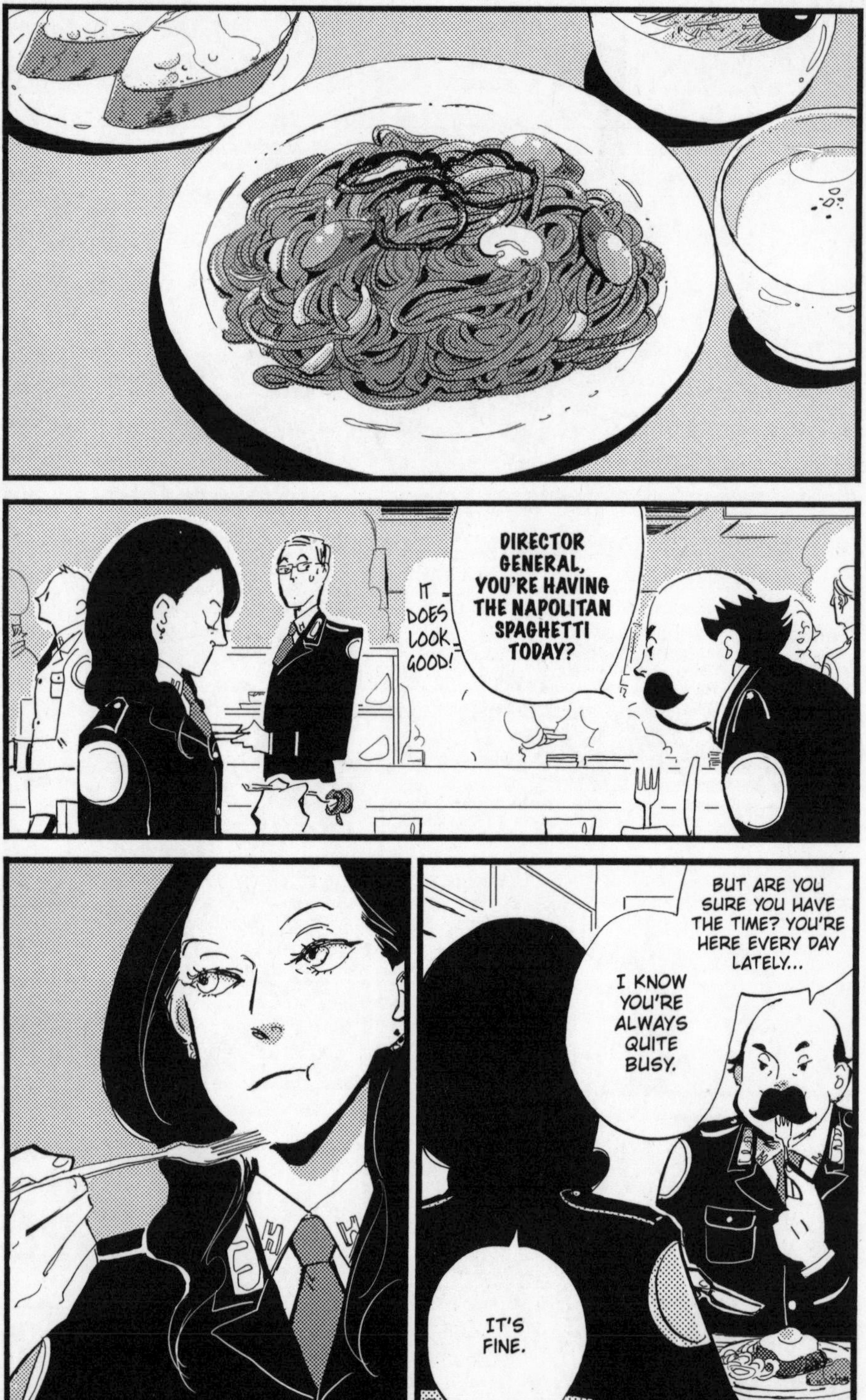
DIRECTOR GENERAL, YOU'RE HAVING THE NAPOLITAN SPAGHETTI TODAY?
IT DOES LOOK GOOD!
BUT ARE YOU SURE YOU HAVE THE TIME? YOU'RE HERE EVERY DAY LATELY...
I KNOW YOU'RE ALWAYS QUITE BUSY.
IT'S FINE.

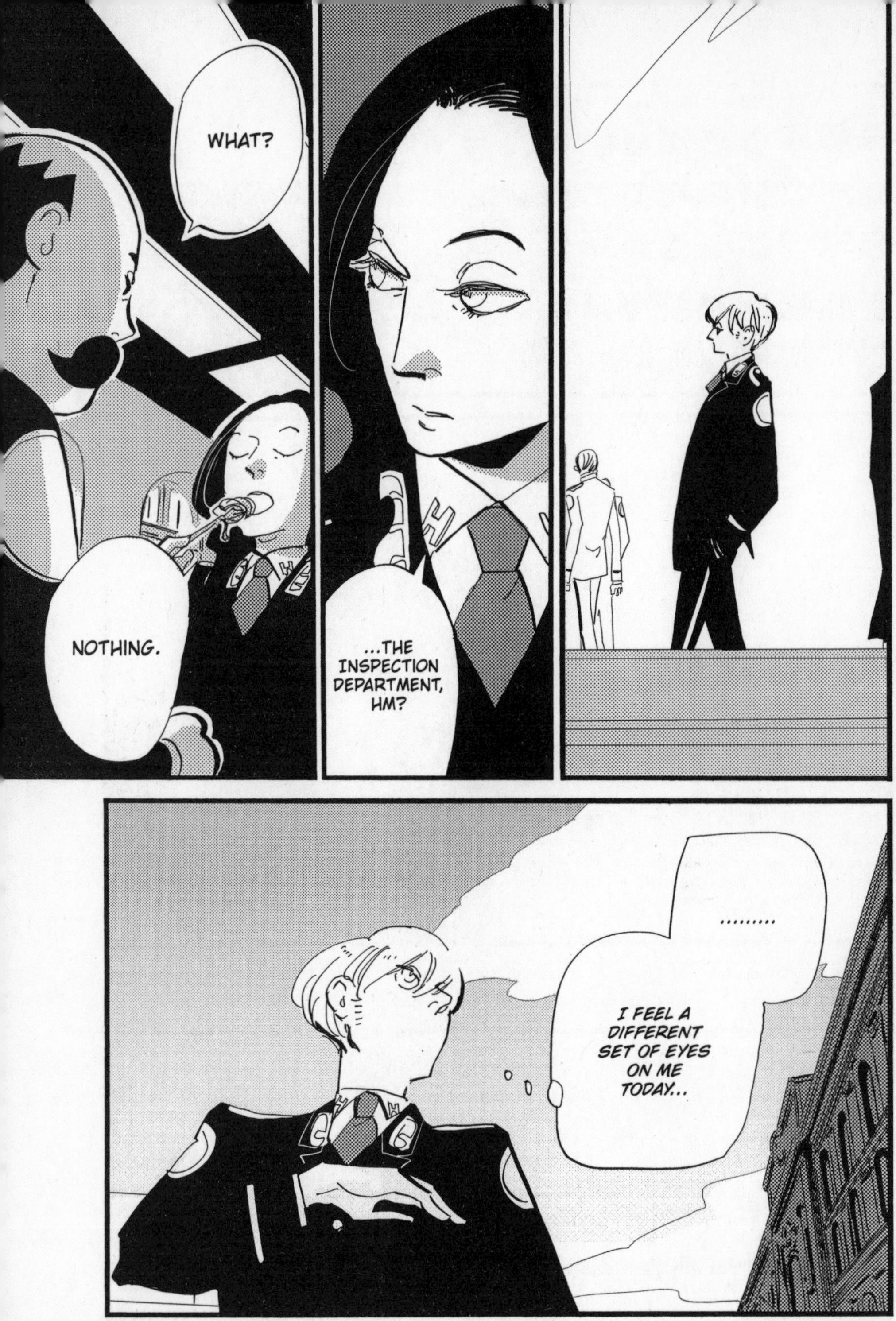

WHAT?
NOTHING.
...THE INSPECTION DEPARTMENT, HM?
....
I FEEL A DIFFERENT SET OF EYES ON ME TODAY...

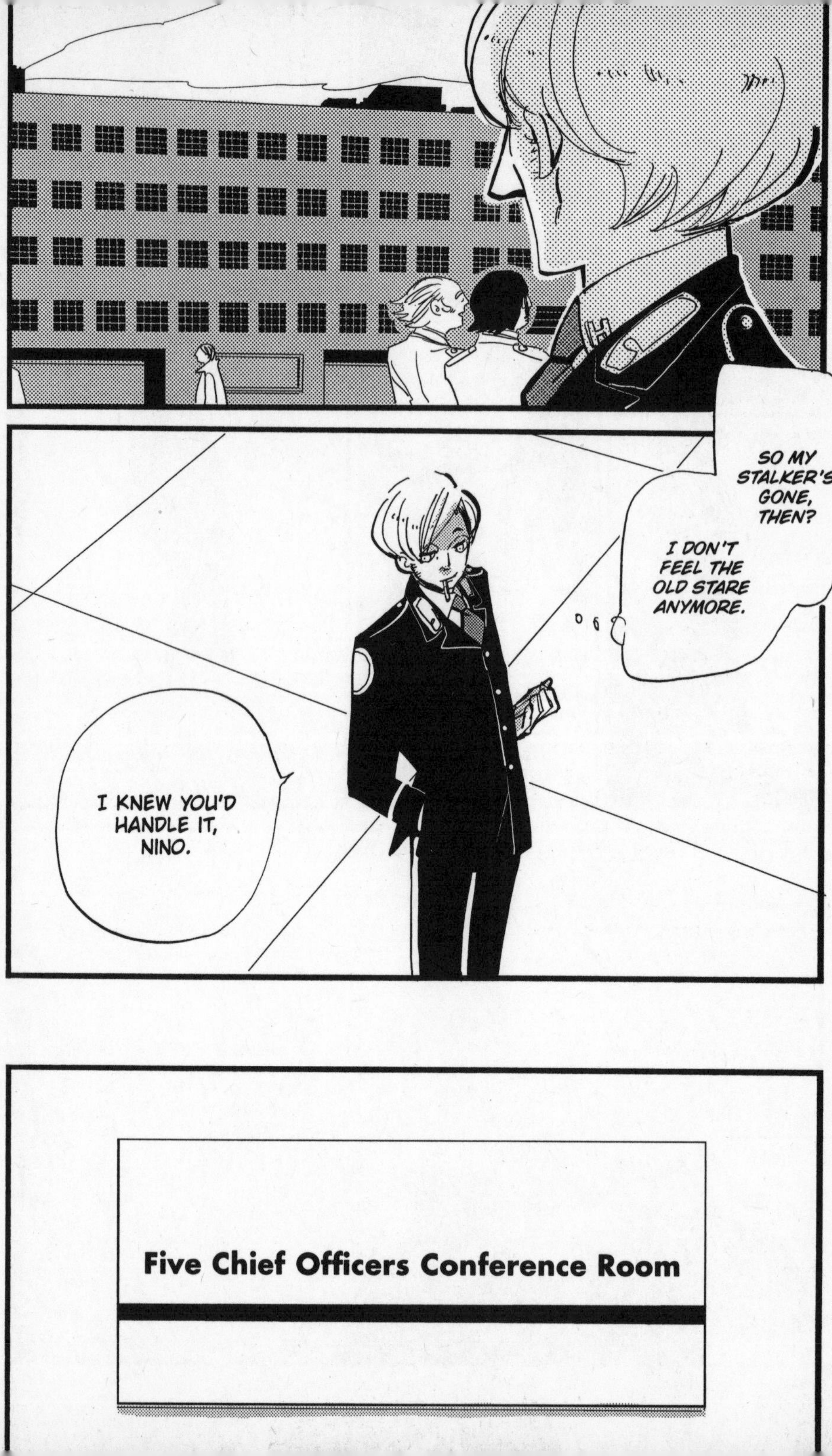
SO MY STALKER'S GONE, THEN?
I DON'T FEEL THE OLD STARE ANYMORE.
I KNEW YOU'D HANDLE IT, NINO.
Five Chief Officers Conference Room

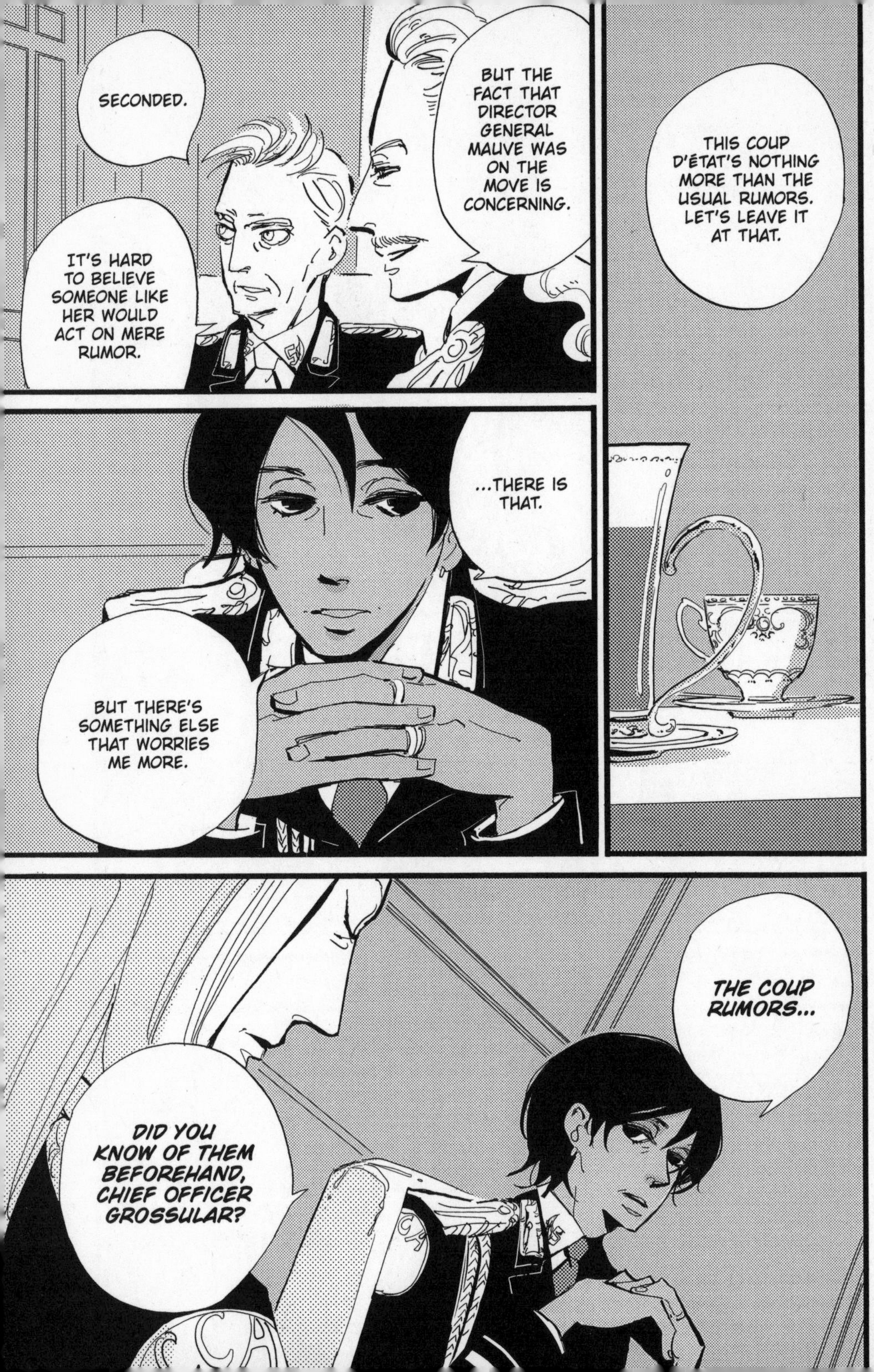
THIS COUP D'ÉTAT'S NOTHING MORE THAN THE USUAL RUMORS. LET'S LEAVE IT AT THAT.
BUT THE FACT THAT DIRECTOR GENERAL MAUVE WAS ON THE MOVE IS CONCERNING.
SECONDED.
IT'S HARD TO BELIEVE SOMEONE LIKE HER WOULD ACT ON MERE RUMOR.
...THERE IS THAT.
BUT THERE'S SOMETHING ELSE THAT WORRIES ME MORE.
THE COUP RUMORS...
DID YOU KNOW OF THEM BEFOREHAND, CHIEF OFFICER GROSSULAR?

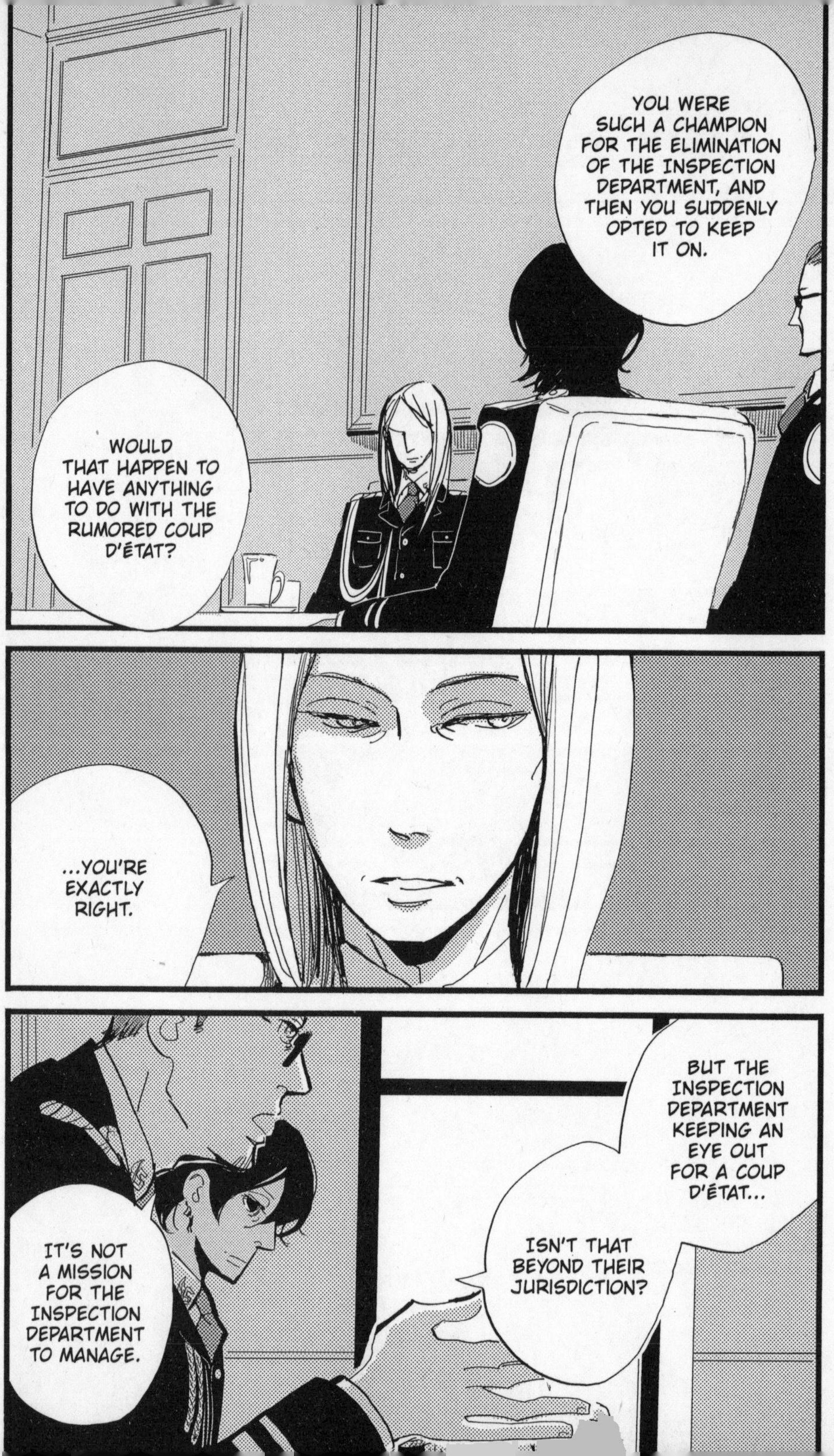
YOU WERE SUCH A CHAMPION FOR THE ELIMINATION OF THE INSPECTION DEPARTMENT, AND THEN YOU SUDDENLY OPTED TO KEEP IT ON.
WOULD THAT HAPPEN TO HAVE ANYTHING TO DO WITH THE RUMORED COUP D'ÉTAT?
...YOU'RE EXACTLY RIGHT.
BUT THE INSPECTION DEPARTMENT KEEPING AN EYE OUT FOR A COUP D'ÉTAT...
ISN'T THAT BEYOND THEIR JURISDICTION?
IT'S NOT A MISSION FOR THE INSPECTION DEPARTMENT TO MANAGE.

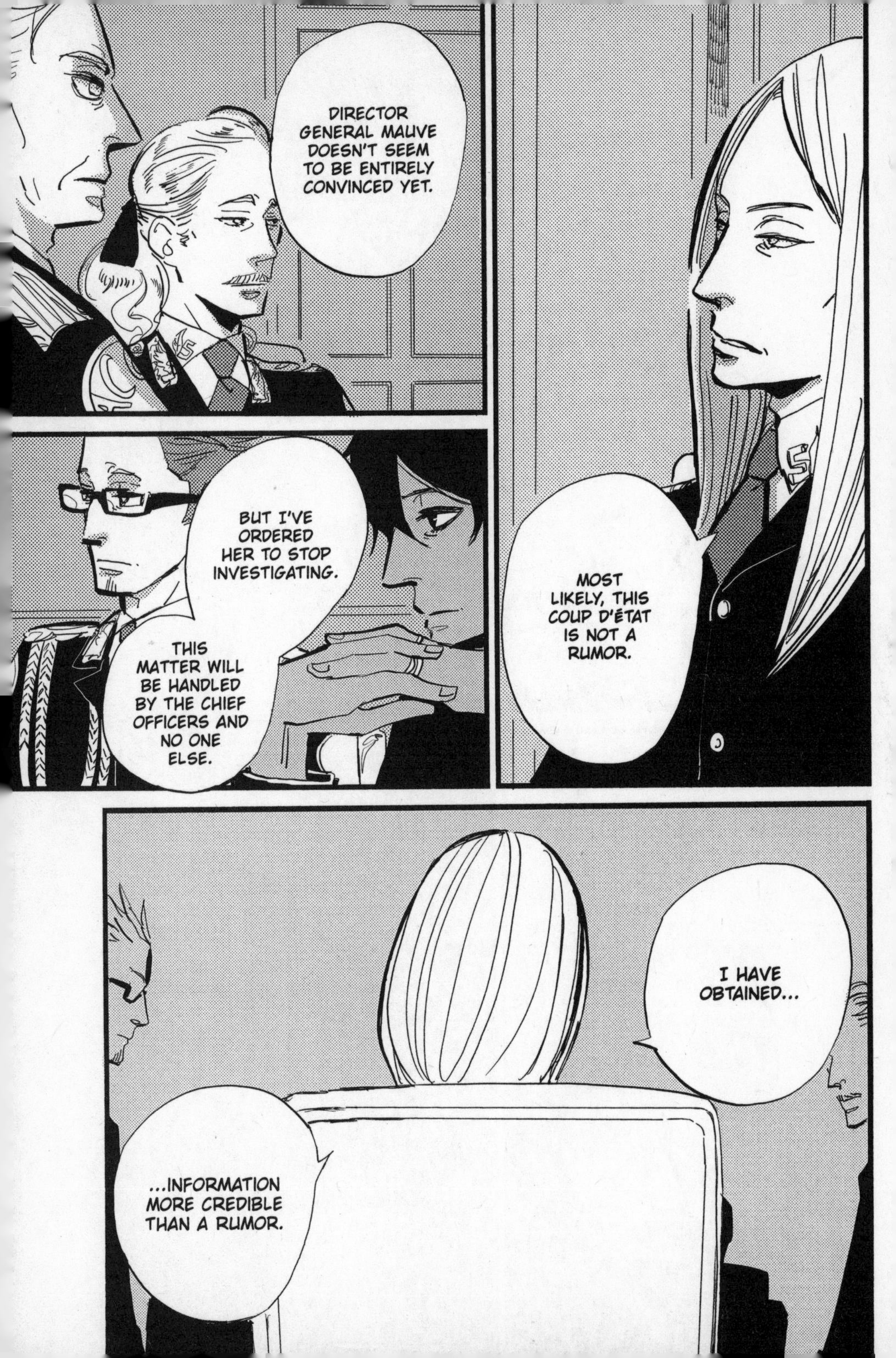
MOST LIKELY, THIS COUP D'ÉTAT IS NOT A RUMOR.
DIRECTOR GENERAL MAUVE DOESN'T SEEM TO BE ENTIRELY CONVINCED YET.
BUT I'VE ORDERED HER TO STOP INVESTIGATING.
THIS MATTER WILL BE HANDLED BY THE CHIEF OFFICERS AND NO ONE ELSE.
I HAVE OBTAINED...
...INFORMATION MORE CREDIBLE THAN A RUMOR.

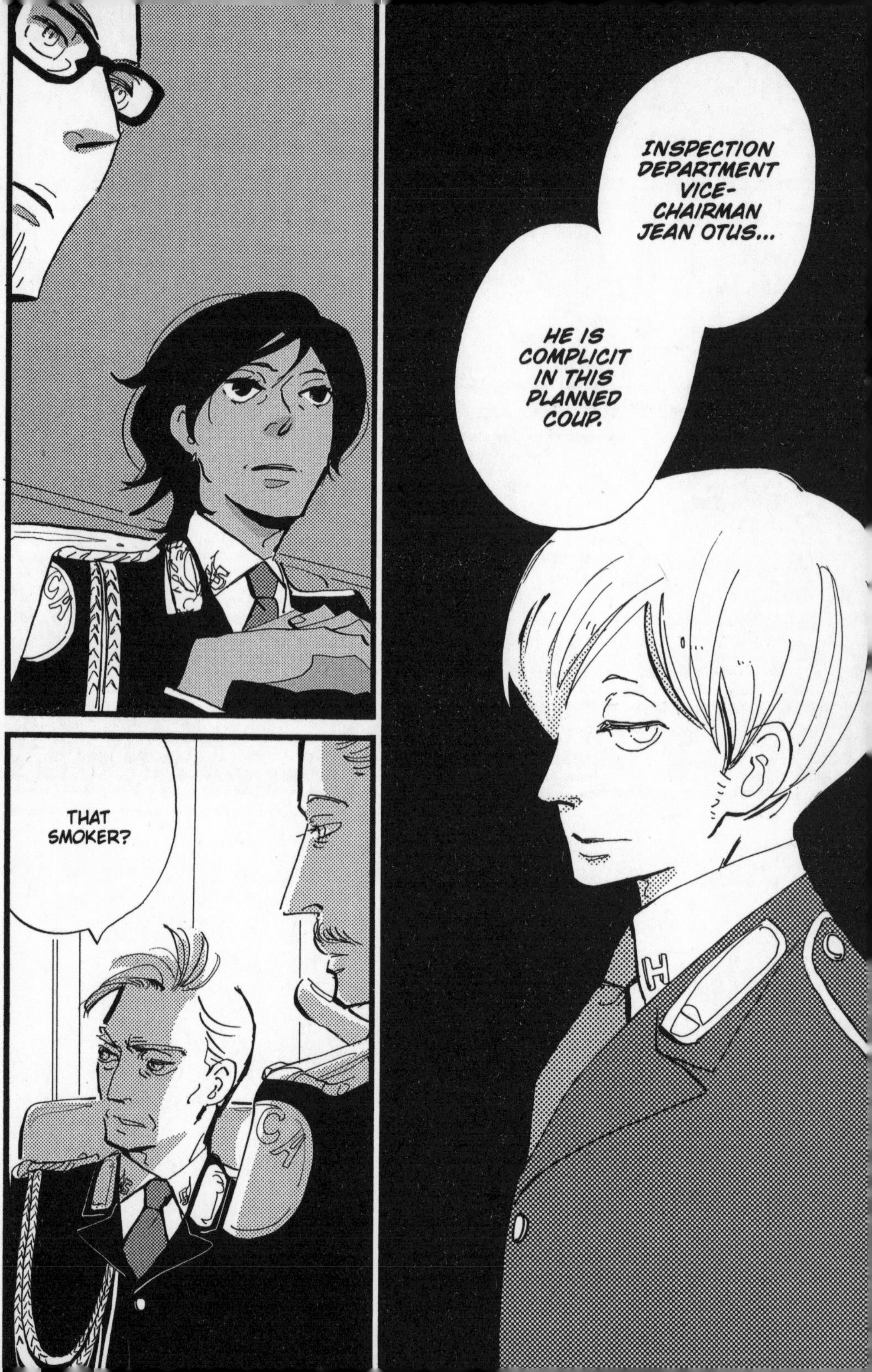
INSPECTION DEPARTMENT VICE-CHAIRMAN JEAN OTUS...
HE IS COMPLICIT IN THIS PLANNED COUP.
...
THAT SMOKER?

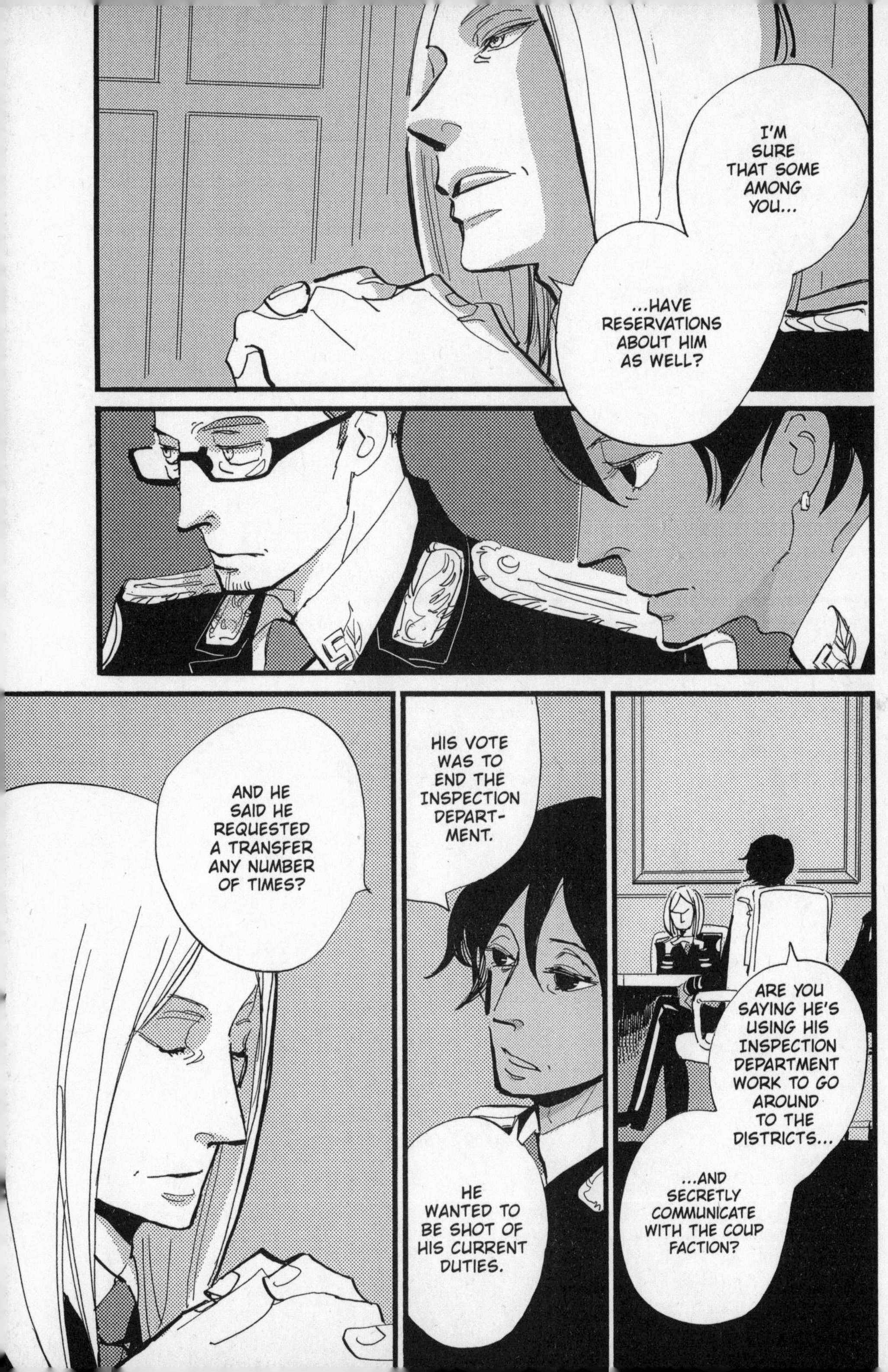
I'M SURE THAT SOME AMONG YOU...
...HAVE RESERVATIONS ABOUT HIM AS WELL?
ARE YOU SAYING HE'S USING HIS INSPECTION DEPARTMENT WORK TO GO AROUND TO THE DISTRICTS...
...AND SECRETLY COMMUNICATE WITH THE COUP FACTION?
HIS VOTE WAS TO END THE INSPECTION DEPART-MENT.
HE WANTED TO BE SHOT OF HIS CURRENT DUTIES.
AND HE SAID HE REQUESTED A TRANSFER ANY NUMBER OF TIMES?

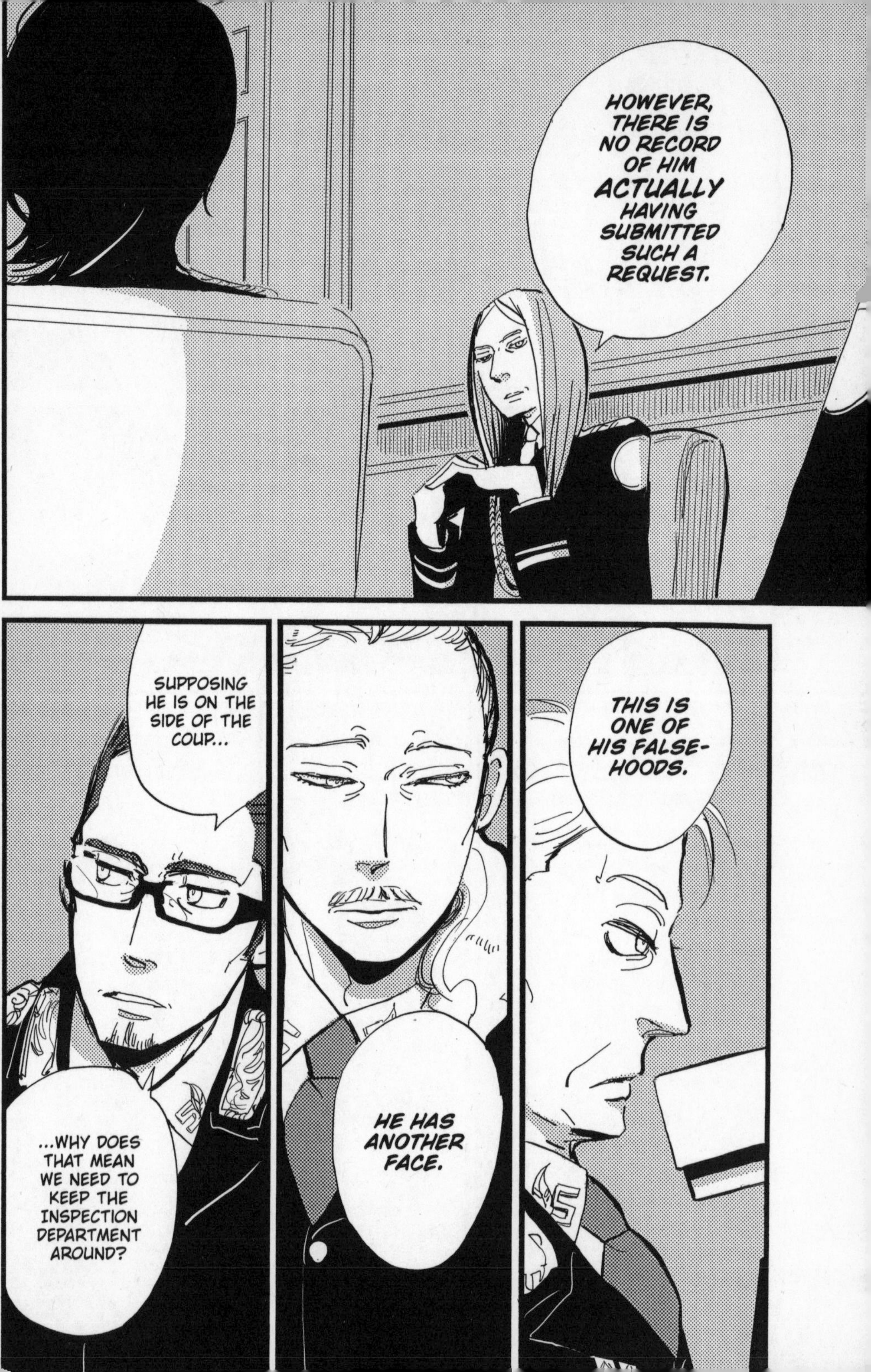
HOWEVER, THERE IS NO RECORD OF HIM ACTUALLY HAVING SUBMITTED SUCH A REQUEST.
THIS IS ONE OF HIS FALSE-HOODS.
HE HAS ANOTHER FACE.
SUPPOSING HE IS ON THE SIDE OF THE COUP...
...WHY DOES THAT MEAN WE NEED TO KEEP THE INSPECTION DEPARTMENT AROUND?

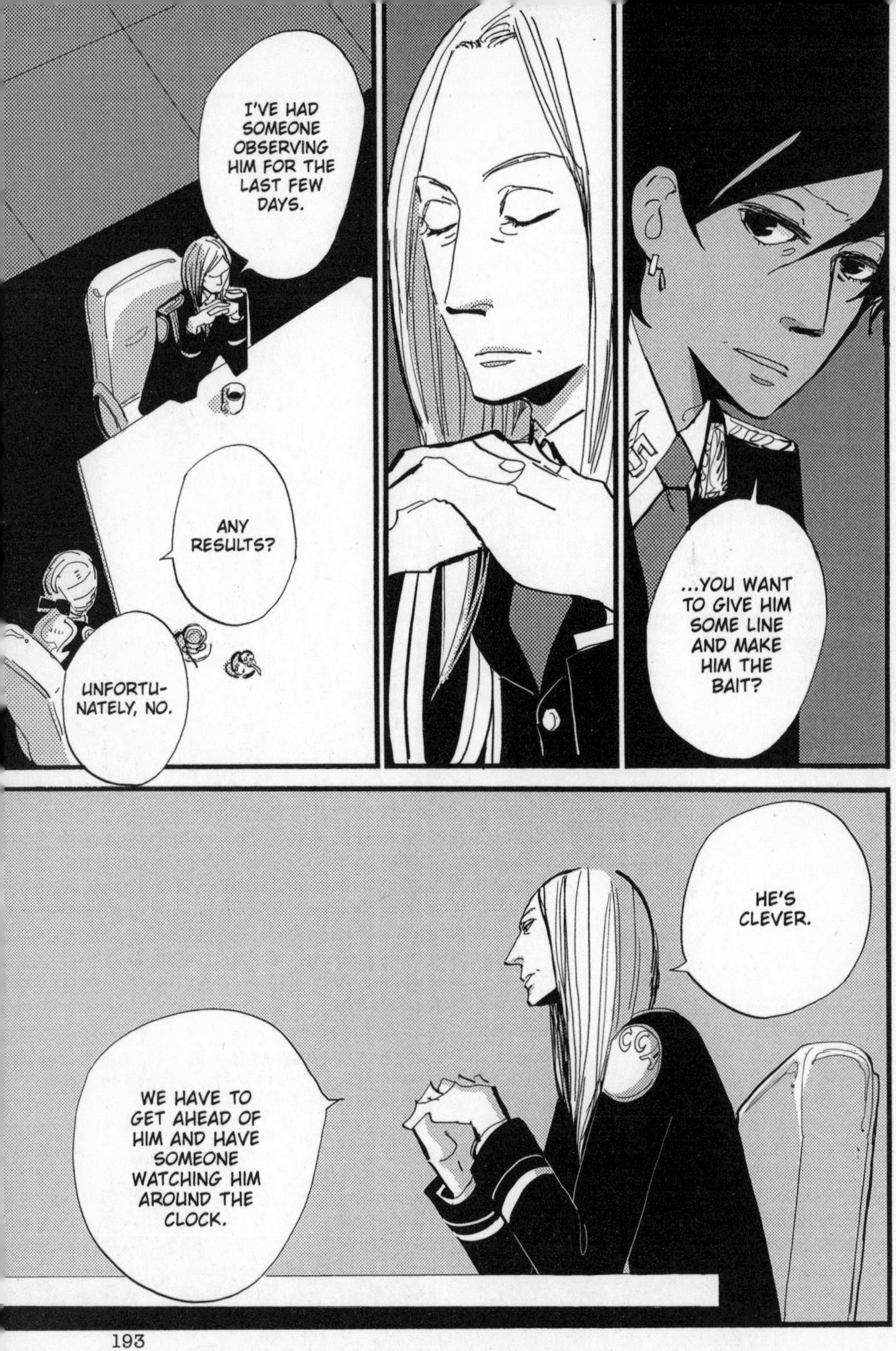
...YOU WANT TO GIVE HIM SOME LINE AND MAKE HIM THE BAIT?
I'VE HAD SOMEONE OBSERVING HIM FOR THE LAST FEW DAYS.
ANY RESULTS?
UNFORTU-NATELY, NO.
HE'S CLEVER.
WE HAVE TO GET AHEAD OF HIM AND HAVE SOMEONE WATCHING HIM AROUND THE CLOCK.

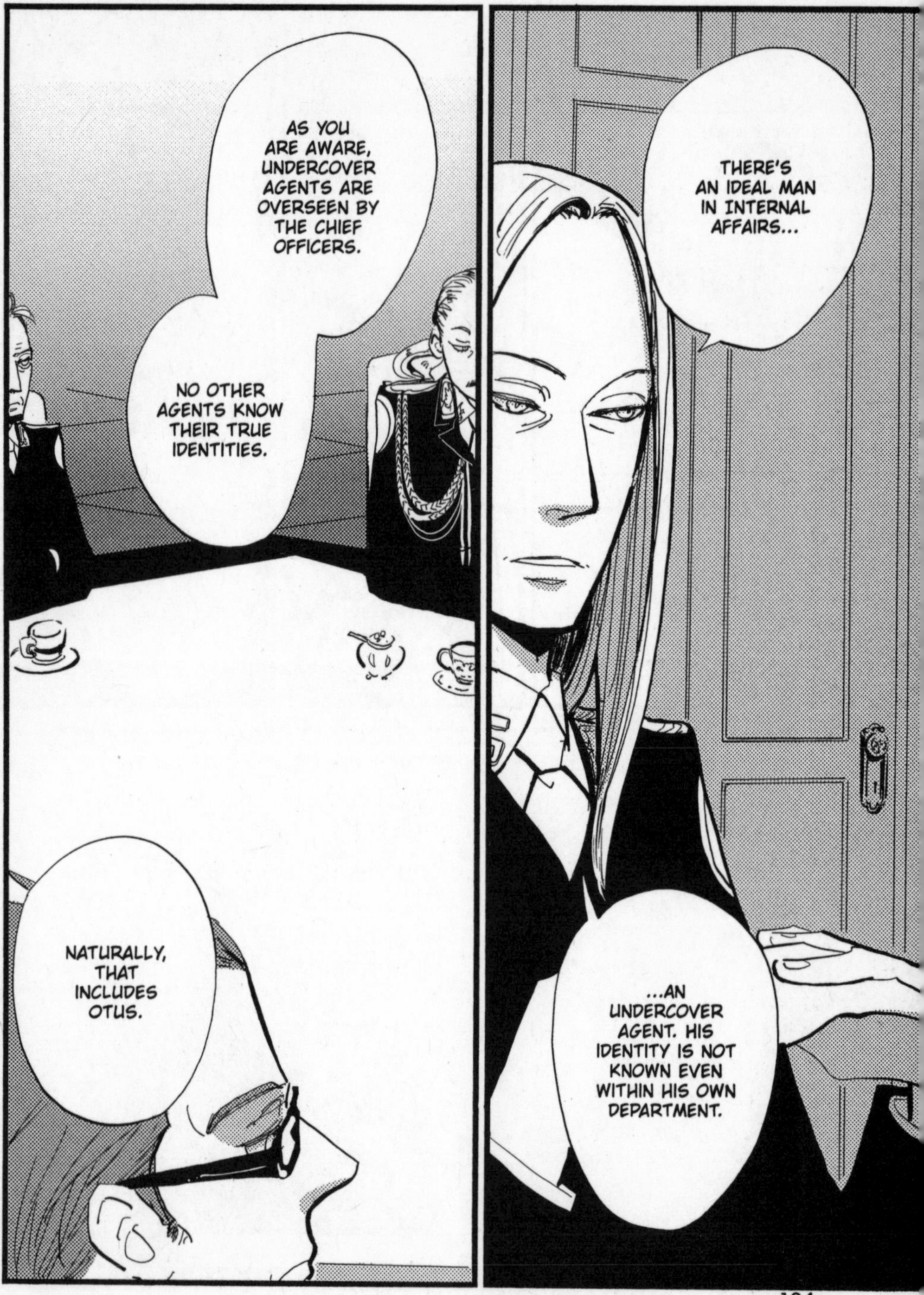
THERE'S AN IDEAL MAN IN INTERNAL AFFAIRS...
...AN UNDERCOVER AGENT. HIS IDENTITY IS NOT KNOWN EVEN WITHIN HIS OWN DEPARTMENT.
AS YOU ARE AWARE, UNDERCOVER AGENTS ARE OVERSEEN BY THE CHIEF OFFICERS.
NO OTHER AGENTS KNOW THEIR TRUE IDENTITIES.
NATURALLY, THAT INCLUDES OTUS.

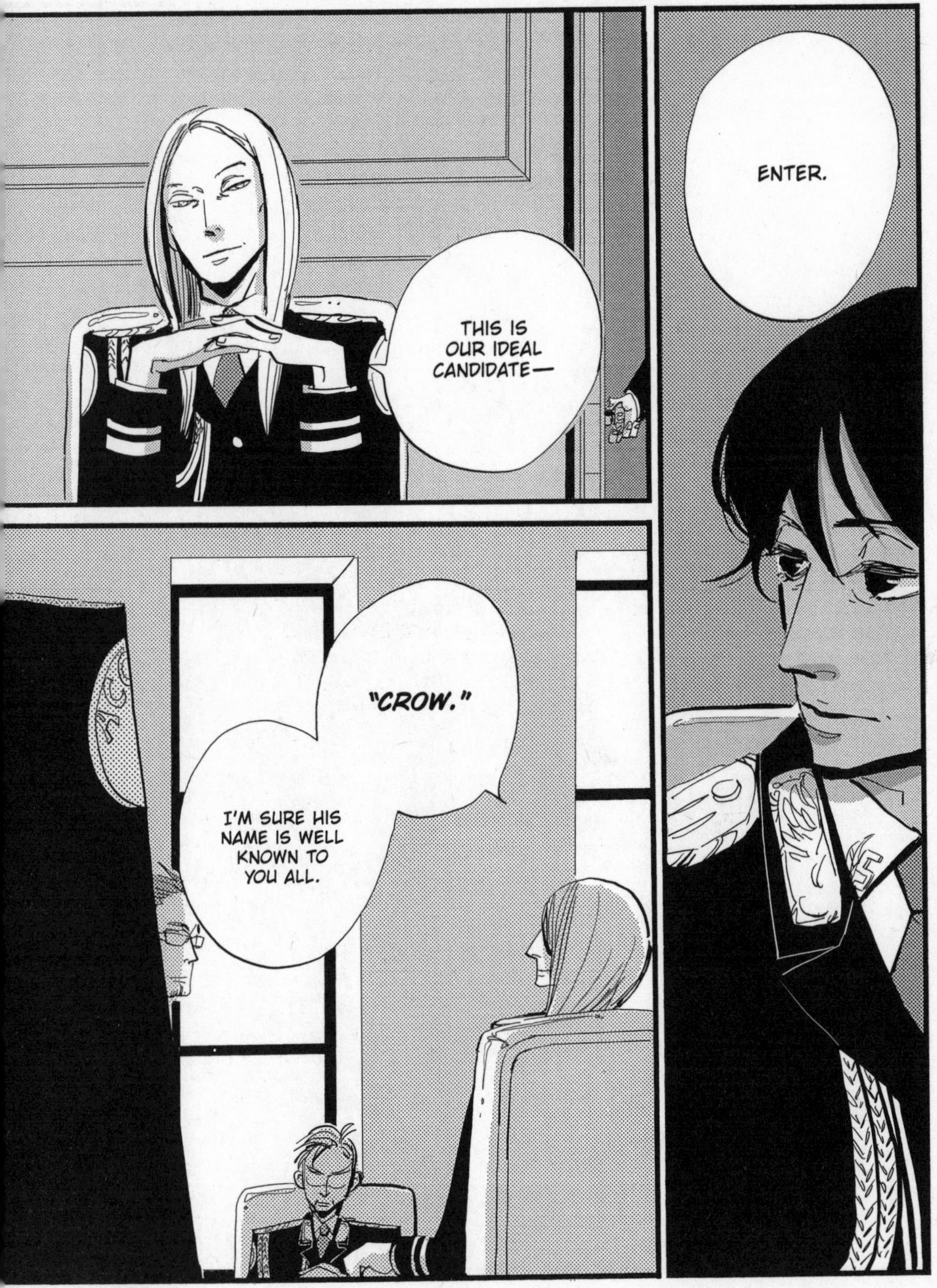
ENTER.
THIS IS OUR IDEAL CANDIDATE—
"CROW."
I'M SURE HIS NAME IS WELL KNOWN TO YOU ALL.

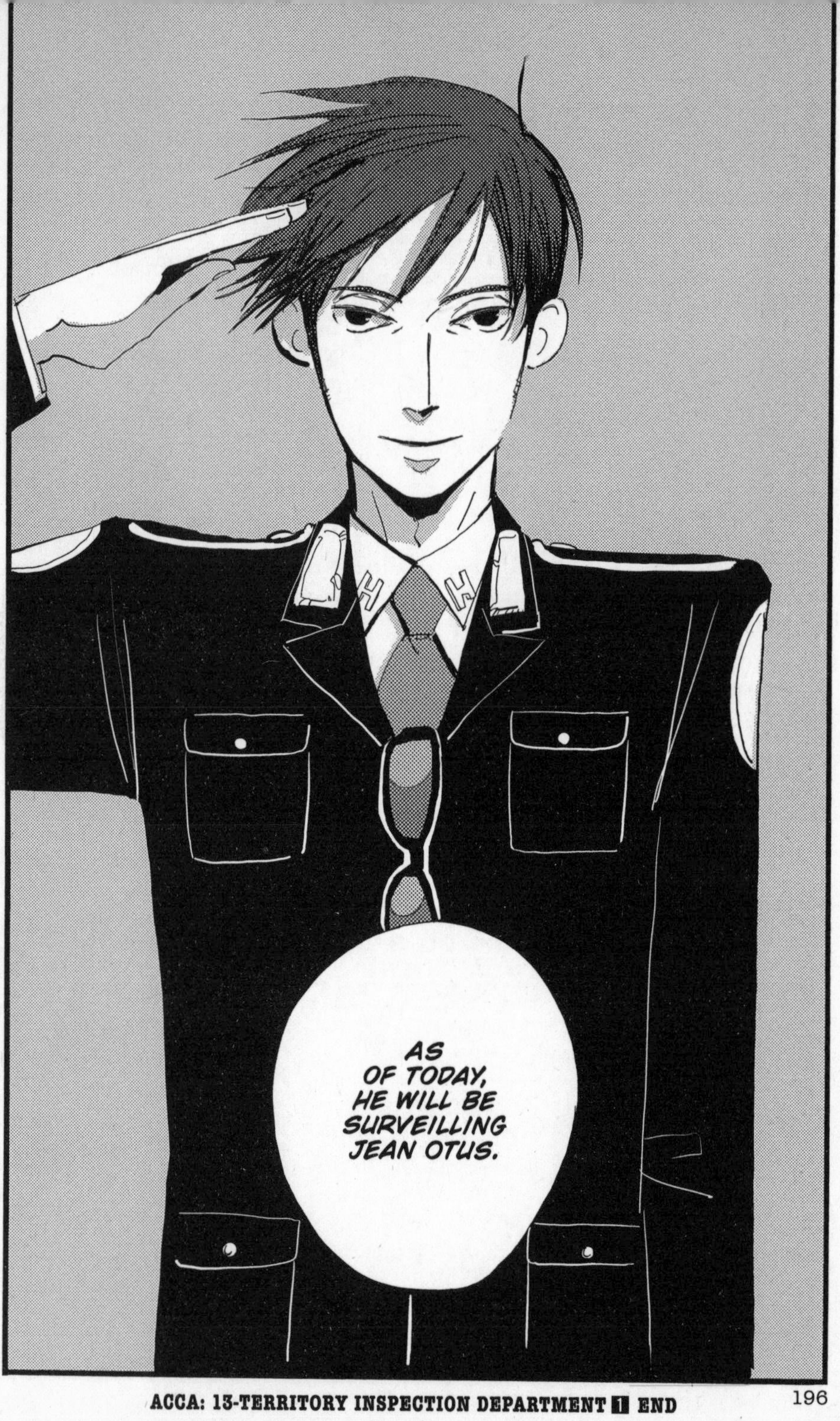
AS OF TODAY, HE WILL BE SURVEILLING JEAN OTUS.

ACCA: 13-TERRITORY INSPECTION DEPARTMENT 1 END